The
Center for
Chinese Studies at the University of California,
Berkeley, supported by the Ford Foundation,
the Institute of International Studies (University
of California, Berkeley), and the State of California,
is the unifying organization for social science and
interdisciplinary research on contemporary China.

RECENT PUBLICATIONS

Lee, Hong Yung. The Politics of the Chinese Cul-
    tural Revolution: A Case Study
McDonald, Angus W., Jr. The Urban Origins of
    Rural Revolution: Elites and the Masses in
    Hunan Province, China, 1911–1927
Pepper, Suzanne. Civil War in China: The Political
    Struggle, 1945–1949
Rice, Edward E. Mao's Way
Wakeman, Frederic, Jr. History and Will: Philosoph-
    ical Perspectives of Mao Tse-tung's Thought

The
Last
Confucian

This volume is sponsored by the
Center for Chinese Studies,
University of California, Berkeley

The
Center for
Chinese Studies at the University of California,

Berkeley, supported by the Ford Foundation,
the Institute of International Studies (University
of California, Berkeley), and the State of California,
is the unifying organization for social science and
interdisciplinary research on contemporary China.

Historical dialectics refuses to acknowledge
the principle that a great revolutionary's
psyche may also harbor a great reactionary;
but psychological dialectics must assume
it to be possible, or even probable.

ERIK ERIKSON
Young Man Luther, p. 231.

The
Last
Confucian

Liang Shu-ming and
the Chinese Dilemma
of Modernity

Second Edition

GUY S. ALITTO

University of California Press
Berkeley   Los Angeles   London

University of California Press
Berkeley and Los Angeles, California

University of California Press, Ltd.
London, England

Copyright © 1979, 1986 by
The Regents of the University of California

First Paperback Printing 1986

ISBN 0-520-05318-4

Library of Congress Catalog Card Number: 75-27920

Printed in the United States of America

1 2 3 4 5 6 7 8 9

for Susan

Contents

Foreword

Liang Shu-ming (or Sou-ming, as his given name is often romanized) is presented in many accounts of modern Chinese history as a conservative nationalist who tried to resist Westernization by restoring China's ancient cultural values (*fu-ku*). Though also known for his important role in the founding of the Democratic League, Liang is most famous for his systematic defense of Confucianism and Eastern civilization against May Fourth iconoclasts in 1921, and for his leadership of rural reconstruction efforts during the 1930s.[1] Both as a defender of China's "national essence" (*kuo-ts'ui*), and as an exponent of traditional agrarianism, Liang consequently appears as a cultural reactionary, defending the indefensible.

> Liang Sou-ming's theory was essentially a reaction to the new thought of the May Fourth period. In spite of advocating the acceptance of certain aspects of Western civilization in these lectures [at Peking University in 1929], he later rejected other Western ideas including both democracy and socialism. In his defense of Confucianism and traditional civilization, he actually deprecated Western learning and advocated in effect a sort of 'Eastward Ho!'[2]

This sort of characterization strongly implies that Liang Shu-ming's praise of harmonic Confucian social values and his effort to preserve the traditional rural economy provided evidence that he had lost touch with the modern world. Moreover, given the conventional distinction drawn between conservative and revolutionary ideologues, it also suggests that Liang was completely at odds with Marxist contemporaries like Li Ta-chao, Ch'en Tu-hsiu or Mao Tse-tung. Guy Alitto's biography of Liang Shu-ming refutes both of these implications. It not only shows that Liang Shu-ming

1. Wing-tsit Chan, *A Source Book in Chinese Philosophy* (Princeton: Princeton University Press, 1963), p. 765; Howard L. Boorman and Richard C. Howard, eds., *Biographical Dictionary of Republican China* (New York: Columbia University Press, 1968), vol. 3, p. 357.
2. Chow Tse-tsung, *The May Fourth Movement: Intellectual Revolution in Modern China* (Cambridge: Harvard University Press, 1964), p. 330.

was very much an intellectual of our times; it also demonstrates that he shared a number of key ideas with Mao Tse-tung. *The Last Confucian* thus breaks Liang loose from his earlier stereotyped mold, and reveals him to be a much more complex figure than had previously been recognized.

For one, Liang Shu-ming no longer seems to be just a champion of China's "national essence," defending a dying culture which he could not personally bear to relinquish. His ideas, while sometimes self-contradicting, do not have to be viewed merely as the means of salvaging his personal identity as a Chinese. Rather, as Alitto analyzes Liang Shu-ming's copious writings on Eastern and Western cultures, we begin to realize that Liang's attack on European utilitarianism also formed part of a global critique of modernity that was expressed as well in the romantic philosophies of Vitalism and Intuitionism in France and Germany. Liang Shu-ming's attachment to Confucian values, then, was not solely a Chinese patriot's search for emotional gratification during a period when many lacked confidence that the nation could survive; it was also a cosmopolitan thinker's quest for intellectual moorings in a society troubled by the anomie and alienation of modern times.[3]

However, Alitto does not expose Liang Shu-ming's foreign ties in order to detach him from his own native roots. While describing the long evening talks that took place between Liang and Mao Tse-tung in Yenan during the War of Resistance, Alitto writes of the "bone-deep Chineseness" the two men shared together. What one therefore sees more than ever before in this sensitive study is the way in which Liang Shu-ming embodied the experiences of a critical generation of Chinese intellectuals, spanning the turbulent years between the decline and fall of the Ch'ing dynasty and the rise and establishment of the People's Republic. Fired by his own messianic conviction that his fate and his country's were one, Liang remained constantly in the political arena during this period, moving across the country as the center of events shifted from north to south and back again.

3. Basing herself in part on Guy Alitto's research, Charlotte Furth has remarked that "a cosmopolitan like Liang Shu-ming saw China, not some other place, as the homeland of universal religiomoral value." Charlotte Furth, "Culture and Politics in Modern Chinese Conservatism," in Charlotte Furth, ed., *The Limits of Change: Essays on Conservative Alternatives in Republican China* (Cambridge: Harvard University Press, 1976), p. 39. See also Tu Wei-ming, "Hsiung Shih-li's Quest for Authentic Existence," in *ibid.*, p. 245.

After joining a number of prominent academic and literary figures in a futile effort to unite fragmented public opinion against corrupt warlord government, Liang Shu-ming joined the 1927 exodus of intellectuals from Peking, where the Manchurian militarist, Chang Tso-lin, had arrested and killed Li Ta-chao. Just as the Chinese Communist Party turned to the countryside then after failing to take over the cities with the help of a relatively small industrial proletariat, so did many liberal and conservative intellectuals, disappointed by their own political weakness in urban centers, begin to seek a new social base among the rural populace. Although Liang Shu-ming was one of the first to detect the untapped power of the peasantry, he initially feared that the notion of village-level social mobilization was a populist dream, a "subjective utopia," which appealed to powerless intellectuals for obvious reasons. But perhaps because one of his students was attracted by the Chinese Communists' promise to arouse the rural masses, Liang experienced an "awakening." If the Communists were turning to the countryside, then Liang too would seek to mobilize the peasantry, and transform the dispersed "village society" of China into the kind of unified national whole that republican politicians had already failed to create by fiat from above.

Alitto thus demonstrates that Liang Shu-ming's rural reconstruction (*hsiang-ts'un chien-she*) efforts were not intended to restore a bucolic past. Rather, they were designed to provide China with the same degree of disciplined social organization that Liang perceived in the West and failed to detect in China. *Hsiang-ts'un chien-she*— which in the Chinese actually reads as "rural construction"—was to be a mode of economic and political modernization, bringing advanced technology to the countryside, while building new social organizations from beneath. There were several models at hand, especially the Hsiao-chuang Experimental Rural School of T'ao Hsing-chih, who was influenced by John Dewey and by the writings of Wang Yang-ming, and who hoped to educate the Chinese citizen of the future with a mixture of scientific training and arduous physical labor. But Liang Shu-ming devised his own particular version of rural social development, combining moral mobilization with economic cooperation. Whereas the Kuomintang's model *hsien* government in Chiang-ning (Kiangsu) was staffed by cadre graduated from the Central Political Academy, Liang's experimental district organization in Tsou-p'ing (Shantung) explicitly resisted the central government's penetration into rural society. And while James Y.C. Yen's "new-style" rural reconstruction project in Ting-hsien (Hopei) was supported with large amounts of foreign funds, Liang's "old-style" and more conservative agrarian effort stressed economic self-reliance and independence from foreign control. Inspired by the Confucian study group (*chiang-hsueh*) which joined teacher and pupils into a responsive moral community, Liang tried to turn Tsou-p'ing into a collective of rural schools, in which the peasants could be morally inspired to create a new communal identity for themselves, thereby transcending their selfish interests as members of individually competing households. Liang Shu-ming apparently conceived of such a new society as a conscious human creation, being the intentional projection of individual wills toward a cooperative existence, reinforced by ritual rather than ordained by law. Society, as Alitto puts it, was to take the place of the polity. As province-wide networks of local schools assumed the functions of local government, farming and credit cooperatives would also replace brokers and moneylenders. Liang thus hoped to renew China as a country devoted to ancient ideals of moral education and composed of thousands of communal economic units.

The most striking characteristic of Liang Shu-ming's conservative rural reconstruction project was its partial resemblance to the Chinese Communist Party's peasant organizational strategy developed during the war against Japan. As Alitto points out, both the Tsou-p'ing experiment and the so-called Yenan model called for economic self-reliance (*tzu-li keng-sheng*), emphasized moral renovation, and sought to educate their cadre to be responsive to the peasants' wishes. Above all, both represented the consolidation of pre-existing forms of collective life in north China's villages: the traditional crop-watching leagues, labor exchange arrangements, and self-defense militia units.[4] For Liang Shu-ming these traditions of rural *Gemeinschaftlichkeit* were ideally represented in the *hsiang-yueh* or "village covenant" system of Neo-Confucian statesmen-philosophers like Wang Yang-ming. Mao Tse-tung, too, may have been influenced by this idealistic Neo-Confucian tradition, so that the notion of a teacher-cadre transforming society into a school-room to study the ethical thought of an inspired leader is common both to a radical strain of Confucianism which goes back to Mencius, and to some of the more voluntaristic forms of Chinese Marxism.

4. Ralph Thaxton, "Tenants in Revolution: The Tenacity of Traditional Morality," *Modern China* 1:323–358.

Another common inspiration may have been what Benjamin Schwartz has called the "muscular Confucianism" of certain nineteenth-century Confucianists.[5] Lin Tse-hsu (whom Liang Shu-ming praised) and Tseng Kuo-fan (whom Mao admired as a youth) were both Confucian patriots who had great confidence in the capacity of a morally inspired populace to repel foreign invaders and overcome social disorder. Dismayed by the prospect of Western treaty ports growing along China's coast, literati like Tseng Kuo-fan praised traditional rural values, and expressed disdain for Chinese who betrayed their Confucian heritage by adopting urban, Western values. Liang Shu-ming and Mao Tse-tung both experienced similar distaste for cities like Shanghai, which (in Liang's words) "tangibly brings together into one place both Chinese and Western corruptions." They also held the new "aristocracy" of Westernized intellectuals in moral contempt for having allowed their native values to become eroded by foreign cultural standards.[6] Just as Mao Tse-tung criticized the urbanites who had joined the Red Army in Yenan for being divorced from the masses and for losing themselves in bookish theory instead of looking after the practical needs of a revolutionary movement, so did Liang Shu-ming accuse Westernized intellectuals of being alienated from the people and of being unwilling to soil their hands by working alongside the masses. Alitto's analysis of these similarities thus implies that "sending people down" (hsia-fang) to work in the countryside was not just a Draconian invention of the Chinese Communist Party. Rather, the policy of hsia-fang may have expressed a more widely held impulse to narrow the gap between urban intellectuals and rural peasants and to overcome the invidious distinction between mental and manual labor.

Yet in spite of these populist similarities, Liang Shu-ming's rural reconstruction project was far from identical with Chinese Communist guerrilla socialism. As Alitto also points out, Liang altogether denied class struggle, which was to be the "key link" in the Communists' view of revolutionary mobilization. Whereas Mao Tse-tung conceived of social organization as a way of consciously

5. Benjamin Schwartz, *In Search of Wealth and Power: Yen Fu and the West* (Cambridge: Harvard University Press, 1964), p. 15.

6. Frederic Wakeman, Jr., "The Patriot," in Dick Wilson, ed., *Mao Tsetung in the Scales of History* (Cambridge, Engl.: Cambridge University Press, 1977), pp. 243–244.

focusing class conflict, so that genuine political struggle helped heighten the collective awareness of members of a peasant association, Liang tried to mitigate conflict in his local schools. Class differences were minimized, and the harmony of the community was made the desired end. Liang and his followers were consequently unwilling to sponsor a militant social movement prepared to assert its independent control of the countryside. The Tsou-p'ing experiment did comprise militia groups, but these were only a police force, not an army. Liang therefore was ultimately dependent upon warlords like Li Chi-shen in Kwangtung, Feng Yü-hsiang in Honan, and Han Fu-ch'ü in Shantung, to protect his rural reconstruction efforts. When abandoned by these sponsors, his social programs were immediately jeopardized.

Moreover, though Liang and Mao both wanted to narrow the gap between intellectuals and peasants, Mao went much further in trying to fuse the two. At times he argued that the only way to obliterate the difference between city and countryside altogether was for intellectuals to give up their very identity and adopt peasant values entirely. Liang Shu-ming, perhaps unto the very present, wished to maintain an ultimate distinction between the intellectuals and the masses. While he, too, deeply desired to narrow the gap between literati and folk, he still thought of the *chün-tzu*, the Confucian gentleman, as being aloof from those whom he would enlighten. Liang and his students may have gone to the people in the 1930s, but they never abandoned their own social identity to immerse themselves in the rural populace, and he himself continued to believe that the sheer moral force of his presence would help to transform the peasants' economic relationships. Insofar as Liang Shu-ming tried to translate that belief into a social program, he truly deserves the title of China's last Confucian political activist.

Frederic Wakeman, Jr.
Berkeley, December, 1977

Preface

The history of the world, it has been said, is but the biography of great men. Samuel Johnson, an illustrious subject of the biographical art if no outstanding practitioner of it, augmented the supposition to say that "there has rarely passed *any* life of which a judicious and faithful narrative would not be useful." As the subject of this biography has yet to have the greatness of a paragraph in world history textbooks thrust upon him, the remark might serve as a minimal apologia for this volume. My own judgment of Liang Shu-ming—and my ultimate motive for writing—is that, his great importance in modern Chinese history aside, he was a profoundly significant human being. His basic concerns, his intellective and emotional responses to his historical situation, and his life, I believe, have vital relevance to our own present concerns and problems. Each reader, of course, makes his or her own evaluation; I have allowed Liang to speak for himself as much as possible, despite his difficult style and the perplexities of rendering it into an English both meaningful and faithful. I have done so also in an attempt to convey some of the tone and flavor of Liang's original writing, as well as to bring forth certain facets of his personality and intellect not amenable to commentary and analysis.

The redoubtable Doctor Johnson further opined that the most valuable biographies "tell not how any man became great, but how he was made happy; not how he lost favor with his prince, but how he became discontented with himself." As Liang was a man of whom the standard reference work of the period states, "little is known about Liang Shu-ming's personal life,"* following this prescription involved more than the usual amount of Clio's legwork. All historians, and especially biographers, strive to make that long leap from the dry, dusty documents to the rich vital stuff of actual human experience. My own attempts to so brace the grasp of historical understanding included some two hundred and fifty hours of leisurely chats with men who had known or worked with Liang. That they all have been living in Taiwan or Hong Kong since 1949

*[107], II, 359.

indicates, of course, that they share a certain minimal level of hostility toward the Chinese Communists and that they have less than objective opinions on certain matters. I have relied sparingly on these interviews for documentation, and only when several interviewees agreed completely and in detail, or when they were corroborated by other sources. Getting to know them, and listening to their anecdotes, opinions, and personal experiences did enliven and enrich my general understanding of Liang. I am grateful to all these gentlemen and particularly to Professor T'ang Chün-i and Mr. Hu Ying-han for allowing me to copy Liang's correspondence to them.

Less successful was my attempt to acquire some existential understanding of Chinese rural life and the problems of rural reconstruction through living in Taiwanese villages and observing rural reform projects; the ethnographic, economic, and political distance between North China of the 1930s and the rural Taiwan of the 1970s proved to be too great. Far more rewarding was a subsequent trip across the Chinese mainland itself, during which I visited several places where the events recounted in this book occurred. I have drawn upon that experience for many physical and topographical descriptions, even, in one instance, of a single room in Yenan (it had reportedly been restored to its original state). Other small details and stray adjectives that the reader might possibly suspect to have sprouted from an overly luxuriant imagination come, in fact, from photos, maps, and corroborated interviews.

The venerable and punctilious rite of academic acknowledgements, never making very racy reading, is often skipped over by the reader; I hope that my own debts, heavier than most, are an exception. The influence of my teachers at Harvard, Benjamin I. Schwartz and John K. Fairbank, is evident on every page. I owe a great and fundamental debt to the Foreign Area Fellowship Program and the University of California Center for Chinese Studies at Berkeley for supporting me through several years of research and writing. Perhaps I owe even more to Chalmers Johnson, Joyce Kallgren, Philip Lilienthal, John S. Service, and Frederic Wakeman for persuading me that the results of those years were worth publishing. In addition, I am grateful to Frederic Wakeman for writing the Foreword to this volume and to John Service for his excellent editing of the final manuscript. Several others also scrutinized parts of the manuscript in various stages of development: Carl E. Dorris, Hong Yung Lee, John Starr, Tu Wei-ming, and Ezra Vogel. The final product benefited greatly from both their perceptive comments and general encouragement. My special thanks to my predecessor in the study of Liang, Lyman P. Van Slyke, for his cordial support. At one time or another I have had fruitful discussions on Liang Shu-ming and modern Chinese intellectual history with David Buck, Charlotte Furth, Lin Yü-sheng, K. C. Liu, Don C. Price, and Laurence Schneider. I am exceedingly grateful to the support staff of the University of California Center for Chinese Studies—Annie Chang, C. P. Chen, Jane Kaneko, Josephine Pearson, and Cordia Schak—not only for their facilitating my work but also for making my sojourn at their institution such a pleasant one. Jane Kaneko, in addition, cheerfully and accurately typed the entire manuscript and several of its revisions. For those mistakes I committed by stubbornly refusing to follow the advice of any of the above, I am naturally responsible.

Finally, and certainly most profoundly, I am grateful to Susan. No customary acknowledgement-of-spouse is this, for I am comfortably certain that few in the annals of academic spousehood have directly or indirectly contributed as much to a work as she has to this one. She edited the entire manuscript in its preliminary stages, made numerous invaluable suggestions on everything from organization to conceptualization, and perhaps most important of all, she willingly shared hearth and home with our often less than entertaining guest, Liang Shu-ming.

Introduction

"I think you stink!" Chairman Mao had wrenched the microphone away from the speaker and burst forth in a stream of technicolor invective against him.[1] A taut hush fell over Peking's cavernous Hall of Benevolence. The several hundred people convened there that September afternoon in 1953 blinked in astonished wonder at the speaker's platform. Almost none of them had ever seen the Chairman in such an unbridled fury. What had the object of his verbal assault, a frail figure clad in an old-fashioned long gown, done to provoke such an unprecedented public tantrum?[2] Waving his finger in the shorter man's bespectacled face, Mao continued:

> Mr. Liang calls himself a man of integrity. The reactionary newspapers in Hong Kong, too, call Mr. Liang the person with the greatest integrity on the [Chinese] mainland. The broadcasts from Taiwan praise him greatly too. . . . They are all your intimate friends. . . . They are all so ecstatic about you that they stigmatize me as a "bandit" and address you as a

1. The incident took place during the twenty-seventh session of the sixty-three member Central People's Government Council, which the national committee of the Chinese People's Political Consultative Conference also attended. My description of the event is drawn primarily from [424f] and [194], pp. 434–436. The text of Mao's remarks has been edited and, in any case, is described as only "the major part" of the original. The published version could well be a composite of two separate sets of remarks before the council. Certainly the piece is extremely disjointed and repetitious. The only published account of the event by an eyewitness ([194], pp. 434–436) reinforces this suspicion. Further, the *Selected Works* specifies several consecutive days (September 16–18) as the time of delivery, a standard method for dating speeches delivered over a period longer than one day.

2. Reportedly, Mao sometimes lost his temper in inner-party councils, but on public occasions such as this, he had never been known to fly into a rage and verbally abuse someone to his face. In this respect, the attack on Liang is unique.

mister.... But what are your meritorious deeds, Liang Shu-ming? What in your entire life have you ever done for the people? Not an iota! Not a mite! Yet you describe yourself as the world's foremost beauty, more beautiful than Hsi Shih [China's Helen of Troy].[3]

Even in the officially edited version published a quarter of a century later in the scriptural *Selected Works*, even with expletives deleted and diction retouched, Mao's remarks on Liang Shu-ming that afternoon appear more tirade than teaching. Any questions Liang had raised seemed to serve merely as an excuse for fresh barbs.

Mr. Liang "asks to know more about the plan." I do not approve of that either. To the contrary, the less people like Mr. Liang are let in on confidential information, the better. This man Liang Shu-ming cannot be trusted. We can let others in on some confidential information, but you, no! When the more restricted conferences of the democratic parties are held, you, Liang Shu-ming, need not attend either.[4]

And so Mao execrated on: "You are this kind of murderer . . . Liang Shu-ming is a greedy schemer, a hypocrite."

Liang had apparently brought on Mao's diatribe with an address he had delivered just previously. Among other things, he had boldly attacked the government for its decision to adopt the Soviet model of economic development because it laid the heaviest burden on the backs of the peasants while making the urban workers a virtual privileged class. Chou En-lai, the chairman of the session, had immediately followed up this first delivery with a vigorous attack on Liang. Mao had mumbled to himself and "looked annoyed." Upon realizing that he had aroused the ire of the nation's most powerful men, Liang requested permission to speak yet *again*.

His previous remarks against the government might best be understood as in the hoary tradition of censorial courage. Liang was remonstrating with the "emperor" in full view of the court. The historian Wu Han, probably in attendance that day, might well have drawn inspiration from this scene for his famous play, *The Dismissal of Hai Jui*. The protagonist of this morality play, Hai Jui, was also a spokesman for the peasantry at the imperial court. Like Liang, he "lived a life of simplicity and was upright and firm in principle.... Uncompromising, he was not swayed by threats of

3. [424f], pp. 107–108.   4. [424f], p. 108.

violence nor intimidated by defeat."[5] Well and good! Liang had
performed as the lone unshrinking representative of the peasantry; he had exhibited the moral heroism for which he was famous.
Why, then, did he attempt to speak again?

Mao had cut off the second speech almost before Liang had
opened his mouth, but Liang's first sentence gives us a clue: "I am
speaking again because I want to test myself."[6] It was the culmination of a lifetime of such tests and perhaps the last conscious public
manifestation of Confucian tradition, for Liang Shu-ming was this
century's foremost Confucian traditionalist. The gesture was Confucianism's epilogue. Liang's little known confrontation with this
century's foremost Chinese Marxist is significantly symbolic. The
Marxist was dominant, the personification of China's future; the
Confucian an impotent vestige, a ghost of the past. Yet the behavior of both men that day remains somehow enigmatic. Why had
Mao reacted so strongly to the empty thunder of tradition? Why
had Liang been so compelled to persist in his hopeless course?

Some Assessments of Liang's
Character and Career

Liang's obsessive concern for self-control and personal integrity is legendary. His life was a continuous struggle to act upon the
moral imperatives he felt. Life was a desperately serious business—a continuous combat with the ever present danger of moral
failure. This moral compulsion made him into a most serious individual. He seldom laughed or even smiled; a joke was beyond him.[7]
This was stange to no one, for his identity as a sage with a capital S
was well known. A Communist critic noted in 1956 that Liang "has
always considered himself a sage and believed that 'Heaven had
begot the power that was in [him].' Is this [self-perception] not
known to many people?"[8]

5. Wu Han, *Hai Jui pa kuan*, p. 5, quoted in [458], p. 30.
6. [194], p. 435.
7. My knowledge of Liang's physical appearance and his dress is drawn
from photographs as well as his friends' verbal descriptions. My understanding of his personality is based in part upon extensive interviews with
those who knew him personally.
8. [101], p. 36. The author might well have had the fracas with Mao in
the back of his mind when he wrote, for the well known quote he used
from Confucius (Analects VII:22) is associated with a certain popular story
about the master. While sitting under a tree teaching his disciples, Con-

Liang Shu-ming

Some people naturally found such sanctimonious stodginess unbearable, but then, do not the sages Confucius and Mencius also sound somewhat holier-than-thou and stubborn at times? No one has denied that Liang was a very special kind of man. The large shaven head, the steely serene eyes, the grimly set mouth, the low yet firm voice—all combined to create an image of quiet, imperturbable strength. Some of his admirers recall his physical presence radiating an aura of calm sanctity so that "one felt in the company of a Bodhisattva." Another wrote that Liang "appeared so awe-inspiring that his students had difficulty speaking fluently in his presence."[9]

Assessments of Liang's career and achievements are diverse and contradictory. His life has been long and complex; it has woven around and through almost all major events and movements in twentieth-century China. And his career and writings have touched on almost all the major concerns in China during the first half of this century. To most of his iconoclastic contemporaries of the May Fourth generation, such as Hu Shih or Wu Chih-hui, he was a muddleheaded defender of Chinese spiritualism against Western materialism—a sort of Chinese Tagore. Some of his foreign-trained confreres in the Chinese rural reconstruction movement of the 1930s patronizingly considered him dedicated but "unscientific." Some of his Marxist contemporaries saw him and his programs as the agrarian feudal clan society's ideological Parthian shot at the inexorably advancing bourgeois industrialization. Under the Communist regime he has been characterized as a subjective idealist who tried to anesthetize the revolutionary rural masses with feudal morality, wanted to keep China weak by opposing industrialization, and worked hand in glove with Western imperialism. In Taiwan he is both quoted in textbooks and condemned as a dupe of the Communists.[10]

---

fucius was set upon by emissaries of the high official Huan T'ui, who ripped down the tree and tried to kill him. His disciples urged him to run for his life, but Confucius—in serene confidence of his divine mission and sagehood—calmly allayed their fears with those words. The second part of the sentence reads: "What have I to fear from the likes of Huan T'ui?"

9. [613]; [311].

10. See, for example, [309b] and [580]. Information on how Liang's colleagues regarded him is drawn from [612]; [615]; [618]; [629]. The Marxist criticism includes: [597], pp. 1–106; [144]; [523]; [455]. More recent assessments from Taiwan and the People's Republic include: [409]; [101];

Liang Shu-ming and Chinese
Cultural Conservatives

In all of these and other appraisals Liang is regarded as a "conservative" or "traditionalist." The reasons for such designations vary from Liang's fervent Confucianism to his insistence on wearing a long scholar's gown even in sweltering heat. Broadly speaking, however, he is regarded primarily as a "cultural conservative." Liang's thought and action seem *prima facie* just another expression of Chang Chih-tung's familiar *t'i-yung* dichotomy: Chinese learning for fundamental principles; Western learning for practical application. This theoretical distinction between principles and practical application provided cautious Chinese reformers with a convenient formula for conservative modernization in the last years under the monarchy. They could uphold their commitment to China's cultural "essence" (*t'i*) and still in good conscience copy Western factories and firearms in order to achieve national "wealth and power." Early references to the nature of the Chinese essence were vague, usually mentioning some fundamental principle of Chinese moral philosophy and social usage. When in the last years of his life, Chang Chih-tung felt compelled by events to take more concrete measures to preserve the *t'i*, he moved to promote the study of traditional literature—indicating that whatever he considered the ultimate nature of the *t'i*, it was somehow inseparable from classical and historical scholarship.

At the same time, some of the anti-Manchu revolutionaries—Chang Chih-tung's political and ideological opposites—began using the same basic concept, "national essence," for their own purposes. They adopted the Japanese neologism *kokusui* (*kuo-ts'ui*) instead of the word *t'i*, but even Chang Chih-tung himself used *kuo-ts'ui* on occasion to refer to the general concept of Chinese essence. The *kuo-ts'ui* coterie, led by such figures as Chang T'ai-yen, Liu Shih-p'ei, and Huang Chieh, persisted until the May Fourth era, when Wu Mi and Mei Kuang-ti of the *Critical Review* (*Hsueh heng*) group took on the mantle. In the hands of the *Critical Review* people, Chinese essence became just another classical "cradle" culture—equal to, but not necessarily superior to, Western classical

---

[532]. Various Kuomintang-connected individuals with whom I talked in Taiwan referred to Liang as a "fellow traveler" because of his political activities before, during, and after the Anti-Japanese War. Except for 1971–1973, his works have not been permitted to be reprinted in Taiwan.

culture. The genealogy of the national essence idea may be extended forward in time to the more instrumental and politicized Kuomintang neotraditionalism of Tai Chi-t'ao and Ch'en Li-fu in the 1930s, and even on to the recent Cultural Renaissance movement in Taiwan.

In all of its various reincarnations, the National Essence school was devoted to the preservation of Chinese "spirit," which adherents believed was embedded in the literary heritage. Thus, their specific activity on behalf of national essence concentrated on classical and textual scholarship, history, and belles lettres, and they often drew parallels between their own endeavors and the revival of Western classical studies during the European Renaissance. Like Chang Chih-tung, they welcomed Western social, political, and economic "forms" as means for protecting China's national essence. Liang Shu-ming, too, was dedicated to the preservation of the Chinese cultural essence (or, more precisely, Confucian ethical values) while accepting, albeit with substantial qualifications, Western political forms and technology. He, too, sought to create an authentically Chinese cultural renaissance.

In the pre-May Fourth phase of this general thought current, the ancient antagonism between the "Old" and "New" Text schools of historical interpretation again flared up—this time over the issue of the establishment of Confucianism as a religion. K'ang Yu-wei, the last great exponent of the New Text school, felt that the Chinese "soul" would be best safeguarded by the institutionalization of Confucianism as a formal state religion, a position perfectly consistent with the New Text school's attitude toward Confucius. The Old Text school opposed the idea of a Confucian religion and maintained that the principal function of scholarship was transmission of the transcendental *tao*—the absolute set of values valid for all people and for all times—which was discovered by the ancients and transmitted through time by sages and worthies.

Liang Shu-ming relates most specifically to this tradition of *tao-t'ung* (transmission of the truth). He had "no respect" for K'ang Yu-wei and the Confucian Church made him "nauseous."[11] Possessed of a sage identity, Liang felt that in the present age he and he alone had fully comprehended the *tao*, and so was under the awful imperative of transmitting it: "The former worthies had a phrase, 'to carry on for the past sages their learning which has

11. [4], p. 137; [4a], p. 4.

become extinct, and to open an age of universal peace for all ages.'
This is the mission of my whole life."[12]

Yet there are fundamental dissimilarities between Liang and
others identified with the National Essence persuasion. In the first
place, Liang was not a member of any scholarly clique, and his
knowledge of China's traditional canons, commentaries, and
chronicles was infinitely inferior to that of a dazzling scholar like
Chang T'ai-yen. In direct contrast to the central thrust of post-May
Fourth cultural conservatism, Liang attached little importance to
the literary heritage and textual scholarship. He dismissed
academic rummagings through traditional literature as misdirected
energy and regarded fiction, belles lettres, and poetry as a lament-
able waste of time. Finally, Liang explicitly rejected the National
Essence group's efforts at cultural persistence, describing it as
"nothing more than simply piling up obsolete curios" and "lifeless
rotten goods."[13]

Even Liang himself was somewhat aware of the tangle of contradictions and ironies in his life and thought. He once noted that
he:

1. Had most despised philosophy and yet ended up talking
philosophy himself;
2. Had never read the writings of Confucius in school and yet
ended up talking Confucian philosophy;
3. Had never attended a university and yet ended up teaching in one;
4. Was born and raised in a city and yet devoted himself to
rural work.[14]

If he had thought further about it, he might have added a few
more. He was a famous pioneer scholar of Buddhism who denounced the modern Chinese Buddhist revival as the baneful work
of "selfish bookworms playing on psychological weaknesses to gain
influence."[15] He was a lifelong antimilitarist who was friend and

---

12. Liang Shu-ming, "Hsiang-kang t'o hsien chi K'uan Shu liang erh"
(Letter to my two sons [P'ei]-k'uan and [P'ei]-shu on my escape from Hong
Kong). This is a letter Liang wrote to his sons after he had fled the
Japanese occupation of Hong Kong and reached Wuchow, Kwangsi. It was
published in a Kweilin newspaper in February 1942, and parts are quoted
in [197], no. 5; [441]; [311].
13. [4], pp. 202, 204–206, 210–211.
14. [564], p. 4; see also [14a].   15. [4], pp. 207–209; [5r].

adviser to four military commanders.[16] He was a "reactionary" who classed Chiang Kai-shek with Yuan Shih-k'ai[17] and thought that the Kuomintang was too conservative and that the Communist movement in the 1930s was meeting the real needs of China. What kind of a conservative could have been a close friend of Communist party founder Li Ta-chao, had personal relationships with Mao Tse-tung and Chou En-lai, but only a nodding acquaintance with the Kuomintang neotraditionalist ideologue, Ch'en Li-fu?

A World-wide Conservative Response?

Perhaps we can see Liang's real significance as an instance in a world-wide response to a common universal "nonconservative," nontraditional phenomenon—modernization, a term I use here in the general sense of Weber's "rationalization" (*Zwecksrationalität*). The main thrust of this ongoing critique of modernization has been an emphasis upon the limits of pure rationalism in solving all problems of the human condition. It might be called a tradition of awareness of certain flies in the cure-all ointment of modernization, or an uneasiness about the "brave new world" of unlimited technological salvation. The reaction has transcended conventional political categories and has included both pessimistic conservatives and optimistic revolutionaries. Because they share a common "opponent," certain types of conservatives resemble Marxist social critics. As Mannheim points out, both the Marxist and Vitalist concepts of reality originate in a common romantic opposition to pure rationalism.[18] This illusive antimodern sensibility has never been satisfactorily defined, although some historians have tried to describe its manifestations with such terms as romanticism, irrationalism, cultural conservatism, critique of modernity, and even literary modernism. When the smoke has cleared from the West's most recent expressions of the modernization critique, savants might add a few more terms.

No definition is ever likely to be definitive. Personal circumstances, the positive content of each premodern tradition, and the specific historical situation shape each conservative's total response.

16. Three were associated with the Kwangsi group—Li Tsung-jen, Li Chi-shen, Ch'en Ming-shu—and one—Han Fu-ch'ü—was originally a Feng Yü-hsiang man.

17. [11n], p. 351.   18. [422], pp. 161–164.

Yet I would suggest that there are certain common themes, regardless of historical circumstances or individual concerns. "Conservatives" all seem to take, and then idealize, a traditional form of
society as the touchstone for social excellence. They share a common enemy in political and economic liberalism (although their
own political stances may be classified as liberal) and a common
antipathy toward individual material self-interest. They are suspicious or outrightly hostile toward the results of industrialization,
especially modern urban life. Such a posture emphasizes society
over the individual and organic group relationships over artificial
legal relationships and individual rights. In addition to their stress
on organic physical community, these conservatives seek, or long
for, common values and a common truth. Most important, they
highly value the nonrational, nonutilitarian aspects of human existence.

A second related yet distinct element in this conservative response to modernization may be discerned in areas outside the
Western European cradle of modernization. When such cultural
units were confronted with modernization, they conceived of it as
"foreign," and thus productive of that tension between "history"
and "value" which Joseph Levenson has identified. Accordingly,
formulations similar to the Chinese *t'i-yung* dichotomy, or the later
"spiritual" versus "material" distinction, appeared in other traditional societies such as India, Japan, and the Muslim world.
These areas were directly menaced by the West's superior military
and economic power and, in self-defense, were compelled to borrow culturally from their aggressors. The making of a distinction
between unique native "spirit" and useful foreign "matter" might
be interpreted as an emotional response resulting from feelings of
inferiority.

In the non-Western societies undergoing these transformations,
"culture" came to be understood in an important new way. Indeed,
within the heartland of bourgeois utilitarian society itself, the idea
of culture also appears and performs a function quite similar in
some respects to its role in the more traditional societies. As
Raymond Williams says in his classic study of the English term:

> Culture emerges as an abstraction and an absolute; an
> emergence which, in a very complex way, merges two
> responses—first, the recognition of the practical separation of
> certain moral and intellectual activities from the driven im-

petus of a new kind of society; second, the emphasis of these activities as a court of human appeal, to be set over the processes of practical social judgment and yet to offer itself as a mitigating and rallying alternative.[19]

Of course, the English did not conceive of the modernizing process as coming from the outside. It evoked no crisis of identity or feeling of inadequacy. But Germany around 1800 was decidedly backward, economically and politically, in relation to the well-established nation-states of England and France. And it was the Germans who most systematically developed a concept of culture which focuses on people's interior feelings in opposition to the social and economic rationalizations that were changing Europe's exterior.

The distinction between interior and exterior is often expressed as a distinction between culture and civilization.[20] The first, culture, is qualitative, organic, normative, emotional, subjective, and particularistic (and includes custom, religion, and art), while the second, civilization, is quantitative, mechanistic, intellectual, accumulative, and universal (and so includes science and technology). The idea of a spirit-matter or spirit-nature dichotomy, which so thoroughly permeates post-*Aufklärung* German thought, is comparable to the dichotomies constructed by conservative romantics and idealists in the non-West. The Russian Slavophiles, sometimes borrowing directly from the German Romantics' fund of ideas, devised similar dichotomies—Russian *sobornost* and spirituality versus Western legalism and rationalism. We could also view the culturally regenerative reform movements of the late nineteenth-century Muslim brotherhoods, such as the Sanusiya, in the same way. In India, China, and Japan, formulas such as harmony with nature versus control of nature or intuition versus intellect were commonplace.

In all of these formulations there are explicit or implicit claims both to the superiority of indigenous spiritual culture as well as for

19. [577], p. xvi.
20. The internal spiritual element sometimes appears as "civilization" (as with W. von Humbolt, A. Schaeffle, P. Barth) and sometimes as "culture" (as in A. Weber's famous formula, and with some others, such as F. Oppenheimer). These contrasted concepts, as well as the general prominence of "*Kultur*," appear as a natural development of earlier German Romantic thought, especially that of Herder and Schiller.

the progress made possible by a selective borrowing from Western material culture. The result of such a combination of the best from East and West would provide the "backward" people with the nature-mastering equipment of the West, and also enable them to retain their higher spirituality (*Kultur, ame slave*, etc.). Thus a distinguishing element in the response of backward areas is the crisis of collective identity. The cliché "Chinese (or Indian, Japanese, or other) spirit with Western technology" in all its myriad forms arose from a fear of spiritual and cultural deracination and frequently culminated in the fundamentally modern emotional and intellectual response of nationalism. For example, German romanticism was inextricable from German nationalism and Pan-Germanism; Pan-Slavism incorporated Slavophile ideas; and the Pan-Islam movement absorbs the spiritual-cultural revival of the Muslim brotherhoods. The ideas of Pan-Asianists became the underpinnings of Japanese imperialism, and even such a man as Gandhi became a nationalist leader. In China, the ideas of the National Essence group became part of the Kuomintang's neotraditional nationalism. In all of these cases, culture came to be seen as a unique, nonrepetitive essence, national in origin and significance, and set apart from the sociopolitical realities of modernization. Cultural renaissance based on the pristine national or people's spirit often became a central concern of the intellectuals associated with these movements and created considerable interest in linguistic, historical, literary, and folk studies.

Agrarianism and Rural Reconstruction

Another characteristic of this world-wide reaction to modernization has been antiurban agrarianism. Liang and his rural reconstruction of the 1930s fit into this response. We should, however, distinguish between the agrarian reform aspects of Liang's rural reconstruction and its underlying agrarianism. In the prewar decade, hundreds of local rural reform programs appeared in China, most focusing on only one specific problem such as education, credit, irrigation, or health. Liang's own projects in Shantung were distinguished by their attempts to solve all such problems and effect a total cultural renaissance as well. Although Liang did indeed emerge in the 1930s as the national spokesman for rural reform in general, and during the war he headed a quasi-political party, the Rural Reconstruction Group (Hsiang chien p'ai), not all rural reformers shared his philosophical agrarianism, which claimed general superiority for rural Chinese life and society.

It took a war with an industrialized nation to force the outstanding American theoretician of agrarianism, Thomas Jefferson, to abandon in part his cherished vision of an agrarian state unspoiled by that "sore on the body politic," the industrialized city.[21] Jefferson, too, was committed to what he considered universal human values that were inseparable from an agrarian form of society, but upon weighing them against national survival, he hedged. What was Liang's response when confronted with a similar conflict between agrarianism and national power at the time of the Japanese invasion of Manchuria in 1931? He pointed to the models he considered suitable for China: India and its unarmed but united moral resistance to British imperialism; and Denmark, which instead of struggling against its shrinking international position, concentrated on improving the quality of life for its people. Confronted with full-scale war in the summer of 1937, Liang's answer was fundamentally unchanged: spiritual solidarity, not industry and military hardware, would save China.[22]

When pressed to make a choice, Liang could not, as Jefferson did, allow the interests of national power to destroy the culture, for he was *au fond* a culturalist, intent on preserving the Way and not a true nationalist dedicated to the Chinese state. The Chinese nation could be a means to preserving the Way, but it could not be an end in itself. To be sure, Liang often presented his case to the public in nationalistic terms, saying in effect that only through revival of China's heritage could the nation-state prosper. But for Liang that heritage possessed not just historical but trans-historical significance. It must not be merely a museum piece which would serve the interests of national identity and pride, but the basis for present action. Like premodern Chinese, Liang believed that China was not just a culture among cultures but the only truly human one. Because he lived in the twentieth century, however, this conviction was hard-won, being reached only after a difficult spiritual odyssey; it was not a mere stubborn clinging to an assumption he was born to.

21. [328], XI, 503–505. In a letter to Benjamin Austin in 1816, Jefferson admits that the war of 1812 caused him to retreat from the stand he had taken against cities and manufacturing in his 1784 *Notes on Virginia*.
22. See [10]; [41]; [42n].

Liang Chi

Liang Shu-ming's Relationship
with His Father

Because of the importance of the relationship between father
and son to many of the issues I consider in this study, a substantial
portion of the book focuses on Liang's father, Liang Chi. This is
warranted, I believe, both because of Liang Chi's influence on his
son's personal development and because he is a character of absorbing interest in his own right.

On another level, a close scrutiny of this father-son relationship
and the peculiar circumstances that surrounded it might also give
some insight into some of the factors that shaped a key generation
in modern Chinese history. Liang Shu-ming was a member of this
critical generation of Chinese whose lives spanned the chaotic
period stretching from the last years of the old imperial order until
well after the new order had been established under the Chinese
Communist Party. This generation has intellectually and politically
dominated May Fourth and post-May Fourth China almost to this
day. Like other fathers of this generation, Liang's father grew up
and was comfortable in a traditional Chinese society that was still
relatively unaffected by Western cultural inroads. In contrast,
Liang Shu-ming himself felt the impact of the West very directly
from the age of six. Although this particular case of generational
conflict and contrast may hardly be typical, in-depth examination
of it does reveal significant symptomatic elements that might aid
our understanding of the emotional matrix in which this prominent generation of Chinese matured.

CHAPTER I

Father and Son

On a wintry blue Peking dawn in 1918, Liang Chi walked in gray-bearded dignity from his study, where he had spent a solitary wakeful night, to nearby Ching-yeh (Pure Dharma) Lake and threw himself into its icy waters. This suicide—a self-proclaimed martyrdom for China's dying traditional culture—brought to a dramatic end the eight-century-long line of Liang family official-literati that had begun with the fifth son of Kublai Khan.[1] Fathers and family background have their place sociologically and psychologically in any biographical study, but are particularly significant in the China of cultural crisis and in the family of a cultural martyr.

Liang Shu-ming, the twenty-third generation of this illustrious line, was born in a small house near the Forbidden City on Peking's Street of Tranquil Bliss on October 18, 1893.[2] Two months later in a rural household free of the burden of such weighty ancestors and untainted by "the fragrance of books," Liang's future student and, in the end, his teacher Mao Tse-tung was born. Hu Shih, Liang's future colleague and antagonist at Peking University, was already a three-year-old toddling around his father's yamen in eastern Taiwan.

1. Kublai Khan's son was named Ho-k'o-ch'i. In 1281 he was enfeoffed as king of Yunnan. When the Mongol dynasty was overthrown, the family went over to the Ming. At the time, the family house was established in Ju-yang (in present-day Hsi hsien, Honan), which in the Warring States period was the site of the Wei capital Ta Liang, so the family adopted the Chinese surname Liang. The family held noble rank throughout the Ming. With the establishment of the Manchu dynasty, the family moved to Chiang-ning in Kiangsu, where it soon started producing officials through the examination system. [99b], pp. 1a–b; [71], p. 3.

2. His given name was Huan-ting. In 1912, a T'ung-meng-hui comrade, Sun Ling-ming (later killed in Shanghai during the spring 1927 Kuomintang purge of Communists), gave him the "style" (tzu) Shu-ming—the name by which he was known for the rest of his life. [99b], p. 12b; [71], pp. 3, 39; [14a], p. 3.

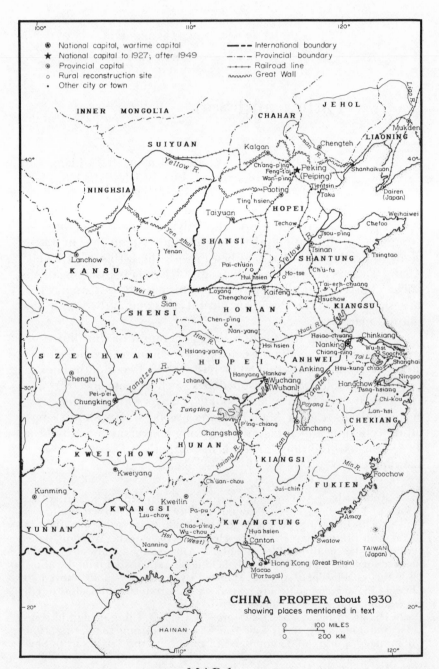

CHINA PROPER about 1930
showing places mentioned in text

Legend:
- ⊛ National capital, wartime capital
- ★ National capital to 1927; after 1949
- ◉ Provincial capital
- ○ Rural reconstruction site
- • Other city or town
- – – – International boundary
- –·–·– Provincial boundary
- +++ Railroad line
- ⌇⌇⌇ Great Wall

INNER MONGOLIA

CHAHAR

JEHOL

Liao R.

SUIYUAN

Mukden

Kalgan

Chengteh

LIAONING

Yellow R.

Chang-p'ing
Feng-t'ai
Wan-p'ing
Peking (Peiping)

Shanhaikuan

NINGHSIA

Paoting

Tientsin
Taku

Dairen (Japan)

Ting hsien

HOPEI

Weihaiwei

Taiyuan

Techow

Chefoo

SHANSI

Tsou-p'ing

Lanchow

Yenan

Pai-ch'uan

Tsinan

SHANTUNG

Tsingtao

KANSU

Hui hsien

Ho-tse

Ch'ü-fu

Wei R.

Loyang
Chengchow

Kaifeng

T'ai-erh-chuang

Sian

Hsuchow

KIANGSU

SHENSI

HONAN

Chen-p'ing

Nan-yang

Hsiao-chuang

Chinkiang

Han R.

Hsiang-yang

Hsi hsien

Huai R.

Nanking
Chiang-ning

Wu-hsi

SZECHWAN

HUPEI

ANHWEI

Tai L.

Soochow

Shanghai

Chengtu

Ichang

Hanyang Hankow

Anking

Hsu-kung ch'iao

Yangtze R.

Wuchang (Wuhan)

Ningpo

Pei-p'ei

Yangtze R.

Hangchow

Chungking

Tung ting L.

Poyang L.

Tsang-hsiang

Chi-k'ou

P'ing-chiang

Nanchang

Lan-hsi

Changsha

CHEKIANG

HUNAN

Kan R.

KWEICHOW

Hsiang R.

KIANGSI

Min R.

Kweiyang

Foochow

Kunming

Ch'uan-chou

Jui-chin

FUKIEN

Kweilin

Pa-pu

KWANGSI

Liu-chow

Chao-p'ing
Wu-chou

Hua hsien

KWANGTUNG

Amoy

YUNNAN

Hsi (West) R.

Nanning

Canton

Swatow

TAIWAN (Japan)

Hong Kong (Great Britain)

Macao (Portugal)

HAINAN

SCALE:
0 — 100 MILES
0 — 200 KM

MAP 1

The Liangs of Kweilin

Since the early nineteenth century, the Liangs had considered the remote southwestern city of Kweilin as their ancestral home, although both Shu-ming's grandfather and great-grandfather lived more of their lives in Peking than in Kweilin. Liang Chi and his children were all born and raised in the shadow of the Forbidden City.[3] Thus the Liangs of Kweilin were more Brahmins of the Imperial City than provincial gentry. In the twilight years of the Celestial Empire the brightest star of the Liang galaxy was Liang Chi's father, Liang Ch'eng-kuang, who like a comet had a short but brilliant life. A distinguished scholar and poet as well as an outstanding horseman and military strategist, Ch'eng-kuang included among his friends some of the most important officials in the empire. He died at thirty-five fighting the Nien rebels in Shansi, tired and burnt out before his time.[4] His death had an instantaneous and decisive effect upon the Liang family; it reduced them to poverty. Ch'eng-kuang's formal wife and his concubine took the only child, Liang Chi, a frail eight-year-old thread of family continuity and its sole hope for the future, from Shansi back to the city of his birth. They did not enter Peking's ancient gates in a manner befitting a proud old family, but crept back in disguise to avoid their creditors. Burning with the shame that only poor relations can understand, the family took refuge in the house of in-laws.[5] In old age, Liang Chi still had memories of crowded quarters and penny-wise frugality, of his formal mother taking in students and his natural mother (the concubine) taking in laundry.

Thus began Liang Chi's life of shabby gentility which did not alter appreciably in his lifetime. The family was also a classic example of that peculiarly Chinese aristocracy: the scholar-official family of many generations. By Liang Chi's generation, the family had lost its wealth and power of former days, but not the tradition of serving as the bearers of ancient ideals and as the society's *custodes*

3. The nineteenth generation Liang, Liang Hou, moved the family to Kweilin in the early nineteenth century. When his son Liang Pao-shu went to Peking in 1849 to take the *chin-shih* examination, he established residence there. [99b], pp. 1–6; [71], p. 3; [14a], pp. 2–3.

4. Liang Ch'eng-kuang had served in the Grand Secretariat for a time and had the rank of "expectant prefect" (*hou-pu chih-fu*) when he died. The court conferred upon him the honorary title *ch'ao-i ta-fu*. His friends included such famous and powerful figures as P'an Tsu-yin, Sun Yü-wen, Li Shou-yü, Hsu Chi-yü, and Weng T'ung-ho. [99b], pp. 1b, 7b.

5. [99b], pp. 3b–4.

morum. Under the stern Confucian eye of his formal mother, Liang Chi received his birthright—a classical education and a classic sense of moral scrupulosity, which instilled in him very early a sense of continuous struggle between selfish personal desire and the moral perfection of a *chün-tzu*. His suicide would be just one more exercise of his lifelong moral athleticism.

These two strains in the Liang family—a tradition of greatness and a sense of moral leadership—permeated Liang Shu-ming's youthful environment and shaped his youthful attitudes. In reflecting upon his childhood, Liang Shu-ming wrote: "The influence of my father's character caused a sense of responsibility toward society and the country to germinate unconsciously in my juvenile mentality, and I felt contempt for that vulgar, profit-pursuing, creature-comfort-seeking life of a selfish fellow."[6]

The memory of family glory seems to have had a further effect on both father and son. The declining patrician family, a familiar theme in modern Western literature and in the lives of many of its writers, often seems to produce children of marked sensitivity. Though modern China has no Mann or Faulkner, both Lu Hsun, its greatest literary artist and trenchant critic of traditional society, and Liang Shu-ming, the saintlike champion of tradition, seem to provide Chinese examples of a relationship between declining family fortunes and spiritual sensitivity.

It has been said that what a father says to his children is not heard by the world, but will be heard by posterity. The fundamental direction of Liang Shu-ming's life, the formation of his persona and his personality, turned upon the poignant point of his relationship with his father. How Liang Chi reached his end is the key to Liang Shu-ming's beginnings. But the path that took Liang Chi to Ching-yeh Lake was by no means a straight one. That he would choose to die for traditional China and the Manchus in 1918 was not obvious from the attitudes he exhibited and the activities he pursued throughout his lifetime. The usual categories of conservative, reformer, and radical do not quite capture Liang Chi.

Liang Chi as Cultural Iconoclast

Liang Chi won the *chü-jen* degree in 1885 at age twenty-four, but not until 1898—a wife and four children later—did he gain an

6. [71], p. 20.

official post as a secretary in the Grand Secretariat. Until then he had eked out an existence as a teacher in private schools, a tutor to children of a Manchu grandee, and a private secretary to Peking officials. He remained in his position at the Grand Secretariat until 1906, when he was given the opportunity to manage the Metropolitan Police Bureau's newly created Bureau of Poor Relief, and later, the metropolitan workhouses. In 1908, he resigned from official life to observe the mourning period for his formal mother's death, and he never held an official post again.[7]

Viewed in the context of his time, Liang Chi appears very radical. In the decade of the 1880s, the major lines of ideological debate were drawn between the few "self-strengtheners," who advocated learning from the West technologically, economically, and diplomatically, and the bulk of somnambulantly conservative officialdom. The most vituperatively aggressive of the conservatives, an amorphous coterie of Peking officials known as the *ch'ing-liu* (the pure party), were hostile to the self-strengtheners and staunchly opposed to compromise with the West on any terms. As a young man in his twenties, Liang Chi not only despised their blind obscurantism, but went beyond even the reformers in welcoming the winds of change from the West. While the self-strengtheners admitted the superiority of Western technology, they still believed that the basic values and institutions of Chinese tradition could meet the problems of the modern world. By 1883, Liang Chi had already concluded that the Chinese Classics did not have the answers for the new problems brought on by the Western invasion.[8]

Liang Chi was well aware that such an attitude toward innovation and change carried certain social and political penalties, as shown by the fate of an official he much admired, Kuo Sung-tao. "Although the newly published books on world affairs and Western learning are despised by 'proper gentlemen,' I absolutely must read them because there is no such thing as a perpetually unchanged state of affairs in the world. I must strive to be realistic and so cannot avoid the ridicule of society."[9]

Liang Chi's "realism" meant that any individual, institution, or

---

7. [99b], pp. 7a–b, 8b, 11b, 16a–b, 20, 22; [193], 346: 20b. Liang Chi served as personal secretary to Ku Ch'i-hsin, Sun Yü-wen, and the *ch'ing-liu* clique conservative, Li Wen-t'ien. He also tutored the Manchu Duke Na's children for a time.

8. [99b], pp. 20, 22; [404b], p. 2b.

9. [99b], p. 9; see also pp. 12b, 13; and [9h], p. 98.

policy must be judged on its ability to achieve concrete results in strengthening China. He despised the effete scribblers of poetry and essay who seemed to believe that Confucian cant, if cast in elegant style, would save China. Liang Chi considered the respected leader of the *ch'ing-liu* coterie, Chang P'ei-lun, a self-serving sycophant who, in quest of personal reputation rather than national salvation, cast ornamented barbs at innovators and innovations. Famous literary scholars like Yü Yueh were also useless for they produced no practical results. Instead, Liang Chi welcomed K'ang Yu-wei's radical institutional reforms of 1898 as "the root of self-strengthening."[10]

The Boxer disaster of 1900, occurring as it did on his very doorstep, brought home to Liang Chi the ignorance and superstition of the masses of his countrymen. Hitherto he had focused his attention upon reform from the top, but now he realized that without citizen-building educational enterprises to influence and involve the common people, there could be no national regeneration. In 1902, he and his friend P'eng I-sun established the *Ching-hua jih-pao*—the first Chinese newspaper aimed at promoting nationalism and reform among the common people. To reach a broader audience they took another revolutionary step and published the paper in the popular language (*pai-hua*). The paper was so innovative that it was popularly known in Peking as a "foreign" newspaper. It, in fact, succeeded in instigating several popular nationalistic movements in the capital, such as the Boxer indemnity contribution movement and the 1905 anti-American boycott. The journal's crusading spirit helped spread circulation throughout North China as far as Shensi, Kansu, and Manchuria. Liang Chi and P'eng also established one of China's first children's magazines, *Ch'i-meng hua-pao*, a pictorial devoted to spreading basic knowledge in science, world affairs, and foreign cultures.[11] Liang Shu-ming later

10. [404b], pp. 9, 11b; [99b], p. 17.
11. Chinese in the treaty ports had established newspapers before this, and a few were even written in the colloquial language, but the ventures of Liang and P'eng were the first of their kind in the capital and perhaps the only ones to stress basic modern knowledge for the masses. The papers stirred up mass patriotic movements over the British mistreatment of Chinese laborers and American exclusion of Chinese laborers. The largest movement was the indemnity contribution movement, in which the papers raised a great deal of money toward paying off China's foreign debts and reducing the interest charges. The paper also established reading rooms and "newspaper lecture rooms" (for the illiterate) throughout the city.

informed the iconoclastic champion of "science and democracy," Ch'en Tu-hsiu, that his father's newspapers had given the people of Peking their first introduction to Ch'en's "Mr. Science."[12]

Liang Chi's cultural pioneering was not limited to the creation of a new journalism. Like many old Peking residents, he had an interest in the theater. In 1904, he wrote and produced Peking's first "new-style play" (*hsin chü*), *The Girl Patriot*, a drama designed to arouse nationalistic sentiments.[13]

Later in 1906, when he was finally given an administrative post in the metropolitan police department, Liang Chi continued to pursue his reformist bent by establishing trade schools in the prisons and instituting an educational program for poor children.[14] Around this time Liang Chi and his wife became acquainted with the founder of China's first socialist party, Chiang K'ang-hu, whom Mme. Liang worked with in women's education. Ch'en Chi-lung, another early socialist leader, was also a frequent visitor at the Liang house for a time.[15]

In no way did Liang Chi depart further from the mores of his peers than in the upbringing of his children. At the turn of the century the relationship between the scholar-official father and his offspring was a very formal affair governed by strict etiquette and inflexible conventions. Many children who had grown up in such households could almost count the times they had actually spoken with their fathers, and then only in an attitude of "trembling respect." Rare was the patriarch who would tolerate argument or even free discussion from his children. In contrast, Liang Chi consciously cultivated a friendly, spontaneous relationship with his children, urged them to talk freely with him, and actively sought

---

P'eng's name became a household word in Peking. The children's magazine was eagerly awaited and read each week by children as far south as Kiangsu. [624]; see also [99b], pp. 19–20; [71], pp. 16–18; [5h], pp. 61–62; [350], pp. 113–176.

    12. [5h], p. 61.   13. Ibid.; also [99b], pp. 19b, 20b.

    14. [99b], pp. 20–22; [193], 496:20b.

    15. In 1904, Mme. Liang [Chang Ch'un-i], a highly educated woman from an old Yunnanese scholar-official family, participated in the establishment of Peking's first modern girls' school, the Nü-hsueh ch'uan-hsi-so, and taught Chinese literature there. She also supported her husband in his reform endeavors. As Chiang K'ang-hu was in Peking working in women's education at about this time, this was probably the period during which he and his colleague Ch'en Chi-lung frequented the Liang home. See [71], pp. 20, 41; [99b], p. 19b.

out their opinions. He purposefully encouraged them to develop an unconventional spirit of independence and taught them to hold their own opinions even in the face of parental opposition. He also forebore inflicting any form of corporal punishment, perhaps aware that there was no accuser so potent nor judge so severe as the conscience within.[16] Early independence brings early feelings of responsibility. Half a century afterwards, Liang Shu-ming still vividly recalled one incident:

> Once when I was nine I lost a string of coins I had saved up. I looked everywhere for it and raised a ruckus with everyone about it, but to no avail. A day later my father found it on a branch of the peach tree in the front courtyard. He knew I had forgotten it myself, but he did not berate me or call me to come see. Instead, he wrote down a message that went something like: "Once there was a little boy playing under the peach tree. He inadvertently left a string of coins hanging from one of the branches and forgot about it. He then went around asking everyone else about it and causing a terrible fuss. The next day while sweeping the courtyard, his father saw the coins and showed them to the boy, who then realized he had been muddle-headed," and so on. Father handed me the paper without a word. I immediately reflected on it, and then ran out and found the coins. I could not help but feel ashamed of myself.[17]

The education of the Liang children and the nieces and nephews in Liang Chi's charge also reflected his cultural iconoclasm and disregard for traditional ways. He sent his oldest son Huan-nai to the Peking College for Interpreters when it first opened its doors in 1903. Three years later he dispatched Huan-nai to Tokyo to study that calling most despised by the traditional scholar class—business.[18] He also sent two orphaned nephews to the Interpreters

16. [71], pp. 5–7; [47], pp. 55–56; [14a], pp. 8–9; [9h], pp. 97–101; [404].
17. [71], p. 7.
18. Liang Huan-nai (K'ai-ming) was born in 1887, six years before Liang Shu-ming. He studied at the Peking College of Interpreters (Ching-shih i-hsueh-kuan)—a government school established to train experts for transactions with foreigners—from its opening in 1903 until August 1906, when he left to attend Meiji University in Tokyo. There he majored in commerce and graduated with honors in the summer of 1911. After working for a half year as an interpreter at the Chinese embassy in Tokyo, he returned to China in January 1912, and the following summer started teaching at Northwestern University in Sian. In 1916, he took a position in

College and later to England for degrees in law, and regretted that he himself had not had the opportunity to study abroad.[19] In a double departure from convention, he saw to it that his two daughters not only received an education, but a modern-style one at that.[20]

Liang Shu-ming's early education was perhaps the most thoroughly unconventional of all. His home education began traditionally enough at age six with a tutor, but instead of memorizing the Four Books, his father instructed the tutor to begin with the *Ti-ch'iu yun-yen* (World geography in rhyme), a kind of primer of world history and geography. Liang Chi, however, did not consider this a wholly satisfactory means to "modern" education. When Peking's first foreign-style primary school, the Sino-Western Primary School (Chung Hsi hsiao-hsueh-t'ang) opened the next year, 1899, he enrolled little Shu-ming in its first class. That same year Mao Tse-tung started his education in rural Hunan, chanting the Classics under the watchful eye and ever-ready rod of a traditional teacher. In the Anhwei village of Shang-chuang, Hu Shih was also engrossed in memorizing the Classics in a traditional family school. But seven-year-old Liang Shu-ming—future defender of tradition—was busily probing into the mysteries of an English primer, learning his ABCs rather than his *Analects*. As a consequence of all

the Ministry of Agriculture and Commerce. After this start on the bureaucratic ladder, he worked his way through several jobs at various railway administration bureaus until he was made the Chief of the Secretariat of the Peking-Liaoning railway administration. Through the 1930s, he lived in Tientsin in the British concession and seems to have had little contact with his brother after 1925 when they finished editing their father's papers for publication. He was married to the daughter of his father's friend and colleague P'eng I-sun. [71], p. 4; [591], pp. 11–64; [99b], pp. 8a, 19a, 24–25.

19. In July 1902, Mme. Liang's uncle, Chang Li-wu, died leaving a wife, three children, and no money. Liang Chi was also related to Chang's wife, and in fact had grown up with her in her father's home. Therefore, the Chang family moved into the Liang household. The next year, Mrs. Chang passed away, leaving the upbringing and education of her brood entirely on Liang Chi's shoulders. He sent them all to modern middle schools and then dispatched the eldest son Chang Yao-tseng to Japan in 1903 for law training and the younger son Chang K'uan-hsi to Edinburgh University in 1904. After sending the daughter to middle school in Tientsin, he sent her to Tokyo for further study. [99b], pp. 16b, 19–20, 22, 26b; [127]; [5c], p. 28.

20. Liang Shu-ming's two younger sisters, Huan-hao (born 1894) and Huan-shen (born 1896), both graduated from the Metropolitan Woman's Normal School (Ching-shih nü-tzu shih-fan hsueh-t'ang, founded 1908) in 1911. [99b], pp. 15, 16, 19b, 24; [71], p. 4.

this foreign education, Liang Shu-ming never memorized the Confucian Classics nor seriously studied them until he reached adulthood.[21]

Liang Chi as Moral Aristocrat

How did Liang Chi, the pragmatic nationalist in the forefront of progressive reform who, even in his personal life, exemplified iconoclastic openness to Western cultural influence, come to kill himself in an anti-Western gesture for traditional Chinese culture? The answer lies in the other side of Liang Chi's personality: the part of his character shaped by the family tradition of duty to and responsibility for state and society.

In theory at least, the true Confucian gentleman held and exercised power through his personal virtue, which was attained by intense moral self-cultivation, maintained by continuous introspection, and brought to bear on society through force of personal example and moral education. This enterprise of forging oneself into an ethical paragon of inner spiritual perfection and outward propriety was a lifelong obsession with Liang Chi, and he set for himself the most stringent standards of proper conduct. Even when alone in his room he would not so much as loosen his collar button or slouch in his chair, for he took in dreadful earnest the hoary warning of Confucian scripture: "the *chün-tzu* must be watchful over himself when he is alone" as there are "many eyes that see and many fingers that point."[22] He doubtless could have obtained office much earlier than he did if he had followed the common practice and called upon any of his father's powerful friends, but to do so would have violated his supersensitive feelings of propriety. When he was finally given a position, he even refused to call on the head of his bureau because he felt that smacked of currying favor.[23]

Liang Chi's personal life was also full of sacrifices made to fulfill

21. [99b], p. 16b; [71], pp. 10–12; [5h], p. 61; [510], pp. 1–2; [14a], pp. 2–3.

22. Ta Hsueh, 6:3. "*Shih mu so shih shih shou so chih ch'i yen hu.*" The passage has been interpreted as referring to myriad spirits of heaven who continually watch the conduct of men. Legge's translation is: "What ten eyes behold, what ten hands point to, is to be regarded with reverence." [378], I, 367.

23. [99b], p. 21b. For instance, only after his father's powerful friend Sun Yü-wen had fallen from power (and so was unable to get him a position), did Liang Chi call on him. [99b], p. 15.

what he considered moral obligations. Despite his own straitened circumstances, he took the widows and children of deceased relatives into his home and raised money for loans to needy associates. When his mother died in 1908, he followed the strictest interpretation of propriety and retired from official life, despite his dire need for money at the time and the fact that the custom of observing a three-year mourning period was long out of fashion.[24]

In 1902, he went into debt to support his friend P'eng's financially disastrous journalistic enterprises. He did so because of his personal relationship with P'eng as well as the responsibility he felt to take up the *chün-tzu*'s burden toward society in general. P'eng's publications aroused the wrath of the Empress Dowager in 1906, and the newspapers were suppressed. The next year P'eng established another paper, the *Ching-hua pao*. His exposés about Yuan Shih-k'ai's Pei-yang army protégés soon provoked Yuan to exile P'eng to the wilds of Sinkiang. In both instances, Liang Chi disregarded the possible effects on his own career and stuck by his friend.[25]

In the same spirit of personal abnegation for public benefit, he risked his life by publicly urging action against the Boxers, even after they had gained the Empress Dowager's backing. When the disaster he predicted occurred and the foreign armies occupied Peking, most of the officials in the city fled with their families and belongings, but again Liang Chi felt the only honorable course was to remain in the city and at his official post.[26]

24. See note 19. In the spring of 1911, a former student of Liang Chi's from the Peking Professional School (Ching-shih shih-yeh hsueh-t'ang, the predecessor to the later Industrial College), where Liang had been preceptor in 1909, asked for a loan to finance a trip home. Although Liang was already strapped for funds himself, he pawned more of his wife's jewelry to raise the money. Liang's only condition was that the student, who had been somewhat of a prodigal, mend his ways and strive to be a useful citizen. Apparently the student did not reform, as the loan was never returned. See [99b], pp. 22a–b, 23b.

25. In August 1906, *Ching hua pao* reported the murders of two Protect-the-Emperor-Society members, Wu Tao-ming and Fan Lü-hsiang, by Yuan Shih-k'ai's military secretariat (Pei-yang ying-wu-ch'u). Yuan closed down the paper and had the Ministry of Justice arrest P'eng (and his son-in-law, K'ang Shen-hsiu) and sentence him to ten years in Sinkiang. Liang attempted to save his friend, and when his efforts failed, he tried to resign from office in protest. Liang also took complete responsibility for P'eng's family while P'eng was in exile. [99b], pp. 19, 20b–21; [71], pp. 16–19; see also [350], p. 172.

26. [99b], pp. 17b, 18. For remaining at his post during the Allied ar-

He evaluated others by the same standards of personal integrity. Virtue, not ideological stance, was his decisive criterion. He had little respect for his employer of the early 1890s, Li Wen-t'ien, not because of Li's anti-foreign conservatism, but because he, like many other Peking officials, had considered fleeing the capital during the 1894–1895 Sino-Japanese war. Liang Chi despised this sort of scholar-official who placed personal considerations above his duty to society.[27] Moral considerations were also the reason Liang Chi could somewhat paradoxically have great admiration for both Wo Jen, who represented the epitome of Sinocentric conservatism, and Liang Ch'i-ch'ao, the revolutionary propagator of Western influence. The two were diametrically opposed in almost every area but one—their moral rectitude, personal virtue, and unselfish fulfillment of their responsibilities as scholars—and that was what was most important to Liang Chi.[28]

Even in his generally enthusiastic response to the 1898 reforms Liang wrote a memorial urging caution, emphasizing that while institutional reform was "the basis of self-strengthening," the basis for effective institutional reform was "the hearts of upright people." Political innovation without moral rejuvenation would simply give more power to the corrupt bureaucrats already in office and so increase their evil influence. Thus, the thrust of Liang's memorial—that good government depended upon good people, not good laws—was identical to the arguments against reform by the ultraconservatives such as Ch'u Ch'eng-po and Chu I-hsin.[29]

Liang Shu-ming—Early Years

Growing up as he did in the capital city Peking, the first few years of Liang Shu-ming's life encompassed such profoundly important events as the disastrous Chinese defeat in the Sino-Japanese War of

---

mies' occupation of Peking, Liang Chi received the title "Shih tu" (Assistant reader of the grand secretariat) and was raised in rank. [99b], p. 19a.

27. Li Wen-t'ien (1834–1895) was a member of the *ch'ing-liu* coterie of Peking area officials who opposed reformist programs and took an unrealistic hard line during the Sino-French War of 1884–1885 and the Sino-Japanese War of 1894–1895, in effect opposing the moderates in Li Hung-chang's camp. See [322], I, 494–495.

28. [404b], pp. 5, 9, 11b; [6].

29. [99b], pp. 16b–17. For Ch'u Ch'eng-po, Chu I-hsin, and other antireformist conservatives on the question, see [491].

1894–1895, the abortive Hundred-Days Reform of 1898, and the Boxer calamity. The impact of the Boxers was perhaps the most direct and terrifying. In the summer of 1900, the "righteous and harmonious fists" surged into Peking fresh from Christian-killing and church-burning in North China. Before and during their famous siege of the foreign-legation quarter, they continued their attempts to eliminate foreign influences and the foreign-influenced in other parts of the city. Liang Shu-ming's Sino-Western Primary School together with many of Peking's Christian churches were put to the Boxers' self-righteous torches. Fearful that he too would be discovered as a reader of foreign books and thus a foreign devils' disciple, Liang Shu-ming furtively burned all his English textbooks.[30]

Shu-ming seems to have had a rather sickly and pampered childhood. At six he still had to have help in dressing, and as his father's favorite, he seems to have enjoyed more than his share of paternal attention. Liang Chi had even personally tended to him during his recurring childhood illnesses. It must have been quite an adjustment for him when he moved away from the family nest for the first time in 1906 to attend the Shun-t'ien Middle School on the other side of Peking.[31]

Genesis of character. Several of Liang Shu-ming's most pronounced personality characteristics were clearly evident by his adolescent years, and they strongly reflected his father's multifaceted personality. His highly developed sense of moral scrupulosity had moved his father to give him the nickname "Hsiao-wu" (the one who resembles me).[32] Like his father, Liang Shu-ming had a compulsive concern for personal virtue and an unremitting desire

30. [71], p. 12.
31. [9h], pp. 98–99; [71], pp. 8–9, 24–31; [14a], pp. 2–3; [99b], pp. 20–22. In the years between 1900 and 1906, Liang attended several primary schools and studied with home tutors as well. In 1901, he went to the Nan-heng Street Public Primary School (Nan-heng chieh kung-li hsiao-hsueh-t'ang). The next year he attended P'eng I-sun's Meng-yang School. In 1905, he went to the primary school run by the Kiangsu *Landesmannschaft*—probably introduced to it by P'eng I-sun, who was from Soochow, Kiangsu. Such an unsystematic primary education was common at the time because modern primary schools were not widespread and the imperial government's new school system was still in a state of flux. See [99b], p. 18; [71], p. 12.
32. [14a], p. 5; [9h], p. 98.

for self-improvement. In his first meaningful contact with any traditional Chinese thought, he had studied the *Te yü chien* (Guide to moral education)—the great compendium of Confucian moralisms on self-cultivation compiled and annotated by Liang Ch'i-ch'ao—and he took to heart the moral maxims he found in it to "establish one's life goal" (*li-chih*) and to preserve and cultivate (*han-ts'un*) virtue through constant self-examination (*shen-ch'a*) and self-rectification (*k'o-chi*).[33] During his high school years, however, Liang sought moral perfection not so much as an end in itself, but more as a means to forge himself into a more efficient instrument for the achievement of patriotic goals.

Single-minded character building cannot avoid having a tint of self-conceit, which prompted his classmates to give him quite a different nickname, "Ao" (proud). Liang admitted that the sobriquet was altogether apt: "Possibly this kind of psychology (of continuous self-cultivation) has its faults—at the least, one cannot avoid divulging to others a kind of arrogant spirit." This tendency toward spiritual priggery, which later in life became more like a schoolmarmish stuffiness, made him admirable to some and unattractive to others. During middle school at least, Liang was still capable of "going out drinking with the boys" on occasion.[34]

Liang's pride, together with his desire to be original and to hold stubbornly to his own views as his father had taught him, formed another lifelong personality trait—tendentiousness. In his Chinese compositions he developed a flair for controverting the generally accepted and was quite free with his criticism of established opinion, which moved one teacher to warn: "Misfortune will inevitably strike one who delights in maliciously opposing others."[35]

Political thought. Liang Shu-ming's youthful political thought also bore the imprint of his father's concerns. Thanks to his father's interest in journalism, Liang Shu-ming developed very early a lifelong habit of newspaper reading and a concomitant interest in current affairs. "The Peking papers like the *Shun-t'ien shih-pao* and *Ti-kuo jih-pao* as well as the out-of-town newspapers like the *Shen pao, Hsin-wen pao,* and *Shih pao,* were all my minimum

---

33. [71], p. 35; [405], II, 1–170.   34. [71] pp. 20–21, 25.
35. [71], p. 27. Many interviewees who knew Liang as an adult emphasized particularly that he was "stubborn," "obstinate," and "opinionated." [612]; [613]; [614]; [615]; [618]; [620]; [622]; [625]; [626]; [629]; [633]; [637].

daily reading material. When it came to talk of current affairs, I was extremely knowledgeable and not at all like the ordinary middle school student."[36] Another uncommon middle school student, Mao Tse-tung, developed a similar mania for newspaper reading at about the same time.

Obsessed by the desire to make China strong against its oppressors, both Liang and Mao were also persuaded by Liang Ch'i-ch'ao and his coadjutors to embrace such Western political institutions as constitutionalism, party government, and rule by law. Liang felt, however, that the specific political and social reform programs had value only insofar as they would build a powerful Chinese nation-state. He read and reread Liang Ch'i-ch'ao's constitutionalist publication, *Hsin-min ts'ung-pao* (Journal of the new citizen), as well as his journal of new literature, *Hsin hsiao-shuo pao* (New fiction), and from them he drew most of what he knew of Western political theories and systems. Later in 1910, Liang Ch'i-ch'ao's last constitutionalist organ *Kuo feng pao* (National spirit) aroused his enthusiasm for other governmental innovations from the West, and he became quite interested in the mechanics of legislative systems, cabinets, budgeting, auditing, and currency systems. China should follow the path of social, political, and economic rationalization and thereby achieve wealth and power.[37]

At this stage in his life, Liang Shu-ming saw no moral limits on the means to force the wavering Manchu court to effect these reforms. Like many young Chinese in the last decade of the empire, he was impressed by the sanitary, surgical efficiency of the Russian Narodnik terrorists. "I held that many kinds of devices could be used in political reform and none was better than assassination as employed by the Russian nihilists."[38] Such a seemingly amoral attitude does not imply that Liang did not consider the moral implications; on the contrary, his attitude toward terror was perfectly consistent with his clear, well-developed moral philosophy. He believed, quite like his father, that all actions must be judged by their results. The ultimate good was happiness, and happiness was the sum of pleasures. Good and evil were synonymous with pleasure and pain, and so he measured any human action by a Benthamesque hedonistic calculus. If judged by the standard of "the great-

36. [71], p. 33; also pp. 15, 20–21.
37. [23f], pp. 253–254; [14r]; [23c]; [71], pp. 14–15, 27–37; [14a], pp. 15–17, 19; [11a], pp. 4–8; [11c], pp. 101–107.
38. [71], p. 33.

est good for the greatest number," then the "pain" that resulted
from an act of assassination was not as great as the pleasure produced by the reforms it would stimulate. He himself described his
adolescent thought variously as "instrumentalism," "pragmatism,"
or "utilitarianism."[39]

In the best, or worst, utilitarian tradition, young Liang considered art and philosophy as self-serving nonsense:

> At the time I devoted myself to saving our nation and people,
> and wanted to do something praiseworthy to establish myself.
> My philosophy of life was very shallow and simplistic. I simply
> ignored the more profound problems of human life. . . I held
> a narrow utilitarian point of view, which valued concrete
> achievement, and I had contempt for scholarship and learn-
> ing per se. I gave some attention to studies with practical
> value, but I considered literature and philosophy as things
> that cheated and deceived people, and so I drove them out of
> my mind.[40]

When, in his freshman year at Shun-t'ien Middle School, the
Chinese language teacher taught the "eight great writers of the
T'ang and Sung dynasties," he was "most unhappy." "I never read
the lecture outlines and above all I detested empty verbiage, like Su
Tung-p'o's fables." He was unregeneratively unappreciative of any
of the treasures of China's literary heritage. "There was not one I
did not despise." He especially disliked China's traditional philosophical greats such as Lao-tzu.[41]

Schoolmates and revolutionary comrades. The Shun-t'ien
Middle School was one of the new-style educational institutions,
which, in Mao Tse-tung's apt remark, "sprang up like bamboo
shoots after rain" after the abolition of the examination system in
1905. The novelty of such schools lay not merely in their Western
format and curriculum in science, mathematics, and foreign lan-
guages. They also brought young Chinese from various regions
together for long periods of time. Of course, China had long had
schools, but the traditional institutions were organized on the basis
of kin or locality relationships. Students in the modern schools
shared a new and unprecedented kind of identity—that of being
"Chinese"—and the student organizations they formed were ex-

39. [23c], pp. 85–86; [14a], pp. 1–7, 16; [71], pp. 14–15, 29–30, 35–37.
40. [71], p. 35; see also p. 29 and [14a], pp. 5–7.
41. [71], p. 27; [14a], p. 5.

"unity of China" not a fixed political idea?

tremely important in the rise of another unprecedented phenomenon—the wave of mass nationalism. The newborn student
class, more than any other single group, was at the heart of China's
first large-scale nationalistic explosion during the last decade of
Manchu rule.

As a new-style student, Liang Shu-ming was part of this new
wave. Indeed, because of his father's influence and his passion for
newspapers, Liang Shu-ming was on the very crest of the wave
rather than one who was passively pulled along by the current.
Even before entering middle school, he had begun his personal
crusade to strengthen the nation. As a mere twelve-year-old he had
distributed leaflets urging participation in various nationalistic
movements. During the 1905 anti-American boycott, he and his
friends had pushed their way through neighborhood shops in
search of the reprehensible American merchandise. Every fresh
incident of national shame made his juvenile blood boil with indignation. Immediately after one such incident, his classmates designated him to confront their school principal with a demand for
extracurricular military training so that student blood and iron
might help "save the nation" against the ravages of the increasingly
rapacious imperial powers. The request was granted, rifles issued,
and a military officer hired to drill the students after classes.[42]

Liang also participated in a more traditional type of association at
his school. Under the stimulus of some of his fellow students, Liang
joined a "self-study group"—an informal association formed to
provide mutual encouragement, criticism, and intellectual benefit
to its members.[43] Here, as so often in the Chinese context, study
refers not only to intellectual learning, but to moral self-cultivation
as well. This small-group discussion of academic and ethical questions, together with mutual criticism of one another's faults, was a
significant part of Liang's adolescence, for the concept would play a
central role in his later educational programs and finally in rural
reconstruction. Such associations were not at all unique in the early
twentieth century. Even revolutionary cells were organized under
such names as the Society for the Promotion of Virtue. Among the

42. [71], pp. 17, 30–31; [14a], pp. 15–16.
43. As a method of warning each other against moral failings, the boys
addressed each other by a nickname that could describe the bearer's worst
tendency. For instance, the group's athlete, Yao Wan-li, was called
"Violent" (Pao), while a group leader, Liao Fu-shen, was called "Lazy"
(To).

reforms Ts'ai Yuan-p'ei later instituted at Peking University was
the establishment of an Association to Promote Virtue to combat
traditional student proclivities for wine, women, and gambling.[44]
In fact, the same technique and pattern recurs throughout Chinese
history; it is based upon the peculiarly Confucian faith in the ability
of the immediate human environment to effect an individual's
internal transformation. The techniques Confucius and Mencius
used in small-group education provide the primal model, and a
similar pattern is clear in the Sung and Ming Neo-Confucianists,
the Ch'ing academies, and even the Communist *hsueh-hsi* (study)
groups.

Through the group Liang Shu-ming participated in, or more
specifically through its leader Kuo Hsiao-feng, Liang was "liber-
ated" to some extent from the narrow utilitarian blinders fastened
so securely under his father's influence. As he was from the same
district, Kuo was good friends with the future founder of the
Chinese Communist Party, Li Ta-chao, and later worked with him
and Mao Tse-tung in the Peking University Library. Kuo was at the
time already quite learned in the Buddhist and Taoist Classics and
the *Book of Changes*, and an enthusiastic propagator of T'an Szu-
t'ung's book, *On Humanitarianism (Jen hsueh)*.[45] Physically, interestingly enough, Kuo looked "like a pretty girl. Everyone who saw him
was startled by his beauty." Liang idolized Kuo and literally wrote
down his every word in a special notebook, which he inscribed
"Quotations from Teacher Kuo." Such pretentious goings-on soon
had their classmates quipping "Liang the Worthy and Kuo the
Sage" (Liang hsien-jen, Kuo sheng-jen).[46]

Inspired and guided by Kuo, Liang started dipping into the
traditional Chinese philosophy he had previously scorned. Liang
read especially heavily in Buddhist works and the writings of Wang
Yang-ming. These adventures into the murky realms of Vij-
nanamatravada Buddhism and Ming period Confucian idealism
did not have an immediate impact on Liang Shu-ming's basic think-

44. The Society for the Promotion of Virtue was founded in Wuhan
and was transformed into a revolutionary organization by Liu Ching-an.
Ts'ai Yuan-p'ei's association (Chin-te hui) was on a large scale, with about
one thousand members at one point, but it still indicates the peculiarly
Chinese concept of the natural combination of scholarship and morality.
See [524b], pp. 108–112; [524c], pp. 172–183.

45. [14a], p. 6; [71], pp. 34–35, 37.

46. [71], pp. 34, 35–36; [14a], p. 7.

ing; he still held firmly to his lucid hedonistic calculus. But the confrontation with the subtleties of philosophical discourse did lead him to the habit of solitary meditation for long periods. What, he began to wonder, really constituted "pleasure" and "pain"?[47]

The self-study group's influence on Liang was not limited to his intellectual development but extended into the realm of politics as well. Throughout his years in middle school (1906 through 1911), two distinct images of China's future came into increasingly sharper focus to China's young student class. In 1905, the scattered republican revolutionary groups had assembled in a less than perfect union under the banner of Sun Yat-sen's Revolutionary Alliance (T'ung-meng-hui). In the summer of the next year the Manchu court set a steady if somewhat slow course toward constitutional monarchy. Liang Ch'i-ch'ao, still the single most influential writer in all of China, was inclined to take these Manchu efforts seriously. The debate between constitutionalism and revolution raged in every Chinese school. For the first time Liang Shu-ming was compelled to defend his faith in Liang Ch'i-ch'ao and constitutionalism, which he had accepted so unquestioningly at the feet of his father and P'eng I-sun. On the revolutionary side, he confronted not only Kuo Hsiao-feng but also many others, including a young cosmopolitan named Chen Yuan-hsi, who had lived in both Canton and Shanghai—the two hotbeds of revolutionary activity.

In his characteristic fashion, Liang Shu-ming met his revolutionary classmates head-on. If people disagreed with him, he could not rest until he understood to his satisfaction precisely what they advocated and why. The Revolutionary Alliance's publications were not easy to come by, but in 1910 he managed to subscribe to its organ, the *Min-li pao* (People's stand). He also got hold of a collection of the debates between the Alliance's stalwart, Hu Han-min, and his own champion, Liang Ch'i-ch'ao, which he read with great care and enthusiasm. Chen Yuan-hsi finally forced Liang to face him in a similar battle of the pens.[48] Liang Shu-ming held to his constitutionalist stand throughout—until the fateful Hsin-hai year (1911). By then Liang Shu-ming, too, had had enough of Manchu foot-dragging and lukewarm reformism, and joined his classmates in the drift toward revolution.[49]

47. [71], p. 30; [14a], pp. 6–7.
48. [71], pp. 34–37; [14a], p. 16; [14r], pp. 196–198; [11a], p. 4; [23f], pp. 253–254.
49. [71], pp. 38–39; [14a], p. 16; [11a], p. 4; [99b], pp. 23b–24; [34], p. 3.

Thus, at the end of 1911, Liang Shu-ming, long committed to national power as an ultimate goal, opted for immediate political action to solve China's modern crisis. He had no interest in Chinese tradition, no conception of Chinese "culture," and only contempt for China's literary heritage. He believed that China would achieve wealth and power only by traveling the same path the West had taken, and actively supported institutional, political, and social reforms based on Western models. How and why did he become such a famous defender of Chinese traditional culture and critic of Western ways ten years later? The answer, in part at least, rests with the influence from his father, Liang Chi.

CHAPTER II

Psychosis, Suicide,
and Sagehood

After Liang Chi resigned from the Board of Civil
Affairs in 1908, he did little except serve a year's stint as preceptor
of the new Capital Professional School (Ching-shih shih-yeh
hsueh-t'ang) and pursue his lifelong love, Peking opera. He had
turned fifty in 1909 and should have approached middle age with
some satisfaction and contentment. That year he built a new house
for his family on Tassle Lane in the pleasant neighborhood south
of the Legation Quarter. His older son Huan-nai was doing well at
the university in Tokyo and his two daughters had entered middle
school. Most gratifying of all must have been his son Shu-ming's
sincere, conscientious character.[1]

Developments on the national scene should have pleased him
too. Death had finally wrenched the Empress Dowager's long-
nailed fingers from the levers of power. After watching this old
woman crush both the 1898 reforms and his own popular education efforts, Liang Chi must have felt some inner relief at her
demise. Yuan Shih-k'ai, who had destroyed his friend P'eng I-sun,
had fallen from power at the same time. By 1909, it was obvious
that the Manchu regents had set an irreversible course for major
change. That year, Prince Tsai Feng decreed sweeping reforms in
the legal codes, the educational system, the armed forces, and the
governmental bureaucracy. Also in that year, China's first local
elections and provincial representative assemblies took place. It
seemed as if China was finally moving in the direction that Liang
Chi had been pointing toward for so many years.

Liang Chi's own attitude, however, began to change, and the
misanthropic bitterness that he would carry to the shore of Ching-
yeh Lake began to emerge. There were reasons. After the long
period without official salary, his financial condition was becoming

1. [99b], p. 22b, [404e], pp. 32, 33–39b; [14a], p. 5; [9h], p. 98.

desperate, and his wife was seriously ill. His earlier popular education movement had failed, and P'eng, his partner and best friend, was far away in Sinkiang. Probably most disheartening to him was the fate of his reforms in the capital police system. Under his successor they had fallen on evil days, and all he had accomplished had come to nothing.[2]

The real turning point was the morning in April 1910, when Liang Chi laid aside mourning and returned to the ministry. "I felt that with my qualifications and past service, I would have no trouble getting a post and a salary to ease my financial difficulties." He was very surprised when he was not assigned a post, but as he recorded:

> Gradually I observed that in every case those who received assignments got them through improper means, by having special relations with high officials or by soliciting help from those in high positions. The high officials of the ministry conduct these unconscionable acts openly. The uncorrupted straight path is completely gone. Even if you should try to move their hearts with sincerity, or ridicule their unrighteous behavior, they would just laugh in your face. Probably no period could equal this one in official corruption.[3]

Public pressure for a national parliament and constitution had been mounting. In May 1910, delegates from the provincial assemblies, provincial chambers of commerce, and other groups surged into Peking waving petitions and making speeches. They submitted ten public petitions to the throne asking for a national parliament. By this point Liang Chi had already soured on such efforts at reform as well as on the nascent Chinese bourgeoisie who were the backbone of the movement. The pressure of these events and Liang Chi's changing attitude toward them opened a small fissure in the father-son relationship so firm just a year before. While Liang Chi fretted at home, Shu-ming skipped school to participate in the petitioning. Liang Chi awaited the October opening of the Provisional National Assembly with crotchety disfavor; he was certain the general moral decadence in government and soci-

---

2. [404d], pp. 8a–b. Compare the police department statistics on the relief and education program before and after Liang Chi's resignation. See [191], pp. 41–42, for the 1906 statistics, and [192], pt. 2, "Wai-ch'eng," pp. 159–161, for the compilation in 1907.

3. [404d], p. 15.

ety, and the assemblymen's lack of virtue, would prevent the assembly from accomplishing anything of value. Shu-ming went excitedly to every session and studied all the proposals.[4]

The contrast between the Confucian faith learned at his mother's knee and the unpleasant realities of a crumbling social order gave Liang Chi cause to reflect upon his family heritage and his own position in officialdom. "The older generation usually considered fame and position obtainable by one's merit, and absolutely not through unscrupulous means, luck, or personal favor."[5] In the Confucian ideal, personal righteousness led to public recognition and political power. Outright competition for power and money was morally inferior. Yet Liang Chi now discovered that the government bureaucracy rewarded the morally inferior. Reform programs or not, he concluded, China was in even greater decline than before. What was the world coming to? Was he to be punished because he upheld family tradition and abided by the standards of morality instilled in him by his parents? Was he to be denied his rightful place in society because he refused to stoop to conduct unbefitting a true *chün-tzu*? In his own observation:

> I've been living in the capital for fifty years and have been having contact with the scholar-official class for over thirty years. Throughout I have never been stained by the fashion of competing [for position and power]. Truly this [refusal to be corrupted] has been brought about by the family training of my youth. When I was seven I listened attentively to the few things my father taught me, and still remember them to this day. The impact of my mother's teaching is even greater.[6]

Liang Chi's Plan for National Salvation

As a Confucian moral aristocrat, it was still his duty to save society, despite its ill treatment of him. He immediately set about forming his own plan for national salvation and resolved to submit it to his former chief at the ministry in hopes of both heading off the moral decline and getting his old position back. He did not start committing his thoughts to paper until 1911, and was still writing in October, when the Republican Revolution rendered the enterprise useless.[7] The manuscript, however, is valuable to us because it

4. [14r], p. 197; [23f], p. 254; [404d], p. 4b.
5. [404d], pp. 26b–27.   6. Ibid.   7. [404d], pp. 15a–b.

shows his thinking during the year that his son, Shu-ming, was slowly following his classmates in their drift toward revolution. It is also relevant to our study of Liang Shu-ming's own solutions to China's problems.

In a way, Liang Chi had not really changed from his 1898 stance on reform, but he had increased his emphasis upon moral renewal and revival. It was all well and good to have constitutional government and administrative reforms, he felt, but "in saving the nation, the task of rectifying people's hearts should be put first." New institutions and laws were not the essential problem in China's decline:

> As for methods of putting China in order, one would have to say that we are quite well supplied indeed. Even the Western nations, when they started building their national power, did not have as many methods to choose from as we have today. And yet the more we try to achieve a good order, the worse things get, and [our efforts even] increase disorder, giving rise to a multitude of corrupt practices [causing] the country to be in such a desperate state that it looks as though it cannot get through another day.[8]

Liang Chi was repeating essentially what he had said in 1898: that the problem was "not inferior laws but inferior people," and that even the most perfect constitutional government would be doomed to failure "because people's hearts are bad." To change people's hearts, Liang outlined a program designed to restore the virtue of the ruler, the official class, and the people.

First, he urged the Manchu regency to actively prepare the people for coming constitutionalism. "The constitutional government is truly a strange thing [to the people], which has never existed [in China], so you must change the people's spirit and promote progressive thought."[9] Moreover, the ruler must take a more aggressive part in learning the real situation of the country and not just rely on ornately written reports completely divorced from reality. One of the problems with reforms thus far, Liang asserted, was that once the decrees left the palace, the regency did not investigate the practical effects in society.

Liang Chi groaned over the people's lack of virtue. Winehouses and brothels flourished; banquets were occasions for obscene language and depraved behavior. As a lifelong moral athlete, he still

8. [404d], pp. 1a–b.   9. Ibid.

retained his puritanical hatred for the sensual. But a new element
had entered his thinking. He linked pursuit of pleasure and material enjoyment with Western influence. He saw the consumerist life
style of the nascent urban middle class as a "superficial imitation" of
Western culture. The new fashion, he complained, raised con-
spicuous consumption to an "honorable" activity, and in such an
environment, the heavenly principles (t'ien-li)—the eternal truths
inherent in the nature of things—would surely perish.[10]

Although leadership at the top was important, Liang Chi saw the
masses as the source of all strength; their present selfishness, greed,
and general corruption must be corrected through moral persuasion and education. Liang Chi's solution was a network of lecture
stations (hsuan-chiang so), which would form the nucleus for local
communities and provide mutual moral supervision and education.
As with his old journalistic enterprises, the aim of the stations was
to imbue the masses with nationalistic enthusiasm, and, using the
vernacular language, provide them with "modern knowledge" in
such areas as basic science and world affairs. The trouble with the
people is: "They do not understand that they themselves are linked
together. Even an urgent national crisis provokes no concern in
them."[11]

Already before the revolution, Liang Chi's thought harbored a
basic contradiction, one which he himself would never notice, but
which his son would dwell upon for years. His plan was predicated
on a resurgence of traditional individual morality, which would
provide the means for making the nation strong. Yet he saw the
moral code as an embodiment of the heavenly principles (the universal human values). Was his ultimate value, then, moral value or
the Chinese nation?

Liang Chi designed his lecture-station system, which would be
administered jointly by the departments of Education and Civil
Affairs, to provide an organizational network for mass moralizing
and mass education. Under this reign of virtuous schoolmaster-
policemen, the current fashion of selfish individualism would give
way to unselfish collectivism. Liang Chi's plan emphasized grass-
roots involvement through a multifunctional local institution, and
was designed to be implemented first in a small area (the capital)
and then gradually extended throughout China[12]—two prominent

10. [404d], p. 6b.   11. [404d], pp. 10b–11.
12. [404d], pp. 21–22b.

ideas in his son's later rural-reconstruction formulas as well. Through the lecture station system, the masses would be trained in self-government and group action; thus mobilized and moralized, they would, under the leadership of a rejuvenated official class, march toward a new, powerful China. The heart of Liang Chi's plan, therefore, was not concerned so much with governmental reorganization and reform as with the transformation of society itself through the efforts and influence of superior men.

Liang Chi's plan closely resembled the traditional *hsiang-yueh* (village covenant) lecture system, which provided for hortatory discourses to the local, rural community and performed certain moral supervisory functions such as public praise or blame of village members. Its principal function, however, was the reading of the sacred edicts (*sheng-yü*) at public gatherings on set occasions. As late as 1906, the regulations for education emphasized the reading of a wide range of materials for ethical education.[13] Liang Chi's plan was built upon this tradition, enlarging its scope and combining it with his two favorite reforms—mass education and a benevolent police system, which included poor relief, rehabilitation programs, and vocational education.

Despite a year-and-a-half of work, Liang Chi's plan was still incomplete when the fateful October of 1911 arrived. Of course, other work had interfered. Liang still went to the ministry even though he had no work, and his wife's illness claimed much of his time because he mixed and brewed her medicines himself. And he still slipped out of the house occasionally to attend the opera at the Chung-ho yuan by the Temple of Heaven, the famous Kuang-te lou near Peking's Ch'ien-men (Front gate), or almost any of the noted theaters throughout the city. Then there had been the matter of his daughter's marriage. Recently, he had finally found a suitable match for his eldest daughter Hsin-ming (Huan-hao). The young man, Tsou Ying-wo, was a landsman of P'eng I-sun's from Kiangsu. In addition, his oldest son Huan-nai had graduated with honors from Meiji University just a few months before and would soon be returning home to help build the new China the old man was envisioning.[14]

Liang Chi was well aware that others had other visions for the future. The "bandit" party, under the leadership of that half-educated, half-Westernized Cantonese, Sun Yat-sen, had staged

13. [452], pp. 231–237. 267–271.
14. [99b], p. 22–24b, 26; [404e], pp. 23b–24, 32–39b.

several armed attempts at overthrowing the monarchy in the past few years. Just six months before, a young bandit party leader, Wang Ching-wei, had tried to assassinate the Prince Regent Tsai Feng, and a month later the whole city of Canton had been in a terrible uproar for days when several hundred revolutionaries assaulted the yamen of the governor-general. In late summer, even more people had been killed in Szechwan.

The Republican Revolution

On the evening of the "Double Ten," the tenth of October, Liang Chi was in his study working on the section of his manuscript called "The Virtue of Officials." It was a pleasant autumn evening in Peking, but a thousand miles away in the Yangtze valley city of Wuchang the weather was rainy with violent winds. There, at nine that evening, a private in the Imperial Army named Ch'eng Ting-kuo shot his platoon lieutenant.[15] The bullet set off the Republican Revolution and relegated the manuscript lying on Liang Chi's desk to the dustbin of history. The event heralded not just the end of the Manchus, who after all had occupied the Dragon Throne for a mere 268 years, but the end of the Son of Heaven, who had stood between the people and the Sky for over three millennia. At the time Liang Chi did not realize these implications; when news of the uprising reached Peking the next day, he regarded it as just another of many recent disorders.

It was another matter entirely to his son Shu-ming and his new-found hope in revolution. With uprisings flaming throughout the entire nation, Shu-ming now felt that the future was on the side of the T'ung-meng-hui and joined some of his classmates in organizing a Peking-Tientsin branch of the Revolutionary Alliance. The area was still under the control of the Manchu court, so their activities were, of necessity, covert. Shu-ming entered the exciting world of secret revolutionaries, replete with assassinations, clandestine meetings, gun-running, and homemade explosives. At eighteen and graduated from middle school, Liang Shu-ming was his own master. He took his first trip outside the walls of Peking to Ch'ang-p'ing on secret revolutionary business, and thereafter made

15. Who fired the first shot and at what time will probably never be known for certain. Western scholars and contemporary Chinese scholars—see, for example, [213], p. 66—accept Hsiung Ping-k'un's account in "Wu-chang ch'i-i t'an" (On the Wuchang uprising), in [287], V, 86–94, but other participants' accounts in [287] conflict with Hsiung's.

frequent trips to the headquarters in Tientsin to get arms and explosives. He was also chosen to run a coal shop as a "front" for the revolutionaries' Peking lair on Tung-tan erh-t'iao Lane. He enjoyed the whole game to the hilt: "In one way our work seemed very violent, as we were playing around with guns and bombs. But at the same time it was very much like a children's game to us. We were by no means aware of its seriousness."[16]

Liang Shu-ming's escapades enlarged the small fissure in his relationship with Liang Chi to a gaping abyss. Liang Chi knew of his son's activities and squarely opposed them. "The establishment of a constitution is sufficient to save the country," he counseled Shu-ming. "Why must [you insist] on revolution? Wait for the mandate of heaven to change. Do not follow [the revolutionaries]." Yet, characteristically, Liang Chi refused to interfere. He had always urged his children to stand firm on their convictions. Even now, when Shu-ming's convictions prompted activities that threatened to put his adolescent neck under a Manchu executioner's sword, Liang Chi expressed his opposition and then said no more.[17]

Events proceeded rapidly. By November all China except the

16. [34]. See also [99b], pp. 23b–24; [9h], pp. 100–101; [14a], p. 4; [23f], p. 253; [71], pp. 38–39. Upon its founding in 1905, the T'ung-meng-hui already had members from eastern Hopei but not until the Wuchang uprising were they active. Liang insisted in several of his writings and public lectures that he had been a founding member of the Peking-Tientsin branch, so there probably was no tightly organized branch in Hopei until after October 1911. Possibly because he used a pseudonym, Liang's name does not appear in any of the surviving first-hand documents of the branch, although some of his classmates' names (Lei Kuo-neng, for example), do appear. At eighteen Liang had to have been one of the youngest members in the branch. The Peking-Tientsin branch's main headquarters were in the Tientsin French concession at the Shen-ch'ang Hotel, which was probably also the newspaper office of the T'ung-meng-hui organ, *Min-kuo pao*, where Liang worked after the Manchu abdication. The hotel headquarters was also used for making explosives and storing arms, but the branch seems to have managed to assassinate no one of any importance, Liang's comments about "pistol and grenade games" notwithstanding. Even the records listing members of the "assassination department" (*an-sha-pu*) are completely blank. The branch was responsible for at least one major uprising (which eventually failed) on November 23, 1911, at Luanchow, but none of their other plans for assassination and yamen seizure got off the ground. An account of the branch's short uneventful life is in [530], pp. 913–915. The surviving documents of the Peking-Tientsin Tung-meng-hui are [543 a–d].

17. [99b], p. 24; see also 23b; [11a], p. 4; [14a], pp. 8–9.

North was in the hands of the revolutionary armies. On January 1, 1912, the Chinese Republic was formally proclaimed in Nanking, with Sun Yat-sen as president. A little over a month later, the Manchu emperor abdicated, and the linchpin of Confucian society was gone forever.

Liang Chi's reaction to the abdication itself was ambiguous: "If [the emperor] is that sincere about it, then it is a good thing. Yet the days ahead hold great troubles. Who will bear them?"[18] Shu-ming's reaction contained no ambiguities. He dashed off to Nanking to join the revolutionary government and to begin his career as journalist for the party paper, *Kuo-min pao*. As a reporter, Liang Shu-ming made contacts with many important personages of the new Republic, such as Minister of Education Ts'ai Yuan-p'ei and Chang Shih-chao. He also became friends with another journalist of the time, Huang Yuan-sheng.[19]

The abdication itself settled none of the real issues facing the new regime: North China was still in the hands of Yuan Shih-k'ai and his clique of Pei-yang military commanders, while the Southern provinces professed loyalty to Sun Yat-sen's Nanking provisional government. Out of his overwhelming desire for national unity and a prudent respect for Yuan's military might, Sun handed the presidency over to Yuan immediately after the abdication was announced. But other questions remained. Would the Republican capital be in Peking—the bailiwick of Yuan and his militarists—or Nanking—the symbol of republicanism and in the hands of the revolutionaries? Would Yuan come to Nanking for his inauguration? On February 29, while matters were still under negotiation and Nanking awaited word from its representatives, elements of Yuan's third division, garrisoned in the capital, and his bodyguard rioted—an event which, by Yuan's design or not, insured that Yuan would not come to Nanking and the capital would remain in Peking.

18. [99b], p. 30; [404a], pp. 10b–11.
19. What Liang was doing in Nanking is not clear. As he didn't really start working for the Tientsin *Min-kuo pao* until around March 1912, he probably went in January with some of his comrades from the North (which was still under the control of the Manchu court until February 12, 1912). [463], p. 63; [5a], pp. 1–2, 17; [9a], p. 7; [47], p. 3; [71], pp. 39–40; [99b], pp. 23–36; [66], p. 5. See also [319], which Liang indicated had expressed the reason for his own *mal du monde*.

Liang Chi's Vow

Liang Chi's house, right in the neighborhood of the most severe fires and ravaging, was not damaged, but the sights and sounds of chaos were all around him. What thoughts could have passed through his mind as he saw the venerable Gate of Eastern Peace go up in a pillar of flame and heard the screams of plunder victims continue through the night? Perhaps he felt that this was the result of their "revolution," a power grab that did nothing but allow gangsters like Yuan Shih-k'ai and his cohorts to hold sway. And his son, his favorite son, was in Nanking, a part of the movement that had brought this about! It was at this time that Liang Chi settled on martyrdom. He and a group of fellow Kwangsi provincials gathered in their *Landsmannschaft* hall on Luan-ch'ing Street and solemnly vowed to defend traditional customs to the death. Then they went to the temples of the two gods of the literati—Wen Ch'ang and Kuan Kung—and, amid incense and flaming tapers, performed the same somber ritual. Later, at home alone, Liang Chi threw himself down before the spirit tablets of his ancestors and vowed to his father, now dead for over forty years, that in this time of crisis he would not disgrace him, but would "exemplify righteousness."[20] Liang Chi grieved not for the passing of the monarchy and the Manchus, but for "customs" and "righteousness." He would defend the heritage of his forefathers with the only means at his disposal, his life. Western influence and the new power-holders were destroying customs and righteousness and so they were the enemy.

The decision to launch oneself into eternity, however, is never so simple a matter. Other emotions, just as deeply rooted in Liang Chi's soul as his faith in Confucian pan-moralism, may have played a role. Liang Chi was facing a problem as old as Confucianism itself. In the Confucian ideal, the superior person's inner moral perfection radiates outward, influencing others by moral example, and at the same time gaining prestige and power for the individual. Yet throughout Chinese history, the upper cymbal of Confucian ideal clashed harshly against the base metal of fact. The discordant tone was especially loud at the end of the Ch'ing, as morale and morals sank to a low ebb.

In his mid-fifties, Liang Chi looked back on a life of scrupulous striving for moral perfection, but also a life that had failed in all its attempts to influence the outer world. He faced a future of unem-

20. [99b], p. 24; [404a], pp. 10b, 11, 1b.

ployment, and his grand design for national reform was made irrelevant by the revolution. He thought back to his beloved mother's high hopes for him—hopes that contrasted cruelly with his present position and his failure to restore his family's glory. Suicide could solve the eternal tension between the inner man and the outer world. He could be famous at last, exert a strong moral influence on society, and accomplish this through the ultimate act of self-discipline. So he decided to die in the hope that this dramatic manifestation of moral rectitude and righteousness "may yet save the country's degenerating moral standards."[21]

As Liang Chi became increasingly bitter over the results of republicanism, he even began to repudiate some of his earlier ideas on reform. Immediately after the abdication, Liang Chi's former superior in the Ministry of Civil Affairs, Chao Ping-chün, who retained the office of minister under the Republic, finally offered Liang the position he had longed for just a few months before. Now Liang Chi angrily refused and responded with a request for early retirement from official life. When the ministry refused to allow him to retire and sent him a salary as well, Liang Chi was further enraged.[22] Ironically, it was his old Westernizer champion, Liang Ch'i-ch'ao, who first articulated some of the vague inner feelings Liang Chi had at this time. Liang Ch'i-ch'ao had come to Peking in 1912 to take part in the new government. In December of that year he published an article, "On National Character," in which he argued that China must resurrect its traditional moral standards based upon its own national character in order to survive. Without a common consensus on right and wrong, any group—family, village, or nation—would disintegrate into chaos. Without its own peculiar national essence—a precious entity evolved over thousands of years—China would perish.[23] Upon this theory of Liang Ch'i-ch'ao's, Liang Chi began to construct his rationale for suicide.

Liang Shu-ming's Crisis and Retirement

Precisely at this juncture, his son Shu-ming, still in Nanking with his comrades rejoicing in their victory, actually did attempt suicide. Shu-ming did so not, as his father planned, as an act of noble will,

21. [404f] p. 1b; [404e], p. 5b; [404a], pp. 38b, 11.
22. [47] pp. 55–56, 61–62; [23c], pp. 86–87; [9h], pp. 98–102; [99b], pp. 25a–b.
23. [404a], p. 62; [406].

but rather in the terrible grip of psychic forces he could not comprehend.[24] Throughout the first inglorious year of the Republic Liang continued to pursue his political and journalistic career, but under a constant burden of growing madness. He seemed continually tottering on the brink of self-destruction. His mother's death in June 1912, after a long, painful illness, did not help his slough of despondency.[25] At the end of the year he attempted suicide again. Unable to continue an active life, he gave up his wandering career and closed himself off in his father's house to "escape the world" (ch'u-shih) and completely devote himself to the study and practice of Buddhism "behind closed doors." This solitary self-therapy continued until the middle of 1916, when he finally reopened the heavy door he had slammed shut four years earlier.

The immediate reason for Liang's resignation from the T'ung-meng-hui, and its newspaper, was its reorganization into the Kuomintang (Nationalist party). As the Peking provisional assembly convened in April 1912, the T'ung-meng-hui and many smaller parties began maneuvering for power. Under the politically shrewd leadership of Sung Chiao-jen, the T'ung-meng-hui successfully absorbed several small parties by reorganizing them into the Nationalist party, which then easily controlled the assembly. Consequently, the Revolutionary Alliance became flooded with unabashedly opportunistic old-style politicians.

During this period of reorganization, Liang Shu-ming was privy not only to the T'ung-meng-hui's smoke-filled rooms, but also to the secret meetings of the smaller parties it absorbed as well. This peek into the seamy side of political life appalled him. Could these shady horse-trading affairs of corrupt old opium-smokers be what democracy was all about, he wondered. This discovery that in politics, as Disraeli said, nothing is contemptible, constituted another source for his crisis:

> I gradually realized that the facts were not at all in accord with my ideals. This was my feeling toward "revolution," "politics," and "great men." I now saw low-class dealings; vile, vulgar mentalities; and ruthless, cruel, and violent things. Before this, [while I was] at home or at school, I had encountered none of these things. This filled me with a disgust and loathing for life.[26]

24. [11a], pp. 3–4; [47], pp. 3–4; [5m], p. 88; [5a], p. 1; [9a], pp. 6–7.
25. [99b], p. 24b.
26. [71], pp. 39–40. Liang attended secret meetings of T'ang Hua-lung and Sun Hung-i's Kung-ho chien-she t'ao-lun-hui (which joined the

Liang was not the only one to leave the party at this stage. Many young idealistic members were revolted at the idea that their organization had now become a haven for self-aggrandizing politicos instead of the nation-saving group of heroes they had originally joined. Rather than be corrupted by those who now claimed their comradeship, they left.[27] Even Li Ta-chao, the future father of the Chinese Communist Party, was so disheartened by the morally flabby body politic that he too was driven to "escape the world" through Buddhism.[28] And Mao Tse-tung, vaguely suspecting that the revolution had somehow failed in its main purpose, left the Hunan revolutionary army and lived aimlessly in Changsha.[29] But the experience seems to have had a more enduring impact on Liang. Although his *taedium vitae* brought on by his disillusionment with politics would pass, he would distrust politicians and their power games for the rest of his life. This aversion prevented him from ever achieving a real understanding of politics and power— an understanding he could have used in his later work as a rural reformer and political mediator.

On many occasions in his later life, Liang Shu-ming wrote about this period of mental turmoil, but always with different explanations and descriptions. Perhaps all are correct. The central event in a person's life—the determinant of one's future identity—is a complex matter, one composed of many layers of reality and many kinds of truth. Perhaps it is folly to attempt a precise clarification of the mental anguish he experienced. Nevertheless, Liang's depression fits into a pattern that Westerners are familar with. Dostoevsky, J. S. Mill, Tolstoy, and many other articulate, sensitive spirits have written in detail about similar crises in their lives.

On the most abstract level, Liang's crisis was the emotional comprehension of a truth he had learned before through his study of Buddhism but had grasped only on an intellectual level: that any increase of pleasure is gained only through an equal increase in pain; no absolute increase in good is possible. Both pleasure and pain originate in desire. Thus, all his strivings for a better future both for himself and for China stood mocked before this eternal balance. Liang must have asked questions comparable to ones John Stuart Mill raised over a century earlier: "Suppose that all your

T'ung-meng-hui during the reorganization) and Liang Ch'i-ch'ao's Chin-pu-tang.

27. [530], p. 130; [600], pp. 58–60.   28. [428], p. 14; [393a].
29. [489], pp. 125–128.

objectives in life were realized; that all the changes in institutions
and opinions which you are looking forward to could be completely
effected at this very instant: would this be a great joy and happiness
to you? The answer came back a thunderous 'no!' "[30]

Such a realization led Liang to a sudden intense and painful
sensitivity to human suffering. Everywhere he turned, it seemed,
he saw new evidence of the essentially evil nature of the world.

> There was another time when I was strolling down a Peking
> street and chanced to see a rickshaw-puller, a white-haired
> old man who was straining to pull forward. No matter how
> hard he tried, he could not run, but his passenger neverthe-
> less urged him to run. As soon as he tried, he tripped and fell
> and bloodied his white beard. Tears welled up in my own
> eyes. . . . I was provoked by so many things and repeatedly
> meditated on them. It made my blood boil. I almost went
> insane that year. . . . Because I was suffering from such out-
> rage and because my mental condition was very unstable, I
> attempted suicide that year in Nanking.[31]

Liang's new awareness of such social evils led him to the Proudho-
nian conclusion that private property was the root of all these social
evils, and for a time he was enthusiastic about utopian socialism.[32]
But the most important result of his awakened social conscience
was "loathing and contempt for life."[33]

There are also many other reasons for Liang's illness. He wrote
of the suicide attempts:

> [They] manifested the contradictions and conflicts within my
> heart. The standards I set for myself were very high and
> when I judged others by my own standards, I had contempt
> for them. But because the standards were so high, it was also
> easy to have contempt and disgust for myself for not having
> lived up to them. I was ambitious, but still had many faults. So
> any misdeeds led to strong feelings of remorse and caused me

30. [433], p. 83.   31. [9a], p. 6.

32. Although during his illness Liang came to the pessimistic conclusion
that socialism, along with democracy, economic development, or even development of Nietzschean supermen would not really significantly alter the
essence of the human condition (see 5a, pp. 14–15), in early 1912 he did
read with enthusiasm a Chinese translation of Kōtoku Shūsui's *Shakai shugi
shinzui* (The essence of socialism), a famous early popular Japanese work
on socialism. This inspired him a booklet of his own on socialism. [9a], pp.
2–4; [14a], pp. 16–17; [71], pp. 42–45; [11a], p.4; [38] p. 289.

33. [5g], p. 39.

to fight with myself. When I had fought myself into a state of confusion, to the point that I could not stand it any longer, then I desired only death.[34]

Guilt (or, as he called it, self-loathing, shame, or remorse) was obviously an important factor in his breakdown. He had contempt for his former heroes because of their mechanistic behavior, which was controlled by their desires and passions, yet he also had contempt for himself for the same reason. He used the term *fan-nao* in the Buddhist sense (temptations or delusions of the passions) so his guilt and remorse were perhaps due to his own slavery to the "delusions of desire and pleasure."[35]

From this point, the antagonism between "mechanistic" and truly "human" behavior became a constant element in Liang's thought. To Liang, all mechanistic views of humankind (and he included most Western thought in this category) regarded the human being as a mere bundle of drives and appetites, an automaton programed by biological urges. To satisfy these needs, the intellect appraises life as means for achieving them, with the result that the ends themselves are lost. Again, Mill's crisis and his reaction against his former Benthamite utilitarianism comes to mind. As Liang said of his own sickness, "an exaggerated utilitarian philosophy easily reacts against itself and becomes negativistic."[36] Mill's crisis over his "exaggerated utilitarian philosophy" seems to epitomize the warning Liang would later give to Chinese youth.

In all his talk at the time of guilt, remorse, and self-loathing, Liang never mentioned his father, no doubt because these were the most profound and poignant guilt feelings of all. Liang Shu-ming had been denied the outlet of rebellion against parental authority available to so many of his generation because his father had refused to interfere with his activities. Unlike Mao Tse-tung's father, for example, Liang Chi refused to beat and bully his son, thus providing him with no firm authority against which to struggle. Liang Shu-ming was forced to act as his own authority figure and punisher.

In the cold clinical eye of psychopathology, Liang's experience was probably psychotic. His attempted suicide in late adolescence, his withdrawal from society, his easily wounded sensibilites, his self-loathing and guilt, and finally his incapacity to function—all suggest a psychosis. Throughout the rest of his life Liang would

34. [47], p. 3.   35. [5a], p. 1; [510], p. 2.   36. [510], p. 2.

bear certain psychological stigmata—megalomania, delusions of power, a touch of paranoia, periods of depression—which fit into a recognizable pattern.

Buddhism

It is not entirely accidental that Liang should choose to seek a cure for himself through Buddhism, and specifically through the Wei-shih (consciousness only; Sanskrit, *Vijnanavadin*) school. Buddhism was enjoying a surge of revival and reform in China at the time and the Wei-shih school was in the intellectual forefront of the movement. The Wei-shih original texts had been recovered from Japan only a few years earlier. In the years that followed, Liang Shu-ming, along with Ou-yang Ching-wu, T'ai Hsu, and Liang Ch'i-ch'ao, became a major voice in the revival.[37]

Liang's Sino-Indian compromise between Western utilitarianism and his father's traditionalism did not heal the break with Liang Chi, who detested Buddhist asceticism as much as Western sybaritism.[38] Liang Chi took offense at his offspring's sutras and prayer beads not only on ideological or aesthetic grounds, but also because Shu-ming's decision to embrace the Bodhi included a vow to eschew meat, marriage, and wine for the rest of his life. No doubt Liang Chi cared little about his son's gastronomical renunciations, but he had a very real and immediate interest in holding a grandson in his arms before he went to face his ancestors. The older son Huan-nai had already put in ten full years of noble connubial effort in vain. Shu-ming's reproductive potential was his only hope. This was serious business, for as the old proverb from the classic, *Mencius,* says: "There are three unfilial acts, but the greatest is to be without progeny" (*pu hsiao yu san, wu hou wei ta*). Further, as Shu-ming was preparing himself for the life of a monk, he had no interest in going to college or furthering his career. This

37. The Wei-shih school (Fa-hsiang or Dharmalaksana) flourished briefly during the T'ang dynasty, but seemed to have vanished, along with its texts, after A.D. 845. Yang Wen-hui (Jen-shan), the father of the twentieth-century Chinese Buddhist revival, was himself responsible for reintroduction of the Wei-shih texts into China. See [607], p. 37; [595]; [572], p. 294. The Wei-shih school remained the intellectual cutting edge of the revival right up until 1949. The leading intellectual figures, as well as Yang Wen-hui himself, were devotees of the Dharmalaksana.

38. [9h], pp. 100–101; [23c], pp. 86–87; [47], pp. 55–56; [11a], pp. 3–4.

greatly disturbed Liang Chi, who was still concerned with the family tradition of glorious public service.[39] Once again, however, Liang Chi refused to interfere, but his dying mother reacted strongly when Shu-ming first proclaimed his decision not to marry to his parents in early 1912:

> She herself knew that she would never arise from her bed again. Crying, she wrung my hand and repeatedly tried to persuade me with emotion-laden words; and again and again I refused to obey. She pleaded that I do as she asked, but I still looked reluctant. My father sat to one side by himself and remained silent throughout. The next day he wrote me saying, "What your mother told you yesterday issued forth from her sickness and her own selfish desires. It might affect your noble ambitions and make you too accommodating and dispirited a person. This is certainly not my desire. [It is all right that] you do not want to marry now. We can always discuss it later."[40]

Liang Chi's conciliatory attitude and Shu-ming's sadder and wiser return to the family house on Tassle Lane produced no reconciliation between the two. The odoriferous incense and infernal chanting that issued from Shu-ming's celibate chamber were quite enough to keep the tension high, but what really drew sparks from Liang Chi was the question of Chinese versus Western culture. While Shu-ming himself had been disillusioned about the new politics, he still felt that China's only hope was through adopting such Western institutions as parliamentary democracy. "My father loathed party politicians and I purposely defended them. He detested assemblymen and moreover was suspicious of the parliamentary system, but I vigorously defended the parliament." Sometimes the two of them would argue all day and far into the night without pausing to eat. The barbs they slung at each other in these verbal bouts were so sharp and hurled with such vocal force that they even reached the ears of passers-by on the street.[41]

The strain in the Liang household was reduced somewhat when P'eng I-sun returned to Peking from his Sinkiang exile, and Liang Chi began to spend more and more time at his friend's house. For

39. [9h], pp. 99–101; [47], pp. 34–35, 55–56; [11a], pp. 3–4; [23c], p. 86.
40. [9h, pp. 100–101. As his crisis did not start until early 1912 and his mother died in June of that year (see [99b], p. 24b), this confrontation must have taken place between February and May 1912.
41. [9h], p. 99; see also pp. 98–100.

some time Liang Chi had been suspicious of his children's spying, and with good reason. Shu-ming had done some prying around in his study and had discovered some of his misanthropic jottings.[42] In order to be free from his offspring's scrutiny and to be nearer to P'eng's house, Liang Chi bought a small one-room cottage on the shores of Pure Dharma Lake, just inside Peking's northern wall. The placid lake and its willow-lined banks proved to be the perfect setting for a man contemplating death, and Liang Chi immediately set to work—free from fear of discovery—on his suicide notes.

Shu-ming's Buddhist enthusiasm lasted only until his father's suicide, but he maintained the practice of self-denial, and the Spartan regimen stayed with him to the end of his days. He remained a vegetarian, never drank wine or smoked, and wore the simplest of clothes to go with his shaven pate.[43]

Back at the house on Tassle Lane, Liang Shu-ming continued to weld the fragments of his shattered personality into an integrated whole. Through Buddhist self-therapy, Shu-ming slowly began to achieve a serenity of indifference toward the transitory show of the illusory world. Via Wei-shih metaphysics, he soared above it all into the sphere of knowing "Thusness," the ultimate nature of things; he achieved a detachment from the tensions within his soul, for now he knew that all the universe, as known to man, was merely phenomena. The noumenon, the Kantian thing-in-itself, was knowable only through direct intuitive realization. His own desires, the evils of man and nature, the notions of good and bad, moral responsibility, and determinism were all relativized by this ultimate unchanging reality.[44]

Against the background of Liang's need to see all things as relative to a Great Void, his lifelong ambivalence toward the formal Confucian moral code (li-chiao) becomes more comprehensible. In the years before and during his time of mental trauma he had broken all Confucian canons on filial behavior. He had defied his

42. [99b], pp. 25–26.
43. Liang's later abstentions were simply exercises in self-mastery, and lacking in religious nature. Nor was he strict in observing them. He ate vegetables from meat dishes and would respond to wine toasts made to him by drinking wine. He shaved his head for convenience as many non-Buddhist Chinese did. [102], pp. 207–208; [510], pp. 3–4; [312], pt. 7, no. 301; [612]; [613]; [619]; [628]; [621]; [640].
44. [5a], pp. 4–14.

father on important issues. Throughout his life he would display a "deep revulsion against the absolutism of Confucian social rules."[45] Viewed from the heights of eternal Thusness, the Confucian code became small and petty, a culture- and time-bound concept unrelated to the true nature of things. For the rest of his life Liang would struggle with such basic dichotomies as those between self-fulfillment and ethical responsibility, between the individual and the collective, and between individual self-importance and authority. His personal situation during these years—caught between guilt for opposing his father and his need for self-development—was the touchstone for his intellectualization of the struggle. Throughout his life he searched for a way in which the individual could avoid suffocation while still enjoying the emotional satisfaction and security of familial bonds.

The months passed quickly. Yuan Shih-k'ai crushed the "second revolution" and gradually consolidated his dictatorship. Throughout 1913 and 1914, Yuan coolly dismissed political parties, cabinets, and finally parliament itself. In 1915, Japan's notorious Twenty-one Demands rocked the entire country, and a new wave of rallies, strikes, and boycotts swept through China. That same year, a young man named Ch'en Tu-hsiu unleashed another kind of revolution by issuing his call to Chinese youth to be "progressive, not conservative; utilitarian, not formalistic; dynamic, not passive."[46]

These events did not pass unnoticed by Liang Shu-ming, but his main attention was elsewhere. It has been said that modern Chinese intellectuals were concerned primarily with China's profound cultural crisis. Yet there were some who oriented themselves toward the universally human questions rather than their specific historical situation. Such choice spirits were more emotionally involved with the perennial problem of the meaning of human existence than with the immediate problems of their environment. Liang was one of these temperamentally transcendental per-

---

45. Benjamin Schwartz has noted that for the transitional generation preceding Liang, "Buddhism and philosophic Taoism both point to an ineffable, inconceivable, ultimate ground of reality which transcends and relativizes all determinate orders and structures or reality." Precisely because the transcendant reality lies beyond all determinate orders, it can become an inspiration for all sorts of anti-orthodox reformist schemes and ideas. [465], p. 210.
46. [151].

sonalities, but, like many great religious and political leaders of the past, he seemed to join together his personal contemplations on the eternal and the problems facing his countrymen. He emerged from his period of crisis and meditation with a messianic sense of identity, as a man with a message of universal significance. Projecting his own encounter with meaninglessness onto China's cultural dilemma, Liang joined his conception of the universally human concerns with the immediate concerns of the particular situation in China.

Emergence from Seclusion

To broaden Liang's base of exploration, his middle school philosopher chum, Chang Shen-fu, recommended some Western works to supplement Liang's collection of Buddhist canons.[47] Sometimes Chang selected well (Bergson, Schopenhauer, and Nietzsche) and sometimes not so well (Gustav LeBon). Liang also read Yen Fu's translations of Mill, Huxley, Jenks, and Montesquieu. So armed, he ventured forth into print with a few short articles on Buddhism in late 1915. His first article was a criticism of Ch'en Tu-hsiu's remarks on Buddhism.[48] In the spring of 1916—with Yuan Shih-k'ai's newly established monarchy in acute crisis—Liang's own crisis drew to a close. As if to signal the end of his psycho-social moratorium, he wrote a major article, which summed up his experience, and the results of his philosoph-

47. Chang Sung-nien (Shen-fu), the leading Chinese interpreter of Bertrand Russell and authority on dialectical materialism, was Liang's classmate at Shun-t'ien middle school. Chang soon went to France to study, but before leaving he supplied Liang with work and information on modern Western thinkers. Chang was later Liang's colleague at Peking University's philosophy department, and during the 1940s, he was associated with Liang in the third party movement. [66], pp. 4–7; [14a], p. 7; [5a], p. 18.

48. [5c]; [1]. In the latter article and other articles, Liang referred extensively to these translations of Yen Fu's. Liang also read Yen Fu's translation of Alfred Westharp's "Views on Chinese Education"—[603]—which advocated traditional Chinese values in education. A decade later Westharp would become Liang's close friend. [9i], p. 105. In 1914, Liang also put together an anthology of Chinese literature in hopes of establishing a simple, functional standard modern Chinese. This work reflects the influence of Huang Yuan-sheng, who had written on the subject. [5b], pp. 21–22.

ical probings and existential suffering, as well as adumbrated the identity with which he emerged.[49]

Liang's article did nothing less than offer a spiritual salvation for the modern world. With all previous standards and beliefs dissolving, contemporary people are left anxious, insecure, and frightened by their spiritual deracination. Liang used his newly acquired knowledge of Western thought to build a case for Wei-shih metaphysics as the means to understanding the true nature of the world. The Wei-shih approach was superior to both Western idealism and materialism because it differentiated between the character of the noumenon and the phenomenon. Only the Wei-shih concept of Thusness could capture the nature of the ultimate noumenon.

After a convoluted metaphysical discussion, the second part of the article turned to the problems of human life. As life was aimless, without purpose or significance, Liang felt that there were only two paths that offered any hope of success. The first was complete asceticism—seclusion from the world and single-minded spiritual training. In this way one could escape the temptations and distractions of the illusionary world. The second approach was to seek a life in accord with the conventional rules of the illusory world, but continue to steel oneself against desire, and devote oneself to the alleviation of human misery.

Liang now felt that the first path, which he himself had been pursuing, was foolish because it was impossible to exclude human life altogether. Moreover, the first approach contained the logical fallacy of striving to elude the pain of birth so as to get the pleasure of not being born. The way of the most courageous people—the second path—called upon one to plunge into the storm of earthly

49. [5a]. Apparently Liang was acquainted with the noted journalist-politician Chang Shih-chao from his time as a reporter, for he sent the article directly to Chang in Shanghai for publication. Chang had left the city, and another man associated with Chang's *Tiger* magazine, Chiang Wei-ch'iao, sent Liang's manuscript to *Tung-fang tsa-chih*, where it was eventually published. The immediate stimulus for Liang's writing this summary of his thought and beliefs was an article by his friend, the journalist Huang Yuan-Sheng—[319]—which discussed the "modern condition," the devaluation of all values by critical rationalism, the disintegration of traditional beliefs and absolute standards into relativism, which results, Huang felt, in a tension between intellect and emotion. Huang was assassinated in San Francisco before Liang's article was published.

slings and arrows. In August, immediately after his article was published in *Eastern Miscellany*, Liang came out of seclusion to take a position as personal secretary to the newly appointed Minister of Justice, Chang Yao-tseng, one of the many orphans who had grown up in Liang Chi's house.[50]

It is not entirely surprising that Liang's protracted late-adolescent crisis of identity should take him from suicide to Nirvana and back to where he started. Erik Erikson, whose research into the late-adolescent psycho-social moratorium of the *homo religiosus* is well known, has observed:

> The youthful crisis of identity and the mature one of integrity makes the religionist's problem of individual identity the same as the problem of existential identity. This concentration in the cataclysm of adolescent identity crisis of both the first and last crises in the human life may well explain why religiously and artistically creative men often seem to be suffering from a barely compensated psychosis, and yet later prove to be superhumanly gifted in conveying a total meaning for man's life. . . .The chosen young man extends the problem of his identity to the borders of existence in the known universe. . . .He acts as if mankind were starting all over with his own beginning as an individual, conscious of his singularity as well as his humanity.[51]

That Liang was a "religionist" of sorts, and that his crisis was a "religious experience" is certain; for the rest of his life he would be, in Western terms, a "messianic" personality. Prophets, saints, and messiahs, however, are sages and worthies in China. Chinese sagehood of all varieties (Confucian, Buddhist, Taoist) involves a merging of the transcendental eternal with the particular temporal. The sage rises to the sublimity of the universal trans-historical *tao* and

---

50. [99b], pp. 26b–28b; [127]; [66]. Chang had returned from Japan after the revolution. After Yuan Shih-k'ai's death in June 1916, the Peiyang clique attempted to restore unity with the South, and Tuan Ch'i-jui appointed several members of the Kuomintang to his cabinet, including Chang Yao-tseng. [380], II, 480–481; [540], 13.8 (Aug. 10, 1916):358. Liang was Chang's correspondence secretary and took responsibility for drafting letters and other documents. See [5e]. Shen Chün-ju, Liang's associate in the third party movement three decades later, was Chang's appointment secretary. See [66].

51. [235], pp. 161–162.

then returns to the common world to teach how the ultimate reality relates to the mundane problems of people. He succeeds in synthesizing in himself the contradictions inherent in the human condition, and so joins the sublime and the common, the universally human with his particular historical situation.

Liang saw himself in these terms. A close reading of his article, together with knowledge of his personal situation, reveals that he compared (perhaps unconsciously) his abandoning a life of seclusion for a life in the world with that of a Bodhisattva who chooses to leave the first way leading to Nirvana in order to offer enlightenment and salvation to others. Liang's stated purpose for writing the article was to share with suffering modern man the path he himself had traveled to reach inner tranquility; his clear implication was that, having achieved enlightenment himself, he felt bound to instruct the still-ignorant masses.

This "delusion of sagehood" was the basis of Liang's personality integration, which would withstand failure after failure in the external world. For the rest of his life he would feel that he held the key to the salvation of not only China, but all humankind and was under the awful imperative to impart it to others. In 1942, with both his rural reconstruction efforts and his political movement destroyed, he could still state publicly: "I cannot die now, for if I do, heaven and earth will change color and history will change its course. . . .Not only will China perish, but the world itself will perhaps be on the edge of extinction."[52]

The article in which Liang announced his intention to reenter the world also proved to be his key for reentry. His subtlety of mind, broad learning, and innovative cross-cultural comparisons of philosophical concepts made an impression on the intellectual community and established him as a major intellectual figure. His circle of friends, so small before, now widened to include many of China's important scholars. Among those who received the article favorably was Ts'ai Yuan-p'ei, the newly installed reformist chancellor of Peking University who was engaged, in early 1917, in collecting together at the university a faculty of both high academic quality and divergent interests. After talking Liang's article over with his recently appointed dean of the School of Letters, Ch'en

52. Liang Shu-ming, "Hsiang-kang t'o hsien chi K'uan Shu liang erh" (see "Introduction," note 12); see also [197]; [441]; [311]; [330], p. 24.

Tu-hsiu, Ts'ai invited Liang to teach Indian philosophy. As Liang was still committed to Chang Yao-tseng, he refused.[53]

If warlord politics had not intervened, Liang might never have had an academic career. Nor indeed, by most standards of the time, should he have had one; he had never gone to college, much less studied abroad for an advanced degree. In any case, the smoldering conflict between President Li Yuan-hung and Premier Tuan Ch'i-jui burst into a roaring flame in the spring of 1917. Li dismissed Tuan, who in turn called upon the Northern militarists to denounce the government. As a result, Li was forced to call for help from the crusty old Anhwei *tuchün*, Chang Hsun, and his pigtailed troops, who immediately marched on Peking. But Generalissimo Chang, it turned out, had come to bury the Republic, not protect it; for he had his own plans for the restoration of the Manchu dynasty. For two weeks in that comic-opera Peking July, the eleven-year-old Henry P'u-i donned the dragon robes and once more occupied the throne of his fathers. As a consequence, the parliament, the cabinet, and Liang Shu-ming's job were dissolved.[54] He was now free to accept the university post. At this juncture, however, his brother-in-law Tsou Ying-wo died suddenly, and it was Liang's duty to accompany his sister and the body back to Tsou's native place in Kiangsu.[55]

Once in the South, Liang decided to avail himself of the opportunity to see Central China, and so took a detour through Hunan on his way back to Peking. The excursion made a lasting impression. That fall it happened that Tuan Ch'i-jui's Northern warlord clique attempted to seize control of Hunan from the Southern faction and, in the process, turned the province into a battleground. Since warlord troops had an uncanny ability for doing more damage to the local citizenry than to each other, Liang saw firsthand, and for the first time, what happened to rural society when armies marched. Enraged, he rushed back to Peking and immediately wrote an anti-militarist pamphlet calling for the formation of a civilian antiwar organization of good people (*hao-jen*) which would pressure the militarists with public opinion to eschew armed force in settling their differences.[56]

53. [5a], p. 18; [66]; [14a], p. 11; [510], p. 2; [2a], p. 1.
54. [5a], p. 18; [66]; [2a], p. 1; [99b], p. 27. Although he was working as Chang's secretary, Liang continued to publish short articles on Buddhism, such as [5d].
55. [99b], p. 26b.   56. [5g], esp. pp. 39–40; see also [11a], p. 3.

When Liang passed through Changsha, he probably saw the towering Western-style building (the only one in town) of the normal school where Mao Tse-tung was studying. It had been occupied by Northern troops, but Mao and some classmates had procured rifles from the local police station and forced the Northerners' surrender. It was both characteristic and portentous that while Liang hastened back to Peking for a pen with which to fight the warlords, Mao rushed for a gun. Mao allegedly remarked around that time: "If the people are weak, what is the use of perfecting their virtues? The most important thing is to be strong."[57]

Hu Shih, just back from Columbia University and the feet of John Dewey, happened to see his new colleague's pamphlet and was moved to write in his diary: "This man Liang will certainly want revolution in the future. How wonderful! How wonderful!"[58] The pamphlet was, in fact, not revolutionary but conservative— conservative of the tradition in Liang's family. Although it might seem arrogant or even ridiculous for a twenty-four-year-old with no power, position, or even fame to come forth with a formula for national salvation, it was the natural thing for Liang to do. Responsibility for the spiritual and material welfare of the people was what he had been born to. It was also natural that he should call on the educated to come forth and fulfill their responsibility to society.

In many ways the proposals Liang put forth in the pamphlet foreshadow the patterns he would follow in future writing and the formula he would adopt for future activities. He first identified a basic problem from which all of China's other problems stemmed (use of military force internally); then systematically examined and refuted other suggested solutions (such as unification under the constitutionalists, or a wait-and-see stance); and finally set up an organizational framework for action by small local groups of intellectuals (local commercial and educational organizations would become the organs of the disarmament movement).[59]

The ideas in the pamphlet further prefigure his future work in that they demonstrate his faith in both the innate goodness of the masses and the ability of an elite—formed along moral (good versus bad) rather than political lines—to elicit the latent power of the people. Finally, Liang's unqualified antipathy toward the use of

57. [148], pp. 43–44.
58. Quoted in [11a], p. 3. Five years later Hu would label Liang a conservative and Liang would call Hu an antirevolutionary. See [11k].
59. [5g], pp. 61–91.

military force in politics, and the urgency with which he stressed the need for social order and rectification of the declining moral climate are consistent with the guidelines he would set forth in future programs in the 1930s and 1940s.

Liang Chi's Suicide

Liang finally arrived at Peking University in late 1917 and proceeded to teach a course on Indian philosophy. Most of 1918 he devoted to making the course outline and notes.[60] His father, too, was busy with a project—the rewriting of local folk operas and rearranging them for the stage in Peking. Aside from writing his notes and suicide papers, Liang Chi had devoted little time to anything but opera in the years from 1913 to 1918. To him, the decline in the standards of Peking opera—the moral as well as aesthetic standards—epitomized the decline of society generally. Years before when he had first written his experimental opera, he had considered it an instrument for the propagation of nationalism. In his later years, he saw opera solely as a mode of moral uplift, as an inspiration for the masses. Even while attending the theater, his acid hatred and bitterness for those in power came bubbling to the surface and he glared at the officials with contempt mixed with envy. Sometimes his thoughts were whimsical: How can an official class so bent on avoiding responsibility and hardship be so hardy and brave when pursuing pleasure as to come to an unsanitary, hot, stinking, crowded theater like this? "What a great pity our nation has wasted so much wealth supporting these officials who only care about pleasure and take no responsibility at all for proper affairs!"[61]

Sometimes his favorite operas, such as *Third Wife Teaches the Son* (*San niang chiao tzu*), caused him to reflect upon his own training in the duties and virtues of his class. Indeed, his mixed emotions of love and hatred toward his mother and her stern reign of virtue, as well as toward the official class and their corruption were reawakened and fed by all he saw. He would return home from the theater sighing at the greatness of traditional virtues portrayed in a work, or shaking his head at the lack of it in those officials he saw or overheard in the audience. Sometimes he would also make observations on the decline of the Peking theater's artistic standards, but

60. [2a], p. 1.
61. [404e], p. 32; see also pp. 23b–24b, 29b; [99b], p. 28.

this would only cause him to reflect upon the morality of the new republican officialdom. They could not distinguish good and bad performances because they simply could not distinguish good and bad. These pleasure-loving opportunists in suits and spats did not even know proper theater etiquette, much less what was a good performance. Good opera, Liang Chi felt, should transmit the virtues of the ancients, "loyalty, filial piety, chastity, righteousness" (chung, hsiao, chieh, i). But all present-day Pekingese understood was "eating, drinking, amusement, and pleasure" (ch'ih, ho, wan, le).[62]

November 14, 1918, was the date of Liang Chi's sixtieth birthday, the most important of all birthdays to a Chinese. His children had been busy for months preparing for the event. At first Liang Chi opposed their gathering birthday poetry, for poetic scribblings were still "empty things" to him,[63] but as the time approached he paid them no mind. His attention was on rewriting folk and other plays for production in modern-style opera (wen-ming hsi). Through this return to the work of his earlier days, he perhaps hoped to make one final contribution to Peking opera and, through the opera, to uplifting the moral climate of the city of his birth. Whenever he had to sacrifice art to make a didactic point, he would do so.[64] The famous Ts'ui Ling-fen and Yang Yun-fu, the same innovative artists who worked with him on his first play back in 1904, again collaborated with him, and the plays opened at the Wen-ming yuan in September 1918.[65] Performances continued through the end of the year, but as a final blow to the already bitter old man, they drew no special praise from the press.[66]

Perhaps the failure of the world to appreciate his masterpieces convinced him not to pass his sixtieth birthday.[67] On October 22, he attended his last opera, drawing from it the usual evidence of

62. [404e], p. 39b; see also pp. 4b, 26b, 35b, 37a–b; [99b], p. 28.
63. [99b], p. 28.
64. [404e], pp. 23b–24b, 26, 37, 38b–39b; [99b], p. 28.
65. [488], Nov. 26, 1918; [278a]. Ts'ui also used the name Hsien Ling-fen.
66. [488], Sept. 4, 7, 13, 22, 28, 29, 1918; Oct. 18, 19, 24, 26, 29, 1918; Nov. 10, 13, 23, 24, 26, 1918; Dec. 1, 12, 22, 25, 1918; Jan. 8, 15, 16, 1919.
67. Liang Chi had, after all, made his vow in early 1912; what kept him from fulfilling it earlier? Originally in 1912 he wanted to wait for the convening of the provisional parliament and to submit his thoughts to the assemblymen. After that he had harbored hopes to visit Hangkow's famous West Lake (he loved southern scenery) and Kweilin (his ancestral home, which he had never seen) before he died. [404a], pp. 1b–2, 10–11b, 13–14b, 57–59; [404f], pp. 1–11b.

moral decline, but also a renewed faith in the power of virtuous example. On the last day of October, Liang Chi went to a relative's house to pay a long-standing debt of twenty dollars. That same day, he also called on an old teacher whose birthday was coming up soon and gave him a present in advance. Then, on November 7, Liang Chi rose early and prepared to leave for an overnight visit at P'eng's.[68] Before he could get away, he ran into Shu-ming, who fell to discussing the latest news from war-ravaged Europe. "Will the world be all right?" Liang Chi asked. Shu-ming answered, "I be-lieve that the world will get better every day." "If it can, then fine!" commented the father, and then left the house.[69]

Two days later his children became anxious that he still had not returned from P'eng's. With the birthday celebration only five days away, they went to the Pure Dharma Lake to fetch him home. He refused to go with them, but assured them that he would return by himself the next day. He wrote feverishly through the entire night, putting the finishing touches on his "Warning to the World," and his last letters to friends.[70] As dawn was breaking, he dressed and told the servant that he would take his usual morning stroll around the lake and return shortly. An hour later, just when the servant was becoming anxious, a policeman spotted a plain blue hat float-ing in the waters at the extreme northern end of the lake near the small island of the High Temple. The servant and P'eng rushed out and immediately recognized the hat. Then they ran back to Liang Chi's study and found, piled neatly on the desk, his notes and letters.[71]

As Liang Chi had planned, his death exerted far more moral influence on society (and gained more personal fame for him) than all his efforts during his lifetime. Major newspapers carried the story; important people wrote tributes and poetry; and follow-up

68. [404e], pp. 40a–b; [99b], p. 28b; [480], Nov. 19, 1918.
69. [14a], p. 18.
70. [99b], p. 28b; [480], Nov. 19, 1918.
71. At the extreme northern end of the lake, there is a narrow inlet in the middle of which is a small high island. On the top of the island is a temple, still standing today. The inlet could be seen from P'eng's house. The area—with its willow trees, temple building and walkways—is the most pleasant and peaceful part of the lake.

It had been Liang Chi's habit to take a dawn walk around the lake, so the servant did not find it strange that he had gone out alone that morning. Although for months it had been obvious that he was writing something, P'eng saw what he was writing only occasionally and it was in such disorder that he could not see it for what it was—a suicide note.

articles, eulogies, and reflections continued to appear long after the event. A grand tutor, still living in the Imperial Palace, issued an edict bestowing an honorific posthumous name on Liang, and even Premier Chin Yun-p'eng penned a votive tablet. Others held memorial meetings, and for years afterward, people could be seen burning spirit money and crying at the lakeside. Liang's act was commemorated with a stone monument erected on the shore of the lake and a mass meeting organized by residents of the lake neighborhood on the anniversary of his death. Inspired by Liang Chi's "Warning to the World," which was published in the Peking papers, an old Mongol bannerman also drowned himself a few weeks later.[72]

Reactions, moreover, were not limited to old scholars and officials and local residents. Even the anti-traditionalist intelligentsia—men such as Ch'en Tu-hsiu, T'ao Meng-ho, and Hsu Chih-mo—were deeply moved by Liang Chi's martyrdom. Their discussions of it appeared soon afterwards in the pages of *New Youth* and continued into the 1920s. As late as the 1970s, remembrances and reflections were still being published in the Hong Kong and Taiwan press.[73]

The masses of people were under the impression that Liang Chi simply had killed himself for the fallen Ch'ing monarchy, according to the ancient Confucian tradition of loyalty (*chung*).[74] Liang Chi himself had written that if his suicide had to be understood in

72. See [488], Nov. 12, 14, 26, 28, 1918, Dec. 4, 1918, Jan. 13, 15, 1919, Nov. 26, 27, 28, 1919, Dec. 2, 19, 1919; [278], Nov. 16, 1918, Dec. 2, 1918; [480], Nov. 19, 1918, Dec. 7, 1918. For the grand tutor's tribute, see [99b], pp. 28b–29; [193], 496:21. The bannerman, Wu Tzu-chien [Pao-sun], was a former official in the Board of Rites and the manager of P'eng I-sun's paper *Ching-hua jih-pao*. See [99b], pp. 28b–29; [488], Dec. 3, 1918, Dec. 8, 1918.

When I visited Pure Dharma Lake in May 1973 (now known by its alternate name Chi-shui t'an), the small temple on the island was still there, but no trace of the monument remained. Several stone monuments in the area had obviously been destroyed, as their bases were still in evidence. After an extensive survey of the neighborhood and a visit to the local neighborhood committee, I finally located an old man who had lived there forty years. He said that as he remembered, the monument to Liang Chi was intact at least until 1945. Probably the monument, being "feudal" but without great artistic value, was destroyed shortly after liberation.

73. See [153]; [516]; [5h]; [307]; [293a]; [517]; [139]; [529]; [205].

74. See [293a], pp. 143–144. This is very curious in that newspaper stories on the suicide did not mention anything about the Ch'ing royal house.

any concrete sense, then it should be the "dying out of loyalty for
(*hsun*) the Ch'ing dynasty."[75] Had he not refused to hold office
under the Republic, much in the traditional style of eremitic protest against ruler and government? Had he not put his hopes in
gradual reform under the monarchy? Yet Liang Chi did not support the restoration attempts of either Yuan Shih-k'ai or Chang
Hsun. To him, Yuan represented the epitome of postrevolutionary
evil, and when he heard of Chang Hsun's plan to put the last
Ch'ing emperor back on the dragon throne, he wrote four letters
pleading with Chang to desist. Liang was aware that the emperors
were gone for good. At another time he stated flatly: "I am not
opposed to republicanism; I heartily welcome it."[76]

In fact, he died for neither the Ch'ing monarch nor the institution of monarchy. He was disturbed because not only was no one
willing to die out of loyalty for the Ch'ing, but no one was willing to
sacrifice for or carry out the ideals of republicanism either.[77] His
death was intended as an example to the Republican generation of
what constituted real personal commitment to ideals, public duty,
and private rectitude.

Liang Chi's various theoretical explanations of his act contradicted each other. He welcomed republicanism, yet said that his
suicide was out of loyalty to the Ch'ing monarchy. He unconsciously linked the universal heavenly principles with the particular
Confucian code of propriety. He dedicated his life to propagating
modern knowledge and died cursing the "new learning." But these
contradictions are not important. His death was determined not by
his theoretical constructs but by the *chün-tzu*'s burden he had
taken up in childhood. The greatest poet of the day, Hsu Chih-mo,
understood this singularly well, for as Shelley claimed in defense of
his art, only the poet "participates in the eternal, the infinite, and
the one." Hsu saw that:

> In the back of the entire body of his [Liang Chi's] ratiocina-
> tions there still gleams an unmistakable something—call it
> what you will, "heavenly principles," "righteousness," faith,
> ideals, or Kant's moral category, which was precisely what
> Mencius "desired more than life"—which in the end imper-

75. [404a], p. 1.
76. [404a], p. 11; see also p. 51b; [404e], pp. 16a–b, 24–26b; [99b], pp.
27a–b.
77. [293a], p. 145.

ceptibly determined his cruel death. This amorphous something cannot be obliterated by textbook knowledge, and even less can it be taught by ordinary education.[78]

Even Ch'en Tu-hsiu, the initiator and main figure in the anti-traditionalist New Culture movement, admired Liang Chi's death for tradition. Perhaps this is not surprising, for although Ch'en had demanded that the heavenly principles be replaced with scientific laws, he had also written passionately about the moral heroism of Christ on the cross. Ch'en correctly understood that Liang Chi did in fact die to propagate the moral principles he had learned as a child and not for the Ch'ing monarchy. He went on to praise Liang Chi's spiritual capacities, his rare integrity, and his essential nobility in sacrificing himself for principles.[79]

Hu Shih, whose last remaining parent had died in Anhwei just a few days after Liang Chi's suicide, returned from his own mourning rites (which he had suitably modernized) in a less sympathetic mood. Claiming that Liang Chi had died because he could not accept the new Western learning, Hu urged the public to take a lesson from Liang Chi's tragedy and "form the habit of welcoming new thought so that new knowledge and new tides of thought can flow unceasingly." Hu, of course, was currently engaged in the business of importing such new thought and knowledge, and his use of Liang Chi's death to emphasize his own importance appears somewhat ludicrous. "Youth of today," Hu proclaimed in a poor attempt at irony, "take a look at a revolutionary of twenty years ago!"[80]

Attempts at purely rational explanations for Liang Chi's act do not succeed. His son's contributions to the discussion ended up in contradiction and vague pleas to remember that his father had been a progressive.[81] Similarly, China's best-known sociologist, T'ao Meng-ho, failed to make any real sense:

> After I read his writings, my admiration increased for Mr. Liang's resolute, unwavering character; his conscientious, incorruptible conduct; and the sincerity of his loyalty to rela-

78. [293a], pp. 146–147. Hsu's allusion is in Mencius VI;10, which reads: "So, I like life, and I also like righteousness. If I cannot keep the two together, I will let life go, and choose righteousness. I like life, indeed, but there is *that which I like more than life* and therefore I will not seek to possess it by any improper ways." [378], I and II, 411.

79. [153].   80. [309a]; [5h], p. 64.   81. [5h].

tives and friends. In our present age when everything is commercialized, that there was, after all, someone like Mr. Liang is a very precious phenomenon . . . but I still feel that suicide should not have been the method chosen by the old gentleman.[82]

T'ao evaluated Liang Chi's act by the bare utilitarian standard of its social effects. "How," he asked, "could such an act be effective?"[83] Liang Chi's character and motives were not the most important point to him.

Liang Chi's suicide was actually not amenable to sociological analysis. Neither Durkheim's classic categories nor his student Halbwachs' modification of them quite capture it.[84] The act was, in Durkheim's sense, "altruistic" because Liang Chi died in a way for the collective, yet it was also what Halbwachs calls "imprecatory," because it was inspired by a hatred for the collective and its treatment of him. Liang Chi did live in the midst of swiftly disintegrating social groupings and rapidly changing social values, which might have produced Durkheim's "anomic" suicide, yet Liang died for a very specific set of social values. Hsu Chih-mo, with a poet's distaste for intellectualization, dismissed any attempts at "scientific" analysis. Hsu answered T'ao:

> [The suicide's genesis and results] are definitely not those that our common sense can measure, and even less can they be evaluated by the criteria of social or natural science. We idiots who believe in spiritual life, as long as we can hold an inch of ground, cannot by any means allow the forces of pragmatism to crush completely any expression of a person's soul, and even less can we tolerate the black shadow of the age's superstition (in the middle ages it was religion, now it is science) to obliterate the unchanging values of the cosmos.[85]

Less flattering an interpretation would be that Liang Chi's suicide was simply the final expression of a displaced patrician's resentment and bewilderment. Another lost Brahmin unfitted for the twentieth century, Henry Adams, had departed from the world just a few months before Liang Chi. Surely he would have understood his Chinese brother's predicament. As Adams often stated in his peevish autobiography, his "eighteenth-century education" and family tradition made him unfitted for the America of President

82. [517], p. 153.   83. [516].   84. See [231]; [255].
85. [293], p. 152.

Grant and steam dynamos; and so Liang Chi's stern Confucian
pan-moralism made him unsuited for the China of Yuan Shih-k'ai
and railroads. Not only was it no longer enough to be an Adams of
Boston or a Liang of Kweilin, but the assumptions and training of
youth were positively harmful to success in the new worlds of
adulthood. Interestingly enough, Lu Hsun, who was living in Peking at the time of Liang Chi's suicide, published a short story a few
years afterwards about a pathetic old man who, having failed
numerous times in the examinations, drowned himself in a lake
while pursuing a mysterious white light. The light, the old man
thought, was guiding him to the buried treasure of his ancestors.[86]

Despite Liang Chi's personal distaste for poetry, perhaps it was
the poets, especially Chinese poets, who could best understand
Liang Chi's death. And perhaps the character of Liang Chi's
suicide is best captured by a comparison with the death of Ch'ü
Yuan, China's first great poet and first famous water suicide (as the
Dragon Boat festival testifies). Ch'ü Yuan died rather than allow the
jewel of his integrity to be destroyed. As the poet poised himself on
the banks of the river Mi-lo, he proclaimed that the world was filthy
and he alone was pure. It is not difficult to imagine Liang Chi at the
edge of the lake, declaiming his own diamond-hard purity to a
corrupt world. (Was it an accident that he chose the Pure Dharma
Lake for his death?) The ancient rhymes of Ch'ü Yuan capture
perfectly what Liang Chi's feelings must have been as he stood on
the brink of oblivion:

> The men in power with their petty jealousy
> Do not know my worth
> I could have borne high office and brought glory
> Instead I am dragged to the bottom and am unsuccessful. . .
> I know that death cannot be put off
> Oh that I could love life no more!
> I proclaim to all superior men [chün-tzu]
> I will be an example to you![87]

86. [419a].   87. [500], VIII, 2487–2490.

CHAPTER III

Confucius and Culture
at Peking University

The Climate at Peita

The year following Liang Chi's suicide, 1919, was a momentous time for China, and especially for Peking University. The World War was over and China was struggling at Versailles to regain its territories occupied by the Japanese in Shantung. When word came that the struggle had failed, a nationalist explosion, set off by the Peking students and professors, ripped through the country. Along with it came a cultural revolution unparalleled in Chinese history.

The young professor of Indian philosophy was in the very center of the movement. His closest friends at the university—Hu Shih, Li Ta-chao, Ch'en Tu-hsiu, and Ts'ai Yuan-p'ei—were the central figures of the May Fourth and New Culture movements. Another, less famous friend, philosophy professor Yang Ch'ang-chi, introduced Liang to his student and future son-in-law, a big Hunanese recently arrived from Changsha named Mao Tse-tung. Although the young Mao spoke with a heavy accent and had a rustic air about him, Liang found him impressive, and it seems the feeling was mutual, for Mao audited some of Liang's classes.[1]

Liang should have felt at home at Peking University. It was in his native city, and he had many friends on the faculty including two middle-school classmates. But he never managed to fit in well with the predominant "New Culture" group. For one thing, he was a Buddhist when Buddhism had not quite gained intellectual re-

---

1. Liang's references to his contact with these figures include: [66]; [4], pp. 1–2, 7, 43, 44; [11a], pp. 3, 8, 9; [5m], p. 80; [51], no. 18, Oct. 5, 1941. Li P'u-sheng, who worked with Liang on the Peking magazine *Ts'un-chih yueh-k'an* in 1929 and 1930, recalled that Liang had told him how impressed he was with Mao at their first meeting and "despite his rough exterior, perceived him to have great ability and talent." [628].

spectability. For another, he was almost alone among his colleagues as one who had never studied abroad or, for that matter, even been to college. At age twenty-four when he arrived at Peita, he was also considerably younger than most of the relatively young faculty. Ch'en Tu-hsiu, for example, was thirty-eight, Li Ta-chao twenty-nine, and Ts'ai Yuan-p'ei forty-one. Even some of Liang's students, such as the later prominent scholars, Fung Yu-lan and Ku Chieh-kang, were older than he. Another student, Fu Ssu-nien, with whom Liang publicly crossed swords in early 1919 over the relationship of Buddhist Hetuvidya (logic) to science, was only one year younger.[2]

The May Fourth Incident

At the time, Fu Ssu-nien was not famous for his scholarship, but for student activism—as the founder of the influential student magazine, New Tide, and as a prominent leader and elected marshal from Peking University in the historic May Fourth demonstrations. Fu did call for restraint when, after the demonstration at the Gate of Heavenly Peace on May 4, 1919, the aroused students cried for direct action against the traitorous government ministers, but he could not control them. The agitated students marched off to the residences of government ministers Ts'ao Ju-lin and Chang Tsung-hsiang where they proceeded to burn down Ts'ao's house and beat Chang senseless.[3]

Events followed rapidly after that. Government repression prompted more student organization and demonstrations in Peking, which then acted as a catalyst for a nationwide movement. The incident itself, and the movement that followed, drew many young intellectual leaders, such as Ch'en Tu-hsiu and Li Ta-chao, into a new life of political activism. Li's would be snuffed out by a warlord's executioner just eight years later, and Ch'en's finale would be rejection by the party he had founded. But they and others made the choice of putting aside some of their own beliefs and principles in the interest of political expediency.

Their colleague Liang Shu-ming reacted quite differently to the May Fourth incident. In his only public comment, he chose deliberately and provocatively to stress the civil rights of Ts'ao Ju-lin and

2. [66], p. 6; [5j], pp. 69–75; [243]; [244]; [136].
3. [155], p. 233; [158], p. 16.

Chang Tsung-hsiang. Although Liang was in complete sympathy
with the students and their motives, he reiterated what he had said
in his anti-warlord pamphlet two years before: if China is ever to
attain stability, then everyone—northern warlords or southern
constitutionalists, police or students—must obey the law and refrain from violence. If China is to have any future, then the con-
tenders for determining that future must work together to establish minimal civil rights. He went as far as to plead with the students
responsible for the attacks to hand themselves over to the police
and "voluntarily accept whatever punishment given them."[4]

Aside from once again exhibiting his penchant for shocking non-
conformity, his statement reflects his lifelong attitude—that he
would only approve of or act on methods that were consistent with
the preservation of his own moral standards. This personal reticence to sully his sagehood with political power, would make him
politically irrelevant throughout his career. After May Fourth,
Chinese youth tended to believe in nationalism, political activism,
and quick solutions to China's problems; before 1911, so had
Liang, but none of the three survived his late-adolescent crisis.

From Bodhisattva to Confucian Sage

Until 1921, when Liang actually announced that he had abandoned Buddhism for Confucianism, the general public regarded
him primarily as a Buddhist scholar. He had launched the contemporary systematic philosophical study of Buddhism with his 1918
book, *A General Discussion of Indian Thought* (*Yin-tu che-hsueh kai-lun*),
and, as China's leading Buddhist layman-scholar, he was frequently
asked to contribute to study and discussion on the subject.[5] He was
also in close contact with the other leaders of the Buddhist in-

4. [3]; [177]; [324], p. 156.
5. [2a]. Liang completed a manuscript based upon his class lecture
notes in 1918; the book was first published in 1919. By 1926 it had had five
printings. It was republished in Taiwan (without Liang's name) in 1966, so
apparently it has retained some of its scholarly value.
    In September 1920, the Young China Association passed a resolution
prohibiting anyone who believed in a religion from membership. This was
part of a larger antireligion movement among the young intelligentsia.
Because of resulting disputes within its membership, the association began
a program of research on the question of religion. As a prominent contemporary religious thinker, Liang was invited to lecture to the association,
and later published an article on religion in the association's journal. [5m].

tellectual revival.[6] In this context, his 1921 announcement had considerable dramatic impact.

It is tempting to focus on Liang's father's suicide as the primary stimulus for his apparently sudden conversion to Confucianism and Chinese culture; scholars have generally accepted this interpretation.[7] Certainly the impact of Liang Chi's suicide and his son's reaction to it cannot be dismissed lightly. The event does provide the most obvious and public indication of a change in Liang Shu-ming. At the time, he publicly beat his breast for having ignored Chinese culture and his father's teachings. "Oh, alas! The son's sin fills heaven and earth!" he repeated over and over; and for years, he wept openly on the anniversary of his father's death.[8] Probably Liang Chi's suicide did provide the final impetus and have the effect of strengthening his son's self-identity and hastening his conscious public declaration of ideological allegiance. Still, it was another two-and-one-half years before Liang Shu-ming finally abjured Buddhism and consecrated himself to Confucianism.

A close scrutiny of Liang Shu-ming's writings prior to his father's death reveals an adumbrated form of his later ideas on Confucianism and Chinese culture. In fact, his 1916 article on Buddhism signaled—however cryptically—his first step toward Confucius and the culture derived from him. Although the main thesis was the superiority of Buddhism, Liang did comment on the simi-

---

The discussion and Liang's contribution attracted considerable comment. See [601]; [538].

Also in 1920, many scholars of Buddhism, such as Chang T'ai-yen and Lü Ch'eng, began comparing the philosophy of the Wei-shih school with various Western thinkers such as Bergson. Li Shih-ts'en, editor of *Min-to tsa-chih*, asked Liang to give his opinion on the matter in a special issue of the magazine on Bergson. See [5n]. A 1921 article on religion [137] referred to Liang's 1916 essay [5a] as a prime example of Indian religious thought.

6. Liang had personal relationships with Chang T'ai-yen, Liang Ch'i-ch'ao, Ou-yang Ching-wu, and others involved in the Buddhist revival. In 1920 Liang visited Ou-yang Ching-wu's newly established Buddhist institute in Nanking, the Chih-na nei-hsueh yuan, where he probably first met his friend and supporter, the Cantonese militarist, Ch'en Ming-shu. See [4], pp. 114–115, 210–211; [423], p. 124; [571], p. 320; [5r], p. 115.

7. See [367], p. 176; [198], p. 331; [548], pp. 9–10; [506], p. 278; [570], p. 118; [144], p. 96. Liang himself said that his own decision to lead a Confucian life was made "in March and April" of 1921. [4a], p. 2; [14a], p. 16.

8. [312], pt. 6, no. 301 (May 16, 1963): 19–20; [9h], pp. 97–103.

larity he found in certain aspects of Buddhism and the *original* Confucian philosophy of life.[9] The following summer, he suddenly decided to read the Confucian Classics seriously *for the first time*, and became engrossed in the thought of Wang Yang-ming and his disciple, Wang Ken (A.D. 1483–1540). In another essay, he described Chinese culture as a transcendent entity transmitted from earliest times and independent of the forms it had assumed in history.[10] This idea of an essence of Chinese culture—an indefinable something created by China's earliest sages—would become the central pillar to all Liang's thought for the next forty years. In contrast to his beyond-good-and-evil Buddhist metaphysical philosophy of the time, Liang's anti-warlord article in the fall of 1917 spoke of a natural innate moral goodness in the masses, suggestive of the Confucian belief that there is an absolute moral standard inherent in the nature of humankind.[11] A month later, when he went to Peking University to take up his post as professor of Indian philosophy, he straightaway and with characteristic provocativeness declared to Chancellor Ts'ai Yuan-p'ei and Dean Ch'en Tu-hsiu that he had come for no other purpose than to spread and elucidate the teachings of Buddha *and* Confucius.[12] Thus, there is evidence to suggest that the crucial turning point in Liang Shu-ming's life began with his late adolescent psycho-social moratorium—his spiritual crisis of 1911–1916—and not his father's suicide.

When, in March 1921, Liang Shu-ming did publicly commit himself to Confucianism, he immediately set about changing his life style from that of a pious Buddhist to that of a pious Confucian.

---

9. [5a], p. 16. Also in this article, Liang had already suggested that all Western thought was "mechanistic" and "superficial." Three years later, at the memorial meeting for Miss Li Chao in November 1919, Liang forcefully expressed his growing antagonism toward Western rationalistic thought and his suspicion of the then current blind faith in rationalism among the young. He pointedly criticized the other speakers—Hu Shih, Li Ta-chao, Ch'en Tu-hsiu, and Ts'ai Yuan-p'ei—for emphasizing intellect at the expense of emotions. Women's liberation (the general topic of the meeting) would never have any real effect as a purely rational construct, Liang insisted; rather, it would succeed only with emotional commitment. See [5k], pp. 76–77; also the reports of the memorial service in [488], Dec. 1, 1919; [480], Nov. 20, 1919.

10. See [4], pp. 135, 138, 214; [5f].   11. [5g].

12. [4], p. 15. Such a shift from Buddhism to Confucianism is a classic pattern, especially among Sung and Ming Confucianists. Liang himself was aware of this tradition. See [47], p. 63.

The major distinction was obvious—he would have to marry. For Liang, of course, seeking out connubial bliss was a stern moral imperative stemming from his new commitment and from guilt over his previous unfilial celibacy. As he wrote to a friend at the time, he was marrying out of love of virtue, not out of sexual desire.[13] Upon hearing of his decision, a Cantonese militarist friend, Wu Yung-po, introduced him to his wife's younger sister, a young Manchu widow named Huang. The girl was not particularly attractive, intelligent, or warm, and due to her aristocratic birth, had never learned to cook or keep house. Liang was not especially attracted to her, but apparently rather than embarrass Wu or go through the process again, he married her. In the winter of 1921, he finally became a filial son: "I led my bride to pay obeisance before my father's picture and wept."[14]

The Cultures Question

The public learned of Liang's new commitment through a series of lectures—"Eastern and Western Cultures and Their Philosophies." The published form of these lectures made him a national figure as the defender of Chinese culture at a time when the culture question was foremost on the minds of many young Chinese intellectuals.

A study of one culture in an attempt to discover its "soul," or a comparative study of more than one culture in order to isolate their special features, was not a new enterprise. "*Kulturduselei*" (speculation about culture) had become very popular in the late-nineteenth and early-twentieth centuries, especially in Germany. In China, with the rise of the New Culture and May Fourth movements, it became not only a popular, but an extremely urgent, subject of discussion. When Ch'en Tu-hsiu founded the *New Youth* magazine in 1915 and issued his clarion call for young China to overthrow all of old China, the new, foreign-trained intellectual establishment hastened to comply. Stated somewhat baldly, the new intellectuals said: China is weak not only because of the lack of firearms and factories but also because of the entire culture, its ethics, literature, and thought. The West is strong because of its culture. Therefore,

13. [389], I, 28.
14. [9h], p. 100; [312], pt. 1, no. 295 (Feb. 10, 1963): 14; [5i], p. 65; [636]; [621]; [623]; [617]; [619]; [628].

to be strong, China must abandon its own culture and adopt that of the West.

Ch'en Tu-hsiu launched *New Youth* with an article on "The differences in the basic thought of Eastern and Western peoples," which compared East and West thus: The West emphasizes war, struggle, the individual, utility, and rule by law, while the East is devoted to peace, repose, the family, and the emotions.[15] Li Ta-chao simplified the distinction even further by saying that the West was a culture of positive action (*tung*), while in Eastern culture, passivity (*ching*) prevailed. Li attributed these differences to geographical influences. He agreed with Ch'en Tu-hsiu that the passive, dependent, restful Eastern attitude was the source of China's weakness and difficulties, but he did not go as far as Ch'en and call for wholesale destruction of the Chinese tradition. Rather, Li joined the growing band of intellectuals who envisioned a future world culture based upon a synthesis of East and West. The active, progressive world view of the West would replace the somnambulant Eastern attitude and, in doing so, solve the problems that had arisen in China as a result of its passive attitude. Conversely, the "oriental spiritual life" would help keep Western materialism under control. Both China and the West would thus undergo reformation, and a superior new culture would emerge.[16]

John Dewey, who was teaching at Peking University for most of the 1919–1920 academic year, spoke of a future blending of Eastern and Western thought in a way quite similar to Li's call for an East-West synthesis.[17] Dewey's most famous Chinese disciple, Hu Shih, likewise predicted the emergence of a world philosophy that would harmonize the characteristics of Eastern and Western philosophy.[18] The university's famous foreign-mind-in-residence the following year (1921) was the English philosopher Bertrand

15. [152].   16. [394].

17. At least this was Liang's interpretation of the remarks Dewey made at the ceremony opening the Peking University school year in 1920 (at which time Dewey was awarded an honorary doctorate). Ts'ai Yuan-p'ei came away with the same interpretation. See [524a], p. 82. Liang also referred to a lecture Dewey delivered at a meeting of the Peking University Philosophy Society, but this lecture was not reported in the press. See [4], pp. 2, 176. Neither Barry Keenan's exhaustive listing of the Chinese publications of Dewey's lectures nor Robert Clopton's collection of Dewey's China lectures has any note of either of these two lectures. See [228]; [343].

18. [310], "Tao yen," pp. 5–6; see also [4], pp. 12–13.

Russell. He expressed the hope that China would somehow absorb Western science and technology while retaining the ethical qualities and humanistic way of life at which China was superior. Although not optimistic about the chances for realization, Russell held up this East-West cultural blending as an ideal the Chinese should strive for.[19]

   Liang Ch'i-ch'ao's and Chang Chün-mai's disillusionment with Western culture. Perhaps the most prestigious, persuasive, and popular proponent of the "blending" theory was Liang Ch'i-ch'ao, who returned from a European trip in early 1919 to report to his countrymen that the West was crying for Eastern spiritual solace.[20] Impressed by the malaise that had settled over the European intelligentsia after the World War and had destroyed much of the Victorian Age's faith in progress and science, Liang Ch'i-ch'ao jubilantly concluded that the West's culture was not so perfect after all, and that Chinese culture might help correct the defects.

   The main target of Liang Ch'i-ch'ao's diatribe was rationalism (or science), which he believed had destroyed all spiritual values by reducing man to a materialistically determined part of nature. If people are just biological mechanisms, functioning according to invariable physical laws, then "how can there be any responsibility for good or evil?" Liang Ch'i-ch'ao asked.[21] An inevitable and spectacular result of the death of virtue, he declared, was the World War, in which the Westerners—whom science had equipped with a colossal technology for destruction while stripping them of moral standards—had almost succeeded in destroying themselves. Yet the war had caused "the majority of the people's philosophy of life to undergo a change. European intellectuals had awakened to the faults of their previous faith in the 'omnipotence of science' and unending material progress through unbridled competition."

   19. Russell advocated cultural synthesis in many of the lectures he delivered during his 1920–1921 sojourn in China. The lectures were published in newspapers, periodicals, and in a journal (edited by Liang's friend, Chang Shen-fu) solely devoted to propagation of Russell's thought, called *Lo-su yueh-k'an* (Russell Monthly). The most succinct expression of Russell's cultural syncretism is [461], which he published after returning to England.
   20. Liang Ch'i-ch'ao's original articles were published as a series in [481] in March 1919. See [407].
   21. [407], p. 10.

Liang Ch'i-ch'ao pointed to Kropotkin's "mutual aid" and Bergson's "creative evolution" as examples of how the Europeans were
modifying Darwin's harsh law of "survival of the fittest." Eucken's
philosophy was his example of renewed interest in "spiritual life."
The Europeans had discovered, according to Liang Ch'i-ch'ao, that
Chinese culture contained humanistic ideals similar to their own,
and so Eastern spirituality would play an important part in correcting Western materialism.[22]

In early 1923, a young German-trained philosopher at Peking's
Tsing Hua University, Chang Chün-mai (Carsun Chang), provoked a full-scale intellectual debate by raising similar doubts about
following the West's path of industrialism, capitalism, and scientism.[23] Since the May Fourth incident, he felt, young Chinese had
come to feel that science could solve all problems—social and personal. But, Chang averred, problems of the human soul, of
morality, of the aesthetic nature, could not be solved by mere rationalism. He put forth a critique of Western modernization, pointing out the ugliness, injustice, and cruelty of industrialized urban
society. Should it be China's goal to become equally dehumanized,
Chang asked.

          Liang's Eastern and Western Cultures. Liang Shu-
ming's statement on the subject, which was first published in book
form at the end of 1921, was regarded by intellectuals at the time,
and by historians since, as the link between Liang Ch'i-ch'ao's 1919
articles and Chang Chün-mai's "Philosophy of life" lecture. The
three stand together in most people's minds as a wave of conservative backlash against the successes of the New Culture movement.[24]
In their anti-positivist bent, their search for the core significance of
Chinese culture under the encrustations of traditions, and their
distaste for the modern industrialized West, the three do share
common themes and approaches.

Although it was Chang Chün-mai's unique speech that set off the
major intellectual fracas of the decade, Liang's lectures and their
publication did create a sensation of their own and attract an un-
precedentedly large audience for a scholarly work. The book gal-

   22. [407], pp. 36–38.   23. [119].
   24. [308]; [150], II, 330; [304]; [580], pp. 121–122, 129; [144], pp.
90–98; [141], pp. 72–82; [155], pp. 329–331; [367], pp. 170–185, 310–331;
[198], pp. 326–337; [376], pp. 135–141; [108], pp. 27–30, 104–105; [345],
pp. 40–42; [324], pp. 155–161.

loped through eight printings in its first four years, and immediately catapulted Liang into national prominence. His regular lectures at the university suddenly drew such numbers of students and outside auditors that he was forced to give his courses in the main hall of the school. His outside lectures became major events worthy of press coverage.[25] Despite his young age and limited accomplishments, his name even appeared in public opinion polls on "the greatest living Chinese."[26] Liang's influence and fame, moreover, was not just in China or among Chinese. The book drew comments in the Japanese scholarly community a few months after its publication, and word of it quickly spread to the communities of Chinese students studying abroad. Even a Western missionary published a summary of it.[27]

Nevertheless, only one of the famous paladins of the New Culture movement—Hu Shih—deigned to review Liang's book. The underlying feeling among the important anti-traditionalist theoreticians was that Liang was something of a harmless eccentric, much like that old champion of foot-binding and illiteracy, Ku Hungming. The intellectual establishment simply did not seem to take Liang as seriously as they took Chang Chün-mai. Perhaps Okasaki Fumio, who introduced Liang's book to the Japanese in 1922, correctly identified another part of the reason for the ambivalent response to Eastern and Western Cultures. In a comment accompanying his summary of the book, Okasaki observed: "The Chinese intellectual world is bewildered by the book and does not know how to respond to it."[28] Indeed, the published commentaries of the time demonstrate this confusion and how differently people understood and interpreted the book.

Liang's contribution to the cultures controversy made an extraordinarily deep and lasting impression in China. It was Liang's book that actually created the "cultures controversy" and perhaps

25. See [161]; [247], pp. 21–26; [637]; [233]; [565]; [488], Mar. 26, 1924. Liang's lectures had been privately printed in 1921; the seventh Commercial Press edition came out in 1926.

26. [203]. Liang tied for tenth place with the "Christian general," Feng Yü-hsiang, who had just pulled off a spectacular coup by occupying Peking when the poll was taken. Considering that Liang had resigned from Peita and left Peking months before the poll was taken, he did rather well. Liang also won a place in another poll taken earlier in Shanghai. See The Weekly Review 23.6 (Jan. 6, 1923): 223–226.

27. See [451]; [246]; [434].   28. [451], pp. 700–701.

set the stage for the public reaction to Chang's speech. People
continued to read *Eastern and Western Cultures* long after most
Chinese had forgotten about Liang Ch'i-ch'ao's and Chang
Chün-mai's arguments. Liang's book became a kind of classic
treatment of the question, provoking public discussion and criticism through the following three decades. And it has maintained its
currency outside mainland China for nearly another thirty years.[29]
In Taiwan, it is quoted in school textbooks alongside the sacred
words of Sun Yat-sen and Chiang Kai-shek, and Liang Shu-ming's
ideas are compared with newer cultural theories such as Soro-
kin's.[30] That, thirty-five years after the publication of *Eastern and
Western Cultures*, the Communist regime should devote almost as
much time, energy, and ink in criticizing Liang Shu-ming as they
spent on the more famous Western-oriented liberal, Hu Shih, gives
further indication both of the appeal of Liang's ideas and their
durability.

   If major intellectuals of the period gave Liang's book such short
shift, how are we to explain its great acclaim and popularity? This
apparent contradiction suggests that perhaps the New Culture intellectuals' impact was really extremely limited among the larger,
less articulate, middle-brow sections of society outside the large
coastal cities. Liang's book seems to have resonated with the structure of sentiments in this literate silent majority of marginal and
middling intellectuals. One hostile critic, for instance, accused

---

   29. See [249]; [374]; [505]; [245]; [309d]; [131]; [149]; [118]. One form
the discussion took was the 1930s debate between those who advocated
"cultural reconstruction on a Chinese base" (*Chung-kuo pen-wei chih wen-hua
chien-she*) and those who favored "wholesale Westernization" (*ch'üan-p'an
hsi-hua*). The most important articles of this debate and a bibliography of
all articles published are in [226] and [227]. See also [309f]; [551].
   Although Liang himself remained indifferent to much of the later debate (see his comment on the "cultural construction on a Chinese base"
question in [47], pp. 120–122), the influence of his *Eastern and Western
Cultures* has been obvious in all subsequent discussions. See, for example,
[155], pp. 329–331; [144]; [141], pp. 72–82; [117], pp. 1, 50–51; [501], Nov.
1, 1941; [445]; [604]; [357]; [443]; [295], pp. 159–180; [589], p. 42; [523];
[508]; [442]; [175b]. The government sponsored "Movement for Revival of
Chinese Culture" (Chung-hua wen-hua fu-hsing yun-tung) on Taiwan in
the late 1960s once again brought the question to the fore and produced a
plethora of books and articles, of which [585] is a fair sampling.
   30. See [236]; [150], I, 330; [569], pp. 16–17, 175–196; [568], pp. 54,
64; [570], pp. 112–145; [304]; [197]; [532], I, 5, 6, 30, 48, 115, 116; [537];
[411].

Liang of using the book to "marshal the masses of musty high school teachers" into a legion of opposition to the New Culture movement.[31] Then, too, unlike those of his confreres who lived and worked primarily in Peking, Shanghai, or Canton, Liang seems to have been at his best and most comfortable in the provinces and among the less sophisticated (and less Westernized) strata of educated people.[32] Perhaps an understanding of what Liang was saying can give us some insight into the nature and feelings of this vast middle section of Chinese society during the tumultuous twenties and thirties.

31. [565].
32. The Occidentalized intellectual mandarinate of Peking had already administered a rankling snub to one such middle-brow provincial bumpkin. As Mao recalled several years later, "I didn't exist as a human being [for them]. . . . They had no time to listen to an assistant librarian speaking southern dialect." See [489], pp. 134–135.

CHAPTER IV

Eastern and Western Cultures

The basic question underlying the discussion of cultures in China, including Liang Shu-ming's contribution to it, was a tension between the values of Chinese culture on the one hand and rationalization of social and economic organization toward the end of world mastery (modernization) on the other. Could both the preservation of Chinese ways and the acquisition of power-producing modernization coexist? The cultural blenders thought they could. The advocates of wholesale Westernization, Ch'en Tu-hsiu and others of his persuasion, made the case that since all Chinese ways—be they ethical or literary systems—seemed incompatible with the modern world, the Chinese had no choice but to abandon their past entirely. Ironically enough, Liang Shu-ming's theory of culture was more compatible with that of the Ch'en Tu-hsiu camp than with that of the cultural blenders.

Will and the Formation of Culture

The category of "culture" was the basis of Liang Shu-ming's theory, which he built on the metaphysical foundations of Wei-shih Buddhism—the concept of the cosmos in eternal flux.[1] He posited an *anima mundi* comparable to Schopenhauer's concept of Will; all life was an expression of this blind force. The struggle between the individual embodiments of the Will (*ta-i-yü*) and encountered obstacles to fulfillment constituted the life process. The spirit—or unfulfilled Will—makes demands on the environment and overcomes the environment's obstacles to fulfillment in a continuous

---

1. Liang admitted that his version of Wei-shih metaphysics was highly interpretive and personal; he also allowed that in matters of Buddhist scholarship he was no peer to specialists like Ou-yang Ching-wu and Lü Ch'iu-i. [4], p. 48; [4a], pp. 4–5.

interaction between demand and response. The life process, then, becomes an unending sequence of problems presented to individual expression of the Will.[2] Culture—"a way of life"—is the way in which people resolve the contradictions between the Will's demands and the obstacles presented by the environment. Cultural differences are due to differences in the "direction" of the Will—or the way the Will attempts to deal with the environmental obstacles.

Liang posited three ideal cultural types—expressions of three distinct directions of the Will—which, in turn, are responses to different ways in which the problems of the environment are perceived (or different kinds of contradictions between the Will and the environment). The first type, represented by the West, is the regular or normal direction of the Will; it is a response to the basic problems of the human as animal: the need for food, shelter, and procreation. Here the Will goes in a forward direction to conquer the environment and satisfy these primal desires. All the characteristics and products of Western culture, such as science, democracy, and power over nature, have developed naturally from this direction of the Will. The second basic direction of the Will is sideways to harmonize itself with the environment—to achieve a balance between the demands of the Will itself and the environment. This cultural type deals with the problems of having an emotionally satisfying life and thus achieves greater inner contentment and *joie de vivre*. It is represented by China. The third type is represented by India; the Will turns backwards into itself seeking its own negation. In the final stage of the third culture, humankind realizes that the world is an illusion and so seeks ultimate enlightenment.

By way of illustration, Liang imagined that the archetypical Westerner resolves the contradiction between the Will's demand for shelter and the environmental obstacle of a dilapidated house by completely demolishing the house and building a new one. The Chinese will repair the old house, and the Indian will attempt to extinguish the desire for housing. Each of the directions should succeed the other at the appropriate stage of human evolution. At the primitive stage of existence, the problem of primal needs is met by a headlong rush forward in an attempt to bend the environment to meet the most basic desires of the human organism. After people have satisfied their basic wants, they become conscious

2. [4], pp. 24, 28–50, 80–87.

of the problem of achieving emotionally rich, satisfying lives—of truly enjoying their material acquisitions while finding joy in life itself. After achieving this state of both interior contentment and exterior wealth, they are still confronted with a consciousness of the truly eternal problems: the world's impermanence and their own inevitable death. In the third stage, humankind frees itself from the illusions of the existence of both the inner self and the outer world, and finally achieves the ultimate joy of Nirvana.[3]

On one level, Liang fashioned his theory in a value-void of pure relativism. Each of the Will directions is an equally valid preoccupation of humanity at the appropriate stage of development and in response to the problems of that stage. "The present victory of Western culture lies only in its being appropriate for the immediate problems of humankind, while the reason for the present defeat of Indian and Chinese cultures lies not in any inherent goodness or badness. It lies in nothing more than the fact that they are unsuited to the times." Liang still seems to cling to the lofty peaks of Buddhist indifference, which he had scaled with so much pain: "I by no means take human life to have any [inherent] good . . . and human culture to have any value. . . . I know that, no matter what, humankind cannot achieve salvation unless it destroys the two fundamental holdings [holding to the reality of self and to the reality of the world]."[4] Yet neither Liang's relativistic metahistoricism nor his recognition of the ultimate unreality of all phenomena prevented him from singling out the essence of Chinese culture and identifying it as an absolute value; it required a tortuous process for him to do so.

To explain the very existence of Chinese and Indian cultures at the present stage of human development, Liang looked back to the early geniuses or sages of the Chinese and Indian cultures: "Actually this thing culture is every bit a creation of genius and accidental exceptional ideas." Unlike their Western counterparts, who saw only the immediate problems that confronted humankind, the Indian and Chinese sages inexplicably anticipated the problems of the second and third paths *before* the problems had actually materialized. As the most brilliant people of their age, their attention to these problems set the direction for their cultures on the second and third paths before the first path had been fully completed.[5]

---

3. [4], pp. 24, 52–55, 66, 166–167.   4. [4], pp. 109, 209.
5. [4], p. 44; see also pp. 45, 145, 154, 159, 199–200. Liang's great-

Although there are several areas in which Liang's theories over-lap with Marxist views, his emphasis on the primacy of conscious-ness places him squarely in opposition to the historical-materialist interpretation of culture, an interpretation just gaining popularity in China at the time. Liang admitted the Marxist claim that the economic substructure determines the cultural superstructure, but he felt that this theory alone did not explain enough. Economic or geographic determinism could only deal with objective factors and so only explain causal relationships (*yuan*).[6] Why, Liang asked, had not China and India developed economically and undergone an industrial revolution as the West had? Obviously, he contended, the Easterner's subjective factor—the underlying attitude or direc-tion of the Will—was the only sufficient cause (*yin*).

Cultural Blending Rejected

On first glance, Liang's metaphysical ramblings would seem to have little to do with his final conclusions about Chinese and West-ern cultures. He claimed, however, that this theoretical speculation about the ultimate nature of the universe "is the center of my whole book."[7] Basing himself on it, he dismissed all the theories of cul-tural blending. If culture in its entirety is an expression of a distinct underlying direction that the Will may take, then individual cul-tural products—such as European science or Chinese ethics—cannot be detached or added. The people can produce the prod-ucts of a certain culture only if they hold the underlying attitude of that culture.

---

man theory on the origin of cultural differences is similar to Russell's, who, when pressed to make a hypothesis, said: "Probably a great deal depends upon the character of dominant individuals who happen to emerge at a formative period, such as Moses, Mahomet, and Confucius." [461], p. 187.

6. [4], pp. 44–47; see also pp. 145, 154, 159, 199–200. Russell's lec-tures might have impressed on Liang the failure of historical materialism to explain the differences in economic development among the world's cultures, or the difference in cultures that share the same physical envi-ronment. Russell noted that although the Chinese, Egyptians, and Babylonians had "similarity in physical and economic circumstances, there was very little in common between mental outlook of the Chinese and that of the Egyptians and Babylonians. . . . People who attribute everything to economic causes would be hard put to account for the differences between [them]. . . . I do not think science can, at present, account wholly for na-tional character." [461], p. 187.

7. [4], p. 43.

As proof, Liang pointed to the failure of China's past attempts to capture Western wealth and power through cultural blending. In the late nineteenth century, China first tried to blend in the most superficial Western cultural products—technology and industry. Following the failure of these early attempts, the Chinese went a step further and, as advocated by the 1898 reformers, copied Western institutions and laws. In 1911, they went still further and overthrew the monarchy to establish a republican representative government and other Western institutions. Yet all these efforts had failed because the underlying Chinese attitude remained unchanged.[8]

Therefore, Liang could dismiss Liang Ch'i-ch'ao's "Reflections on a European Journey" as simply a celebration of the recent European concession that certain elements in Chinese culture and philosophy had some value. "Actually," he declared, "not one word of what Liang Ch'i-ch'ao said is right."[9] As Liang Shu-ming elaborated:

> [All who advocate a blending of East and West] feel that both cultures have their faults, so they think up [a culture] that meets their subjective demands and call it perfect. They do not understand that the reason one culture is that culture in the first place is certainly not due to anything else but its [underlying attitude]. Their mistaken ideas [about blending] arise from this [misunderstanding]. Really, how can one fundamental spirit be combined with the fundamental spirit of another culture?[10]

Thus, at least on the surface, Liang Shu-ming rejected the "select the best from East and West" formula. Joseph Levenson has suggested that the only motive that a Chinese could have in celebrating the beauty of blending cultural values would be a desire to see China and the West as equal partners, a desire for Chinese "equivalency."[11] Liang rejected the formula, not because he detected Chinese hypocrisy in denying an interest in the national origins of adopted values, but precisely because he felt that no value could be truly borrowed without also taking on the national consciousness that had created it.

Because, however, the direction of the Will in China was different from that in the West, China could not be viewed as "behind"

8. [4], pp. 4–5, 8–9.   9. [4], p. 14; see also pp. 2, 13.
10. [4], p. 198.   11. [379], I, 109–116.

the West on a path of development common to all humankind. On the contrary, China was on its own track, completely different from the West's. Because China's direction was different, science, democracy, and industry were not inevitable for China.

> I can state categorically that if Western culture had not made contact with us, and China had completely shut itself off from foreign contact, then China would have gone another three hundred years, or five hundred years, or even another thousand years, and absolutely would not have produced these steamboats, railroads, airplanes, scientific method, and democratic spirit. That is to say, the Chinese have not been traveling on the same path as the Westerners. Because, if China were just traveling more slowly on the same path, then there would be a day when we would, walking slowly, catch up. If each [culture] is going along separate roads, or in separate directions, then no matter how long [China] travels, it will never reach the point the Westerners are at now![12]

In effect, Liang was saying that any dysfunctional elements in Chinese culture had to emanate from the outside, not merely as catalytic agents, but as basic sources of change. Chinese social institutions themselves had no built-in *vis a tergo* to produce change. "Unchanging China," Liang felt, would have remained unchanged forever if not for the West.[13]

Now, however, the world *was* in communication. The West—because of the wealth and power its attitude enabled it to produce—was very rapidly becoming the cultural model of the entire world. Thus, Liang's cultural schemata also had the potential for a radical doctrine. Now that all cultures were in contact, the three cultural systems based upon the different directions of the Will could no longer coexist; one would emerge as the culture for all of mankind. Therefore, he concluded, "unless [Chinese culture] can become the world culture, it cannot exist at all."[14]

The radical anti-traditionalists, Liang believed, saw the problem most clearly. Ch'en Tu-hsiu, for example, had realized that if China was going to import Western science and government, it had to import the rest of the culture as well; the Chinese must fundamentally adopt Western culture in its entirety and change the underlying direction of the Will.

12. [4], p. 65. 13. [4], p. 203; see also pp. 64–65, 145.
14. [4], p. 9; see also pp. 3–4.

I cannot but praise and admire the clarity of Mr. Ch'en's
mind! Although it is easy for people to be confused about the
differences in these two cultures, Mr. Ch'en is very able to
recognize them clearly, and moreover, sees that Western culture is an integrated whole that cannot be looked at superficially and piecemeal. Because of this awakening [of Ch'en's],
everyone now advocates that the best thing to have is a
thought revolution, a culture movement.[15]

One can imagine the hush that must have fallen over Liang's
audience after he said this. In the end, even Liang Shu-ming, a
profound philosopher who admired Buddhism and Confucianism,
also agreed with the New Youth coterie! He even agreed with his
arch-rival, Ch'en Tu-hsiu.

Science and Democracy

Liang also agreed with Ch'en that the essence of Western culture
is science and democracy: "Western culture is a culture in which
these two distinguishing characteristics—science and democracy—
are produced by the spirit of the Will moving forward."[16] By following the "first path" of human culture, Western culture con-
fronts the normal concerns of humankind—those related to survival:

Since the physical necessities of clothing, food, and shelter are
all taken from the natural world, this [Western] attitude is one
in which the demands [of individuals] were directed forward
[toward the natural world] changing the external environment and conquering obstacles with force. If people had not
thought up methods to do this, then they would not have
succeeded . . . or been able to survive.[17]

This direction of the Western Will toward the satisfaction of
appetites and desires produced two fundamental attitudes, the
crystallizations of which were science and democracy: the attitude
of intellectual calculation toward the external world led to the development of science; the attitude of individual self-interest and
desire to obtain one's rights led to democracy. Modern Western
culture is the logical culmination of these attitudes, which go back
to the ancient Greeks. The Sophists' skepticism set up "benefit to
the individual" as the only criteria for evaluating action; Socrates

15. [4], p. 6.   16. [4], pp. 22, 24.   17. [4], pp. 166–167.

equated knowledge with morality and placed primary emphasis on
the intellect. Western culture is entirely selfishness and the use of
intellect. Most of Western philosophy since the Greeks has been
concerned with rational calculation of the natural world—
epistemology, cosmology—and such questions. All features of
Western culture—its rationalized competitive economic and political systems, the decline of religion, the emphasis on law, rights, and
the individual—developed naturally from this.[18]

Liang neatly disposed of the gaping inconsistency presented by
the other-wordly ascetic European Middle Ages with the analytic
aid of the Reverend Frederick Robertson's distinction between Hebrewism and Hellenism. Between the Romans and the Renaissance,
Liang blithely explained, the West was temporarily under the influence of Eastern (third path) Hebrewism. (If the good Reverend
Robertson could have known what purposes his sermons served in
heathen Chinese hands, he must have turned over in his proper
Anglican grave!) "Hebrew thought came from the East," Liang
claimed. "I suspect that it might have had some distant connections
with India."[19]

The Renaissance was the Westerners' return to their normal cultural development, and with it, their underlying attitude reverted
to the Greek pattern. Liang quoted Hoffding's saying that "the
greatest achievements of the Renaissance were the discovery of the
world and the discovery of man." "Discovery of the world," of
course, was the rebirth of science, this time the pure rationalism of
the Greeks supplemented with English empiricism. Critical rationalism destroyed the religion and supernationalism of the Middle Ages. The English empiricists wedded the two fundamental
tendencies of self-interest and rational calculation with the West's
Promethean will to possess, and gave birth to modern industry.[20]

The Renaissance's "discovery of self," Liang continued, provided
for the development of democracy—a system Liang praised for
allowing both maximum personal freedom and maximum collective action. Democracy was based on the individual's rights: positively, the guarantee of an opportunity to develop oneself; and
negatively, the guarantee of freedom from interference from society or other individuals within a defined sphere of action. The
development of the individual (*ko-hsing ti shen-chan*) was actually the

18. [4], pp. 155–158, 76–77, 142–152.   19. [4], p. 56.
20. [4], pp. 66–67.

other side of the coin to the development of the individual's social nature (*she-hui-hsing ti fa-chan*). Democracy provided for effective organization and at the same time protected individuals from having their individuality smothered by the organization.[21]

It was, according to Liang, the Western awareness of the self that produced this greatest of Western democracy's achievements: the guarantee of individual freedom of expression and development along with provision for the organization of corporate bodies. Since individuals have the right to share in the decision process, they are not an anonymous part of the organization. The organization's guarantee of specific individual freedoms enables individuals to feel that they can obey the decisions of the organization without giving up their own freedom. Individuality and the organization are mutually dependent on each other; one cannot exist without the other.

Individual freedom and consciousness of self are valuable not just to the individual, but also to the collective, for they allow for the release of individual energies that are the means to a more powerful corporate body. Without this unleashed selfishness, the West's economic development and wealth would have been impossible. Without the active participation of the individual in society, the famed Western public spirit and democracy would have been impossible.[22] These themes, which run through the "liberalism" in the pre-1911 writings of Yen Fu and Liang Ch'i-ch'ao—when Liang, as a middle-school student, first began to think about the West—informed Liang Shu-ming's understanding of democracy.

The Consequences of the Western Way

This recognition and affirmation of the self (*tzu-chi*) and the ego (*wo*), Liang explains, naturally leads to the Western attitude of self-interest and desire to enjoy for oneself the various things from the natural world. As a consequence of the Westerners' habit of intellectual calculation: "The ego and the cosmos in which the ego is located—both of which had been blurred together without distinction in human intuition—are cleaved cleanly in two, never again to coalesce." The Westerners now view the natural world only in terms of satisfying desires, as an object for utilization and conquest. This attitude informs their whole outlook on the world and their attitude toward fellow human beings as well. The modern West-

21. [4], pp. 37–41.   22. [4], pp. 37–42, 61–62.

erners' intellect is just too strong and overpowering. While it has achieved enormous increases in knowledge and wealth, made life comfortable, and accomplished many other undeniably admirable things, it has also damaged "spirituality" and caused "existential suffering."[23]

In places Liang sounds like a philosophically inclined ecologist:

> The Westerners' life attitude brought about a great fissure between individual and individual, as well as between individuals and nature . . . profoundly alienating individuals from each other and from nature. With this attitude, it appears [to them] that nature is indifferent toward people and so they in turn are even more ruthless toward nature, until they have lost entirely their former feelings toward a humanized universe that nourished and brought forth all things, had good intentions toward them, and that they in turn respected. [Before this] they and the universe were mutually dependent and mutually affectionate. Moreover, because the Westerners' intellect classifies the whole of the cosmos into [intellectual] categories, they transform [the cosmos into mere] matter. Looking at nature, they [now] see only a great pile of splintered dead things, and themselves as [merely] compounds of these unrelated dead things.[24]

Westerners' intellectual calculation for individual profit has "cut [them] off and alienated them from the cosmos, placing them in conflict and contradiction with it, so that [they are] without emotion and weary unto death."[25]

Westerners can obtain no spiritual solace from their fellows either because "the divisions between man and man are so clearly drawn, and each individual's calculations are so important, that each is split off from, and set in opposition to and in competition with, others. . . . It is as though each feels that only he himself [really] exists. . . . All others [are] aliens or enemies." Even the family itself is not immune to this mean-spirited haggling. "As soon as you open your mouth, you must speak in terms of rights and obligations, legal relationships through which everybody keeps accounts with everybody else, even extending to the relationship between parent and child or husband and wife.[26]

By now it was obvious to Liang's audience that he had not come to lavish unqualified praise on the modern West, but rather to call attention to the price paid for its achievements. It must have been

23. [4], p. 63.   24. [4], p. 177; see also pp. 178, 179, 186.
25. [4], p. 186.   26. [4], pp. 178, 152.

comforting to them to hear that the much envied Westerners, whose empires spanned the globe, and whose days were passed in luxury, were after all pitiful, Scrooge-like creatures incapable of enjoying the affluence their aggressiveness had produced. "Their lives are rich externally, but internally they are still poverty-stricken to the extreme!"[27]

Intellectual calculation. Liang spoke of the first element of the Western attitude—intellectual calculation at the expense of emotion—as one that could lead to a loss of the integrity of life itself:

> Intellect is a tool for life, for convenience in arranging and calculating and for creating the [imaginary] hypothesis of dividing life. But to take such a division as real is not merely a mistake, but a gravely dangerous one. Life is a whole. If you divide it into segments and make one contingent on another, then it loses its relish. When life's integrity is maintained, all parts have their own inherent meaning or interest. If this attitude [of calculation] is taken, the individual moments of life all become means. Living in a house becomes merely for the sake of eating and sleeping [in it], and eating and sleeping, in turn, become merely a means to the end of reproducing, and gradually a person's whole life has meaning only in something external to itself. The fun of living would no longer be in the living itself, but in some other purpose extraneous to it. . . . In reality, life has no ulterior ends, but is for its own sake. Each moment of life is an end in itself, and not for the service of another moment, and does not derive its significance from some later phase of life. Intelligent people are especially prone to make this mistake, and [consequently] find the flavor of their lives drying up. Then they start searching for life's meaning, its significance, its value, and so on, so much so that their emotions and will are shaken, convulsed, and broken.[28]

This utilitarian calculation "turns people into machines, and suffocates and kills [their vital force]."[29]

Individual self-interest. The other dominant strain in bourgeois utilitarian culture—selfish calculation—led to anxiety

27. [4], p. 178; see also p. 152.   28. [4], pp. 133–134.
29. [4], p. 135.

about the external *results* of all actions. When life's center of gravity is thus in the external world, Liang said, one is prey to life-destroying anxiety. Focusing on one's personal profit, of course, produces such anxiety; even an altruistic but result-oriented concern over the benefit to one's nation, or even to humankind, would cause it.[30] (After all, in Liang's own crisis, much of his anxiety had been over the success of the Republican Revolution, and not his own individual interests.) The utilitarian's dependence on external results is one of the connecting strands between Liang's Buddhist conversion of 1912 and his later Confucian stance of the thirties and forties. When the adolescent Liang made the existential discovery of the "relativity" of human happiness, it led him to seek ultimate truth in Buddhism. Pleasure was a consequence of satisfying some desire in the external world, but desire was also responsible for pain and unhappiness. In 1921, the Confucian Liang felt that the old Schopenhauerian trap of desire, fulfillment, ennui was valid only for utilitarians, whose joy was "relative."

> What is relative joy? This [kind of] joy stands in opposition to and is consequent upon suffering. . . . Ordinary people traveling the road of [intellectual] calculation always want to use *means* to attain their end. Consequently, they must first get something, and only then are they joyful. If they do not get it, they suffer. Their joy is completely tied to the thing that is their goal, and so it is dependent on the external. When their joy departs, suffering begins, and vice versa, so it is obvious that this [joy] is relative.[31]

Clearly, Liang was putting himself into a position that has to be described as anti-intellectual. He uses the word "intellect" in much the same tone as, for example, the nineteenth-century European Romantics. Like Shelley's "calculating faculty," Liang's intellect could dissect and so destroy life. An attitude of selfish calculation, Liang claimed, led to a person's very life becoming a means to external ends, with the result that one's interior vital force became dissipated in the external world. What Marx called the "icy waters

30. [4], p. 138; [5r]. There is little doubt that Liang was, at least unconsciously and perhaps consciously, referring to his own past personal crisis. The phrase "to fight with oneself" (*tzu-chi ken tzu-chi ta-chia*) he used only twice in all his writings: once in describing his own crisis—see [47], p. 3—and once in describing the conflict between intellect and emotion in those who did not lead a Confucian life—see [4], p. 124.

31. [4], p. 137.

of egotistical calculation," Liang believed, was the Westerner's very blood, and it drowned not only ecstasies and enthusiasm, but life itself.

Liang must have appeared a bit overly emotional to his audience in his shrieks of pity for the spiritual suffering of Westerners—especially for one who had never been abroad. "It is really too sad a life to lead!" he exclaimed several times.[32] Liang was probably quite sincere, for the roots of these emotions went back to his own crisis. Liang felt he had known the Western path and its suffering firsthand, and so knew whereof he spoke. This image of the spiritually and psychologically shattered utilitarian (pragmatist, hedonist—Liang drew no distinction) would recur repeatedly in his lectures and writings. His choice of words in each instance clearly indicates that he had his own experience in mind.

Western machines and capitalism. The logical consequence of the wedding of the two tendencies of self-interest and material intellectual calculation was industrial capitalism. The Faustian spirit's drive for knowledge of the external world (science) uniting with the drive for satisfaction of material desires gave birth to the Machine, which, in the tone of a Ruskin, Gandhi, and other critics of industrial society, Liang termed "really the devil of the modern world." Liang's critique of capitalism is in that area where the conservative and Marxist traditions overlap:

> When the machine was invented . . . the small-scale industries were destroyed one after the other . . . the small-scale capitalists became workers one after the other, and went to large factories to work for their living. Society became virtually split into two classes. . . . The relationship between the capitalists and their workers appears to be a free contract. . . . Actually the capitalists have the power to oppress the workers and control their existence completely. The workers have only the freedom to starve, because if they do not work, they do not eat. . . . There are continuous crises of unemployment; they [the capitalists] stockpile production surpluses of food and clothing while people are starving and freezing.[33]

That Liang's conservative critique of Western capitalism would

32. [4], p. 178; see also pp. 152, 166; [4a], pp. 3–4; [5r], p. 115.
33. [4], p. 163.

avail itself of such obviously Marxist-inspired analysis is not surprising. As Karl Mannheim pointed out, the Vitalist and Marxist concepts of reality originate philosophically in a common romantic opposition to pure rationalism.[34] The early Marx and Marxists had a Janus-like attitude toward the machine, and Liang, too, has an aversion to modern industry. Anti-industrial feeling is the basis of Marxist emotion, just as its opposite—worship of science and technology—is the basis of Marxist logic.[35]

In China, as in the West, this basic emotional reaction to the philosophical implication of bourgeois rationalism and its attendant economic system would express itself in both radical and conservative forms. In his various anti-capitalist animadversions, Liang was actually talking about "alienation," believing that Westerners were compelled by their social and economic environment to act in a way destructive to human nature *(jen-lei pen-hsing)*.[36] Liang is another example of how a conservative's groan of despair could sound, to use Durkheim's phrase, much like a socialist's "cry of pain."[37] But Liang believed that all classes of Westerners were equally alienated: "The present economic predicament and its destruction of human nature . . . is just intolerable. It makes no difference whether people are workers, those who are better off, or even capitalists. The vital force of all of them is just about exhausted; life is unnatural, mechanical, and insipid for all in the same way."[38]

Other aspects of industry bothered Liang too—as they did the early Marx. Liang saw the dehumanizing potential in the division of labor, and in machine production which made workers into appendages of machines and allowed them no creative satisfaction. He pointed to the social problems that were thus generated, such as suicide, crime, drunkenness, anomie, and the decline of the family. After a day of repetitive, dull, boring work, the workers still had to seek pleasure "urgently." Leisure was just another kind of suffering, for the workers could find pleasure only in stimulating the most vulgar corporal desires. "In all cases, if it is not lewd and in

34. [422], pp. 161–164.   35. [547], p. 63.
36. [4], p. 181, 63; [5r], p. 116.
37. After carefully studying socialism, Durkheim concluded that it was inspired by moral passion, by emotional revulsion to capitalism, and not by any objective scientific conclusions: "Socialism is not a science . . . it is a cry of pain." [232], p. 5.
38. [4], p. 165.

excess, then it will not be pleasurable." But what bothered Liang most, it seems, was the constant competition with others, which forced all people to put their entire spirit single-mindedly into economic struggle, and constantly filled them with anxiety and fear.[39]

Chinese Culture: The *I CHING* and Intuition

The tremendous prestige of Western Ideas in post-May Fourth China led traditionalist thinkers of all shades into some strange contortions. Despite their antipathy toward things Western, they seemed to go to great lengths to try to tack the name of a Western thinker or theory onto the ideas in China's past they wished to exonerate. Liang Shu-ming was no exception; he sought to substantiate his theories with "evidence" he found in recent Western intellectual trends.

For example, Liang found support for the ancient Chinese cosmology of the *I Ching* (Book of changes)—in which there was no absolute, ultimate, single, unrelated existence—from that "uncommon Western scientific genius," Einstein and his theory of relativity.[40] Liang also suggested that Henri Bergson (at the time very influential in both Europe and China) had discovered with his philosophy of Vitalism what the ancient Chinese had known all along. To an extent, the opposite process took place—Liang interpreted Chinese metaphysics with the aid of the Frenchman. Bergson's central epistemological idea was that intuition could catch the flux of reality "on the wing" so to speak (instead of congealing it by intellectual analysis into fixed, inflexible categories), and so reach absolute knowledge and truth. Liang, in effect, fashioned his own theory of the Chinese mind and of Confucianism with this and other Bergsonian concepts.[41]

39. Ibid.; see also pp. 166, 178, 191.
40. [4], p. 118. Liang also claimed that Einstein's new theory affirmed Wei-shih Buddhism's concept of a world in which basic reality is manifest in the changing phenomena of successive events acting according to the law of cause and effect (*yin ming*). [4], p. 87. A few years later other theoreticians of the Wei-shih school, such as the famous Abbot T'ai Hsü, also asserted that their interpretation of Wei-shih was in accord with the theory of relativity. See [113], pp. 124–125.
41. Liang had read Bergson by at least 1915, while he did not seriously study Chinese philosophy until late in the summer of 1916. See [5a], pp. 11–13, 18–19; [4], p. 135. Liang also noted that his first reading of Bergson was "one great joyous event of my life." [47], p. 23.

Liang was quite ready to admit that, on superficial examination, China appears to be just plain backward, or simply a less evolved form of culture.

The majority of people consider China to be purely and simply inferior to the West. They feel that the Westerners have evolved quickly . . . while Chinese are stupid and have not evolved. . . . When I first looked at [the situation], I thought the same thing. Take, for example, the matter of mastery of nature; at the stage when humanity has not evolved [very far] and is still unenlightened, it cannot conquer nature. The less evolved, the less able to master nature, and the more evolved, the more able to master nature.[42]

But, said Liang, the underlying Chinese attitude is harmony, yielding, and compromise. In this attitude, people do not set themselves in opposition to nature, but rather harmonize with it and rejoice in it. Instead of stimulating desires (as Westerners do) or repressing them (as Indians do), Chinese take the middle way and achieve contentment. Thus, inner satisfaction and happiness are the special achievements of the Chinese second course.[43] The heart of Chinese culture, according to Liang, is its metaphysics, which, in both the questions it focuses on and the methodology it uses, is fundamentally different from either the Indian or Western varieties.[44] While the latter two focus on ontology—the problem of substance (is the ultimate reality of the cosmos mind or matter, monist or pluralist?)—the Chinese metaphysics *ab initio*

The gist of Bergson's intuitional metaphysics is found in his 1903 essay in [106], pp. 177–227. From the terminology and images in Liang's writings, it is obvious that he was most familiar with and most influenced by Bergson's *L'Evolution creatrice* [104], which was the first of Bergson's works that Liang read. See [5a], p. 11. Liang ignored entirely many of Bergson's fundamental ideas, such as his distinction between "mechanical time" and "duration," or his ideas on memory and self. But Liang seemed to have grasped thoroughly *L'Evolution creatrice*'s exegesis of intuition, intellect, and language. Liang seems to have had no familiarity with Bergson's other important pre-1921 works, such as [103] or [105].

Liang also compared Wei-shih metaphysics and Bergsonism. Although he felt that the concept of a universe "in continuous flux," and "of fluid reality" was central to both, he thought that they differed radically in methodology. He pointed out that while Wei-shih relied solely upon sensations and intellect to reach understanding of this fluid reality, Bergson relied solely on anti-intellectual intuition. [5n], pp. 97–101; see also [4], pp. 78–79, 86–87, 119, 169.

42. [4], p. 64; see also pp. 34–38, 65, 151, 200–204, 208.

43. [4], pp. 65–66, 151–152.   44. [4], pp. 80, 114–115.

seeks to understand *change*. Liang claimed that since the Chinese metaphysicians did not think in terms of static substances, the ideas they formed never dealt with concrete questions of substance. Western and Indian thinkers, on the other hand, used intellectual analysis with clearly defined, exact concepts, but it is impossible to understand or describe pure change with logic-bound concepts and precise words that are fixed and static by their very nature.

Chinese philosophy uses intuition to capture the abstract principles underlying the physical universe. These principles could only be expressed in suggestive "ideational flavors." The *I Ching*, the foundation of all Chinese thought, describes cosmic life as a ceaseless flux, given form and motion by mutually antagonistic, interpenetrating, dualistic forces; these were expressed by suggestive signs, such as the *kua* (trigrams) of the *I Ching*, or other symbols, such as the opposing forces of *yin* and *yang* or dragons and horses.

The intuitive process whereby the Chinese metaphysicians got the feel or taste of the ebb and flow of the cosmos was, of course, nonrational; intellectual reasoning, by its very nature, fixed and deadened whatever it touched. Consequently, Liang asserted, because the Chinese mind has never enmeshed itself in the tangle of ontology and epistemology, it has remained unscathed and impervious to the modern critical rationalism that has destroyed Western metaphysics.

Liang's contrasting of Chinese metaphysics with science is worth noting, for the distinction reappears in different form later. Chinese metaphysics, he said, is based on intuition, which is a "disinterested" human capacity (*wu so wei erh wei*). The basis for science, on the other hand, is the intellect, which is a purposeful tool, an instrument for dealing with the Will's struggle with the environment. Thus, the exercise of the intellect always has an ulterior motive (*yu so wei erh wei*) and is directly related to the material interests of the individual.[45]

Confucius' Intuitionism and
Bergson's Vitalism

Liang's direct link between the Chinese metaphysical foundations and Chinese culture is Confucius, whom Liang credited with formulating a philosophy of life based on the principles of the *I*

45. [4], pp. 80, 114–119.

Ching and then developing the means for instituting it in society. And it is the substance of Confucius' philosophy that enabled Liang to assign an absolute, universal value to Chinese culture, despite the metahistoric relativism of his cultural schemata. The process might be summarized thus: the universe is life; life is a ceaseless flux; so the ultimate reality is pure change, and to comprehend change in itself, is to comprehend the essence of reality. According to Liang's interpretation, Confucius had grasped the nature of pure change (and so of life) from the *I Ching*. One underlying universal principle emerges from the flow of life—harmonization of all elements of existence.[46] (The fundamental value of harmony would inform his later reformist thought and projects.)

For Liang, this basic concept of harmonization provided the much debated "connecting thread" (*i kuan chih*) in all Confucius' thought. Expressed as a philosophy of life, it is *jen* (benevolence, true humanity, or perfect humanness), the quintessential expression and essence of Confucianism.[47] Like Bergson, Confucius supposedly saw intuitive feeling as the infallible guide to a life of harmony with nature. Liang's Vitalist interpretation of Confucianism—derived from the Wang Yang-ming school and suffused with Bergsonian images and terms—is a defense of absolute value against pure rationalism similar to that in the German conservative-romantic origins of Vitalism and "philosophy of life."[48]

The inherent irony of Bergson's intuitionist philosophy is that it recognized human consciousness as permanently intellectual. To Bergson, humans are intent upon intellectual calculation of natural events because of the anxiety they feel when confronted with uncertainty and disorder. Only occasionally can they coax into full flame that "almost extinguished lamp," the intuition, which reveals to them the existence of another natural order based not on cosmic mathematics but on *élan vital*. In a more completely evolved, perfect humanity, Bergson suggested, intuition and intellect would

46. [4], pp. 118–120.

47. [4], p. 121. The phrase, which appears in the Analects IV:15 and XV:2, has been interpreted in various ways by commentators throughout Chinese history. Liang specifically took issue with Hu Shih's interpretation that it referred to Confucius' "way of knowing." Liang asserted that Confucius, as an intuitionist, never concerned himself with rationalistic epistemological questions. See [4], pp. 121, 126–129.

48. [422], pp. 83–93, 157–164.

have been more perfectly blended together. The implication we draw from Liang is that Confucius had achieved precisely that—a "leap" in the evolutionary process which landed him in the realm of a more perfect humanity.

The antagonism between intellect and intuition is crucial to Liang's Confucianism. Bergson held that intellect was an evolved faculty, which, since it enabled people to deal with their environment, was instrumental to the control of material objects. Liang agrees:

> Intellect provides humans with a tool for calculation, and calculation from beginning to end is for selfish purposes [*wei wo*]. When the intuitive, emotional function is strong, the intellect withdraws; when the intellect is active, then intuition and emotion quiet down. The two thus have mutually antagonistic tendencies.[49]

The difference between *jen* and the absence of it was precisely whether the intellectual or the intuitive side of a person prevailed. As soon as intellect starts to function, it carries with it the possibility of selfish calculation, which makes life and its joy dependent upon satisfaction of the desires.

> Confucius was different from this. From the very start he had no concern for fixing [the external material environment into calculable quantities and certain categories], or calculating [and thus] connecting his emotions to the external. He had not the slightest concern for success or failure, but an abundant, rich zest for life. His vital force was very strong. There was no situation in which he was not at ease and self-possessed. Never for a moment was his heart not elated.[50]

The idea of living and the breath of spring permeated Confucius' universe, Liang said, and Confucianism is nothing more than living a full, rich life in accord with the principles of nature. Because he based his philosophy on change, Confucius avoided any sort of certainty, which contrasted sharply with "others" (referring vaguely to Westerners or to Mo-tzu, Liang's Chinese philosophical equivalent of the West). Since reality was constant flux, no invariable rules could be derived, and thus, Confucius did not try to find fixed, objective principles, for they departed from the central principle of the middle way (*chung-yung*). Any principle or rule, when carried straight to its logical conclusion, violated the mean.

49. [4], p. 128.   50. [4], p. 137.

Because Confucius based his life on intuition—that faculty which was "disinterested" and completely free of the practical necessities of confronting the environment—his actions were "without ulterior purpose" (*wu so wei*). "Confucius most emphatically advocated and taught people this [doctrine] of action without specific purpose (*wu so wei erh wei*). Keeping accounts itself is not necessarily bad, but it is the thing that can hinder *jen*."[51]

Confucius, according to Liang, had only two devices by which to institutionalize his way of life—rites and music (*li* and *yueh*). He used intellect to design these institutions to achieve the blending of intellect and emotion, or to modify and adjust the raw instincts of humankind. The effect of Confucian rites and music is to create an emotional and spiritual stability for human life. Confucianism has, Liang said, performed the functions of a great religion without the faults of religion (such as superstition and other-worldliness). Confucianism used aesthetics instead to achieve its goal. Ts'ai Yuan-p'ei and others at the time advocated providing for one's spiritual life by substituting art for religion, but Liang believed that Confucianism was much more reliable than ordinary art, as it had a systematic philosophy and way of life behind it.[52]

Diametrically opposed to the Confucian philosophy of life was utilitarianism, which, in Liang's view, represented all Western philosophies of life. Thus, Liang established the fundamental dichotomy that would be at the center of his thought for the next thirty years. The West was the equivalent of mechanistic positivism, intellectualization, purposeful (*yu so wei*) action, selfishness, and ethical nihilism. All these conditions were inherent in pragmatism, which he saw as the logical culmination of all Western thought.[53] The alternative was China and Confucianism—the equivalent of emotion, intuition, noncalculation, ethics, unselfishness, and absolute value.

The Failure of Chinese Culture to Fulfill Itself

Confucius' intuitionism and its corollary, indeterminacy, had important implications for the concrete expression of this "religion that is not a religion." If Confucianism was based on an intuitive grasp of the constant flux of reality, then it could have no fixed

51. [4], p. 134.   52. [4], pp. 140–143, 153–154, 193, 196–197.
53. [4], pp. 157–158, 193.

objective rules of conduct (which in themselves were attempts to classify experience into inflexible categories of intellect). Thus, conventional Confucian morality has been basically antagonistic to the true spirit of Confucius; and all the *formal moral codes* and rules of behavior throughout the two thousand years of Confucian Chinese history have actually been anti-Confucian.

Liang's intuitionist interpretation of Confucianism enabled him to relativize its concrete historical expressions, such as the formal ethical codes (the *li-chiao ming-chiao*). Relativism then allowed him to retain the underlying spirit of Confucianism, its absolute value or heavenly principles (*t'ien-li*), while dismissing the specific cognitive definitions for moral behavior derived from these absolute values (the *li-chiao* code) as a perversion of the "true" Confucianism.[54] Everyone must understand, Liang said, "that the heavenly principles are not fixed objective doctrines such as 'a minister should be loyal' or 'a son should be filial.' "[55] (The two examples of traditional morality that he unconsciously chose to mention both have a direct relationship to his own life experience: he had not been a filial son; and loyalty had been responsible, at least on one level, for his father's suicide.) Liang is thus able to solve his father's contradiction between the universalistic heavenly principles and the particulars of Chinese morality. The heavenly principles were both universal to humankind and still particularly Chinese, but they were not the formal historical Chinese morality.

Liang's Vitalism had another purely Chinese element in its emphasis on the family and its relations. The rites and music were society's methods for putting Confucius' way of life into effect, but all of this was based upon the process of cultivation of emotions springing from the most natural of all sources—the emotions of child toward parent. The first emotions in one's life should be cultivated to become the basis for all emotions. In other words,

54. [4], pp. 152–153. "*Li chiao*" and "*ming chiao*" refer to "ethical education," as well as the rather concrete "rules of decorum," which acted as a quasi-legal code. With the rise of the Neo-Confucian dualistic rationalism in the Sung dynasty, these rules of etiquette (*li fa*) were regarded as external expressions of the internal principles of man and nature (*t'ien li*). Because of this, in the Sung period the *li chiao ming chiao* became, and continued thereafter, rigid inflexible codes with the force of sacred law. Much of the main thrust of the anti-Confucian criticism in the early Republican period was directed toward these external expressions of Confucian morality.

55. [4], p. 127.

Liang said, although the *Classic of Filial Piety* (*Hsiao ching*) is not an authentic Confucian work, its famous statement that "filial piety is the source of virtue and the root of teaching" is true. All Confucianism could indeed be said to be nothing more than an extension and amplification of filial piety (*hsiao*) and fraternal submission (*t'i*).[56]

While on the one hand, Liang held filial piety to be the basis of "true" Confucianism, on the other, he echoed the May Fourth anti-traditionalists' condemnation of formal Confucian precepts of family life. "The ancient ceremonial regulations and lifeless precepts tended strongly toward creating a dark and tomblike oppression [of the individual] and caused quite a bit of suffering." There had been no concept of "self"[57] (*tzu-chi*) in traditional society, Liang claimed, and so there had been no room for individuality to develop. In the authoritarian family structure, the individual had been "buried and lost."[58] Liang applauded the attack of Tai Chen (A.D. 1724–1777) on "the various sorts of extremes in thought and the obdurate dogmatism" that had led to increasingly oppressive social life since the Sung.[59] In condemning the formal ethical code born in the Sung, Liang wrote: "For thousands of years it has made us impotent in any attempt to liberate ourselves from various authorities, and so individuality could not develop. Society could not develop either. This is [our] biggest point of inferiority compared to the West."[60]

Yet because of his ambivalence toward his own conflict with his father, Liang probably could not completely adopt the New Culturists' totalistic condemnation of the traditional family. "Within the family," Liang believed, "and in society in general, it was always possible [for the individual] to achieve a certain kind of satisfaction, not of the cold, indifferent, hostile, and calculated kind [but of a kind that] gave much vigor to the spirit of life." Thus, "although in this respect [to individual development, the family was] a failure and not to our benefit, yet, looking at it from another angle, it was very successful" because through it the Chinese were able to avoid the alienation from their fellows and the withering of human feelings that afflicted the Westerners.[61]

56. [4], p. 140; [539a], chap. I "K'ai tsung ming i."
57. [4], p. 140.   58. [4], pp. 37–40, 152.
59. Liang wrote that Tai Chen's attack on the formal codes was "a budding of the [true] Confucian philosophy of life." [4], p. 150.
60. [4], p. 152.   61. [4], pp. 153, 152.

Liang's ambivalence toward formal ethics and traditional family organization was only one corner of a larger contradiction in his defense of tradition. He simultaneously ascribed absolute universal value to Confucianism and condemned its concrete historical expression. How did he explain the obvious gap between what China had been historically, and what, according to his theory at least, China should have been?

The Premature Birth of China

The problem, Liang said, lay in precisely the same reason for China's only and greatest achievement: Confucius and the early sages had transcended their physical environment to achieve a more perfect understanding of humanity than China's level of cultural development had warranted. The birth of Chinese culture had been premature; the Chinese environment of the time had provided insufficient foundation (economic or intellectual development) for Chinese culture fully to realize itself. The historical result was a kind of half-baked attempt at fulfilling the underlying spirit, which neither succeeded nor failed, but rather stagnated in a vague state of limbo. "The Chinese have been clearly under the sway of the problems of the first road. Since they still must go through the first road, they have only been able to make compromises with the [external, material] situation and produce [a kind of] ambiguous, vague culture."[62] Thus, Confucius' basic ideal of harmony had become a mere easy-going slovenliness and produced only "sproutings" of his true spirit. Historical Confucianism and Chinese culture, based only on "dregs" and "inflexible doctrines," had succeeded only in bringing forth a dim shadow of itself. Nothing in Chinese culture was "clear-cut" as in the West.[63]

No one had ever really understood Confucius' original spirit, Liang averred (implicit in this judgment was that he was the sole exception). Hsun-tzu, for instance, completely misunderstood Confucius when he concluded that human nature was bad, and that objective external rules were needed to make people good. As a result, the main emphasis of Confucians after Hsun-tzu had been on external restraints and rules of conduct. Liang reviewed Chinese history dynasty by dynasty, pointing out the mistakes of all Confucian thinkers. Although he allowed that Wang Yang-ming,

---

62. [4], p. 200; see also pp. 199–203, 297.
63. [4], pp. 154, 180, 145, 200.

and especially his disciple Wang Ken, had "just about" understood Confucius, the inescapable conclusion was that for these many centuries there had been precious little Confucius in Confucianism.[64]

Even if someone had understood the master's true spirit, the unsolved problems of the first road would have prevented its institutionalization. A high level of intellectual development is necessary to put the rites and music—Confucius' original method for institutionalizing his spirit—into effect: "The rites and music have not flourished, and so the philosophy of Confucius had no way of being institutionalized." The result was that "for thousands of years of Confucian-dominated Chinese history, the life attitude of the ordinary people had actually been Taoist."[65] Consequently it had always been impossible to achieve a truly Confucian social order.

The Imminent Sinification of Humankind

At this point, Liang's audience probably wondered what hope Chinese culture had to survive at all in even half-realized form, since the alienating Western culture obviously had the answers to the problems of the first road. But Liang had more to say—rather startling news: "In a word, the future world culture will be a revival of Chinese culture."[66] Precisely at the present time, he proclaimed, Western culture has played out its historical role. The West has solved the problems of the first road—survival, primal needs, material want—and is encountering the problems of the second level—problems that only the Chinese attitude can solve:

> Many faults have appeared in the first road [the West] has taken and now the present generation wants to abandon it for the second road . . . because when the first course is completed, the problems of the second course arise; and so the Chinese attitude, which previously was not suited to the times, comes into an age when it is really essential.[67]

The West has developed the means of supplying humanity with

---

64. [4], pp. 138, 145–150; [47], p. 123. A reading of Wang Ken (Hsin-chai, A.D. 1483–1540) first attracted Liang to Confucianism. Along with his fellow student Wang Chi (Lung-hsi, A.D. 1498–1583), Wang Ken is sometimes regarded as almost a Ch'an Buddhist. See, for example, Huang Tsung-hsi's criticism in [317], 32:1. What seems to have attracted Liang most, however, was Wang Ken's dynamic interpretation of knowledge, which emphasized that action in the external world was the completion of inner knowledge.

65. [4], pp. 145, 147.   66. [4], p. 199.   67. [4], p. 200.

"all physical necessities, from the natural world, [but now] the Western attitude, like the problem of physical survival itself, will cease to exist." "Humankind," Liang claimed, "will turn from an epoch of material want to one of spiritual unrest." The future world culture would represent "a decisive basic change" for Western culture, which would adopt "completely the Chinese road." This was, "no matter what, undeniable."[68]

This prediction, Liang emphasized to his audience (which was no doubt stunned by it) was based on irrefutable "objective" evidence he found in recent Western intellectual and cultural trends. The shift was discernible in many ways, but "in general the basic key lies in that [the Westerners'] line of vision, [which had been] directed externally, has now been turned around." Now Westerners are seeking inner satisfaction, inner joy, inner life. Now they must "deal with the inner workings of the minds of others," with "human affairs," and not with material problems.[69]

Liang pointed to the "Oriental character" of the new intellectual atmosphere.

> [The West's thinkers are] unconsciously changing direction.
> . . . Before they talked about absolutes; now they have
> changed and talk about relativity. Before it was in-
> tellectualism; now it is emotionalism. Before [they] wanted to
> use intellect; now [they want] intuition. Before [philosophical
> study] was static; now it is dynamic. Before it was centered on
> knowledge, now on action. Before they looked outward; and
> now their vision is directed toward the self, toward life. . . .
> Oriental philosophy has always wanted to understand life,
> and the Westerners have always wanted intellectual knowl-
> edge. But now there are none [in Western intellectual circles]
> who do not turn toward the path of [understanding] life.[70]

Liang's list of specific examples strikes a Westerner as a bit strange, for he includes not only the obvious foes of positivism, such as Bergson, Nietzsche, and Eucken, but also the American pragmatists, John Dewey and William James, and the revisionists of Darwinian evolutionary theory, Alfred Wallace and Thomas Huxley. Another of Liang's favorites—Bertrand Russell—aside from his positivist roots, was a famous polemicist against both Bergson and pragmatism. To Liang, such widely diverse currents as instinct psychology and guild socialism pointed unambiguously to a spiri-

68. [4], pp. 166–167, 196, 198.   69. [4], pp. 176–177.
70. [4], p. 176.

tual sinification of Western culture.[71] Was there an inner logic to
Liang's vision of the post-World War intellectual climate, or were
his conclusions due to a combination of wishful thinking and an
unsophisticated knowledge of the West?

Both answers are valid. The only shared characteristic of the
bewildering spectrum of movements and figures Liang identified
was their prominence in China at the time. Although Liang believed he had surveyed all the leading Western thought, his "objective evidence" was really a most subjective interpretation of the
Western ideas and thinkers he happened to encounter. He had, of
course, with the help of Liang Ch'i-ch'ao, put his finger on that
reaction to late nineteenth-century materialism (or mechanism, or
scientism), which H. Stuart Hughes has called a "revolt against
positivism."[72] Yet Liang failed to detect that the *fin de siècle* critique
was really just another expression of an unremitting tension in
Western consciousness that had been going on since before the
Enlightenment. From where Liang sat, mechanism-positivism-
naturalism was the expression of the very essence of Western culture and any questioning of it was only a very recent and quite
unprecedented phenomenon. Since he conceived of Chinese culture as generally the antithesis of Western culture, then naturally
any attack on that Western tradition—no matter what the real nature of the criticism—had to have affinities to Chinese cultural
attitudes.

The way Liang interpreted Western intellectual trends, and the
way his own elucidation of Confucianism reflects the influence of
such disparate Western thinkers as Dewey and Bergson, are both
instances of a characteristic phenomenon among the intelligentsia
in twentieth-century Chinese history: "the selective borrowing of
particular ideas from many different Western ideologies for purposes that were often far removed from the premises upon which
they were based."[73] The phenomenon is not limited to China. In
the West, too, religious thinkers and political movements have
selectively borrowed foundations and scaffolding for their theories

71. [4], pp. 164, 166, 169–187, 191–194.
72. [321]. Although Hughes limited his study to major social thinkers
of Western Europe and focuses primarily on the prewar era (and so ex-
cludes such men as Kropotkin, Eucken, James, and the postwar Bertrand
Russell), his book does outline an intellectual trend identical with what
Liang perceived.
73. [428], p. 13.

and programs. In the early twentieth century, Syndicalists grasped on to Bergson despite the philosopher's own opposition to direct-action politics. Some religious thinkers and humanists took to the physicist Heisenberg's indeterminacy principle as a secure scientific fortress for free will. Yet because of the Chinese intellectuals' spotty understanding of the West and its intellectual history, their eclectic borrowings appear stranger to us. An interesting example of how the process worked is the use Li Ta-chao and Liang Shu-ming each made of Kropotkin and Bergson.

Kropotkin. Li Ta-chao utilized Kropotkin's concept of mutual aid explicitly to reinterpret the Marxist theory of class struggle into something more amenable to Chinese nationalism. Liang Shu-ming proclaimed Kropotkin as a prime example of the imminent Confucianization of Western civilization. Prince Peter Alexeivitch, he exclaimed, "truly can be said to be a great worthy" because he has shown that people's moral and altruistic impulses spring from an inherent biological faculty. "Is this not precisely the same as Mencius' likening of propriety and righteousness to people's sense of taste? Kropotkin is just brimming over with Chinese flavor and Confucian temper."[74]

Liang's sincere surprise at Kropotkin's theories was possible be-cause of his distorted comprehension of the Western intellectual world. Only the Chinese, Liang thought, had ever really had an abiding faith in the ultimate goodness of humanity, and now there was, of all people, a Westerner, expressing that same faith!

> Chinese have always been deeply colored by the theory of the goodness of human nature. Westerners, while they might not specifically oppose the theory, still never propagated it. But he [Kropotkin] loudly sings out the theory of the goodness of human nature. Because of this, he advocates anarchism and holds that people themselves all have the potential for good-ness; it is not necessary to call for some alien force to control them. [He holds that] not only is this possible, but moreover [will come about] quite smoothly. He very much opposes any system of punishments.[75]

Thus, Kropotkin becomes a fine example for Liang of how the

74. [428], pp. 13–14, 140–146; [4], pp. 185–186.
75. [4], pp. 185–186.

West is changing from the "way of the tyrant" (*pa tao*)—which took human nature to be naturally evil and therefore had to rely on punishments to rule—to the Chinese ideal, the "way of the king" (*wang tao*), which relied on moral influence and the creation of a proper environment in which humanity's true nature could manifest itself.[76]

Bergson. Li Ta-chao used Bergson's concept of free will to inject a strongly voluntarist strain into his historical materialism. Liang seized upon Bergson's anti-scientific intuitionism and his activism as the perfect companion to his own left-wing Wang Yang-ming Confucianism. Liang could also believe that the popular acceptance of Bergsonian Vitalism was a sign of a profound revolution in what he understood as Western culture. As Bergsonism was, in Liang's mind, the equivalent of Confucianism, he could say: "the waxing and waning of the influence of intellect and intuition is [the equivalent of] the waxing and waning of the Western school and the Chinese school." Liang perceived of the Westerners as madly scrambling about in their spiritual misery searching for "a way out. [Their] only savior is the Vitalist school of philosophy. . . . Intuition will rise up and replace intellect in the world."[77]

Russell. The role Liang accorded to Bertrand Russell—a philosophical child of the Enlightenment-born rationalism that Liang saw as the apotheosis of Chinese culture—seems most inexplicable; Liang, nevertheless, designated the Neo-Realist as the modern Westerner "most like Confucius." Right up through 1949, decades after Liang had dropped Bergson and Kropotkin completely, he still quoted Russell.[78] Russell actually won his place in Liang's consciousness and in his list of Western cultural bellwethers somewhat by chance. Russell happened to be teaching at Peking University precisely during the period (academic year 1920–21) when Liang was preparing his lecture series on Eastern and Western cultures. Since Liang's old friend, Chang Shen-fu, was China's leading Russell scholar, Liang had listened to Chang expound at

76. [4], p. 180.
77. [428], pp. 21, 23, 25, 145, 155–156; [4], p. 178.
78. [4], p. 181. See examples in [14a], p. 31; [86], pp. 8, 68, 128, 290, 292, 322; [84], pp. 3, 10.

great length upon Russell's writings and had read them for him-self.[79] Moreover, Russell's ideas on China and the West were quite similar to Liang's own.[80]

Undoubtedly Russell's greatest attraction was his enthusiastic praise for traditional Chinese culture and his equally ardent criti-cisms of the West. That a renowned Western philosopher found delight in almost everything of old China was maddening to many modern-minded Chinese intellectuals, but was welcomed by many conservative and not so conservative elements. Sun Yat-sen, for one, said that Russell was the only Englishman who had ever un-derstood China.[81]

Russell was, nevertheless, a rigorous intellectualist and the founder of logical positivism, the antithesis of Liang's intuitionist Confucianism. But there were two Bertrand Russells: the disem-bodied intellect of *Principia Mathematica* and the publicist whose witty eloquence on ethical and social questions manifested an al-most mystical passion and tenderness for humanity. Liang pro-bably found repugnant much of what even the second Russell had to say, but he unerringly focused on what he wanted in Russell. For example, in his ethical philosophy of the time, Russell posited "growth springing from life's central principle" as the ultimate human good. This ideal of "full growth," Russell said, "cannot be defined or demonstrated. It can only be felt by a delicate intuition."

79. See [524a], pp. 61–62; [598]. Liang had definitely read the Chinese translations of Russell's *Problems of Philosophy* [459] and *Principles of Social Reconstruction* [460]. See [5d], p. 31; [4], p. 170; [5p], p. 104. Although Liang attended some of Russell's lectures, he never became personal friends with him. Conversation in April, 1974, with Professor Chao Yuan-jen, who was Russell's escort-interpreter in China.

80. Russell's description and analysis of China's cultural dilemma, put forth in [461], is quite similar to Liang's. Russell saw that China must somehow make itself strong enough to resist foreign aggression, yet avoid the problems of Western-style nationalism. China must use science to con-quer poverty, yet avoid the vices of Western industrialism. Russell's own view on how humanized industrialization might be possible is expressed in [462]. Compare also [461], pp. 194–198, 200–202, with Liang's description of Western and Chinese life attitudes. Other striking similarities with Liang are in [461], pp. 187, 212, 213, 242, 252. Russell, however, seems to have valued most what Liang felt to be the worst—the influence of Taoism among the masses. [461], pp. 42, 83–84, 187–194. Russell's attitude toward, and interpretation of, Confucianism was also quite different from Liang's.

81. See [198], p. 237; [578], p. 120.

So, despite Russell's virulent attacks on Bergsonism, Liang was not without some basis when he described Russell's "visions and opinions" as "very much in accord with those of the Vitalist school."[82]

Russell identified harmony—both within the individual and between the individual and society—as the goal for human institutions. He looked to education as the means for nurturing the healthy creative impulses in people and inhibiting the unhealthy possessive impulses. Although he hated formal religions, he still favored those that "would bring into human existence something eternal . . . remote from strife and failure and the devouring jaws of time." So Liang was not really distorting Russell's thought as much as being discriminating in his reading of it when he pronounced Russell's ethical and social views as "completely the same as Confucius'."[83] Confucianism, too, Liang pointed out, had harmony as its central ideal and, through the rites, music, ancestor worship, and sacrifice, sought to nourish the good impulses of people so that they would be dominant over the bad. Although not really a religion, Confucianism did bring that "something eternal" into human life.

William James and John Dewey. Liang's inclusion of William James (1842–1910) and John Dewey (1851–1952) in his list of the Western thinkers who provide evidence of changing Western attitudes might seem even more incongruous. After all, Liang had already identified pragmatism as the final "completion" and "rounding out" of the Western attitude.[84] Yet James did have mystical leanings toward the end of his life; and pragmatism itself, together with Vitalism, does oppose pure intellectual knowledge, stress the emotional rather than the intellectual aspects of life, and make knowledge subservient to action. The pragmatists' view that real knowledge comes only from action in the real world, and their "dynamic" interpretation of virtue shares important qualities with the thought of Wang Yang-ming and particularly that of his student, Wang Ken. Other modern Chinese commentators have also remarked on the similarities between Wang Ken and pragmatism.[85]

In his book, Liang reports only that Dewey, in a lecture at Peking University, had said that Western philosophy one-sidedly studies

82. [4], p. 177; [460], p. 24.   83. [4], pp. 182–183; [460], p. 245.
84. [4], p. 193.   85. For example, see [337], p. 152.

nature while "Orientals one-sidedly study human affairs." Liang's belief that the coming problems of Western culture would be in the realm of human affairs made it possible for him to construe Dewey's statement to support his thesis on the changing of the Western direction.[86]

Tagore. Liang found further evidence of the Western change in the great popularity the Bengali poet, Rabindranath Tagore, enjoyed in the West. The Nobel Prize winner's anti-intellectual intuitionism "was just the thing for treating the Westerner's sickness." Liang further explained, to his own satisfaction at least, why it was an Indian and not a Chinese poet who was receiving Western acclaim: "Original Brahmanism was not at all like this [Tagore] . . . so this path of his is not the Indian or Western one. Although in form [Tagore] is unrelated to Chinese philosophy, nevertheless, I want to say that he belongs to China and the Confucian road."[87]

Eucken. "The whole significance of [Rudolf] Eucken's [1846–1926] philosophy," Liang said of this other Nobel Prize winner, is its attempt "to change the Western attitude of life. He opposes the Western road and [embodies] the Chinese Confucian road. . . . It is easy to see that he wants to transfer the center of gravity in Western life from the external to the internal. . . . This is rather similar to Confucius' central meaning." Eucken's emphasis on personal action and courageous, heroic moral struggle and his militant activist idealism seems—like pragmatism—to have struck deep resonances with Liang's own Confucianism, which stemmed from the strong activist tenor of Wang Ken. "Only Eucken," Liang said, "deserves to be called resolute and courageous."[88]

Psychology. Liang even claimed that recent Western psychology helped prove his point with its discovery of the unconscious and irrational side of humanity. Research has now discovered, Liang observed, that one's rational nature "is superficial and that the hidden, unconscious part is really the important basis." The realization that instincts and emotions are the true determinants of behavior has deposed the traditional Western concept of people as rational beings who calculate their actions for their self-

86. [4], p. 176.   87. [4], pp. 186–187.   88. [4], pp. 179, 180.

interest—the concept upon which liberal economic and social thought had been built. With the demise of the idea of humans as calculating machines (the root concept most "diametrically opposed to the Chinese way") the culture built upon it would certainly change. The philosophical underpinnings of economic free competition, which have caused so much suffering in the West, have been destroyed.[89] Liang asserted that this new emphasis on the nonrational aspect of human life proves that:

> The line of vision of the Westerners is gradually coming ever closer to the vision of Confucius. Confucius wholeheartedly focused upon the emotional side of humanity. The difference between Confucius and the Westerners—their basic point of conflict—lies precisely in this! Therefore, I do not doubt that [the Westerners] will take Confucius' path.[90]

Darwinism. Liang was aware that the image of people as animals driven by their instinct for survival into continuous combat with others of their kind (social Darwinism) was another basic support for capitalist liberalism. He pointed to those revisionists of Darwinism—the older Thomas Huxley, Kropotkin, Alfred Wallace, and Benjamin Kidd—as proof that the West had now discovered that mutual aid and altruistic, virtuous behavior were based on instinct too, the social instinct. If society, rather than the individual, is taken as the unit of competition, then morality could be conceived of as a product of the struggle for survival. Wars and economic competition, thought Liang, had been legitimized by the old theory of evolution. But now that the new theories have destroyed that legitimacy, reform of the capitalist economic system is inevitable.[91]

Socialism. This remodeling of economic life, Liang predicted, would take the form of socialism. In "most recent" socialist doctrines he detected a major change of direction which provided further evidence for impending Western Sinification.

> Socialist thought is no longer so simplistic. They previously thought that fulfilling material needs was the equivalent of fulfilling human needs. They thought that if the economic situation was reformed in accord with their ideal, humankind

89. [4], pp. 168–171.   90. [4], pp. 170–171.
91. [4], pp. 171–174.

would then have a full, rich life, that it would create a golden
world. . . . They mistakenly believed that as soon as the external environment was completely reformed, there would be no
more problems. . . . But now their focus has advanced from
the material to the spiritual sphere, from the external to the
internal. . . . Socialism, which has followed the Western path,
has now changed its direction to the Eastern path.[92]

A good example of this new awareness, Liang said, was the recent popularity of guild socialism.

I got a book from Li Ta-chao on guild socialism. . . . That
school's view of life manifests even more how Westerners are
invariably discarding the way of life of rushing ahead in pursuit of things, and how they desire the Chinese attitude of
peaceful contentment. Who would dare deny that this [school]
is flourishing because the Chinese attitude is replacing the
Western attitude?[93]

Just three years prior to Liang's development of his theory, the
Bolshevik revolution had shaken the world. Precisely at the time
Liang was giving these lectures in Tsinan, Mao and eleven others
were meeting in the Po-wen Girls' School in Shanghai's French
Concession; the outcome of their meetings was the Chinese Communist Party. Li Ta-chao, the man who had introduced Liang to
guild socialism in the first place, was the Party's chief theoretician
and had publicly and privately espoused Marxism for the past
three years. Yet Liang dismissed Marxist socialism as a passé form
that had already failed: "Even the predictions of the socialism with
the scientific temper [i.e., Marxism] have not come true to this day.
Because social revolution through class struggle has not come
about, it [Marxism] has split up and collapsed." On the other hand,
he pronounced guild socialism more "realistic and at the same time
full of idealism."[94] Underlying this summary dismissal of Marxism
and definite preference for the cooperative path to socialism was
Liang's metaphysically derived Confucian predilection for harmony and rejection of struggle.

Since the Westerners had already achieved abundance, their
economic organization now would try to provide "a more contented, more leisurely style [of life] much as the Chinese attitude
has always been. . . . Enterprises in the material life will recede into

92. [4], p. 184.   93. [4], pp. 184–185.
94. [4], pp. 154–155, 177.

a subordinate position. . . . Again this is the Chinese style." Liang even went as far as to suggest that in an effort to provide some human satisfaction, the West might revive handicrafts: "If they really do revive handicrafts and abandon big machines, this too would be just like the Chinese way."[95] (As with other of Liang's outlandish predictions, he was fifty years too early.)

Chinese rites and music. Before reform of the economic system could be realized, Liang said, the entire Western social system had to be destroyed. First on the list was law and punishment, which Liang called "control-style" law and likened to methods used for "controlling animals." Law upheld the present social order by "using force to supervise everyone, and make people still have a psychology of calculating profit and loss. Law is founded upon and relies upon nothing more than turning to account everyone's mental calculations." Rather than rely on the external restraints of law and force, the society of the future must rely "on personal character . . . on the social instincts . . . on emotion, on a psychology of togetherness between the self and others, and not on calculating one's own benefits."[96]

But how will society be able to train and cultivate effectively the character and emotions of the individual? Liang answered that "there are only two things—art and religion—which have the power to affect the emotions in this way." Yet religion in the usual sense had been destroyed by rationalism, and all other bases for it, such as guilt or *Aberglaube*, will be destroyed by the inevitable advance of human knowledge. Moreover, aesthetic methods alone had never really been effective.[97] What will be needed, Liang predicted, is something that uses aesthetic techniques but which is based upon a systematic philosophy, that will have the existential effectiveness of a religion without its faults. So, Liang triumphantly concluded, the only possible institution and practice that could fill the bill was Confucian rites and music (*li yueh*). They would inevitably replace law in the future world civilization. The Confucian system, which "is like a religion and yet is not a religion, not art and yet is art," would be able to create social order and discipline without relying on law and punishments, for its nature was to "train the instincts." "Although I do not dare predict that [the West] will import [the

95. [4], p. 194.   96. [4], pp. 194, 195.
97. [4], p. 195; see also pp. 94–113; [5m], pp. 133–136.

original] Confucian rites and music part and parcel, I do predict
that the general idea [of the future Western institution will have to
be] like [Confucian rites]."[98]

As Confucian rites and music will replace law in Western social
life, Confucian philosophy of life will replace Western religion in
spiritual life. The spiritual need will be for "something like religion,
which is able to stabilize one's life and give emotional comfort.
[People will need] a religion that has no tendency toward other-
worldliness . . . something that can solve doubts and difficulties."
Only Confucianism, Liang predicted, can perform such a function,
and so the West will be forced to adopt it.[99]

Liang Shu-ming's prophecy on the imminent Confucianization
of the West appears similar to Liang Ch'i-ch'ao's 1919 call for the
Chinese to rush to the West's spiritual salvation. "Forward march!"
Liang Ch'i-ch'ao had written in "Reflections." "On the other shore
of the ocean are millions of people bewailing the bankruptcy of
[their] material civilization and crying piteously for help, waiting
for us to save them!" Even before this, Ku Hung-ming, that redoubtable reactionary champion of Manchu monarchy and con-
cubinage, had called out, in elegant English, for similar Chinese
evangelistic zeal. Two decades before that, the Indian Swami
Vivekananda had called to his own countrymen in exactly the same
vein: "Up India, and conquer the world with your spirituality! The
world wants it; without it, the world will be destroyed." His followers had continued to hope that Hinduism might yet dominate the
world.[100]

Liang Shu-ming's prognostications, however, did not wait on
Chinese missionary activity or even the existence of China. The
West would necessarily and naturally Sinify itself through the
inexorable evolution of the human condition. In explaining this
process and qualifying his original prediction, Liang adumbrated a
crucial idea in his later rural-reconstruction theory. The West, he
emphasized, is not "choosing" to change cultural direction, but
rather is being forced to do so by the problems created by its present culture. The "objective realities" (shih-shih, a term he usually
used to refer to economic factors) would determine the speed of

98. [4], p. 196; see also pp. 153–196.   99. [4], p. 197.
100. [407], p. 38, [353], "Preface," p. 5; [354]; [344]. Swami Vivekananda
quote in [257], p. 24; see also [257], pp. 25, 37–44, 271.

cultural change, he said. "Not until the objective realities change will the time of necessary [cultural change] arrive." For the Westerners, the "change in objective realities" is "most important," so until the economic system changes, a general change in culture cannot come about. "The objective realities do not permit the adoption of this second road attitude just yet."[101]

This position seems to contradict Liang's previously stated philosophical basis: that the ultimate determinants of cultural developments were subjective—that is, consciousness determined existence. He had implied that the early Chinese sages had been able to transcend existence (their environment and the level of economic development) to achieve a consciousness that they had expressed in creating Chinese culture. He now seems to say that *in the West* the consciousness is determined by social being, by economics. In other words, he seems to accept historical materialism as valid for Western society, but not for Chinese society.

China's Cultural Dilemma and Liang's Conclusions

Liang had presented China's cultural problem in such a way that no solution seemed possible. He summarized the dilemma thus:

All our points of inferiority are due to the disorderliness of our cultural evolution; [our culture] matured prematurely. We did not continue to struggle with the forces of nature and conquer nature; as a consequence, we are now, in every way, thralls to nature. We did not wait to develop a concept of ego, but just passed over [that stage] and put value on compromising the self and yielding to others, so now we are enslaved by myriad kinds of authority. We did not wait for the development of the intellect, but skipped [that stage] and went on to esteem illogical spirit and favor the use of intuition alone, so now our thought is muddled and our scholarship is unsystematic. Because we took the second course before the first, we are suffering [various] afflictions. We have no capacity to resist nature and so are at the mercy of natural disasters. . . . We are [as a people] bullied internationally [by imperialism] and domestically [by warlords]. [We have] an oppressive military and a poverty-stricken national economy. . . . In a world

101. [4], pp. 168, 191–193; also p. 203.

dominated by problems of the first course [we] have walked
but a few steps on the first course.[102]

Liang had some surprising recommendations for the resolution of
this dilemma. In the process, he also rejected the positions of most
of his contemporaries.

Attitude toward other cultural conservatives. With his repeated emphasis on his perception that China's present desperate
straits were the logical consequence of its culture, Liang emphatically disassociated himself from the other cultural conservatives of
the day. He derided their muddled defense of tradition in the face
of Ch'en Tu-hsiu's "lucid mind and sharp pen." "Try tracking
down the source of these [present] afflictions and you will find that
all are clearly brought upon us by our own culture," Liang
exclaimed.[103]

> There still are some ignorant people who insist upon slough-
> ing off responsibility by saying that it is not our culture that is
> bad, but just that it has been ruined by [the sages'] posterity.
> [The conservatives] sigh with regret that the way of the an-
> cient sages has not prevailed. . . . It is just because and only
> because the ancient sages' doctrines *have* prevailed to some
> degree that this kind of [situation] has come about. . . . Ac-
> tually the Chinese [situation] today is due entirely to [our] own
> culture and there is no way to repudiate its faults.[104]

Liang criticized the conservatives, however, not for defending
tradition but because they had failed to do a creditable job of it.
Confronted with the New Culture onslaught, they could only sput-
ter with "nothing more than curses and anger . . . but have no
positive program with which to good-naturedly proceed with advocating tradition." This was because "their own thought is
poverty-stricken and . . . they have not discovered where the fundamental spirit of the old culture lies." Instead, they can only engage in classical scholarship and literary studies, "pile up stiff rotten goods," and call that Chinese culture. At the same time they
made the same mistake as the advocates of cultural blending. The
conservatives "always seem to want science and democracy to depart from [their basic] principles and meet them halfway."[105]

102. [4], pp. 202–203, 208.   103. [4], pp. 204–206, 203–204.
104. [4], p. 203.
105. [4], pp. 205–206. The "rotten goods" Liang specifically had in mind
were the kinds of articles carried in the short-lived Peking journal *Kuo-ku*

Attitude toward Buddhism. Liang's most violent attacks were reserved for the adherents of Buddhism and specifically the Buddhist revival, which, until his recent conversion to Confucianism, he himself had participated in. According to his theory of cultural evolution, the Indian "third course" of ultimate enlightenment was not suitable until after humanity had secured a satisfactory material life (by completing the first course) and achieved a satisfying inner life (by completing the second course). So the actual result of propagating Buddhism at China's present stage would be to distort Buddhism—"turn it into a low, despicable, mean thing"—because "the proper motives for [turning to] Buddhism can arise only after life is satisfying and complete."

He did not deny that there has been a "revival" of Buddhism, but commented that: "Of those who are Buddhist today, very few have pure motives. Most people's motives are selfish and evil. It is clear that [the propagators] are taking advantage of people's psychological weakness to gain converts. [They are] taking advantage of the bad times [which have] induced an escapist mentality in people." Therefore he pleaded with the leaders of Buddhist reform and revival to cease their efforts. "I oppose the propagation of Buddhism, and moreover, I oppose the reform of Buddhism," Liang proclaimed. "If there is a revival of Buddhism, then China's disorders will be without end."[106]

A Contradictory Solution

Liang saved the answers to the apparently insoluble paradoxes he had raised concerning China's future for his final lectures. He had admitted that China's cultural spirit and the West's cultural spirit were mutually incompatible, but faced with the pressing problems that Western culture had already mastered, China's course was clear, to Liang at least: his recommendation was an

---

[370], devoted to propagating and studying traditional literature and scholarship and the idea of "national essence" (*kuo-ts'ui*). The magazine vigorously opposed the colloquial literature movement. Many of its editors, such as Liu Shih-p'ei, Ma Hsu-lun, and Huang Chieh, had been associated with the *Kuo-ts'ui hsueh-pao* (Journal of national essence, Shanghai, 1905–1911). The *Kuo-ku* ceased publication in 1919 after the death of Liu Shih-p'ei, but the same tradition was carried on through the 1920s and into the 1930s in *Hsueh heng* [298] under the leadership of Liu Po-ming, Wu Mi, and Mei Kuang-ti.

106. [4], pp. 209–210, 202.

"attitude of 'complete acceptance' of Western culture. . . . The two spirits [of science and democracy] are completely correct. We must accept them unconditionally. The urgent task facing us today is [to know] just how to introduce [them effectively]."[107]

The specific current difficulties Liang chose to emphasize in his lectures reflected his previous concerns. The mass crusade for minimal civil rights that he had called for in his anti-militarist tract of 1917 was still his first order of practical business in 1921:

> Because of the rapacious acts of the warlords, life and property do not have an iota of protection. . . . Our most urgent present need is for domestic tranquility and the establishment of the individual's rights to life, property, and other such rights. . . . More urgently needed than anything else is to know how to make the individual's rights secure and how to achieve a tranquil social order. Not only are these [two conditions] more precious than anything else, but they are also prerequisites for meeting all our other needs.[108]

As a means to achieving these two preconditions, Liang still advocated an effective liberal democracy, just as he had before the revolution and his crisis:

> We have already adopted a Western system of government. The Westerners have produced this system by having an attitude of struggle. But most of our citizens still have the same attitude they have had for these several thousand years. They are not the least interested in politics and do not demand their rights. Our worry today is not that people will struggle for rights and power, but that they will not. Only if the majority of citizens rise up and demand their rights can we [effectively] establish this political system, and so gain domestic tranquility and rights to life and property.[109]

Liang likewise implied that only Western science and technology could raise the standard of living for the masses—his second immediate concern. "Take a look at the lower classes of people—they would virtually be better off in hell. Natural disasters often strike, and when they do, the people are utterly defenseless and must just endure them."[110]

Possibly because of the heightened anti-imperialist atmosphere generated by the May Fourth movement, Liang now manifested a

107. [4], p. 206.   108. [4], pp. 208, 204.   109. [4], p. 208.
110. [4], p. 203.

greater awareness of the dangers of foreign aggression. It was bad enough that "We have had to take their bullying and insults," but now, Liang felt, the greatest danger was that the imperialist powers would "use their great [accumulations of] capital and other economic means to keep the Chinese in perpetual economic thralldom, and so force the Chinese to serve them with no chance of ever throwing them off."[111]

In effect, Liang was saying that China must Westernize to survive. He recognized the antagonism between nationalism and culturalism, between preserving the Chinese nation (*pao-kuo*) and preserving Chinese values (*pao-chiao*). Yet he had also ascribed universal absolute value to Chinese culture and predicted that the modernized nations were on the verge of taking the Chinese road. The dilemma seemed insoluble: China could not retain its culture because it was directly responsible for the present problems that threatened to destroy it; yet if China abandoned its culture for the West's, then China would suffer the dehumanization and spiritual distress inherent in Western culture precisely at the time when world culture was turning to that of the Chinese. Moreover, culture to Liang was a holistic expression of one unified underlying human attitude, so he had denied himself the easy solution of advocating a blending of Chinese and Western cultures.

In the end, Liang could not escape from the corner he had so painstakingly painted himself into. The solution with which he concluded his lectures muddled the central issue: "Completely accept Western culture while fundamentally reforming its mistakes (*ch'üan-p'an ch'eng-shou erh ken-pen kai-kuo*)." At the same time, "Critically reappraise and bring forth anew China's original attitude."[112] Although this formula would allow for both the nation's survival and for retention of China's original cultural attitude, it flatly contradicts his concept of culture as a holistic entity created by one underlying attitude or Will direction.

The thrust of Liang's 1921 book was that Chinese culture was both on a higher spiritual level than Western culture and compatible with modernization. For the next three decades he would rephrase and rework the same message through thousands of published pages. He would replace intuition and *jen* with rationality (*li-hsing*) as the essence of Chinese culture, and he would alter the concrete programs for practical application of the theory, but not

111. [4], pp. 203, 208.   112. [4], p. 202.

the substance: China could preserve the heritage of the sages—the discovery of true humanity—and still acquire "wealth and power." Underlying all his ratiocinations runs the unrelenting, unresolved contradiction: Chinese culture was truly human precisely for the same qualities that had prevented it from achieving what the Chinese people now needed. There is nothing particularly Chinese about this contradiction, of course. In one form or another, it has been the central issue of most modern Western philosophy and literature.

Science, for instance, was produced by intellectual calculation of the external world; such an attitude *by its very nature* had made the universe "a pile of dry dead things" for the Westerner, and was the diametrical opposite of what Liang described as the Chinese attitude. Democracy was produced and maintained by "clearly demarcating the division between self and others" and by selfish struggle for one's rights; yet this was the exact opposite of the Chinese spirit of emotional merger of the self with others and of yielding (*jang*).

In a way, Liang's 1921 theory seems to end up advocating what he had set out to oppose—the blending of Chinese and Western cultures. At one point, even he himself inadvertently came dangerously close to blurring the distinction between himself and the advocates of cultural blending. "Our urgent needs at present . . . all require that we take the first course. . . . But if we do not blend [*han-jung*] the life of the second course into it, we will not be able to avoid its dangers and mistakes." (The cultural blenders usually used the word *t'iao-ho*—to blend or to harmonize—but *han-jung* is close enough to translate as "blending.")[113]

Liang does seem to imply that while historical Chinese culture might be incompatible with modernization, his own ideal of China's *original* attitude is not. He has tried to describe and establish an attitude that would embody "the original Chinese spirit" and enable the Chinese to avoid the pitfalls of the Western road, but which at the same time would allow them to get what they truly need from the Western culture.

> The attitude I want to put forth is the "resoluteness" [*kang*] of Confucius. . . . Only this sort of dynamism can make up for

113. [4], p. 212; see also p. 205. Although *han-jung* may be translated as "blending," the term may be taken to imply a process whereby the two elements to be blended together are not equal and would still retain their own integrity.

the former Chinese shortcomings, save the Chinese from
their present afflictions, avoid the faults of the Westerners,
and enable the Chinese to cope with the needs of the world.
The Chinese originally walked this road, but [later] they
tended too much toward passivity, softness, subordination,
quiescence—that is [they were] nearer to Lao-tzu's way. It has
not been the vigorous, resolute, active way of Confucius.[114]

This attitude would in one stroke solve China's material inferiority
and also revive the original, true Confucian life; it would both serve
the purposes of modernization and, after all these many centuries,
finally close the gap between China's "true" cultural spirit and the
facts of its actual historical expression.

A common characteristic this solution to China's cultural crisis
shares with the ones Liang would develop and advocate later is
pragmatism; Liang sought always to identify the practical with his
prescriptive values. He hinted that successful reform and effica-
cious action depended upon all Chinese firmly internalizing a securely based philosophy of life (*jen-sheng t'ai-tu*): "A man must establish his life on a firm foundation before he can move forward."
Before reform can be successfully implemented, a firmly rooted
mass emotional commitment must be established; for practical
reasons, modernization must wait upon spiritual reconstruction
and reintegration. As China was lacking this essential prerequisite,
it was natural that the New Culture and May Fourth movements
had so far failed to produce real results. "The new party [*hsin p'ai*]
advocates nothing more than Ch'en Tu-hsiu's science and democracy and Hu Shih's 'critical spirit'. . . . I approve of all of this, but I
feel that these alone do not provide [us with] a philosophy of life.
Superficial methods [that do not reach the inner person] are of no
practical value."[115] Various new thought currents and reform programs had come and gone, passed around "by word of mouth and
pen . . . [but] never do they affect the real situation nor have actual
influence. Only if [we] solidly establish a way of life, can we really
absorb and digest science and democracy effectively. If we do not
[first have a secure philosophy of life], then I dare predict that the
New Culture movement cannot produce any results."[116]

Only with an enthusiastic mass commitment to a dynamic positive Confucianism (that is, Liang's) could China achieve the wealth
and power of modernization. Only with a renaissance of China's

114. [4], pp. 212–213.   115. [4], pp. 213, 205.
116. [4], pp. 213–214.

original spirit—"a religion which is not a religion"—can "the oppressive atmosphere of death be stripped away from our vital core,
and allow the Chinese people to be resurrected." (Some thirty years
later Liang used precisely the same metaphor to describe the
transformation wrought by the Communists.)[117]

At this time Liang put forth no concrete program for just how to
go about instituting his quasi-religious mass movement, but his
general direction was clear enough: "What I want is a re-creation of
the custom of philosophical discourse [chiang-hsueh] like that of the
Sung and Ming [dynasties] using the [way of] life [and relationship]
of Confucius and Yen [Hui, Confucius' favorite disciple] to solve
the melancholy problems of life that afflict our youth today."[118]
Chiang-hsueh—the custom of disciples living and learning together
in a small group formed around a teacher—contains two key ideas:
the small, intimate group as the basic unit of moral and intellectual
improvement; and the student-teacher relationship as the organizational form. The statement also illustrates how Liang had transferred his own past "melancholy problems of life" onto all the
youth of China.

Liang emphasized that what he had in mind was a *mass* movement, not the exclusive *chiang-hsueh* institution that had existed
historically. "It should not become an enterprise just of small
coteries; it should exert effort to become widespread [throughout
society]. . . . We can make Confucius' path broad and universal."
Liang pointed out that the school of Wang Yang-ming's disciple,
Wang Pi (Tung-yai), had a lot of artisan and peasant students.
Liang was silent on just where these *Analects*-thumping educator-
revivalists would come from, how they should organize, how they
should go about approaching the masses, and other details, but
promised to talk about the matter later. "Confucianism is not a kind
of thought, but rather a way of life. I am still alienated from this
way of life; allow me to try it a bit and I will have something to say
later."[119]

These lectures clearly implied that Confucianism is a universal
value; Liang also implied that no one before him had ever really
understood Confucius. He was in sole possession of this message of
salvation for humankind. That messianic streak—the "delusion of

117. Ibid.; see also [87]. Liang used the same phrase in a private letter to
a friend about a year after this. [90].
118. [4], p. 213.   119. [4], pp. 213–214.

sagehood"—is clearly evident in the preface Liang wrote for the book:

> I see the pitiful condition of the Westerners . . . [who], desiring spiritual restoration, are running all over searching. It is really [a case of] "not yet learning the great doctrine." Should I not guide them to this path of Confucius? I also see Chinese slavishly imitating the shallowness of the West, and some [of them] mistakenly studying Buddhism. . . . [They are also] searching everywhere. . . . Should I not guide them to that best and most beautiful of lives, the Confucian one? . . . Really, if it were not for my coming to propagate [Confucius], would there be [anyone] to do so? This is the reason that forced me [personally to change and] lead a Confucian life.[120]

That old image—already present in 1916—of the Bodhisattva abandoning the comforts of Nirvana has now reappeared as a Confucian sage who bears responsibility for transmitting the eternal *tao*.

120. [4a], pp. 3–4. The phrase is from Mencius 7B:29. In the original text, the "great doctrine" is that of the "superior man" (*chün-tzu*).

CHAPTER V

Public Reaction to
Eastern and Western Cultures

The three most famous critics of Liang's book repre-
sented a wide spectrum of political views: the liberal Hu Shih, the
Kuomintang leader Wu Chih-hui, and the Communist Yang
Ming-chai.

Hu Shih's Review

Since Liang's book had severely criticized Hu's recent work on
ancient Chinese thought and had even cast aspersions upon Hu's
intellectual integrity,[1] it is natural that Hu should come forth with a
public response. His sarcastic review accused Liang of using over-
simplified generalizations and vague abstractions to construct a
fundamental solution.[2] The thrust of Hu's critique was basically the
same as his oblique attack on the Chinese Marxists in his 1919
"Problems and Isms" exchange with Li Ta-chao. From where Hu
and like-minded Westernized liberals stood, Liang's conservative
"fundamental solution" and what the Communists advocated did
indeed look much like the same animal.

Hu agreed with Liang's definition of culture as the form of
human struggle with the environment, but he emphasized that the
demands on the environment were physiologically determined.
Since all humans shared the same physiological make-up, their
demands on the environment were fundamentally the same.
Human thought was not, as Liang suggested, an expression of
cultural direction, but simply a tool for satisfying these demands.
Thus, according to Hu, all cultures and their ways of satisfying
these demands "differ only in detail" (*ta-t'ung hsiao-i*). "Take the
problem of hunger, for instance. The only solution for it is 'to eat.'
Now, the thing to be eaten might be rice, or bread, or corn meal,

1. See [4], pp. 1–2, 12–13, 121, 126–128, 130–134, 138.
2. [309b], pp. 158, 162–163, 166–169, 171, 174.

but in any case it has to be animal or vegetable. Certainly one cannot eat stones."[3]

Principle of limited possibilities. Because human needs are everywhere the same, Hu implied, any statement about the special character of a particular culture (such as Liang's distinction based on different underlying attitudes) is by its nature "arbitrary" and invalid. There is only one set of needs to be met and the ways in which these needs can be met are limited. The same principle held true for social systems, political systems, or metaphysical ideas. "The big difference between me and Mr. Liang," Hu declared, "is just that I hold that all peoples walk the 'original road of life' [while] Mr. Liang holds that China and India walk two other roads." "Because we accept the 'theory of limited possibilities,' " Hu sneered, "we do not dare try to lay down any formula about the cultures of peoples."[4] Apparently Hu changed his mind soon afterwards, as three years later he made the same generalizations about the characters of Chinese and Westerners which Liang had made.[5]

Hu gleefully produced exceptions to Liang's generalizations. Had not Liang claimed that the Chinese philosophy of life was one of "contentment" and "moderation"? Such ideals, Hu pointed out, existed in Western culture too; the Chinese, with their wine-worshipping poets, concubines and prostitutes, came no closer than the Westerners to realizing the ideal.[6]

If China was, as Hu suggested, on the "original road" along with the West, then it was still incumbent upon him to answer that dreaded question which Liang's theory had answered: Why were the Chinese so far behind?

> Because of environmental difficulties or lack of them, and because of the [different degrees of] urgency of the problems [facing the various peoples], there are differences in the speed with which they [the peoples] travel. . . . We can only say that, in the past three hundred years, the European peoples were confronted with an urgent coercive environment [which made them] get ahead a few steps.[7]

Just what this sudden alteration of the seventeenth-century European environment was or why it occurred, Hu left to the reader's imagination.

3. [309b], pp. 171–176.   4. [309b], pp. 172, 176, 175.
5. [309d].   6. [309b], p. 168.   7. [309b], p. 175.

Liang's rebuttal. Liang steadfastly refused to respond to the criticisms leveled at his book. The supercilious flippancy of Hu's review, however, did hurt him and provoke a rejoinder. Hu had also openly classed Liang together with Chang Chün-mai as an enemy of the New Culture movement, a distinction that Liang deeply resented.[8] Liang's counterattack added nothing new; it was more a protest that Hu and the others had neither read his book carefully nor tried to understand it. "Everybody read my book as though they were reading the *Peking Morning Post*, rushing through it in five minutes. . . . What kind of answer do [they] want me to make to this kind of criticism? [If Hu] now insists that I reply, I still have no other way of answering but to point to the original book and ask him to examine it [more thoughtfully]." Liang repaid Hu's sarcasm in kind: "Ah, [Mr. Hu]! . . . What harm would there have been in understanding [my book] with an open mind! If [you] really did not have the time to read it, then [why did you not] drop [the matter] and forget about it? . . . Why did you have to insist on dashing off a sloppy job of criticism?"[9]

In contrast to the way he saw his critics, Liang portrayed himself as humble and intellectually conscientious, and as giving all critics the benefit of the doubt. "Because of this [attitude]," Liang said, "I very much like to seek opinions different from mine, and I want to understand clearly the reason why the other person does not agree with me. Yet everybody [else] is not [this way]."[10]

While not denying that Liang's paranoiac streak surfaced a bit in this rebuttal, it is fair to say that he was justified in his accusations. Hu had, for instance, completely ignored Liang's many pages of arguments refuting the kind of environmental determinism upon which Hu had based his criticism. Liang also despaired over Hu's dismissal of the possibility of the existence of cultural attitudes just because exceptions to the general rule could be found. "Oh, alas! Mr. Hu, oh, do desist! You, sir, basically do not admit the existence of things like 'a kind of style' [or] 'coloration' [or] 'tendency' [or] 'spirit,' and regard all those who speak in such terms as muddle-headed, so who dares argue with you, sir?" Liang happily referred several times to the use that Dewey, Hu's revered teacher, made of such terms when he discussed cultures.[11]

8. [9c], p. 54. See also the exchange of letters between Hu and Liang on Hu's review in [309c].
9. [9c], pp. 22–23, 54.   10. [9c], p. 22.
11. [9c], p. 37; see also pp. 36–38, 42, 46.

On the whole, Liang defended himself quite well, demonstrating that at least Hu's facile commentary had begged all the questions the book had raised. Yet one implication of Hu's "theory of limited possibilities" had hit home: If culture was nothing more than the methods by which peoples satisfied their physiologically generated desires, then the effectiveness of the process each adopted became the clear, objective, absolute standard for judging the value of cultures. Liang tried mightily to demonstrate that such a standard was not possible by claiming that human subjective demands on the environment were not wholly determined by a physiological make-up common to all. For instance, Liang said, "hunger" was not "the problem" for the Indians, but rather it was "eating that was the problem, that is, life [itself was the problem]." In ancient India, Liang said, starving oneself was a common custom. Yet Liang obviously could not deny that almost all Indians did and still do eat, just as the Westerners and Chinese do, despite their different attitudes toward life.[12]

Liang's ever sensitive feelings were also wounded by Hu Shih and Ch'en Tu-hsiu's pigeonholing him with the conservatives as an opponent of the New Culture movement. "The way [they] talk, I am an obstacle to their thought reform movement. . . . This makes me feel very sad. I do not feel that I oppose their movement! I applaud and encourage their efforts!"[13]

Other Criticism

Liang's emotional plea for mutual understanding was not very successful. Crusty old Wu Chih-hui snorted that "it is not he who is the enemy; it is what he says!" Yang Ming-chai was so incensed at Liang's accusation that people had not really read the book that he was inspired to write a book almost twice as long as Liang's.[14]

Wu Chih-hui. Wu claimed that Liang Ch'i-ch'ao and the authors of certain books had "swindled" Liang into a misconception of the West, so Liang had ended up "making a joke of Western civilization in the same way that Ts'ao K'un [the warlord then controlling Peking] is making a joke of the constitution." This estimation was echoed by others with a Western education, even

12. [9c], pp. 46–48.   13. [9c], pp. 19–20. See also [154].
14. [580], pp. 16, 127; see also [565].

those sympathetic to Liang. If Liang had ever been to the West, one remarked, he would never have opposed Westernization. Because they had a more sophisticated understanding and personal experience of Western society, many critics pronounced Liang's characterization of Western history and philosophies to be oversimplifications. Some pointed to clearly anti-utilitarian strains in Western thought, such as mysticism and romanticism. Others faulted Liang for ignoring Christianity in his analysis and assured him that modern rationalism or no, religion in the West was not the corpse Liang had made it out to be.[15]

Yang Ming-chai and others. As befitted a good Marxist, Yang Ming-chai attacked Liang for claiming primacy of the "spirit" or life attitude over economic and geographic factors.[16] But Yang also criticized literally everything else in the book, almost page by page. Of all the critics, only Yang and Liu Po-ming, an editor of the conservative journal, *Hsueh heng*, thought to use the obvious anti-intuitionist argument that Julien Benda had leveled at Liang's champion, Bergson. Benda had argued that if Bergsonism were to remain "faithful to its principles," it could "logically do nothing more than utter simple negations or mere cries of enthusiasm" and so could not really explain anything. In the same vein, Liu pointed out: "Mr. Liang truly esteems intuition, but his writing a book to elucidate the value of intuition was an affair of the intellect."[17]

Most reviewers tended to side with Hu Shih on the question of Liang's "three roads" metaphor. Although they accepted the validity of terms such as "tendency" or "style," they pointed out that life was a struggle in all cultures, and the Will by its very nature had to go "forward." Unconvinced by Liang's subtle metaphysical gyrations, they felt that "there is only one great road—the road forward . . . only the methods and speed [of walking it] are different."[18]

Most also agreed with Hu Shih that Liang's cultural ideal types were a bit too ideal, especially the Chinese one. The real Chinese

15. [580], p. 17; see also [144], p. 96; [413]; [391]; [597], pp. 15–20, 37–38.
16. [597], pp. 8–11, 20–24.
17. [102a], pp. 101–102; [597], p. 74; [413], p. 8.
18. [391], p. 10; see also pp. 11–12, 15–16; [390], pp. 437–440; [597], pp. 7–8, 11–14, 32–36; [144], pp. 93–94.

simply did not measure up to Liang's characterization of them. Even Liang's most sympathetic reviewer bluntly stated:

> [Liang's description of Chinese family and social life] overly compliments the Chinese. . . . Do not tell me that Mr. Liang has not heard of those many kinds of hostility and enmity [which exist], such as brothers fighting over property inheritance or friends breaking up [because of] calculating [self-interest]. Do not tell me that Mr. Liang does not know about the jealousy, the secret plots, and the many kinds of misery almost universally present in family life? . . . In reality, cases of cold, selfish calculation are by no means less than among the Westerners; the only difference is that [the Chinese] give more consideration to face, whereas the Westerners openly wrangle [with each other].[19]

In this same vein, Yang Ming-chai pointed out that the Confucian scholar-officials had been, in fact, creatures of inexhaustible greed, by no means without the habit of selfish calculation.

Liang had allowed, of course, that the true Confucian spirit had not prevailed in history, nor had it been properly understood. But in side-stepping attacks on historical Confucianism, Liang walked squarely into assault from the opposite direction:

> During these several thousand years, the Confucianists have controlled politics and education, and they still have not been able to implement the [true] meaning of their own ancestor's doctrine. . . . Was this not because the [doctrine's] ideals were too high and had no relation to [actual] human life? Since they have not been able to realize it in these thousands of years, how do we know they will not go on for ten thousand years more and still be unable to adopt [the doctrine]? Of what value is a culture that cannot be adopted in several thousand or perhaps several ten-thousand years? [Then] is it not a waste of time for Mr. Liang to elucidate [this culture]?[20]

Liang was too naive, the critics noted, to see that even though in theory he had disassociated his "true" Confucius from the superstitious, hypocritical, and corrupt encrustations of traditional Confucianism, the publication of his book would, in practice, support and encourage the warlords, bureaucrats, and other reactionary forces that used the "false" Confucius to bolster their positions.

19. [602], p. 6; see also [391], pp. 9–10; [390], pp. 94–95.
20. [597], p. 106.

Philosopher Li Shih-ts'en, the most thoughtful reviewer of the book, reduced the dilemma to its inevitable conclusion:

Mr. Liang . . . has special insight into the true value of Confucian philosophy, and so he has decided to propagate and advocate it. But I feel that [in doing so] he should not mention [the name of] Confucius. [That way, Liang] can publicize and exalt the essential message of Confucius all he wants, and it will not be taken advantage of by the "false" Confucianists.[21]

Not all commentators were so caviling. Some were unqualified in their praise of the book and even attacked Hu Shih and Wu Chih-hui's criticism.[22] Indeed, the book created a corps of devoted disciples throughout China, some of whom would become cadre in Liang's later rural reconstruction movement.

The Contradiction and the Critics

The book's fundamental contradictions naturally escaped the admiring young neotraditionalists, but they escaped many of the book's more exacting critics as well. Perhaps, Liang's subtlety and skillful use of vagueness succeeded in obscuring the contradictions to most. Even Liang's semantic dodge on the issue of cultural blending got past many reviewers. Some, of course, did perceive that Liang had contradicted himself. One man "agreed in general with Liang's thought" but admitted that he did not understand why Liang opposed cultural blending, since "Liang himself says as much."[23]

Only a very few observers thought long and deeply enough on the book to see the ultimate contradiction underlying Liang's solution to China's cultural dilemma. One observed that Liang's two proposals—advocating wholesale acceptance of Western culture, but qualifying this acceptance with the requirement of "changing it basically" to accord with the Confucian spirit—"cancel each other out." If, as Liang advocated, the Chinese accept science completely, then logically they "must rid themselves completely of the Chinese-style attitude." If the democratic spirit is propagated, then "how can [we] again lead the people down the Confucian road, and

21. [391], p. 20; see also pp. 16–19; [390], pp. 94–97.
22. See [381]; [280]; [248], pp. 3–4, 6–11; [602], pp. 5, 9–10.
23. [602], pp. 9–10; see also p. 5; [391], pp. 22–23; [390], pp. 95–98; [580], pp. 124–126; [144], p. 90.

mix into their brains that sort of anti-democratic spirit of . . . Confucius?" he asked.[24] Even this criticism, however, does not clearly identify the full nature of the contradiction.

One man—the professional philosopher Ho Lin—did appreciate both Liang's skill and the contradiction. Liang had postulated that "the Confucian life attitude had unique, universal, eternal value," Ho pointed out; yet Liang avoided "falling into a narrow debate on the superiority and inferiority of Chinese and Western cultures. He ingeniously avoided the biased, narrow, reactionary opinion that Eastern culture is better than Western culture." Instead, Ho observed, Liang had used the method of "vaguely hinting that the Oriental life attitude was more profound and superior to the Western one." But in the final analysis, Ho judged, Liang's "advocating a resurrection of the Confucian attitude while at the same time advocating science and democracy still does not completely escape the snare of 'Chinese learning for the basis; Western learning for utility' [*Chung-hsueh wei t'i, Hsi-hsueh wei yung*]."[25]

This reference to the old *t'i-yung* formula was obviously not altogether inappropriate. Yet in Liang's theory the *t'i* was no longer something the Chinese presently had in their possession; it had become an unrealized potential, and the effective acquisition of the *yung* was consequent upon the realization of the *t'i*. The *t'i*, now a universal product of human evolution, was Chinese only because Confucius had discovered it first, and it survived only because of Confucius' modern successor, Liang Shu-ming.

The historical significance of Liang's book and the response it aroused may be assessed in various ways. At the time, an American missionary said it signified that "the Chinese have reached a reflective stage in their contact with Western civilization. . . . They have now begun to make critical and scientific study of the civilizations of the West, of India, and of their own country in the hope of building up for themselves the very best type of civilization for the future." Ho Lin thought that "at a time of wholesale Westernization" and "total loss of confidence in Chinese culture," Liang was able to restore some measure of Chinese confidence and self-esteem. Ts'ai Yuan-p'ei judged the book to be of universal human significance and said that "Mr. Liang has raised the most important problem in the contemporary philosophical world."[26] Ts'ai's statement is no

24. [391], p. 24.   25. [261], pp. 10–12.
26. [434], p. 698; [261], pp. 10–12; [524a], pp. 82–83.

exaggeration; the central issue connecting all of Liang's thought is, after all, the crisis of modernity.

Perhaps the most perceptive appraisal was from Liang's friend, Li Shih-ts'en; Li somehow sensed that Liang's theories were answers to Liang's own existential questions. "Liang is a man," Li said, "whose life is unsettled and so [he] has gone forward searching for [an answer]. . . . By careful investigation, he found that the reason for the unsettled nature of his personal life lay in this degeneracy [moral crisis] of modern life, so he raised up Confucian philosophy . . . as salvation for it."[27]

The book *was*, in fact, a projection of Liang's own encounter with meaninglessness—his own spiritual odyssey through "Western utilitarianism," the comforts of Buddhism, and its final resolution in Confucianism. While the expressions of this solution—the concrete measures Liang would advocate—would change after 1921, the solution itself would not. His search was over.

27. [389a], pp. 8–9.

CHAPTER VI

Liang's Quest for a Program, 1922 – 1926

Liang felt that he had solved China's cultural crisis on the philosophical level. But a sage, especially if he is a disciple of Wang Yang-ming, knows that completion of inner knowledge is action in the outer realm. The eight years following the publication of *Eastern and Western Cultures* were a period of tentative groping for a concrete program of action that would embody and fulfill his abstract conceptualizations. The book itself contained suggestions for immediate action in two areas: politics—the establishment of political and domestic stability; and education—revival of the *chiang-hsueh* custom. Immediately after publishing his book, Liang acted to implement his ideas in both these areas.

A Plan for Political Reform—"Our Political Proposals"

The failure of the Republican Revolution to achieve its goals and Liang's own involvement in it had implanted in him a deep and abiding suspicion of politics of any kind. Yet he had served in the Ministry of Justice in 1916 and had tried to promote a political movement of sorts in 1917. That he was again willing to involve himself in political matters in 1922 is an example of his lifelong ambivalence toward a personal political role. In the following decades he would hold several other political offices and himself initiate a political party during the Anti-Japanese War—an action that put him in the thick of political infighting and maneuvering for a decade. Nevertheless, he always approached politics with enormous reluctance and with a feeling of being forced by his own sense of duty.

Although Liang conceived of China's crisis primarily in cultural terms that demanded a cultural solution, the warlord-ridden chaos of the early 1920s did move him to act politically. In early 1922,

Liang, along with Li Ta-chao, proposed to Ts'ai Yuan-p'ei the publication of a political manifesto assessing the current conditions
and solutions to China's dilemma.[1] Other influential Peking
intellectuals, such as Hu Shih and Ting Wen-chiang, were also
enthusiastic about the project, and a group comprising sixteen famous intellectuals soon formed to carry it out. Their final document, entitled "Our Political Proposals" and drafted by Hu Shih,
became a standard for liberal politics for more than a decade.[2]

That Liang Shu-ming, a cultural conservative, could agree on a
common political platform with Western-oriented Hu Shih and
Ting Wen-chiang, as well as with Communist Li Ta-chao, is not
as surprising as one might first think. Whatever his opposition to
Western influences, Liang maintained what can only be called a
"liberal" political stance throughout his life. His position was not
unlike that of idealistic cultural conservatives in other parts of the
world and in other times. The opposition of such persons and
groups to the political status quo caused them to uphold vigorously
liberal political principles and ideals. The mid-nineteenth-century
Russian Slavophiles, who fought for liberal political goals against
the autocracy of Nicholas I, are a case in point.

The document the liberal group produced in 1922, in fact, contained many of the ideas Liang himself had already publicly advocated. The main theme of the manifesto—that good people (hao-
jen) had a responsibility to set aside petty political differences and
involve themselves at least minimally in the affairs of the government—is strikingly similar to ideas Liang had expressed in his
1917 pamphlet. In the pamphlet Liang had blamed the "good
people" for the dismal situation because of their noninvolvement
and defeatist attitude, and pleaded with them to rise up and join
together to work for a solution through the force of public opinion.
Although Hu Shih had been so scathingly critical of Liang's culture
theories, the enthusiasm with which he had received Liang's 1917
treatise obviously carried over into his drafting of the 1922
manifesto.

Even some of the specific ideas from Liang's book on culture can
be found in the manifesto. Liang had stated that he hoped all
would develop a spirit of struggle for their political rights. The
manifesto read: "We firmly believe that the first step toward politi-

1. [11k], p. 333; [198], p. 240.
2. This manifesto was first published in [540] and then three weeks
later in Hu Shih and Ting Wen-chiang's liberal journal [447]. See also
[308b].

cal reform is that good people must have a fighting spirit. It is necessary to have a militant and decisive public opinion." The manifesto also recognized the significance for good government in the development of individuality (*ko-hsing ti fa-chan*), another concern Liang had belabored in his book. In addition, the proposal for a disarmament movement that Liang had put forth in 1917, along with his lifelong abhorrence of the use of military force in politics, both found expression in the manifesto.

Chiang-hsueh

In the long run, however, Liang's innermost identity was not that of a maneuvering Confucian strategist like Chu-ko Liang, but rather with Confucius himself. The ultimate model for the Sung-Ming *chiang-hsueh* was the relationship of Confucius and Mencius and their followers. As in the prototype, the students traveled with and generally involved themselves in the affairs of the master. The *Analects* portrays a Confucius who was intimately involved with the emotional and moral problems of his students. It was with this Confucius that Liang identified. Immediately after his book was published, Liang started personal experimentation with *chiang-hsueh*. In 1922, he formed a kind of commune-cum-academy with some of his students, and whenever circumstances permitted throughout his life, he maintained this life style.[3] (It would be interesting to know how his recent bride reacted to having a dozen strangers move in with them, but unfortunately that has not been recorded.)

Within the group, the students and teacher kept watch on each other's moral failings, just as Liang's group of middle-school friends had done with each other and for the same reasons. As Liang explained:

> Even though [one] is aware of one's sickness, it is not easy to supervise oneself. The ancients say, "the wise man cannot see his own face; the strong man cannot lift his own body." That is to say, a person cannot easily see his own appearance; and even if he can see it clearly, it is still not easy for him to be able to discipline himself at all times of his own accord. There-upon, at such times the only method is "to become close with one's teacher and choose one's friends from those who are morally and intellectually superior" [*ch'in shih ch'ü yu*]. Aside from this there is no other way. Why? Because every person is

3. [47], p. 1; [9e], p. 78.

apt often to ignore his own [actions]. Therefore you need
your teacher and friends to remind you constantly to keep
you from ignoring [your own actions] . . . . [One must] rely on
one's friends' good examples to subdue, become aware of,
and respond to one's own faults, and to cultivate [the friends'
strong points]. Suppose I am rash and impatient, and I live
together with someone whose temper is very tranquil and
calm; I can [then] get rid of my rashness and impatience. [If] I
am discouraged but have spirited friends and am in their
midst, then [I] will naturally and unconsciously become spirited and enthusiastic.[4]

Chiang-hsueh provides a connecting thread with which to link
Liang's personal life, his educational ideals, and his approach to
rural reconstruction. It is also the keystone around which he would
construct his plans for cultural revival and rural reform. The
chiang-hsueh tradition had a tremendous appeal for this man who
had experienced such a devastating emotional crisis in his youth
and now transferred that crisis onto his own students and all
Chinese educated youth. This experience created a deep and abiding concern in Liang for the moral and spiritual well-being of
youth. The faith underlying *Chiang-hsueh* in the transformative
power of moral criticism, exhortation, and example in the small
group is something Confucian Liang would share with Marxist
Mao.

Socialism

Another element in Liang's eventual rural reconstruction program, which was also already present in the early 1920s, is the
primacy of economic revolution and socialism. He warned other
reformers:

Unless the economic system is fundamentally changed, the
efforts of educationalists, moralists, public-health workers,
and religionists all are useless. . . . If you really are sincere in
your desire to reform society, you should apply your efforts
to this area [of economic reform]. . . the rest is vain verbiage.[5]

And Liang admitted that his own efforts at cultural and moral
revival, as well as his quest for a philosophy of life for the young,
were all hopeless unless he could also find a way to change the

4. [47], pp. 18–19.   5. [9a], pp. 1–10.

economic basis of society. Under the existing economic system, based on individualism and private property, "everyone quite naturally becomes mean and petty, selfish and egocentric." Thus, in Liang's estimation, the economic system was the cause of all the social disorders, crimes, and spiritual dehumanization: "Hollow preachings are ineffective. Only a radical reform of this [economic] system will suffice."[6]

Although the Chinese had not yet undergone an industrial revolution, and thus were not yet subject to the same intensity of dehumanizing mechanization and class conflict which existed in the West, the problems were still acute. Liang believed that both China and the West needed socialism to resolve their existing social and economic problems: "The symptoms are not completely the same. But the suffering is just as bad and as urgently in need of a cure."[7]

Once Liang had worked them out to his satisfaction, his commitment to *chiang-hsueh* and socialism became unalterable. But the evolution of his comprehensive program for the reconstruction and salvation of Chinese society took much longer. Although he considered the problems extremely urgent, he could not bring himself to follow the course taken by many of his contemporaries who seemed to latch on to, try, and discard a succession of schemes and ideas in their impatient search for some solution to China's desperate conditions. Liang seemed to recognize the destructive potential in pursuing half-thought-out proposals, and so was much more cautious and deliberate in his efforts. He would not commit himself to any endeavor—even rural reconstruction, which had tremendous emotional appeal to him immediately—until he had had a chance to analyze every aspect and persuade himself of the *practical* efficacy of the entire program.

He was well aware of the scattered attempts that had surfaced in the wake of the May Fourth movement to shift the focus of China's reformers from the eastern urban areas to the countryside. In 1919, Li Ta-chao had called for educated youth to "go to the villages" with their efforts to build a new China. In the same year, the pioneer theorist on rural education, Hsu Chia-chü, published his essays stressing the urgent need for adapting education to meet the particular problems of the rural areas. In 1923, the founder of the influential *Tiger magazine* and an old acquaintance of Liang's, Chang Shih-chao, came forth with a scheme to turn China into a

6. Ibid.   7. [9a], p. 10.

kind of agrarian Taoist utopia in order to escape the evils of industrialized Westernization. In spite of the appeal of these ideas, Liang doubted the practicality of an agrarian state in the modern world. Only industrial development, he believed, could alleviate China's poverty and make the country strong enough economically to ward off the imperialists.[8]

Criticism and Reform of Education

Instead, Liang concentrated most of his attention in the early 1920s on the next logical extension of his concern for the demoralized state of society and the educated elite: the question of educational reform. In both his 1917 pamphlet and his book, Liang had limited himself to simply identifying and describing the problem. By 1922, he had begun to explore more deeply its probable causes and effects. The villain, he found, was Western influence in general and on the educational system in particular. As Liang assessed the situation, Western influence, centered primarily in the big cities but now gradually spreading throughout the country, was eroding traditional Chinese concepts of morality. This insidious cancer was being further exacerbated by general adoption of the Western-style educational system and the misguided efforts of some of the present-day educated elite involved in the New Culture movement.[9]

Although Liang admitted that the members of the traditional Chinese educated class (*shih*) had not always been the moral paragons that they were supposed to be, they had at least had some idea of proper conduct, self-cultivation, and being a moral influence on society. They had held their positions partially through esteem for their personal character; their role as political governors (*cheng*) had been linked to their role as preservers and teachers of the moral standards (*chiao*). Although their own advantage and profit may have directed their actions, they were conscious of appearances and would have been ashamed to speak openly of their desire for private gain.

Now, however, Western influences had created an atmosphere of open avarice that permeated everywhere and blinded the people to "the real meaning of life." Education had become simply another commercial transaction—the process of obtaining a diploma that

8. See [393b]; [393c]; [339], p. 36; [122]; see also [123]; [124]; [11a].
9. [5r], pp. 113–116; [8].

could be parlayed into a "sybaritic life of ease."[10] It encouraged habits of decadence and luxury at the same time it trained the young in skills that were basically useless to the real needs of the masses.

Middle school graduates cannot manage farms or factories. For the most part, neither can the graduates of special institutes for commerce, industry, or agriculture. Among the most impractical are the agricultural schools. Aside from enabling the graduate to get some job, the education is worthless. So it is that the peasants say "one more student in a family is one more useless person."[11]

The educated class of the day, like its traditional counterpart, was still an aristocracy, but it had lost its sense of moral responsibility for the masses and had become merely an intellectual elite based on money and material consumption. Worse than the traditional elite, who might have paid only lip service to moral considerations for the sake of appearances, the modern elite did not even have a sense of appearance to forget. Before, the educated could not speak publicly of profit; today, they "wrangle openly over private advantage. Their ability to become rich in business is not only considered proper and justified, but even praised as really making use of what one has studied."[12] What kind of moral example for the people was that?

Liang quite consciously chose the term "aristocracy," for he felt that the new education was so expensive that now only the very rich could educate their children. So the traditional distinction between mind workers and body workers threatened to become a hereditary one; Chinese society would bifurcate permanently into two classes, just as Western society has done. Education now imparted only bad habits and moral flabbiness. Thus, the Chinese educated class, unredeemed by any sense of propriety or social duty, was living an exploiter's life in the cities which was totally alienated from the life-style and interests of the masses:[13]

Once a child from the countryside goes to higher primary school in the city, he can no longer live the old, simple life. He cannot eat the old food, wear the old clothes, drink the tea, or smoke the tobacco. He looks down on everything and has no patience with it. But, as for the knowledge and ability that a

10. [9d], pp. 57–68; [9m], pp. 151–152.   11. [9d], p. 66.
12. [9d], p. 61; see also pp. 57–68; [9m], pp. 151–152.
13. [9e], pp. 83–84; [9d], pp. 55–57, 60–62, 67; [9m], pp. 149–154.

rural family needs, he has not a whit! Instead he has some
half-baked, irrelevant, scientific knowledge in English,
physics, and chemistry. He cannot actually do any farm work;
instead he can play ball and do [Western] calisthenics and has
developed the habit of lazy loafing.[14]

Liang concluded that the present educational system in China
combined the worst in both Western and Chinese traditions. While
Chinese educators had discarded all that was of value in their
traditional education, they had clung to its weaknesses. Western
intellectuals, for example, were not ashamed of doing manual
labor, but the new Westernized Chinese intellectuals, even those
who studied agricultural or industrial arts, considered it just as
shameful to do manual work as their literati ancestors had.
Another example was that Westernized Chinese intellectuals still
wanted to be officials, a profession that Western intellectuals did
not find necessarily desirable. Thus, while Western influence had
created problems, it had not "corrected the old faults of the intellectual class, and the new Chinese intellectuals even lacked the
good points of the Western intellectual class."[15]

Liang also criticized the Westernized Chinese educators for their
Western-style concept of a teacher as one who simply imparts
"knowledge and techniques," with no real concern for the psychological, physical, and moral development of the student. Significantly, Liang used the image of a youth so overwhelmed by
emotional problems that he turns to suicide: "[The teacher today]
can remain completely ignorant of his student's psychological and
physical pathology to the extent that he can only be surprised after
one of his students commits suicide." In contrast, Liang maintained: "If you want to educate, then you must become intimate
friends with the student, and only after that can you understand
him and be a guide to him." Liang's solution, of course, was the
small-group intimate student-teacher relationship on the *chiang-
hsueh* model.[16]

Liang Shu-ming's criticisms of the modern educational system
sound much like the ones his father raised a decade earlier. As his
father had done, Liang condemned the deleterious influence of the
West for its *embourgeoisement* of the educated class. His rage at the
resulting loss of any sense of moral obligation among the present-
day educated leaders also has the same tenor as his father's. The

14. [9m], pp. 151–152.   15. [9d], pp. 63–64.
16. [9e], pp. 74–76.

modern intellectual class was a decadent, parasitic aristocracy unjustifiably supported by society:

> In their conduct and their lavish spending, [they] are just like bureaucrats. I am wounded in my heart. Although things like clothing, food, and amusements are trivialities, yet therein lie the differences between the common man and the aristocrat. . . . I cannot [bear to] be an aristocrat! I cannot watch the operas of Mei Lan-fang. I have never gone to the Chen Kuang cinema. This is an aristocrat's life. I watch the hubbub of the automobiles and carriages at the door and the thought of my coming and going with them makes me really ashamed. Those who lead an aristocrat's life are decadent![17]

In sum, Liang condemned the failure of the Western-style educational system to meet the real needs of Chinese society, while at the same time, it alienated the intellectuals from the masses. Because the educational system was imported from a society in which conditions were very different, it "not only fails but also creates many social problems . . . it virtually [is a case of] the schools educating people for another society."[18]

Liang's attack anticipated the criticism others would make years later. Tawney arrived at many of the same conclusions in his 1930 report for the League of Nations Educational Commission. In 1928, Mao observed how the peasants of his home area rose up against their useless Western-educated teachers and replaced them and their schools with their own kind, which were more suited to their own real needs.[19] The general thrust of Liang's educational thought had already set him traveling on a path that would converge at many points with Mao's later vision. That same path would carry Liang even further away from the Westernized Dr. Hu Shih, who, during those years Liang was taking the educational establishment to task, was residing in Shanghai's foreign concessions,

17. [9d], pp. 67–68. A few months after writing this passage, Liang wrote another piece praising his father specifically for never frequenting such places of amusement. This suggests that he had had his father in mind when writing the passage. See [7].

18. [9m], pp. 149, 153–154.

19. Tawney's critique of Westernized education as unsuited to the needs of Chinese society reached the Chinese reading public in [163]. Other of Liang's criticisms—such as the lack of physical education, agricultural education, or vocational education—are also found in Tawney's critique. Liang also prefigured Mao's attack on "foreign-style schools" and their being "entirely about urban things, unsuited to rural needs." See [424a], pp. 39–40.

traveling to Europe, associating with foreign and "foreignized" intellectuals, and dining at "one or another of the city's better restaurants, sometimes with an evening of cards to follow."[20] In short, he was leading the "aristocrat's life" Liang so fervently despised.

Liang Meets Two Colleagues

Because he was dissatisfied with the narrowly intellectual Westernized education of Peking University, and because he never really intended to be an armchair sage cloistered in academia, Liang tried to resign his post several times between 1921 and 1924. Each time Ts'ai Yuan-p'ei had cajoled him into staying on, but Liang could never restrict his activities to just his teaching responsibilities. After the death of his father's old friend P'eng I-sun in 1921, Liang took over the management of P'eng's Peking newspaper, the *Ching-hua pao*. He also was in great demand as a speaker because of the success of his *Eastern and Western Cultures*, so he traveled extensively throughout the country giving lectures and attending meetings.[21] In the course of his travels, he encountered two people who would have a particularly significant effect on the development of his thought and the direction of his future activities.

Alfred Westharp. Liang's first and only foreign friend was an eccentric German educator-musician. Alfred Westharp ran a school in the remote Shansi capital city of Taiyuan, where Liang met him in 1921 during a conference of educators. Liang found Westharp's educational style most interesting, for it coincided with his own ideas. Westharp stressed the students' psychological and physical health. Moreover, the students did all their own housework and cooked their own meals. They even ran a small factory at the school where they manufactured some of their daily necessities, such as shoes and stockings. They also took over the school administrative and maintenance responsibilities.[22]

---

20. [253], pp. 216–220.

21. Liang continually protested that he had neither the qualifications nor the inclinations of a scholar or a philosopher; he was instead simply "conscientious about solving problems," and this was regarded by others as scholarship or philosophy. [9p], pp. 189–193, 197–199; [4], p. 2; [11a], p. 2; [14a], pp. 1–3, 11–12; [510], p. 5. See also [66]; [71], p. 19; [463], p. 63.

22. Westharp had emigrated to America and then to China around the turn of the century. He was given to such bizarre behavior as performing piano sonatas nude, in a dark, heated room; his theory was that no other

Wang Hung-i. Liang first met his close friend and future colleague, the Shantungese politico-educator Wang Hung-i, when he delivered his series of lectures on Eastern and Western cultures in Tsinan in 1921. The two men hit it off immediately, and over the next decade they cooperated together on several reform and educational ventures. Not really a scholar or very articulate himself, Wang found that Liang was saying precisely what he had been feeling. Only after hearing Liang's lectures, Wang observed, "did my understanding progress." Under Liang's influence, Wang shifted his chief concern to the question of culture.[23] At the time, however, Liang was still unprepared to provide Wang with a specific program of action. Left to work one out for himself, Wang eventually hit upon a program for rural reform, and, in the end, he was the one who finally succeeded in winning Liang over to rural reconstruction work.

Wang Hung-i had been traveling a long road in his quest for solutions to his lifelong concerns—inequality and poverty.[24] Before the 1911 revolution, Wang blamed the "slave literati" mentality in

---

sensations should be allowed to interfere with the appreciation of the music. (The audience, however, was not required to join him *in puris naturalibus.* Nevertheless, his efforts failed to rouse in Liang any appreciation of the glories of Beethoven.) His other artistic firsts included music written to accompany the classic *Book of Poetry* (*Shih ching*), which he trained his students to perform. Years before Liang met him, Westharp—an ardent Sinophile—had had some of his anti-Western ditherings translated and published in Chinese by the famous translator Yen Fu. See [47], p. 118; [9k], pp. 121–143; [9i], pp. 105–112; [603].

23. Wang first heard of Liang through a former student of his who later was Liang's student at Peking university. Interested by what the student told him, Wang persuaded the Shantung Department of Education to invite Liang to lecture on Eastern and Western cultures. [555], p. 2; see also [557], p. 1; [558]; [11j].

24. As a student in Japan in the early 1900s, he supported the revolutionary cause and joined Sun Yat-sen's Tung-meng-hui. With the establishment of the republic, Wang became the provincial commissioner of education for Shantung, and in that capacity established a network of new-style schools throughout the province. When the KMT "second revolution" against Yuan Shih-k'ai began in 1913, he resigned his post and devoted his time to his middle school in Ho-tse and to work with many like-minded KMT members for the overthrow of Yuan Shih-k'ai. He and his fellows, who controlled education in Shantung, succeeded in frustrating Yuan's 1915 conservative education policies in the province. When Yuan died in 1916, Wang emerged as a major figure in the Shantung provincial assembly. He established a network of experimental factories throughout the province in another attempt to raise the income of the poor.

late imperial China, and the subservience of Confucian ethics to bureaucratic legalism. At that time he began putting his efforts into educational work, but concentrated on what he felt would have the most practical results in raising the income level of the rural poor. He believed it was necessary to learn about Western science to make up for existing Chinese deficiencies, but felt that traditional Chinese political and educational thought were sufficient in other areas. His central doctrine was to "nourish [the people] first and then educate [them]"—ethical concerns could be taken care of only after seeing to their economic well-being. The schools he founded included the Ho-tse (Ts'ao-chou) middle school, a bandit reformatory, an industrial school, and various handicraft centers scattered throughout the province.[25] The industrial school, at least, was also a center for revolutionary propaganda and activity, and as such, was closed by the Manchu government in 1907.

In the early republican period, Wang came to know the Mi family of Chai-ch'eng (Ting hsien, Hopei), where they had been running a model village since 1904. In 1914, the new magistrate of Ting hsien, Sun Ch'un-chai, became interested in the Mi family activities and helped them move beyond reform of education and customs toward a village self-government program. In 1916–1917, Sun went to Shansi, where he served a brief tenure as chairman of the provincial government. For whatever reasons, Sun's ideas appealed to the Shansi warlord Yen Hsi-shan and his adviser Chao Tai-wen, so they continued some of the programs after Sun's departure.

Basically, the Shansi local government system was organized according to Yuan Shih-k'ai's 1914 experimental code (which apparently was actually adopted only in Shansi). It consisted of a four-tiered sub-hsien administration: districts (*ch'ü*); villages (*ts'un*—

In 1919 Wang became aware of the "new thought currents" at Peking university and sought out Hu Shih, Ts'ai Yuan-p'ei, and others in the hope that they might provide him with the answers to his concerns. He also read all the new books. Gradually (and rather perceptively) he came to the conclusion that the new thought was moving toward communism. Such a violent way to equality was not in accord with his own Confucian ideals. [555]; [557]; [554]; [556]; [475], II, 1–19; [11j], p. 325.

25. These schools were also centers of revolutionary propaganda and activity. The school in Wei-hsien was closed by the government in 1907 because of its political nature. [555], pp. 1–3; [558], p. 1; [520], pp. 419–420; [157], pp. 15–16; [471], II, 221–231.

some of which were "incorporated" together for administrative purposes); *lü*, made up of twenty-five households; and finally, a five-household unit called a *lin*.[26] Through this administrative system they implemented the Mi family's programs against banditry, opium-smoking, foot-binding, etc., which Sun Ch'un-chai had transported to Shansi. (In the 1920s, the Nanking government adopted a modified form of this basic administrative framework.)

In 1922, shortly after his first meeting with Liang Shu-ming, Wang Hung-i visited Yen Hsi-shan and Chao Tai-wen. From what he saw and heard in these areas, Wang began to see village self-government as the key to solving China's problems; it provided a program that was both consistent with Wang's values and was also able to solve China's economic and political problems. He then set about organizing other North China gentry with views similar to his own. In 1924, Wang moved to Peking and, with Mi Ti-kang, founded a newspaper to publicize their ideas on village self-government. The two also collaborated with others on a manifesto calling for rural political and economic reforms that would make the village the basic unit of sovereignty. This informal association of northern Chinese gentry became known as the Village Government Group (Ts'un-chih p'ai).[27] They were eager to gain Liang's support and participation, but at the time he refused. Liang was not unsympathetic. Already in early 1923 (and completely independently from Wang), Liang had given a lecture suggesting agrarian revival as a solution to China's problems. Yet, not only had Ch'en Tu-hsiu warned him that such a plan was a petit bourgeois chimera, but even Liang himself "greatly feared that it was a subjective utopia, a useless illusion. . . . I dared not believe [in it]."[28]

26. The documents dealing with the provincial regulations for village self-government and reform are found in [470]. Wang, Mi, and Chao had all studied in Japan at about the same time and had joined the T'ung-meng-hui while there.

27. The group's membership and influence seem to have been limited to the provinces of Shantung, Shansi, Hopei, and Honan. Yen Hsi-shan, who contributed some articles to their magazine, could be considered a member. The group's most active members were Chao Tai-wen, Mi Ti-kang, Wang Hung-i, Ju Ch'un-p'u, Lü Chen-i, Wang Hsing-wu, Yin Chung-ts'ai, Yang T'ien-ching, Sun Tse-jang (Lien-ch'üan), Yen Lan-t'ing, P'eng Yü-t'ing, and Liang Chung-hua. See [279], p. 59; [217], p. 99; [111]; [297]; [142]; [555], pp. 2–3; [557], pp. 1–2; [533a]; [9q], pp. 228–230, 237–255; [11a], pp. 13–15.

28. [11a], pp. 10, 13.

Liang Leaves Peking for Shantung, 1924–1925

Wang did, however, win a partial victory over the other various causes competing for Liang's attention. In 1924, there were two main forces pulling at Liang: one from the south in Canton, where Sun Yat-sen's reorganized, Russian-backed Kuomintang was preparing to march north to unify China; and one from the east in Shantung, where a group of culturally conservative officials and gentry were planning to establish a traditionalist counterweight to the Westernized Peking University. The new institution, which symbolically they wished to establish at Ch'ü-fu, the birthplace of Confucius, would be devoted to the preservation of national essence (*kuo-ts'ui*).[29]

From the south, the Kuomintang militarists, Ch'en Ming-shu and Li Chi-shen, both of whom had befriended Liang before they had gone south, repeatedly appealed to him to come and join their efforts for national salvation. When Li Ta-chao returned to Peking from Canton in early 1924, he told Liang about the new Kuomintang and assured him that at this point Li's own Communist party, which had allied itself with the KMT, only wanted democratic revolution.[30] Yet in the spring of 1924, when faced with this choice between revolutionary South and conservative East, Liang could not reconcile the KMT *military* solution with his personal ideals. Much to the chagrin of his Canton admirers, he made a public statement to that effect, and in it, he criticized the KMT's reliance on force.[31]

In April 1924, about the time Liang made his final decision to go

29. [109], 228/3277, third quarter, 1921; [488], Nov. 30, 1922; [9e], pp. 72–73.

30. Li Chi-shen (1886–1959), an important member of the "Kwangsi generals Clique," taught at the Peking Military Staff College during the first decade of the Chinese republic. During that time he audited Liang's classes at Peking university and became his lifelong friend and admirer. Li left Peking for Canton in 1921. Ch'en Ming-shu (1890–1965), prominent Cantonese militarist, was a devotee of Buddhism; he first met Liang at the Buddhist scholar Ou-yang Ching-wu's Nanking Metaphysical Institute (Chih-na nei-hsueh yuan). They became lifelong friends. Another personal tie was through Ch'en's friend, the Cantonese Wu Kuan-ch'i, through whom Liang had met his wife. Both Li and Ch'en greatly admired Liang and tried continually to persuade him to join the KMT Canton government in the early 1920s. See [233]; [312], pt. 1, no. 295; [11a], p. 9; [628]; [635]; [636].

31. [233].

east, the Bengali poet Tagore visited China to preach his message of unified Eastern spirituality against Western materialism. For his evangelistic pains, the Indian was severely denounced by all wings of the Kuomintang and most other new intellectuals. In the last days of his professorship at the university, Liang attended the reception for this prophet of Asianism, and was accorded a private interview with him. Not really interested in Tagore's ideas on Asian spiritual revival, Liang devoted the interview to lecturing the visitor on the nature of Confucianism.[32] A month later, Liang left the red-brick halls of Peita, never to return.

In the fall of 1924, Liang led his three favorite students to Shantung in response to Wang Hung-i's invitation to him to take over the management of the Sixth Provincial Middle School in Ho-tse. Wang regarded his middle school, together with an affiliated higher research institute (Ch'ung-hua shu-yuan), as the precursors of the proposed Ch'ü-fu University, but apparently he was the only one of the original promoters who continued to support the project. Regardless of the prospects for Ch'ü-fu University, the middle school venture attracted Liang for the opportunity it offered him to test in practice his still vague ideas on educational reform and to experiment with *chiang-hsueh*.[33]

32. [47], pp. 70–72. For a description of Tagore's 1924 visit to Peking and reactions to it, see [257], pp. 155–245.

33. The three original sponsors of Ch'ü-fu university were Chin Yun-p'eng (b. 1887), P'an Fu (b. 1870), and Hsia Chi-ch'üan (b. 1883), all from old, powerful Shantung families. All had held important provincial and national government offices prior to 1921. Chin Yun-p'eng had been governor of Shantung from 1913 to 1916 and premier of China from 1919 to 1921. These three men formed an anti-Japanese political force in opposition to Tuan Ch'i-jui's policy of appeasement. Although they had already bought the land and gathered part of the endowment for the university by 1922, the project was abandoned by 1925. Wang alone among the university's backers persuaded Liang to go to Shantung to found Ch'ung hua shu-yuan as a preliminary step toward the establishment of the university. See [555], p. 3; [9e], pp. 79–81; [9j], p. 118; [488], Nov. 30, 1922; [471], II, 1–19.

Liang's initial contact with rural life was in the summer of 1923, when he lived for two months in the house of his student Ch'en Ya-san in Ch'en-po, a small town in Ho-tse hsien. His second rural sojourn was during 1924–1925, when he headed the Sixth Provincial Middle School in Ho-tse. Precisely during these years (1923–1925) the maladministration of Shantung warlord governor Chang Tsung-ch'ang brought about a great increase in rural banditry. Because of the resulting popular demand for law and order, dormant secret societies—the Red Spears (Hung ch'iang hui) and the

The Ho-tse middle school reforms. In a sense, the reforms Liang instituted at the middle school were a kind of microcosm of the method he was seeking for the reformation of society in general. At the center was his *chiang-hsueh* idea, which would combine moral and intellectual improvement through the mutual interaction, encouragement, and criticism experienced in small student-teacher groups. Thus, in contrast to the mechanical intellectual training one received in Western-style schools, Liang's school was dedicated to providing education for the whole man—emotional and moral guidance as well as intellectual nourishment. Even in its intellectual training the school would stress small groups and self-study, reducing as much as possible the reliance on the formal academic lecture as a pedagogical tool. Liang significantly and specifically mentioned his own middle-school self-study group as an example of what he intended—the nonstructured interaction of students with each other and with teachers should replace what he considered the rigid, inflexible class-hour-credit system.[34]

To guard against turning his students into members of the new aristocracy that was divorced from the life of the masses, the students engaged in daily manual labor and were responsible for the physical maintenance of the school without the aid of the usual service personnel: "We feel strongly that a situation in which one part of society has more material enjoyment than the rest is wrong. Therefore, our food, clothing, and lodging will be very plain and simple. If a boy from a rich family comes to us, we must change his habits and have him learn to be more frugal and thrifty."[35]

In accordance with his socialist ideals, Liang eliminated fixed fees and tuition; instead he set charges according to the family circumstances of the student. And he insisted that "students would be treated exactly the same, regardless of what they paid." The school would be run on the basis of human feelings (*kan-ch'ing*), not on legalistic rules that provided the framework for the management of Western-style schools.[36]

Big Sword Society (Ta tao hui)—spontaneously revived and greatly expanded their membership; they formed village self-defense corps, often associated with and organized around traditional local rural schools. Liang's later rural reconstruction plan also featured people's militia organized and maintained through a system of local schools, so it is conceivable that his experience in Shantung during this period influenced him. [109]; [617]; [619].

34. [9e], pp. 71–86.   35. [9e], p. 83.   36. [9e], pp. 83–85.

Admission to the school would depend on how the candidate scored on two tests: the usual test to measure intellectual capacity and achievement; and the more important interview with a school representative to determine the prospective student's "personality and attitude." Morals and morale would be the final criteria for admission, not intellectual power or academic preparation.[37]

Ch'ü-fu University. Liang hoped that through the institution of his reforms at the school, a group of students and teachers (for the latter were also to seek moral and intellectual self-improvement) would be inculcated with the values of his system and become the foundation with which to build the later Ch'ü-fu University. He also expected the program to provide him with core cadre to work for his larger purpose—the revival of the entire country.[38]

Liang took special care to distinguish the Ch'ü-fu University he envisioned from that previously supported by Wang and his associates. The original concept had combined the National Essence group's stress upon traditional literary and historical studies and K'ang Yu-wei's concept of Confucianism as a national religion. In fact, the group had first invited K'ang to head the school and recruit the faculty. Perhaps K'ang's stubborn monarchism stuck in the throats of the culturally conservative but very republican-minded Shantung politicians, for nothing came of the plan.[39]

Liang specifically disassociated his own ideals from K'ang's, proclaiming that his Ch'ü-fu University would be free from any "religious stink." Nor would it be a "preservation of antiquity academy" (*ts'un-ku hsueh-t'ang*) devoted to literature and scholarship. Neither did he envision any den of obscurantism, full of "hollow talk about Chinese and Indian philosophy." Rather, the very first departments would be in mathematics and biology for the "thorough study of modern learning" and only later would other specialties be developed at the school.[40]

---

37. [9e], pp. 81–82.   38. [47], p. 1; [9e], pp. 78–80.

39. [488], Nov. 30, 1922.

40. [9e], p. 72. The idea of a "Ts'un-ku hsueh t'ang" (Preservation of antiquity academy) was usually associated with the "national essence" (*kuo-ts'ui*) school of cultural conservatism. Chang Chih-tung first suggested that, after the civil service examination system was abolished, such an academy should be established to protect and sustain the "national essence" through a concentration on classical scholarship. [116], 68:23–32.

Liang's Second Retirement, 1925–1926

Perhaps Liang's brand of cultural conservatism was also not in accord with what the Shantung group envisioned, for Ch'ü-fu University never materialized, and Liang returned to Peking in the spring of 1925, disappointed and melancholy over the failure of his plans. He took with him some of the students from the middle school, who would become his lifelong disciples. In a very deep depression, he planned to retire from any activity for a period of three years, which he would spend living together with his disciples on the bucolic Tsing Hua University campus in Peking's western suburbs. He would continue his *chiang-hsueh* with the students until a suitable opportunity for action arose.[41]

Liang's three closest disciples, however, did not stay with him in Peking. Even while he was still in Shantung, the KMT generals Ch'en Ming-shu and Chang Nan-hsien had kept up a steady stream of letters and telegrams urging Liang to go south and join the Northern Expedition. Depressed and pessimistic, Liang refused to leave, but he did send Hsu Ming-hung, Wang P'ing-shu, and Huang Ken-yung to investigate the real nature of the new Kuomintang and its Northern Expedition.[42]

For the rest of 1925 and into the next year, Liang steadfastly refused offers of teaching positions and lecture series from various universities in North China, and began the long-postponed task of editing and collating his father's papers for publication. Early in 1926, he and his students moved into the house of his old German friend Westharp, who himself had recently moved to Peking from Taiyuan. Liang read the enthusiastic reports on the Northern Expedition sent to him by his three disciples, but he could not reach a decision on going south.[43]

There were also other reasons for Liang's period of semi-retirement and depression. The whole country was in upheaval; the armies of the Northern Expedition were surging northward under the twin banners of national unification and anti-imperialism. Throughout the South, the Communists prepared the way by organizing labor unions and peasant associations. The situation was ripe for decisive change. Yet Liang, whose self-identity as

41. [11a], pp. 4, 9–10; [47], pp. 1, 55; [9j], p. 118.
42. [11a], pp. 4, 9–10.
43. [9g]; [47], pp. 55, 57; [11a], pp. 4, 9–10; [9i], pp. 105–107; [9k], pp. 122–124.

sage was still unshaken, was himself without a design for national (and, ultimately, human) salvation. He was convinced neither by Wang Hung-i's plan for rural self-government and agrarian reform nor by the Kuomintang's foreign import of military unification and party rule. Most disheartening for him were the grave doubts he began to entertain about whether any remnant of the original Chinese spirit—the gift of the sages—existed at all. What hope could he have of its regeneration?

The period also held personal misfortunes and difficulties for Liang. His eldest son was suddenly stricken with a strange disease and eventually died from it. Liang blamed the death on the deficiencies inherent in Western medicine, yet he himself had chosen the doctor. Could he have secretly berated himself for his lack of faith in Chinese medicine? He was also poverty-stricken; he had no income, yet was unable to rouse himself to accept any of the many offers he received for academic employment.[44] Even his chosen undertaking of editing his father's papers gave him no comfort. He was smitten with overwhelming guilt for his past unfilial behavior and for his refusal to realize the value of the tradition for which his father died.[45]

By September 1926, KMT armies had already crossed the Yangtze. After Ch'en Ming-shu's troops occupied the strategic Wuhan area, Ch'en urged Liang to come meet him. Liang consented. Still doubtful about the KMT, however, Liang went first to Shanghai, then to Nanking, and in the end, returned to Peking, so he ended up not going into any KMT-controlled areas.[46]

44. [9j], pp. 118–120; [47], pp. 125–126; [11a], pp. 8–10.

45. This guilt is quite obvious in a piece he wrote at the time. See [9h], pp. 97–103.

46. While in Shanghai in October, Liang chanced to meet Tseng Ch'i, the leader of the nationalistic anti-Communist China Youth Party, which, at the time, was allied with the conservative Western Hills faction of the KMT. Tseng tried to win Liang over to his party's program, but Liang did not find Tseng's platform any more satisfying than the KMT's. [11a], p. 10.

CHAPTER VII

Kwangtung and Honan: The Beginnings of Rural Reconstruction, 1927–1931

In January 1927, while Liang was still struggling with his indecision and despair, two of the students he had sent south returned to Peking from the Left-KMT capital at Wuhan. The third of the original trio—and Liang's favorite—Hsu Ming-hung, did not return; he had joined the Communist party.[1] The other two, especially Wang P'ing-shu, had also been deeply impressed by the Communists, but had not actually joined them. After a time with Liang, Wang's and Huang Ken-yung's thought gradually "returned to normal," but Liang had already seen how the Communist program appealed to "youths of courage and spirit."[2]

The Communists and Liang's "Sudden Awakening"

With all these factors working on his mind, Liang and his students continued in their daily routine of study and discussion in the spacious halls of Ta-yu Manor in Peking's Western Suburbs. In this

---

1. The intrepid Hsu Ming-hung was to be a key figure in the Fukien Rebellion six years later. He had served with and was close to Ch'en Ming-shu, Ts'ai T'ing-k'ai, and other leaders of the Fukien uprising, and also had connections with the CCP (of which he might have continued to be a secret member). In this unique position he attempted to engineer an alliance between the Fukien insurgents and the Kiangsi Soviet. When the revolt failed, he disguised himself as a peasant and ran for the area controlled by the Communists, but was captured on the road. Because he had made so many enemies through his impulsive ways (he had had hsien magistrates summarily executed for graft), intercession failed and he was executed. Local peasants maintained that the vengeful ghosts of the executed officials had seen to it that he was caught. [563]; [314]; [622]; [636].

2. [11a], pp. 10–11; [563]; [38], p. 346; [14a], pp. 26–28.

tranquil setting Liang experienced a sudden and dramatic "awakening," which ended his spiritual paralysis:

> What did I awaken to? Actually I did not awaken to anything particularly new and fresh. I merely swept away the clouds of doubt and [went through them] to an open and straightforward self-confidence. What did I repudiate? I repudiated the whole line of Western gadgetry and was not again to be infected with any hankering [after them]. What did I believe in? I believed in our own way of shaping our country and was no longer to be timid and meek [about it].[3]

Liang deceived himself (and many others) with this announcement of a lightning-flash conversion.[4] He was, in fact, no less insistent than he had always been that China desperately needed to learn science and democracy from the West. Yet there is a decided difference: he no longer believed that *specific* Western social, political, or economic institutions—such as industrialized cities, representative assemblies, or schools—should or could be imported into China. Perhaps because of the influence of Wang Hung-i and his group, Liang adopted a conservative particularist rationale for opposing Westernization. The Chinese people's spirit (*min-tsu ching-shen*—a term he borrowed directly from Wang), their habits, customs, and psychology, as well as the present material conditions obtaining in China (such as poverty, poor communications, little

3. [11a], p. 12.

4. The dramatic phraseology in which Liang cast the description of his "awakening" has attracted historians to quote it and to mistakenly believe that, as one put it, Liang had undergone "a radical internal transformation." See, for example, [518], p. 48; [257], p. 61; [548], pp. 37–38. Actually, Liang's cultural solution for China remained fundamentally the same as it was before this awakening experience. After 1927, he sometimes substituted the words "technology," "development of intellect," or even "economic development," for what he had called "science" in *Eastern and Western Cultures*, but in effect, both before and after his "sudden awakening," he was referring to the same type of cultural borrowing from the West. Democracy later became "organization" (*tsu-chih* or *t'uan-t'i*) and implied the involvement and influence of the ordinary person in the affairs of the commonweal, as well as the guarantee of minimal civil rights. This, of course, was precisely what he had found valuable in "democracy" in the 1921 book. After 1927, he continually declared that science and organization were what China must learn from the West, just as before his "awakening" he had declared that science and democracy must be learned from the West. This was the very basis for his rural reconstruction. A few examples from Liang's writings: [19]; [38], pp. 50, 56, 175; [25], p. 47; [11h], p. 250.

industrialization and urbanization) would not *permit* the adoption
of these "Western gadgets."[5]

This kind of argument is, of course, reminiscent of the reasoning
employed by Yuan Shih-k'ai (and his advisor, Frank Goodnow) to
support his revival of the monarchy. It is also similar to that of
several KMT ideologues, such as Tai Chi-t'ao and T'ao Hsi-sheng,
who put the same conservative particularist argument into
Marxist-inspired categories. Similarly, late nineteenth-century Russian conservatives, such as Constantine Pobiedonostsev or Feodor
Dostoyevsky, opposed democracy on grounds of Russia's historical
and cultural uniqueness.

The awakening Liang spoke of was primarily an awakening of
confidence in China's ability to survive with modified forms of its
own institutions. He now "dared to believe" that something like
Wang Hung-i's program for a rural revival-reform movement
could enable China both to survive and also to revitalize what was
left of China's "original" culture. His most serious doubts had been
about whether any program of rural reform could be economically
realistic. How could a self-consciously agrarian nation survive in a
world of industrialized imperialist powers? How could rural self-
government lift the masses out of poverty? "I dared not believe that
the subjective, simplistic ideals of Wang Hung-i and his group
could solve China's economic problem, and the economic problem
is the problem that affects all problems." Not until over a year
later—in 1928, when he was already engaged in promoting rural
reform in southern Kwangtung—did Liang's doubts "for the most
part" disappear.[6]

Viewed in the context of his whole life, the sudden insight Liang
experienced was perhaps the final step in a gradual process—
starting in 1916—of resolving the guilt he felt for opposing his
father's anti-Western traditionalism. But a more immediate factor
was the realization—brought home to him by his own students—of
the enormous attraction communism had for young China. "It was
not really until the Communist party enlightened us that we finally
saw through to the ultimate nature of everything about the Westerners and their whole bag of tricks; afterwards, I had this sudden

5. Liang's first statements of this theory on the unsuitability of Western
institutions to Chinese material and spiritual environment were in [11b]
and [11c].

6. [11a], p. 15.

realization and then sighed deeply that the Western bag of tricks truly could not be used."[7]

Liang saw in the West only the Enlightenment assumption common to both Marx and Smith—that any reform can succeed only if based on material self-interest. But from his perspective, communism was the logical conclusion of Western culture; it explained "all social phenomena" in terms of the individual's material self-interest. Yet the obvious appeal of the Communists and their programs among the young Chinese intelligentsia stimulated his commitment to rural reconstruction. Unless he himself provided the young with a truly satisfactory program of action, they would definitely follow the Communists. The irresponsible, nonrevolutionary KMT, the soulless liberals such as Hu Shih, and the irrelevant conservatives provided no real alternative.[8]

Kwangtung, 1927–1928

In May 1927, Liang finally responded to the standing invitation from the Kwangsi clique militarists to go south. That year, in fact, saw a mass exodus of modern intellectuals from Peking, which was then under the control of the Manchurian warlord, Marshal Chang Tso-lin. Possibly the immediate stimulus for Liang's own departure in May was the execution the previous month of his friend, Li Ta-chao, by Marshal Chang's troops.[9]

Liang and his students first went to Shanghai to meet Ch'en Ming-shu and together they all made an excursion to Hangchow's famous West Lake. Liang then proceeded to Canton for a meeting with Li Chi-shen, at the time a member of the Kuomintang Central Executive Committee, president of the Whampoa Military Academy, and governor of Kwangtung. After meeting with Li, Liang proceeded to a small village near Canton and the family home of his disciple, Huang Ken-yung. He had intended to stay at the Huang's home in Hua hsien for just the summer but ended up remaining there for the rest of 1927.

Liang had no great hopes at first of being able to experiment

7. [11a], p. 12.
8. See [11j], p. 329; [11a], pp. 11–12, 19–21. That Liang saw himself as being in direct competition with the Communists for the souls of China's young intellectuals did not pass unnoticed by later critics. See [250]; [582]; [456]; [402], p. 161; [264], p. 211.
9. [428], pp. 258–260.

with rural reconstruction in Kwangtung. He reasoned that the new
Leninist mold in which the KMT was now cast would not permit
programs that diverged from its own ideology. Li Chi-shen, however, had great faith in Liang. Without his knowledge, Li secured
approval from the central government in Nanking for Liang's appointment to the Kwangtung provincial government. Liang, however, was not yet prepared to come out publicly with a rural reform
program. Nor had he decided on whether to initiate action in
Kwangtung, so he refused the appointment.[10]

Rural discontent. As it turned out, Liang's refusal was
opportune. His extended sojourn in rural Kwangtung allowed him
to see firsthand the Communists' successes in mobilizing the peasantry—an experience that reinforced his conviction that unless his
own efforts at revitalizing China succeeded, victory would go to the
Communists. His actual witnessing of the armed clashes between
the peasant associations organized by the CCP and the local
landlord-controlled militia (*min-t'uan*) strengthened his faith in the
potential of a peasant movement and persuaded him that the future belonged to whomever could harness the peasants' rage and
frustration.[11] "A peasant movement is what China definitely must
have at present. If anyone ignores the peasant movement, then he
does not understand the present situation." Only after the success
of his own "revolutionary" peasant movement—aimed at revitalizing China's ethical society as well as remedying the political and
economic backwardness—"would the other peasant movement be
useless, and only then would it be possible for the Communist party
not to exist."[12]

It was in 1927, too, that Mao Tse-tung was profoundly struck by
the discontent he observed in rural China, and the experience de-

10. [11a], pp. 15–17; [9m], pp. 146–147.
11. [14p], pp. 131–132. P'eng P'ai, the first important Communist to
work with peasant organizations, was the dominant figure in the reorganized Kuomintang Peasant Department, in which Mao Tse-tung was also
active. The peasant associations that he and his followers organized dominated much of eastern Kwangtung for the period before the Canton
uprisings of December 1927.
12. [38], pp. 179–180, 184. Post-1949 attacks on Liang continually point
out that he conceived of his rural reconstruction movement primarily as an
alternative to the Communist movement. See, for example, [296], p. 36;
[173], p. 53; [260], pp. 196–197; [302], p. 79; [590], p. 32; [351], p. 131;
[414], p. 282; [342], p. 177.

termined his future strategies as well. The different reactions of Liang and Mao to the phenomena is revealing. Mao perceived it as a motive force for an armed political movement of spiritual proletarians and immediately set about developing an army.[13] Liang heard it as a call for moral leadership and immediately set about designing a program that would fill the countryside with *chün-tzu*.

Li Chi-shen. In December 1927, General Chang Fak'uei seized Kwangtung in an attempt to overthrow Li Chi-shen. Li, who was in Shanghai at a meeting of the Kuomintang Central Executive Committee, ordered Ch'en Ming-shu to return to Canton and attack Chang. In the meantime, some of Chang's troops joined with Communist organizations in Canton and succeeded in seizing the city and proclaiming the famous Canton Commune. Ch'en eventually crushed the revolt and Li himself returned to Canton in early January.

Li now sought further discussion with Liang, who came forth as a Mencius, a sage with a vision of a good society who promised universal dominion to the power-holder who would put into practice his program of reform. "I hope," Liang said to Li, "that you will be able to open up a viable economic and political path for the Chinese people. . . . How [could you] go about opening up this path for the people? With none other than this so-called rural government of mine!"[14]

The canny militarist was too much of a realist to accept all his scholarly friend's idealistic notions, but Li did "express acceptance" of Liang's hopes for him and gave Liang permission to experiment with rural government in Kwangtung. With this commitment, Liang decided to stay in Kwangtung and to participate officially in the government. He replaced Li as the chairman of the Canton reconstruction governmental committee and presented a proposal for the establishment of a rural government training institute as well as an outline for an experimental plan for rural government.[15]

Liang apparently grew impatient with the slow turning of bureaucratic wheels (the proposal had to be sent to the central government in Nanking, approved, and returned before the

13. The gist of Mao's important writings immediately after his classic 1927 report on the success of the Hunan peasant associations point precisely to the absolute necessity of independent military power. See [424b–c].
14. [11a], pp. 16–17.
15. [375], 13.20 (May 25, 1936); [9m], p. 147.

Kwangtung provincial government could put it into operation). He concluded, therefore, that "the opportune time had not yet arrived." In addition to his innate suspicion of government-sponsored reform, two other factors held him from pursuing a government-run rural program at the time. He had just started working on a systematic formulation of his disjointed ideas on the subject and still had little in the way of specific blueprints for what rural government should be. He had also heard about several other rural reform projects that had started in northern and central China and he wanted to visit these sites before launching his own programs.[16]

In the meantime, Li had offered him the position of Kwangtung commissioner of education. Liang refused and recommended the old classical scholar, Huang Chieh, who did accept. Liang agreed, however, to head the Kwangtung First Provincial Middle School in Canton (the best middle school in the province) in the hope of using it as a testing ground for training workers in rural reform. Hearing that Liang would be in Canton, the Sun Yat-sen University philosophy department tried to recruit Liang back into scholarly life, but Liang refused, insisting, as he often did, that he was no scholar or philosopher.[17]

T'ao Hsing-chih and the Hsiao-chuang Experimental Rural Normal School

Liang left Canton in mid-1928 for a trip to Shanghai and Nanking to visit educational innovators and to gather advice and personnel for his own rural work in Kwangtung.[18] He twice visited

16. [11a], p. 18; [9m], pp. 148–149.
17. He made his first series of public lectures on rural reconstruction in Canton in 1928. [38], p. 2; [636]; [9m], pp. 145–168; [9p], p. 191. Huang (1874–1935), an old classical scholar, had been a member of the revolutionary National Essence Protection Society (Kuo-ts'ui pao-ts'un hui) and the Southern Society (Nan she). See [416]; [107], II, 465–468.
18. In Shanghai he visited Kao Chien-szu, an education specialist who was, for a time, the head of the Kiangsu government and its commissioner of education. He also conferred with Chu Chia-hua, a high-ranking Kuomintang official who was a member of the central government in Nanking and on the National Committee of Reconstruction. [11b], p. 39; [23i], p. 281. He also tried to recruit Li P'u-sheng (later an important Kuomintang leader), who was teaching in Shanghai at the time, to go to Japan for three years to study agricultural economics. Liang promised Li

T'ao Hsing-chih's famous Hsiao-chuang Experimental Rural Normal School (Hsiao-chuang shih-yen hsiang-ts'un shih-fan hsueh-hsiao) outside Nanking. T'ao's was the only rural reform program that ever elicited Liang's unqualified praise and approval. It achieved this rare distinction, of course, by happening to coincide with Liang's own ideas and inclinations. T'ao had reacted in much the same way as Liang to the urban-oriented "book education" system of the early Republic. A disciple of John Dewey, he had worked out a more practical alternative based on the Deweyian concepts of "education is life" and "education is society." T'ao, however, went even further than Dewey, and proclaimed that "life is education" and "society is education."[19]

Like Liang, T'ao believed that the nature of modern Chinese education had alienated the Chinese intelligentsia from the rural masses and left them as parasites unfit to perform any service for society at large. Thus, China needed a new form of education, which would immerse the intellectual in rural life where he could "learn by doing" and transform himself into a new kind of man "with the skills and physique of a peasant . . . the brain of a scientist . . . the interest of an artist . . . and the spirit and enthusiasm of a social reformer." Although T'ao was explicitly a Deweyite, his philosophical roots, like Liang's, were anchored in Wang Yang-ming; Wang's doctrine of "the unity of action and knowledge" was reflected in T'ao's own chosen name, Hsing-chih (action-knowledge).[20]

Since "life was education," there were no formal classes at Hsiao-chuang. The students worked in the fields daily and participated as much as possible in the entire range of village life. They provided for their daily needs through their own physical labor: for example, they raised and prepared their own food and wove their own sandals. Their training was simply to learn how to solve resourcefully the problems of rural life and how to impart this knowledge to the peasants through personal example. The local village school and other institutions established by the students— such as the communal teahouse—were multifunctional centers of political and educational activity. Propaganda and peer-group

---

funding from the Kwangtung provincial government, but Li refused for family reasons. [628].

19. [514], pp. 1–10; [366], pp. 319–320.

20. [184], p. 162; [512], pp. 1–5; [513], p. 182; [9m], pp. 156–157; [421], p. 7.

pressure were applied against such village life vices as gambling, foot-binding, and opium-smoking. Through the students, the peasants learned new organizational forms and political procedures by *doing* them, just as they learned new agricultural techniques by using them. "Learning, teaching, and doing" were all one process at Hsiao-chuang.[21]

Liang returned to the Canton middle school fairly bubbling with enthusiasm for what he had seen:

> What attracted my attention right off was its doctrine—"the unity of teaching, learning, and doing." They believe that the educational theory should be: however life is, so should education be. Therefore, the educational method is: however one does things, so does he learn; and however he learns, so should he teach. In my opinion, this is quite the right way of education.[22]

Liang found all aspects of the Hsiao-chuang experiment congenial to his own ideals; much of T'ao's project, in fact, resembled Liang's own reforms at the Shantung Sixth Middle School. Liang noted with approval that the Hsiao-chuang schools were managed by the students themselves, just as they managed their own lives. The teachers merely served as supervisors and advisors. Students and teachers shared the hard life of the peasants as equals and changed their urban life styles for the rural one. "Their purpose lies in enabling the student to withstand hardships as well as the peasants can, and moreover, to really understand the peasants' problems. So their lives have all been transformed into the life of the common people. They wear short clothing, and often go barefoot like the peasants."[23]

Thus inspired by T'ao's work, Liang immediately set about re-creating his own Kwangtung First Middle School as closely as pos-

---

21. [9m], pp. 157–167; [366], pp. 181–185, 321–322.

22. [9m], p. 157.

23. [9m], p. 166. Hsiao-chuang had other aspects that attracted Liang's attention and which would become important components in his own rural reconstruction program. For example, the school concerns extended to diffusion of agricultural technology as well as organization for community improvements and welfare, such as cooperatives, roads, village unions, and fire departments. [9m], pp. 161–163; [366], pp. 283–296. Possibly the most important aspect of Hsiao-chuang was the stress placed upon local village joint action, promoted through the "center" schools (*chung-hsin*) and tea house.

sible in the image of Hsiao-chuang. First, he reported his decision to the assembled faculty:

We may conclude that this kind of school [Hsiao-chuang] will certainly be effective. The students trained this way will have at least two advantages. The first is ability. [They will] have three kinds of ability:

(a) The ability to do manual labor—[at our school] we do not have any manual labor [to do] and cannot do manual labor.

(b) Intellectual ability—all that they study [at Hsiao-chuang] is real learning. They learn themselves, they act themselves, and so obtain real learning. [I am] afraid that the learning we inject through [our] teaching is not real learning. If we have any intellectual ability, it is false intellectual ability.

(c) The ability to make a communal life [t'uan-t'i sheng-huo]—this refers to their self-management and the students sharing in running school affairs. [At our school] the students and teachers form two classes, a ruling class and a ruled class. This [situation] cannot develop the ability for making a communal life.

The second advantage is a reasonable life. They [at Hsiao-chuang] have made their life the life of the common folk; this is the difference [between them] and us. We! We have neither [real] ability nor democracy. We cannot perform [real service] and yet want to enjoy the aristocratic life. Society's faults come from the school system! My visit to Hsiao-chuang interested me very much. I do not know whether or not our colleagues and classmates cheerfully and voluntarily want to reform our school [along these lines].[24]

Quite possibly the faculty of the First Provincial Middle School was not prepared to "cheerfully and voluntarily" follow Liang's reform plan, but he had already placed many of his friends and students from the North in key positions. Westharp, for instance, was appointed principal of the affiliated normal school, and Huang Chieh was appointed dean of studies. Liang's disciples, Hsu Ming-hung (who had now repented joining the Communists and returned to Liang's fold), Huang Ken-yung, and Chang Shu-chih, were given teaching positions and full authority to innovate.[25]

24. [9m], pp. 167–168. Liang never really acknowledged T'ao's influence, although he professed great admiration and respect for T'ao's dedication and originality. The two men knew each other but never had a close personal relationship. [78].

25. Liang seems to have relied throughout on Huang Chieh and his

Liang set forth a complete reform program, which aimed at training the students "to use the strength of their own minds, ears, eyes, hands, and feet to make their own lives, and to form their own communal life, so that no matter what problems they might face later on, they would be able to find ways of dealing with them independently. . . . The present system just turns the students into incompetent, useless things."[26] All student services, such as school repair, laundry, the canteen and dining halls, were abolished or reduced, and the students and teachers themselves took them over. They cooked, laundered, and repaired for themselves; they organized cooperative stores and class kitchens. Students took over the school's administration, enforced their own disciplinary rules, and established (together with the teachers) a common agreement (*yueh*) for all. The lecture-and-textbook style of education was kept at a minimum; Liang ordered more "active learning" instead of "passively sitting, listening to lectures."

Most significant for Liang's eventual rural-reconstruction formula was his attempt to instill in his students the organizational forms and habits of communal life. Each class constituted a self-sufficient unit under the guidance of a faculty adviser; all matters of discipline, the class-kitchen system, academic work, and so forth were under the jurisdiction of the class unit. This version of Liang's old *chiang-hsueh* concept of the small group banded together for mutual intellectual and moral improvement was built upon the figure of the class director (*pan chu-jen*). The students kept a daily diary of emotional, ethical, and scholastic problems which they submitted to the class director. Thus in touch with his students' inner lives, the director was better equipped to help them.

Finally, Liang made another attempt at promoting a "socialism" of sorts. All able but poor students, and even inferior but "conscientious" poor students, would be exempt from tuition and fees. Their fellow students and teachers would join together to provide for their living expenses.[27]

---

other students to manage the school. He himself did not even move into the school until December 1928 and left for the North two months later. [9n], p. 187; [9m], pp. 145–149; [636].

26. [9n], p. 175.

27. [9n], pp. 176–186. Apparently these reforms were not carried out under Liang's personal supervision (he left Canton in February 1929, just when the reforms went into effect), but by his disciples at the school. Students also did agricultural work, handicrafts, carpentry, and metal work, all for the practical purpose of supporting the school. [636].

On balance, these reforms at the Kwangtung First Provincial Middle School were not informed by Liang's visit to Hsiao-chuang as much as inspired by it; their fundamental direction was the same as his experiment at the Shantung Sixth Provincial Middle School.

Liang Returns North

In February 1929, Liang set out on a tour of rural reform projects in central and northern China. He left Kwangtung with the intention of returning to pursue his rural government training programs there, but perhaps the possibility of remaining in the North was lurking in the back of his mind. Wang Hung-i and his associates had been sending letter after letter urging Liang to return to Peking, where they were establishing a new journal devoted exclusively to discussion of rural reform and village government.[28]

Leaving his disciples behind to carry out his reform plan at the school, Liang and a party of Cantonese officials and intellectuals interested in rural work went first to visit the China Vocational Education Society's (Chung-hua chih-yeh chiao-yü she) project at Hsu-kung-ch'iao in K'un-shan hsien, Kiangsu. Huang Yen-p'ei, who had founded the organization back in 1918, had recently come to the realization that the agricultural specialists trained in urban schools were worthless in the countryside itself.[29] Once accustomed to city life, they were unwilling to work in the fields and had proved utterly ineffective in improving rural productive capacities. Huang's organization was now reorienting their programs toward training the peasants themselves *in situ*—"creating new peasants."

From Hsu-kung-ch'iao Liang went to Ting hsien in Hopei. He had long known of the Mi family's work there, but during the time he had been in Kwangtung, the China Mass Education Movement Association (Chung-hua p'ing-min chiao-yü ts'u-chin hui), led by James Y. C. Yen, had moved into the Mi-sponsored model village

28. For Liang's observations and comments on his trip and the three projects he visited, see [9q]; also [96].

29. Huang Yen-p'ei, long active in educational reform efforts even before the 1911 Revolution, remained active in rural work throughout the 1930s. The project at Hsu-kung-ch'iao was begun by his association in early 1927. Another major project, comprising thirty-eight villages, was started at Huang-hsü in Chiang-ning county at the end of 1929. The association started another project at Shan-jen ch'iao near Soochow in 1931. For a capsule description of these three projects, see [366], pp. 140–157.

of Chai-ch'eng. Yen had expanded the old urban mass-literacy campaigns of the past into a broader program of general rural reconstruction, which included village self-government and agricultural improvement.[30]

From Hopei, Liang traveled into the mountainous province of Shansi, where a rural self-government system had been in operation for years. As soon as Liang arrived in Taiyuan, Governor Yen Hsi-shan, who was resting in his home village to the northeast, wired an invitation to Liang to come and join him for an exchange of views on rural reform. After a few days with Yen, Liang proceeded through the province, visiting some of the more successful village governments and talking with the provincial officials who administered the village self-government program.

Although he was hostile to the bureaucratic centralization thrust of the Shansi system of rural self-government, Liang admitted that it had succeeded in some areas. Thanks to the systematized village system linked by good communications, and the highly developed local militia system, Yen had greatly reduced banditry.

Assessment of Existing Rural Work

In May, after about two months on the road, Liang returned to Peiping to reflect upon what he had seen. In one sense the trip had been personally gratifying and encouraging to him, for it showed him that others, independently and from radically different approaches, were gradually coming around to conclusions similar to his own. Both the mass education leader, Jimmy Yen, and the vocational education leader, Huang Yen-p'ei, had realized, as Liang had, that China *was* its countryside, and had shifted the attention of their respective organizations from the cities to the rural areas. Moreover, they had discovered that their earlier programs—aimed at solving a single problem, such as illiteracy or the lack of vocational skills—were useless by themselves. As a result, to Liang's great happiness, they had all broadened the scope of their programs into general rural reform movements. Thus, Liang returned from his field observations with even greater confidence that he

30. [9q], pp. 224–232; [366], pp. 67–75; [240]; [241]. The Mass Education Movement had already established itself in Chai-ch'eng in 1926 but did not expand its operations to embrace a greater area and more varied programs until James Y. C. Yen returned from a fund-raising trip abroad in 1929.

was on the right track and that it was the only possible means to solving China's problems.

Yet, on the whole, Liang was quite dissatisfied with the rural reconstruction projects he visited. Although he admired the efforts of the workers, he felt basically that the model-village method was hopelessly inadequate. On the other hand, he found the educationalists' approach unrealistic and out of touch with the peasants' actual needs. "The mass education movement has now shifted its attention to the peasants and expanded its content and significance. Naturally this is great progress. I approve of it. Yet the problem of China will not be solved by education or by any kind of social service enterprise." Such efforts did not even come close to solving the basic problems of the countryside—low productivity and poverty. Mass literacy was an expensive proposition, yet it did nothing to alleviate the peasants' problems; it just "harmed the people and wasted money. . . .They [the peasants] are taught to read, then they go do their usual work and forget [what they have learned]. . . . Mass education will be needed in China, but the time has not yet come. Maybe we should wait until the need for it actually arises, and then do it."[31]

Liang was most dissatisfied with the adoption of Western-style bureaucratic and legal systems, especially in Shansi. Other faults Liang found with the projects were seemingly insoluble problems that would bedevil his own efforts as well. For example, the method of concentrating effort on the reform of just one or a few model areas, although a practical and necessary approach that Liang had to resort to himself, was also artificial and grossly inadequate. "How many villages does China have?" Liang asked. Certainly creating a few model areas here and there was not the final answer.

Then there were the problems of funding and staffing. Both personnel and money for even the few existing projects came from the outside. Ting hsien's project received a provincial government subsidy as well as funds and personnel from the Mass Education Association. Huang Yen-p'ei's project was financed and staffed by his own organization. Liang saw two harmful effects in such arrangements. First, the whole program was maintained artificially; once the outside source of trained staff and money was cut off, the projects would cease to exist. Second, they did not sufficiently involve the peasants. "The villagers see public property—either from

31. [9q], pp. 265–266.

the government or another outside source—as something that has nothing to do with them. And because the expenses do not come from their own pockets, they are ignorant of and apathetic toward public affairs."[32]

But the Shansi alternative to private financing—a direct land tax—was even worse. It was still a government-run and -staffed project, with the role of the bureaucracy too large and that of the people too small:

> The more the government does, the more it pushes the people, and the more the people are pushed, the less they will move. . . . This cannot be regarded as self-government. The various [self-government] programs easily lead to abuses because of this. In a word, the official power is too strong and the people too weak. Although there are good policies, the people always end up getting cheated, intentionally or unintentionally.[33]

Because he considered "official" local government as an exploitative alien force, Liang concluded that the land-tax system of financing local government was "the worst method of all. . . . The people are already paying national, provincial, and hsien taxes. Now the village wants to tax them too! How can they go forward to self-government enthusiastically and cooperatively?" Such monies would be better spent, Liang suggested, "by the people themselves for such things as fertilizer to improve productive capacity. Rather than solving the problem of poverty, [this method] increases poverty."[34]

Liang's conclusion was that unless the rural reconstruction and village self-government movement was a mass mobilization of the people by themselves from the grass-roots upward, it would inevitably fail. Moreover, any governmental or official role in the rural movement would inevitably have a deleterious effect. Extend-

32. [9q], p. 234. Huang Yen-p'ei attempted to answer Liang's criticisms a year later by saying that the injection of men and money from the outside was not envisioned as a permanent method, but only an emergency measure, like artificial respiration, to help the patient revive and recover. If the methods experimented with at the projects are effective, then other locations would certainly imitate them, said Huang. Obviously, he had skirted the issue raised by Liang. Even if the methods did prove effective, it would only have been with the aid of trained men and outside funding, which other places would not be able to duplicate. See [318].

33. [9q], pp. 271–272.   34. [9q], pp. 264–265.

ing provincial or hsien bureaucracy downward into the lower levels of rural society was not local self-government, but its exact opposite: bureaucratization, which was, in Liang's view, incompatible with mass mobilization.[35] The keystone of Liang's own concept of rural reconstruction was precisely this: it was to be a movement of *society* not only independent of the government bureaucracy, but in some circumstances a movement *against* bureaucracy. These principles became unalterable tenets throughout his career as a rural reconstruction leader.

After his visit to Shansi, Liang used a vivid simile to describe his concern over governmental interference in rural work:

> The Chinese people may well be compared to beancurd, and the strength of the officials likened to an iron hook. One may take the iron hook and with the best of intentions come to help the beancurd. But no help at all is better [than this kind of help], for once helped, the beancurd will certainly be damaged. Today "reconstruction" [*chien-she*] is a fashionable term in party and government circles. They do not know that the common people fear this word more than anything else. Does this mean that we should not have reconstruction? Naturally not. When [the people themselves] have cultivated the habit and ability of self-government, the great way of government will be opened, and then reconstruction will come naturally. All that is needed will be there.[36]

Perhaps the problem of local leadership was the most crucial, for all the people who might have been capable of generating the kind of spontaneous peasant movement Liang envisioned had left the countryside. "People with money have gone to the cities and foreign concessions. People of ability have left because the local villages cannot support them. Even the good people have left. Thus, if elections were held, the local bullies and bad gentry [*t'u-hao lieh-shen*] would inevitably win and use the position to their own advantage." As for the potential of the young idealistic students as leaders of the rural movement, Liang somehow overlooked their successes in organizing the peasantry during the Northern Expedition. Instead, he insisted that the young intellectuals were too easily disillusioned: "Because the peasants are apathetic, and set in the

35. [9q], pp. 262–263. For Liang Shu-ming's later elaborations of this idea, see [38], pp. 6, 66; [47], pp. 44–50; [11h], pp. 246–248; [14r]; [20], pp. 301–302; [39].

36. [9q], pp. 272–273.

old ways, it is like pouring cold water on the young reformers' heads, and they give up." Liang also noted that young students "easily incur the hatred of the peasants."[37]

Again, Liang offered no answer to the problem of leadership at the time, but certainly his private thoughts must have been on the inspired, robust, cultivated, young *chün-tzu* he would train through the new *chiang-hsueh* tradition he had been developing in Shantung and Kwangtung middle schools. Had not Liang been dreaming for years about how he, the new Confucius, would cultivate the young people, who in turn would save China and the world through a comprehensive program he was yet to work out? Would not such youth be the natural leaders for his newly arrived at rural reconstruction schemes?

The Village Government Group

As events turned out, Liang did not return to Canton, for the ongoing swirl of military-political alliances changed the situation even before his trip was over. Early in 1929, the leading generals in the Kwangsi clique, Pai Ch'ung-hsi and Li Tsung-jen, broke openly with the Nanking government. Liang's supporter, Li Chi-shen, although associated with the Kwangsi group, had not participated in the rebellion. In mid-March, Li went to Nanking, ostensibly to attend the Kuomintang Third National Congress, but in reality to mediate between Chiang and the Southwestern generals. Chiang, however, was not as amenable to mediation as supposed. He placed Li under house arrest on March 21 and kept him there for some time. With his Kwangtung support now gone, Liang was more readily persuaded by Wang Hung-i and his Village Government associates to abandon his plans for Kwangtung and join their rural reform movement in the North.[38]

Much had happened in the northern rural reform movement in the two years Liang had been away. The successes of the Com-

37. [9q], pp. 258–260.
38. [164], I, 197–198; [176], p. 103; [214], pp. 59–63. Li P'u-sheng, who worked with Liang in the period after his return from Kwangtung, felt that Liang would have gone back if Li Chi-shen had remained in power. [628]. Since another of Liang's friends, Ch'en Ming-shu, replaced Li as governor of Kwangtung, Liang probably could have returned if he had not found staying in the North and working with Wang Hung-i's group more attractive.

munist organizers among the peasantry during the Northern Expedition seemed to have drawn the attention of both the northern militarists and the Kuomintang officials to rural problems. As a result, Wang Hung-i and other like-minded men suddenly found a new respect and interest for their village government schemes. This new interest focused especially on the problems of poverty and the absence of a viable local leadership, perhaps because these are the two factors that had contributed most to the Communists' successes.

Feng Yü-hsiang's role. How Liang's rural reconstruction projects eventually ended up in Shantung under the sponsorship of militarist Han Fu-ch'ü is a complicated story. We must start with the burly, reform-minded warlord of China's Northwest, Feng Yü-hsiang. Feng seems to have been something of a major, if shadowy, figure in the emergence of the rural reconstruction movement; various strands of the movement mysteriously converge on the "Christian General's" own person. He was a close friend of T'ao Hsing-chih's and even had a house built for himself at Hsiao-chuang.[39]

By 1927, Feng had rebuilt his People's Army (the Kuominchün, shattered by Chang Tso-lin in 1926) and controlled, through subordinates and allies, all of Honan, Shensi, Kansu, and Suiyuan provinces. When, in that year, he realized how Communist-led peasant organizations were flourishing in his area, he became greatly alarmed. Fear of the strength and impact of these radical mass organizations was at least one of the reasons behind Feng's decision, in June 1929, to ally himself with Chiang Kai-shek against the Communists and the Left-Kuomintang.[40] Although his interest in rural reform preceded this decision, there is little doubt that the success of the CCP-controlled organizations heightened his concern.[41] In August, almost immediately after allying himself with Chiang, Feng launched his own program of rural reconstruction in Honan with the establishment of a rural-work training school and

39. Feng was an early admirer of T'ao's; he possible supplied T'ao's project with arms for the militia. [495], pp. 5–6; [494], pp. 1–2; [366], p. 283; [504], pp. 41–47.

40. [477], pp. 203–232; [467], pp. 28, 30–35; [327], pp. 252–256; [417], pp. 703–795.

41. The report on Feng's rural reconstruction program by one of his secretaries would support such a hypothesis. See [611], p. 523.

two model villages. Marshal Feng's chief subordinate, Han Fu-ch'ü, administered the rural reconstruction program as part of his responsibilities as the governor of Honan.[42]

P'eng Yü-t'ing. Another strand connecting Feng to rural reform was his secretary from 1921 to 1927, P'eng Yü-t'ing. (A young Szechwanese named Teng Hsiao-p'ing was also a colleague of P'eng's in the Kuominchün at the time.) In the fall of 1927, a few months after Feng had opened his rural training school, P'eng was on his way to his home village for the first time in six years to attend his mother's funeral. On reaching Hsiang-yang, Hupei, he discovered that bandits held the towns and villages along the entire route to his home town near Chen-p'ing in southwestern Honan. "I can say that it was the biggest shock of my life," P'eng said of his discovery that his home neighborhood had "become a bandits' domain." But the worst was yet to come. Alarmed by the bandit kidnapping of a person in the next village, the relatives rushed to carry out the funeral before P'eng could get there. For any Chinese, but especially one from the still very traditional gentry class of rural Honan, this was a misfortune of staggering proportions, and "added yet another layer of incensed hatred toward the bandits."[43]

When P'eng finally arrived in his home village, he quickly set out to organize militia in the neighborhood villages and launch a bandit extermination campaign. In the process he launched himself on a new career—that of a rural reconstruction leader. In the summer of 1928, Han Fu-ch'ü's provincial government appointed P'eng as a district chief in his home area.

Like other single-problem-oriented rural workers at the time, P'eng soon learned that the banditry problem he had set out to eliminate was tightly interwoven with a larger rural problem:

> When I first started bandit extermination, I thought to my-self, "If the bandits can be wiped out, the people's troubles will be immediately solved." Who would have thought that after the bandits had been exterminated, there were still more problems! How should agriculture be reformed? How should

---

42. [611], pp. 523–525; [270], pp. 76–80; [269], pp. 252–255; [107], II, 52. Feng Yü-shang designated Han Fu-ch'ü, the civil governor in Honan in 1928, to take charge of supervising the school graduates and their placement as village heads. [611], p. 524.

43. [366], pp. 185–187.

industry be promoted? How should the village economy be adjusted? How should all of society's problems be solved?[44]

Thus, P'eng proceeded to expand his village self-defense work at Chen-p'ing into a broader rural reconstruction program. Other Honanese, such as Liang Chung-hua and Wang I-k'o—both members of Wang Hung-i's Village Government Group—soon joined P'eng in his work.[45]

The linking together of Wang Hung-i's and Feng Yü-hsiang's respective northeastern and northwestern village government movements came in the same year, when Feng invited Wang to meet with him to discuss the question. Earlier, Wang had also visited the other power-holder in the Northwest, Yen Hsi-shan. Then, in January 1929, Wang founded the periodical *Village Government Monthly* (*Ts'un-chih yueh-k'an*) in Peiping.[46] It was one of the first of the many rural reform journals that would appear in the following decade.

The Honan Village Government Academy. By the time Liang arrived back in Peiping in May 1929, Feng Yü-hsiang and Han Fu-ch'ü had given a commission to Wang Hung-i, P'eng Yü-t'ing, and Liang Chung-hua, to set up an institute devoted to research on rural problems and the training of young rural reconstruction workers. They in turn persuaded Liang Shu-ming to join them in the undertaking, and he immediately proceeded to write a tract explaining and advertising its purposes.[47] In October 1929, the doors of the Honan Village Government Academy were officially opened. It was located at Pai-ch'üan, Hui hsien, in the extreme northern part of Honan, sandwiched between Hopei and Shantung on the east and the dusty loess hills of Shansi on the west.

First Formulation of Rural Reconstruction Theory, 1929

After October 1929, Liang divided his time between the academy in Honan and the Peking offices of the *Village Government Monthly*.

44. [366], p. 188.
45. For a description of P'eng's program and its development, see [366], pp. 183–218; [336]; [562], p. 2.
46. [557], p. 1; [13], p. 31; [11j]; [473], p. 1.
47. [11a], pp. 18–19; [9r]; [38], pp. 1, 346; [472], pp. 1–2.

His lectures at the academy and his writings in Peking afforded
him an opportunity to begin the systematic formulation of his ideas
on rural reform, an enterprise that would occupy his attention for
the next eight years.[48] He first presented the fundamentals of the
rural reconstruction idea to the public that fall in his tract on the
purposes and principles of the Honan Village Government
Academy.[49]

"Chinese society," the piece began, "is a village society. The entity
known as China is nothing more than three hundred thousand
villages." Although some villages still existed in the West, it was not
such a society. From this statement Liang explained his ideas on the
two contrasting cultures, which had been determined historically
by their underlying attitudes. Because Western culture originated
in an attitude of struggle, well-defined, organized groups (classes)
arose as instruments for struggle against other groups. This naturally evolved into capitalism, which at a higher stage of its development produced imperialism. China was a pacific, dispersed society without classes or nonkin organizational forms or strength, for it
lacked the attitude and social structures that produced classes.
China had never even been a nation in the Western sense. Thus, all
Western institutions, which had developed naturally and historically from Western culture, were basically unsuitable for China.

Identifying, as he always did, the practical with the prescriptive,
Liang then argued that China neither *could* nor *should* become a
"modern nation." It could not for two reasons: economic imperialism would not permit the development of Chinese industry
and capitalism; and the institutions and habits of urban industrial
society were incompatible with the spirit of the Chinese people.
China should not take the path of the Western nations because it
would lead to imperialism, class war, economic inequality, and a
grotesque overdevelopment of industrialized cities. But most important, the spirit of the Chinese people was a treasure to be pre-
served. It had the potential for altering the entire world in the
future. To seek to be an aggressive power and so lose this spirit
would "truly be a case of falling from the heights into the dark

48. Liang seems to have spent little time at the academy. He was in
Peiping during most of 1929–1930. See [14a], p. 34; [38], pp. 106, 321;
[11e], p. 177; [8], p. 1. In February 1930, he began writing what was to be
his major work on rural reconstruction, and which he would not complete
until seven years later. [38], pp. 1–2.
49. [9r].

depths." The Chinese should realize that "the strengths of the West are not necessarily good and our weaknesses are not necessarily bad."

Socialization and democratization. China's material inferiority and lack of social organization can be corrected, Liang claimed, through democratization (*min-chu-hua*) and socialization (*she-hui-hua*)—the concepts that replaced science and democracy as his cultural palliative. He stressed the advantages of China's "poor and blank" state in accomplishing this economic and political transformation. Western democracy had achieved individual freedom and civil rights, but it was not truly democratic, Liang pointed out, because of the economic inequities inherent in its capitalistic production modes. "We can socialize both production and distribution simultaneously and so achieve true democracy. Is this not better than what the Westerners [now] have?"

The combination of these two processes of democratization and socialization was rural reconstruction. The villages must first be collectivized economically in order to form the economic basis for a new organization of society. This reorganization would increase production as well. After such grass-roots reorganization was complete, the same processes would be carried out on ever higher levels until the whole nation was socialized and democratized. The opposite—reform from the top—was "like building castles in the air," Liang said.

Finally Liang argued that rural reconstruction was already commonly recognized as the only way for China to develop. He referred to recent rural reform efforts by educationalists (the Mass Education Movement and the Vocational Education Association) and by KMT leaders. This proved, claimed Liang, that "everyone's thinking is moving in the same direction simultaneously."

In July 1930, Liang lost one of his staunchest supporters with the death of Wang Hung-i. Due to his friend's failing health, Liang had already taken over the editorship of the *Village Government Monthly*.[50] He subsequently launched a second journal, *Rural Reconstruction (Hsiang-ts'un chien-she)*.[51] These journals became the major

50. [533b]; [11j]; [11a], pp. 15–23; [375] 13.20 (May 25, 1936); [8].

51. *Hsiang-ts'un chien-she* was first published in Peiping in January 1931; later the publication was moved to Tsou-p'ing, where it continued until the Japanese invasion in 1937. *Ts'un-chih* changed from a monthly to a biweekly in August 1930; it was issued irregularly after June 1931. Its last

forum for discussion of rural reconstruction in the 1930s. Liang's aim was to promote a kind of national movement through them and join together all the varied programs that had already emerged and would continue to spring up in ever increasing numbers in the coming decade. Through these journals and his many books, pamphlets, and articles, he would gradually emerge as the dominant theoretician of the rural reconstruction idea.

The Shantung Rural Reconstruction Institute. Liang had expected to continue his work from the base in Honan, but the kaleidoscopic world of warlord politics again took matters out of his hands. The conflict that had been brewing since the spring of 1929 between Feng Yü-hsiang and Chiang Kai-shek burst into open war in the spring and summer of 1930. Feng's prospects were first dimmed by the defection of two of his chief subordinates (including Han Fu-ch'ü) and then utterly destroyed when the "Young Marshal" of Manchuria, Chang Hsueh-liang (the son of his old foe, Chang Tso-lin), joined the battle against him in September. Chiang's troops immediately occupied the cities of Honan, bringing to an end Feng's last bid for power in North China. When Chiang's troops entered Kaifeng, the capital of Honan, in October, one of their first acts was to close down the Honan Village Government Academy.[52] All was not lost for Liang's project, however. Han Fu-ch'ü, awarded control of Shantung for his timely sellout, had always been a strong supporter of the academy while he was governor of Honan. Upon ensconcing himself in his new dominions in the east, he immediately cabled Liang an invitation to move the academy to Shantung. Before October was over, Liang was in Tsinan discussing the details. By November they had settled on a site.[53] For the next eight years, Liang and his Shantung Rural Reconstruction Institute would be paramount among several attempts to find a non-Communist alternative to the KMT blueprint for China.

---

issue appeared on Aug. 1, 1933. The reason given for ceasing publication was lack of personnel and financial support.

52. [533c].

53. [533d]; [472], pp. 1–2; [204]; [13], p. 31; [533b]; [11h], p. 224.

CHAPTER VIII

Chinese and Western Cultures: Part Two

In a profluence of some six books and hundreds of articles between 1930 and 1949, Liang formulated an expanded culture theory that was more complex, intricate, and detailed than he had written in *Eastern and Western Cultures*. A casual reading through this mass of ratiocinations would give the impression that Liang had totally abandoned his cultural theory of the early 1920s; gone were the metahistorical continuum, Wei-shih metaphysics, India, intuition, Vitalism, and *jen*. Western thinkers and their ideas played no role. In their place were new key terms and concepts. Closer scrutiny, however, reveals not a denial and demission of the message he had conveyed in *Eastern and Western Cultures*, but rather an elaboration and amplification of it.

If the content was the same, the whole approach and points of analytical emphasis had shifted from philosophy to sociology and history. Society and its structures had been neglected in past attempts to define Chinese culture, Liang explained.[1] Indeed, this second version of his cultural theory might be dubbed "Chinese and Western Cultures and their Societies." Chinese culture, Liang pointed out, has been something historically unique: a *sui generis* way of life that has lasted longer, spread farther, assimilated more people, and shaped more neighboring cultures than any other. What has been the essential core of such awesome power?[2]

---

1. [86], p. 115; [38], pp. 326–327. Between the May Fourth era and the 1930s, Marxism emerged as the dominant intellectual influence in the Chinese intellectual world. In a kind of inverse way, Liang was a bellwether for this general trend toward sociological historicism.

2. [86], pp. 2–4, 75, 221; [38], pp. 20, 39–43; [10]; [74]; [49]. The ideas discussed in this chapter appear in one form or another in most of Liang's writings between 1930 and 1949. The most systematic expositions appear in [86], [38], and [11]. A synopsis of Liang's second theory of Chinese culture appeared in a 1964 Taiwan publication under a pseudonym, no

Explication of Occidental Society

To arrive at an answer, Liang systematically compared Chinese and Western social development. Religion was the great historical watershed that set the two off on different paths. Liang would have agreed with such cultural conservatives as T.S. Eliot that the beginning of *any* human culture is dependent upon and inseparable from religion.[3] But Western religion—because of its strictly organized, disciplined form—created the "habit" of corporate life, which then provided the basis for all later political, social, and economic organization.[4] Constant competition and struggle among corporate groups forced their internal cohesion to become extremely strong, which in turn obliterated the individual. On a large scale, this became the nature of the nation-state, the ultimate Western corporate group.[5] Liang claimed that this totalitarian corporate life and the medieval asceticism enforced by religion eventually induced a violent reaction, which took the form of individualism, democracy, and hedonism.[6]

Liang's general analysis of the evolution of Western society was actually quasi-Marxist. The dynamic of Occidental history, he wrote, has been dialectic struggle among groups formed along economic lines. The state has been simply an instrument of the ruling class.[7] And Western history has been a story of struggle, competition, and antagonism among individuals, classes, and nations. In the resulting social changes, the superstructure of political forms, religion, and culture has followed the evolution of modes of production. Liang was, in fact, totally in agreement with historical materialism.

> Marx's explanation of history relies on mechanistic force. . . .
> I believe that Marx's employment of the mechanistic viewpoint to explain social changes and social evolution is suitable for Europe. This is because [when] human consciousness is in the blind service of life, then economic necessity

---

doubt by one of Liang's students who wished to carry on his teacher's message without alerting the KMT (Liang was still officially a non-person in Taiwan). See [443a].

3. [234], p. 47; [86], p. 98; [55].
4. [86], pp. 51, 55, 75, 306, 318; [25], p. 62; [38], p. 23; [55]; [32]; [21].
5. [86], pp. 19, 62, 223–224; [16]; [42n], p. 65; [14r]; [55].
6. [86], pp. 46, 91–92, 126, 136, 236, 301; [9k], pp. 138–139; [14k]; [38], pp. 23, 118; [25], p. 62; [11b], pp. 40–42; [11c], p. 119; [47], p. 61; [32]; [57].
7. [86], pp. 27, 143, 146, 155, 163, 168, 174–175, 183–185, 197; [11d], pp. 173–176; [11g], p. 207; [55]; [38], pp. 2, 88; [16].

operates mechanically. If [one] can grasp the economic mainsprings [of society], then deducing [that society's] inevitable development is possible. Because of this, historical materialism is quite reasonable.[8]

As he had done in *Eastern and Western Cultures*, Liang still characterized Western society as one that operated completely according to the principle of mechanistic calculation of profit and loss. Before the Enlightenment, the ledger had dealt with spiritual concerns: gain or loss of heaven or the grace of God's aid. Later the calculations had become economic and hedonistic. The principle was identical. Throughout history, Westerners have been ruled by one external alien force or another—by God through priests or by the state through law—and have made their calculations accordingly. Through the struggle and interplay between individual and individual, individual and group, and class and class, a rigidly legalistic concept of "rights" had emerged. As a consequence bonds do not exist among people except in legal form.[9] The other result of the Westerner's externally focused attention and demand for satisfaction is modern science.

China: The Death of Religion

Why did China not develop in this normal pattern? Chinese culture, too, had been born of a religion—one that had provided the supporting ideology for the feudalism of the Shang and early Chou dynasties. Yet the early Chinese sages—especially the Duke of Chou and Confucius—were men of extraordinary insight. Realizing that religion was an alienation of the individual from his essence, they began the process of replacing it with pure ethics. People had to rely upon themselves, not some external force, to maintain their humanity. As a consequence, the Chinese produced no great religions and—extremely crucial for the nature of their culture—developed no habit of corporate life or extra-familial collectives.[10]

8. [11d], pp. 146–147.
9. [14k]; [38], pp. 23–32, 65, 114–118, 140; [11c], pp. 119, 125; [47], pp. 9, 32, 61; [86], pp. 18, 65–69, 91–92, 205–210, 267, 285, 290, 301–306; [55]; [57].
10. [86], pp. 2–3, 7–8, 16–18, 49, 66–67, 70–73, 78, 84–85, 98, 134, 170–175, 185, 220–221, 262, 289–292, 329–333; [11b], pp. 47–49; [11c], p. 131; [11d], pp. 170–175; [25], pp. 47–50; [38], pp. 34–43, 50–56; [14k]; [14r]; [21]; [29]; [23c].

At the end of the Chou, China was still following the normal course of societal development. It was a feudal society made up of two mutually antagonistic classes—serfs and aristocrats. Its social order was maintained by brute force, and the *Weltanschauung* of the time was tending toward the production of scientific thought. During the Warring States period, it produced competing nation-states of the modern sort; at the same time, however, the "gentleman" or "scholar" class (*shih*) was bearing forward the sage's discovery— rationality (*li-hsing*). Neither aristocrats nor serfs, these unattached intellectuals had no fixed economic position in society. They respected neither the aristocrats' hereditary right to rule nor their military power. They themselves were qualified to hold political office but did not necessarily do so. Because of them, the old feudalism broke down (land was now on the free market), yet no new bourgeois class emerged to replace it. Chinese society then entered into two thousand years of circular stagnation: not quite forming classes, but not achieving economic equality either; not quite forming a nation, but maintaining its integrity as a cultural entity; not quite realizing the ideals of Confucius, but unable to abandon them. As Liang had described in his first theory, China had been in a kind of limbo, its natural development set awry by the sages' premature leap of consciousness.[11]

Because of *li-hsing*, there were no fixed hereditary aristocracy and no primogeniture, but there was high social mobility in the rural economy and through the examination system. Instead of a class society, Liang insisted, China produced an "occupationally differentiated" (*chih-yeh fen-t'u*) society. Instead of a legalistic society based on force, China had a society based upon ethics and morality (*lun-li pen-wei she-hui*).[12]

Because there were no corporate bodies and classes, China never became a real nation-state. The government has been a do-nothing entity that has merely collected taxes and occasionally used force to maintain order in the face of external or internal disorder. In times of peace, however, the ethical system itself, not military force or the threat of it, has maintained the social order. In contrast to Western

11. [86], pp. 2, 13, 23–24, 32, 62, 184–185, 207, 223–224, 254, 298–302, 321–322, 329; [11b], p. 42; [11d], pp. 170–176; [25], p. 47; [38], pp. 41–61, 77–78; [57].
12. [86], pp. 18, 49, 84–85, 118, 159, 185, 254, 321–322; [38], pp. 23–29, 47, 70, 77–78, 184, 197, 394; [11b], p. 28; [11d], pp. 170–175; [9d], pp. 56–57; [42a], p. 10; [42e], pp. 26–28; [24]; [23f], pp. 257–258; [16]; [14j].

society, in which individual self-interest and its attendant rights have required law backed up by armed force, Chinese society has been held together through inner discipline and ethical consciousness.

Liang's tendency to idealize the social mobility of traditional society again emerged. According to his reasoning, since anyone could take the examinations, and since there were no legal or hereditary barriers to mobility (except for the imperial household—hardly a "class"), there were no hereditary ruling classes.[13] He did not dismiss out of hand the CCP's division of rural society into classes according to land holding. He admitted that such a theory was "not unreasonable"; nevertheless, he concluded that the majority of the population (who were neither landlords nor tenants) have not belonged to clearly differentiated classes of the kind that have existed in Western society (master-slave, noble-serf, bourgeois-proletariat). After all, Liang pointed out, there had been countless rebellions and many changes in dynasty, but not one genuine revolution.

Obviously, the thrust of Liang's theory was to exempt China from Marxian analysis. It was not overly difficult for him to demonstrate that China does indeed defy attempts to put it into the conventional analytical framework. Over the two thousand years since the Ch'in dynasty, Chinese society had changed of course, but the basic modes and relations of production had not changed that much. Liang mocked the determined 1930s efforts of the social historians to force the facts of Chinese history into their Marxist Procrustean bed. The question was not, Liang argued, whether the prerequisites for capitalism had existed in traditional China; he admitted that the sprouts of capitalism, democracy, science, and all other "Western" products had existed, but the crucial and unanswerable question was why for two thousand years they had remained only sprouts. Since China's development was not in accordance with the Marxist normative stages of societal development, some Marxists turned to the absurd category of an "Oriental mode of production" in order to explain it. Others went the equally awkward way of designating the bulk of Chinese history as "semi-capitalist" or "semi-feudal." "It seems that anything one says about China must be preceded by the prefix 'semi-,' " Liang chortled.[14] All these manifestly inadequate efforts, he felt, proved his point. Ev-

13. [38], pp. 75–76, 340–341; [57]; [16].
14. [11d], pp. 142–150; [11e], pp. 177–184; [47], pp. 132–135; [86]; pp. 175–177; [38], pp. 357–359; [16].

erything in China is such a "riddle" precisely because Chinese society has continually striven to realize its potential while lacking the material prerequisites necessary for the task. Confucianism has been like a religion yet not a religion; China has been like a nation yet not quite one; Chinese society has had a tendency toward the formation of classes yet never quite produced them.[15]

The difference between Chinese and Western societies was not simply the difference between traditional and modern societies, Liang inferred; rather, the difference rested in the model of humankind upon which each had been built.[16] Having yet to evolve "reason" (*li-hsing*), the Occidentals' actions are determined solely by material self-interest. Their lives consist only of interaction between the body's demands and the external physical and human environment. Since in contrast, Chinese society is based upon truly human reason, so all Western theories and modes of analysis are inappropriate. For Liang, *Homo economicus* had been extinct in China for over two thousand years, so what the likes of Adam Smith and Karl Marx had to say about society were equally irrelevant.

Since Westerners have taken for granted that all humans are capable only of acting in their own self-interest, they naturally have created political systems in which selfish interests are counterpoised against other selfish interests. At the core of constitutionalism and liberal democracy are "checks and balances" and "rule by law." But Confucius had seen that humans are capable of ethically motivated action. He had placed responsibility upon the individual's moral faculty and specifically not relied on any external force—laws or majorities—to insure proper behavior.[17] (Liang was, of course, resurrecting the old "rule by man versus rule by law" debate of the late Ch'ing.) Such reasoning prompted Liang to oppose Chinese constitutionalism, despite his own "liberal" political position and activities—an incongruity that paralleled his father's seemingly contradictory attitude toward the 1898 reforms.

Liang attempted to explain the irrelevance to China of Occidental political and social institutions and thought by developing further an idea he had vaguely suggested in his first book—that *in*

15. [86]; pp. 27–42, 178–186; [38], p. 41; [11c], p. 119; [11d], pp. 170–175; [9r], p. 275.
16. [86], pp. 27–40, 197, 284–285, 290–291.
17. [11b], p. 31; [11c], pp. 117, 125; [86], pp. 83–86, 122, 132–136, 205–210; [38], pp. 114–118, 182–188; [47], p. 9; [14r]; [16].

the West human consciousness is determined by social existence, but *in China* consciousness transcends existence. He now clearly implied that in China the superstructure had determined the economic substructure, while in the West the substructure had determined the superstructure. Some of the cognitive modes he used to express this idea come quite close to the old "spiritual versus material cultures" rigmarole. After Confucius, Chinese culture and society developed "from the mind to the body," "from consciousness to matter," or "from the higher plane to the lower"; in the West, the opposite was true. The Occident have a "corporal" culture determined by physical factors and forces; Chinese culture is determined by moral and mental ones. Precisely because Western social and cultural development is "unconscious," objective laws of development can be deduced; in China this is impossible.[18]

Human Culture and *Li-hsing*

The keystone of Liang's second cultural theory is the concept *li-hsing*—a word certainly not translatable by the usual English equivalent "reason," except perhaps as Coleridge distinguished it from "rationality." Similar to other vague terms that served as cornerstones in the thought of Liang's spiritual brothers—Matthew Arnold's "culture," Cardinal Newman's "illative sense," or Gandhi's "truth"—*li-hsing* became the functional equivalent of *jen* and intuition in *Eastern and Western Cultures.*[19]

Liang's second theory has none of the systematic quality of his first; its essence lies in subtle implication and oracular innuendo. Liang did not substitute another specific system for the former West-China-India continuum; rather, he implied the existence of a

18. [86], pp. 183–185, 210, 267, 293; [9r], pp. 275, 276; [9k], pp. 138–140; [16].

19. The earliest public reference Liang made to *li-hsing* (and his first published adumbration of his new cultural theory) was in the second half of 1930, so he must have formulated the concept sometime during late 1929 and early 1930 while he was teaching at the Honan Village Government Academy. [11c], pp. 137–138; [11d]. Liang had often used the term *li-hsing* before, but always in the conventional sense meaning "power of reason," or "rationality." The word itself is a Japanese neologism used to translate the Western term "rationality" or "reason" and was not used extensively in Chinese until the early twentieth century. For examples of Liang's previous use of *li-hsing*, see [4], pp. 33, 45, 75, 76, 79, 173; [9k], p. 133.

grand cosmological evolutionary plan. The "ten-thousand things" were evolving upward by their very nature into more complex and higher forms. Inherent in them is a tendency toward *li-hsing*, which runs through and directs this ongoing advance. At the level of vertebrates, a tendency toward reason in the sense of intellect (*li-chih*) was already present; even farther removed from the lower forms of life, the higher primates had "sproutings" of this capacity. With *Homo sapiens*, true intellect appeared. It is this faculty of reasoning which distinguishes people from animals because it separates human consciousness from concrete physical things: people can think abstractly, analyze, deduce, and invent. This ability to transcend one's biological self and physical environment is "the great liberation of life."[20] Yet there is still a gulf between this animal with intellect and the true human. Intellect does indeed mark humans from beasts and is a prerequisite for *li-hsing*, but "while the two are intimately and inseparably connected" they are distinct faculties. "For example, in mathematics, the mind that does the calculating is intellect, while the mind that seeks accuracy [in calculating] is *li-hsing*."[21] The latter, Liang implied, is the true essence of humanity, the ultimate product of the evolutionary vital force.

At one point Liang explained *li-hsing*'s relationship to intellect with the *t'i-yung* formula: "*Li-hsing* is life itself; it is essence [*t'i*]. Intellect is a tool for [the maintenance of] life; it is utility [*yung*]."[22] Liang came quite close to implying that intellect without *li-hsing* is simply a higher form of animal life; it lacks the moral capacity that distinguishes true humanity. He described *li-hsing* as "the normative sense that directs moral action . . . the sense of right and wrong which makes man human." Humans are not animals precisely because they can achieve this "sphere of disinterestedness" or "impersonal feeling" which transcends biological instinct or self-interest; it is "liberation from instinct."[23] Obviously, *li-hsing* is that capacity for "action without ulterior motive," which Liang described in his first book as stemming from intuition and the essence of *jen*.

As in his first theory, Liang was somewhat vague about specific behavioral standards. (This is because, one surmises, fixed objective standards are the apotheosis of true morality.) He did say that *li-hsing* is embodied in Confucian rites and etiquette (*li*), and con-

---

20. [14i], pp. 75–77.   21. [86], p. 128.   22. [30].
23. [86], pp. 128–132, 133, 333; see also pp. 129, 185, 247, 260, 287, 321.

sists of extending familial emotions to all social relationships, emphasizing the "other person," and putting priority upon fulfillment of ethical obligations.[24] Yielding (*jang*) and self-abnegation are the heart of *li-hsing*'s manifestations. As humans are born only with the potential for *li-hsing*, the essence of Chinese culture lies in the process by which this potential is cultivated in the individual. The heart of culture is ethical education (*chiao-hua*).

In the final analysis, it was the Chinese sages' premature discovery of *li-hsing* that foreordained all differences between Chinese and Western cultures. Both had cultivated reason and intellect to a degree, but in the West, intellect was strong and well developed, while reason was "shallow" and "weak"; in Chinese culture, the opposite was true.[25] Western cultivation of intellect eventually produced science, while in China it remained only a latent tendency. Just as Confucius' replacement of religion with pure ethics had a permanent effect upon China's history and society, so the West's retention of religion determined its particular path. When religion collapsed under the onslaught of critical rationalism, legal codes and bureaucracies arose to maintain social order and to define the relationships between the individual and group and between individual and individual. In China, ethical relationships, inner discipline, customs, and traditions have served to maintain social order. In ordinary times, government has had no real role in the process.

Another dichotomy Liang employed to express the fundamental Sino-Western divergence was between the basic Western cultural point of departure—"externally directed force" (*hsiang-wai yung-li*)—and the Chinese one—"inwardly directed force" (*hsiang-nei yung-li*).[26] Liang set up many other such dichotomies (most of them similar to those drawn by non-Chinese cultural conservatives such as the Slavophiles or Gandhi): law versus custom and mores (*li-su*); political group versus family; individual versus family; rights versus duties; physical force versus moral force; and personal desires versus ethical obligation.[27] All are the result of *li-hsing*.

Liang perceived the modernization process as developing from

24. [86], p. 254.
25. [86], pp. 129, 289–293; [38], pp. 39–43; [11d], pp. 174–175; [23c], p. 79; [47], p. 61.
26. [38], pp. 35–38, 41, 61, 65, 114, 118, 140; [11c], pp. 119, 125, 131; [11d], p. 147; [86], p. 267; [47], pp. 9, 61, 147; [23b], p. 31; [57].
27. [38], pp. 37–38, 41, 61, 140; [11c], p. 131; [86], pp. 84–85, 98, 185, 262; [55]; [57].

Western cultural characteristics. China's own culture had prevented that process from coming about. Therefore, *li-hsing* was at
once China's greatest achievement and its greatest fault:

> The greatness of China is only the greatness of human rea-
> son; [its faults are only the faults of the premature rise of
> reason and the prematurity of its cultural maturation] . . . .
> The spirit of the Chinese people, in my understanding, lies in
> "the rationality of humankind." I often say that if the Chinese
> have not lived for several thousand years in vain, if the
> Chinese have made any contribution at all, then it is that they
> first understood why humankind is human. That is to say, the
> Chinese ancients precociously understood humankind . . .
> and the spirit of the Chinese people in its entirety is the bring-
> ing into play this *li-hsing*.[28]

Again, as in the first theory, the abortive leap in the normal
evolutionary process was the root of all China's difficulties; without
first laying the necessary material foundation for realizing its
ideals, Chinese culture had moved onto a higher level from which it
could not retreat.

> Humans are rational animals, but reason in humankind must
> develop gradually. . . . Speaking in terms of the life of a soci-
> ety, it must slowly develop following economic development
> and other cultural conditions. To say that, in Chinese society,
> reason developed prematurely means that the proper time
> had not yet arrived. [Material] conditions were still insuffi-
> cient.[29]

Thus in both of his schematizations of the history of culture,
Liang implied that because of the great insight of its early sages,
Chinese culture had achieved human ethical perfection while
bypassing the basic task of mastering the physical environment. It
was as if the "literary intellectuals" whom C. P. Snow decried appeared in China some three thousand years ago and, before the
people had developed the capacity to completely satisfy their primal needs, turned the direction of their whole culture toward—to
use Coleridge's famous definition of true culture—"the harmonious development of those qualities and faculties that characterize
our humanity." Although they evolved a more human existence
than the West evolved, they have suffered materially because of it.

28. [23c], pp. 92–93.   29. [38], p. 39.

The second formulation of Liang's theory also shows how the universal absolute heavenly principles (expressed in human beings by intuition—*jen* and *li-hsing*) can be universal to humankind and still be particularly Chinese. Chinese culture is simply the development of a universal and eventually realizable human potential. He accorded China a privileged role in the total cosmic-historical process. A historical community, the Chinese people are unique in history in having a cultural and spiritual life that represents the culmination of human moral possibilities. Underneath the corruption of externals this moral community still lives in the present, at least in the villages.

In essence, Liang was expressing the traditional Chinese attitude toward their culture; it was not Chinese culture, but literally the *only truly human* culture—a way of life valid for all people for all time. His attitude toward the West was virtually the same as the anti-Western nineteenth-century Chinese conservatives': Western technology might indeed be resorted to; the important thing was that eventually the Western barbarians *would* realize the superiority of the Chinese way and adopt it.

Yet a deep gulf separated Liang from these traditional Chinese conservatives: they were sure of what they meant by Chinese culture; they could refer to specific political and social institutions, definable codes of conduct, a particular literary and artistic heritage, and certain native customs and usages. They were, in other words, quite happy to accept yesterday as Chinese culture. Liang, in his first book, had already disowned historical Chinese culture. In this second formulation, he again disassociated historical Chinese culture and society, especially that of the most recent centuries, from his own concept of true Chinese culture. Just exactly when degeneration commenced (from Chinese culture's very inception?), Liang never quite said. Regarding the past few centuries, however, he was unequivocal:

> By the time of the Ch'ing dynasty, as I have often said, Chinese culture was superficially stupendous, glorious, elegant, uniform, and in perfect order. Yet its internal spirit was completely empty and decayed. Its surface was a dead varnished shell; inside, it was already utterly rotten. . . . Take a look at the educated class [*shih*] who represented the Chinese spirit. By the Ch'ing, they were unbelievably corrupt. They worshiped the god of literature and the god of war; they promoted the reading of [books based on superstition and

greed]. . . . This whole line was the thing most discordant with
the spirit of the ancient Chinese. The Chinese ancients were,
above all else, against greed and superstition, and yet [this
stuff] was done by combining greed and superstition. So it was
the diametric opposite [of the spirit of the ancients]. By this
period Chinese culture was withered up, rotten, empty, and
hollow on the inside.[30]

Even the doctrines of Confucius and his methods of moral education had become empty formalisms. Like his father, Liang never
lost his loathing of scholarship for its own sake:

The Ch'ing dynasty caused the whole empire to do eight-
legged essays, established a unified orthodoxy according to
Chu [Hsi's] notes [on the Classics] and made the writings of
Confucius and Mencius into literary playthings. The scholarly
community took the study of terminology and texts as their
[primary] task and seldom touched upon the principles [of the
terms and texts]. So, "the study of human life" in higher education turned increasingly inflexible, formalistic, and rotten
until it became nothing but a corpse. At the same time, the
more stern and severe the ethical codes [li-chiao] became, the
more the true meaning of human feelings [jen-ch'ing] declined
and weakened, so that in ordinary society, this ethical education, too, became formalistic and had little vitality.[31]

Its very prematurity had doomed Chinese culture to failure in
completely realizing itself, and, as time went on, those social mores
and institutions based upon reason had become stultified and
"mechanized." Although originally the diametric opposite of religion and law, they had become a means to social control similar to
that in other societies.

Their parochial narrow-mindedness was no less than that of a
religion; their inflexible ruthless cruelty was greater than that
of law. For instance, according to Chinese mores, a child
should be filial and a wife should be chaste. Originally, as
personally self-initiated behavior, it was truly a lofty spirit . . .
but later . . . [the mores and traditions] changed into methods
of maintaining social order. By that time the original spirit
and significance were lost completely, and they resulted in

30. [38], p. 137; see also [86], pp. 299–300; [23c], p. 75.
31. [11h], p. 251.

becoming merely means—formalized, withered, and without zest. At the same time they became extremely intractable, inflexible, and strict.[32]

At times, Liang suggested that the "ideals [of Chinese culture] had always far exceeded the objective realities and had the fault of being unrealistic. . . . Thought was often very far from the actual state [of society], and so was self-contradictory." As he had suggested in *Eastern and Western Cultures*, Liang claimed that China had hovered between the two levels of human development unable to succeed in either. All of China's past achievements "can only be considered a mere shadow of the culture of the second level. Because economic development was insufficient, it really had no hope of successfully becoming the culture of the second level."[33] Well, could not China have just returned to the culture of the first level?

> It could not do that either. Going from the second [level of human culture] back to the first is going from rationality back to biological [corporal culture], substituting the external use of strength for the internal use of strength. . . . This would be a regression in Chinese history; it could not return to a state untempered by reason. . . . It could not advance forward, nor could it retreat. It could only go round and round in hesitation.[34]

That Liang detached his own version of the sages' message from the historical Confucianism does not, however, negate his authenticity; like many generations of sincere Confucians before him, Liang was attempting to go back to the essence, the original Confucianism, and, in the process, was discarding its accidental historical encrustations and baggage.

The Future of China and Humanity

Liang's second theory, then, set up the same dilemma that *Eastern and Western Cultures* had: China had to imitate the West in order to survive, and yet preserve its true culture. In this second version, however, the terms "scientific technology" and "group organization" replaced science and democracy as the mandatory imports. China's most serious problem in meeting the modern challenge was

32. [38], p. 61.   33. [38], pp. 77–78; [86], p. 295.
34. [86], p. 295.

its lack of the forms, habits, and mentality of collective life.[35] Echoing Sun Yat-sen, Liang described Chinese society as diffuse, disorganized, and completely lacking in a tradition of organizational discipline or cooperation.[36] Since ethics has always been a private matter, there has been no concept of public morality or spirit of the commonweal.[37]

In contrast to his pronouncements in *Eastern and Western Cultures*, Liang marshaled no detailed arguments for the imminent Sinification of the West. Rather, he simply assumed that it *must* change. The "post-modern era" is the "great turning point in human history, one from which no country can escape." The evolution of "objective realities" is forcing Western culture to change its direction, just as it is now compelling China to borrow from the West. In the future, "a concrete blending of China and the West" will inevitably occur and humanity will develop a common consciousness based upon *li-hsing*.[38] Is this not once more akin to the kind of cultural blending theory that he had long deprecated?

Yet this great wrenching of human history out of its historical groove would allow Chinese culture to finally resolve the curious paradox it had harbored since its inception; the challenge of the West and the power of its science would enable truly human culture to realize itself fully at last. Liang's unduly optimistic prediction reflects a striking transformation in Chinese thought, one which, according to one student of Confucian tradition, was shared by scientistic liberalism, Marxism, as well as tradition-oriented humanism: "What the West quite definitely did bring was not the concept of social and economic transformation per se, but the belief that with modern technology and modern techniques of political participation, the 'outer' realm of economic and political problems . . . could in fact be formed."[39]

As he had done in his first book, Liang still insisted that a mass cultural revival was a *sine qua non* of successful Chinese modernization. China should build upon *li-hsing* to create a new world culture, one that would capture Western modernization's strengths

35. [38], pp. 50, 56, 145–148, 282, 442; [16], p. 48; [9r], p. 275; [25], p. 47; [86], pp. 70–73; [11h], p. 250; [24].
36. [86], pp. 65–69; [38], pp. 50, 175, 368–369; [25], pp. 47, 50; [274], III, 52–59; [21]; [29]; [16]; [55]; [57]; [19].
37. [86], pp. 65–69, 94, 329–331; [38], pp. 52, 145; [55].
38. [38], pp. 22–23; see also p. 144.   39. [431], p. 119.

while avoiding its epiphenomenal scourges. In his 1921 book, Liang had only hinted indistinctly at a mass movement. By now he had already determined and defined one; it was rural reconstruction.

If Liang's essential message was identical to that in *Eastern and Western Cultures*, why did he abandon Vitalism and intuition for *li-hsing*? His post-1949 Marxist critics have claimed that he had been forced to because such goods had "gone out of fashion," or because such flagrantly obscurantist thought had been decisively and permanently discredited in the 1923 Science and Philosophy of Life debate. All have agreed that the actual content of *li-hsing* was exactly the same as the intuition of his first book.[40] Although this is true, Liang also sometimes used *li-hsing* in the colloquial sense of "reasonable," implying that Chinese culture was just the only reasonable way for a human to live.[41] This axiomatic quality in his use of the word is very similar to the premodern Chinese sense of absolute cultural superiority.

If the message remained unchanged, so too did its underlying and inescapable contradiction. Liang still could only perceive it as irony:

> The various weaknesses of the Chinese which you gentlemen see now are all due to their strengths. The present defeats suffered by China are due to its past successes. The weaknesses of the Chinese come from none other than their strengths. In the future, these many strengths can save the life of our ancient race and revive our nation.[42]

40. [331], p. 9; [195], pp. 112–113; [559], p. 125; [212], I, 179; [101], pp. 47–48.
41. See, for example, [86], pp. 289–292; [14k].
42. [42e], p. 26.

CHAPTER IX

Rural Reconstruction:
Confucian Modernization

Liang's ultimate solution to China's unique cultural dilemma was modernization through cultural revival. The rural reconstruction scheme of the 1930s developed logically from his general ruminations and educational experiments of the 1920s, as well as from his cultural theory. He drew up the actual blueprint between 1930 and 1936. This program of total economic, political, and social revolution, Liang promised, "will develop a new kind of civilization, the likes of which has never existed before"—a *li-hsing*-based "normal human civilization" which he predicted would be the inevitable fate of mankind.[1] Liang's "start of a new life for humanity" would avoid the faults of the "abnormal," "money-based," "distorted," overly industrialized, overly urbanized civilization in the West, where "humanity has lost its control over matter."[2] "This is our historic mission. . . . Our movement is both for the Chinese people and for the world."[3]

Liang's theories naturally find parallels with other antimodern, conservative thinkers, but what is striking about this Confucian response to China's predicament is the degree to which it resembles the Communist-led revolution—both during the War of Resistance (1937–1945) and after 1949—especially in its more clearly Maoist phases and tendencies. This is especially astonishing because most of these recognizable Maoist characteristics had not yet been developed by Mao or the CCP at the time Liang was writing.

---

1. [38], pp. 146, 143; see also pp. 176, 184, 197, 291; [14g], p. 69; [11f], p. 202; [42e], p. 32.

2. [38], pp. 143, 445–447; see also [11g], p. 207.   3. [472], p. 6.

Justifications for Rural Reconstruction: Historical and Practical

To prove the inevitability of his program, Liang interpreted the century after the Opium War in a particular way. The late-nineteenth-century Self-Strengthening movement, the 1898 reforms, the Republican Revolution, the May Fourth movement, the 1924 KMT reorganization, the Northern Expedition, and the Communist movement had all been led by intellectuals who believed that, through imitating the West, China would gain wealth and power. All had subscribed to imported foreign theories that were unsuited to Chinese reality. Each phase had departed progressively further from China's own cultural roots and created disorder, havoc, and destruction of the old institutions and social structures. Yet each failed to achieve its objective. The peasant masses, not the intellectual elite, had paid the price. Their sweat bought the modernizing reforms; the bandits and warlords spawned by the elite's deleterious mischief spilled peasant blood. Imperialism and government taxes reduced the peasants' standard of living and destroyed their livelihood. Most recently, economic imperialism had ruined the peasant handicraft industries and commercialized their crops so that they were liable to the fluctuations of the world market.[4]

The most insidious Western bourgeois influence had been in the spiritual realm. The treaty-port-borne cancer of Occidental individualism and selfishness ("taking oneself as important and ethical relationships as unimportant; regarding rights as important and duties as unimportant") had begun to metastasize throughout society. The descendants of the educated class (*shih*) and the moral aristocracy had deserted the villages for the hell-born urban sinks of depravity, and had been corrupted. "Since Western utilitarian thought has entered," Liang lamented, "the educated class is not only unashamed to speak of profit, but positively glories in it."[5] One consequence was the concentration of wealth and educated talent in the cities, while the villages were being progressively ravaged.[6] These Chinese cities were not production-oriented, as West-

---

4. [47], p. 10; [38], pp. 6, 359–364, 369–371, 379–385; [42a]; [11f], pp. 195–196; [9r], p. 285; [14h], pp. 71–74.
5. [38], pp. 60, 71.   6. [38], p. 394; [17].

ern cities were, but were only centers of consumption for a privileged class (much as Mao later cautioned). All these tendencies had destroyed the countryside's old social order and subverted its underlying customs and morality.[7]

Unless the educated class of the old tradition could be reborn in rural reconstruction, Liang warned, China and its revolution were doomed. "If the intellectuals still loll about in the relaxed atmosphere of the cities and the foreign concessions, then they will not make revolution. Only if they go to the countryside, where the problems are the greatest and the suffering most intense, will they be certain to make revolution."[8] That intense hatred of the privileged, soft-handed life of urban luxury, divorced from the life of the masses, is as pervasive in Liang's thought as it is in Mao's.

Liang believed, however, that after decades of peasant suffering, the intellectuals were finally becoming conscious of the futility in imitating the urban industrialized civilization of the West and were turning toward China's countryside. Now that the "numbed nerves have suddenly become aware of the pain," the Chinese intellectuals were awakening to reality. "The first step of our people's [new] consciousness is to become aware of the villages. After this step, they will naturally awaken to everything else—to the special character of our original social structures and to our inevitable future."[9] Thus, rural reconstruction would be, as Liang entitled his first book on the subject, "the final awakening in the Chinese people's self-salvation movement"—the last of the several attempts in China to meet the Western challenge. In plotting this "inevitable" future, Liang sought to identify the pragmatic with his prescriptives:

> We are forced to make a precise design [for the future] according to the objective realities. Our plan is not subjective, but actually as though predetermined. [The facts] leave us only one path to follow, and coincidentally it also happens to be the most ideal one. It is not that we are [subjectively] choos-

7. [14h], pp. 72–75; [11d], p. 164; [14p], p. 135; [38], p. 294; [39], p. 6; [31]; [21].

8. [11e], p. 190. Before 1927, the old established mass circulation weekly, *Tung-fang tsa-chih*, carried almost nothing about the peasantry. Suddenly in August 1927 (24.6) it published an entire special issue on the subject. Thereafter through 1935 it carried a very large number of articles on rural problems.

9. [38], pp. 321, 363–364, 394–395; [11d], p. 158, 176; [11k], [47], pp. 88–90, 122.

ing the ideal path but that, aside from this one direction, all others are blocked and impassable to us. I often think, sighing: This is really "created by heaven and put in its place by earth". . . . It is really as if [heaven] feared that we would take a wrong turn, and so left us only one road which forces us toward the ideal.[10]

Unlike other nativist conservatives in China and elsewhere, who generally tended toward openly irrationalist appeals, Liang insisted throughout that his plan was formed by observation and analysis of the intractable facts. "Seeking the truth through study of the facts" was as much his watchword as Mao's. His ultimate justification for rural and cultural revival was not national identity and solidarity or romanticism, but the "objective realities," of which the economic considerations were the most important. Compared to other conservatives, the Westernized liberals, or many KMT thinkers, Liang's orientation seems almost Marxist. "Economics is the essential part of the external realities; it is the central skeleton to the external realities. . . . Only after the external realities have developed to a certain point can they produce this new [social] system." He even implied that rural reconstruction was the result of a kind of dialectical development, for he confidently asserted that "the forces for bringing about the solution exist naturally within the problems themselves."[11]

As such a realist observing the facts, Liang emphasized practical considerations in arguing for a primarily agricultural China: it made sense economically to have an "agriculture first" policy because the masses of China lived in the villages, not the treaty ports. Emphasis upon agriculture, therefore, was the best method for achieving national as well as local economic self-sufficiency and self-reliance.[12] Underneath his realistic assessment, however, ran a prescriptive philosophical agrarianism.

Agrarianism has been a common attitude among anti-modernist conservatives; it goes hand in hand with abhorrence for one or several aspects of industrialized urban life. Indeed, it might be more accurate to speak of anti-urbanism or anti-industrialism than of agrarianism.[13] Certainly Liang's agrarianism also reflected his

10. [38], p. 395.   11. [47], p. 90; [38], p. 321.
12. [38], pp. 14–16, 291–295, 372–375, 401–405; [9r], pp. 275–277; [42f], pp. 34–40; [42g], pp. 41–44; [17].
13. Agrarianism in this sense, of course, is a modern phenomenon.

deep loathing for modern urban life. Now that the Chinese city had
become a model of Western bourgeois society—an artificially
created place of selfish, competitive individualists with "no feelings
for others"—it was the enemy. How could a "rational" civilization
be built upon such a foundation? Liang's rural reconstruction was
an attempt to prevent the China of the future from becoming what
the great treaty port of Shanghai had already become. "Shanghai
tangibly brings together into one place both Chinese and Western
corruptions; it is the most condemnable place! Fortunately China
has only one Shanghai, and has not yet become completely
Shanghai-ized." "A bit" of ethical spirit, human feeling, and community spirit still lingered on in the rural hinterlands.[14]

Liang, however, has none of that almost pantheistic regard for
nature, that aesthetic delight in the bucolic that has characterized
Western agrarianism. The pristine primitiveness of village life held
no particular charm for him, and in his way of thinking, "nature"
was no specially charged moral metaphor. After his 1936 visit to
Japan, for instance, he observed with approval (among much general disapproval) that the physical differences between rural areas
and cities were far less in Japan than they were in China. The goal
of rural reconstruction was a kind of reverse *rus in urbe* rather than
a primeval Taoist utopia. Like Mao, Liang was hankering after
"rural cities and urban villages. . . . They should not be two kinds of
things but should blend together."[15]

These parallels with Maoist ideas—such as anti-urbanism, anti-
consumerism, general stress upon overall rural development, closing the urban-rural gap, local self-initiative, and self-sufficiency—
continue through much of Liang's writing on economic development, including his plans for industry. Although firmly committed
to a "rural based" civilization—the countryside as font of rationality
and wisdom—he was just as firmly convinced that, without a great
increase in economic productivity, China's new "rational" civilization would have no chance of realization. "Some people mistakenly
believe that I am opposed to material civilization and industry. I
have never had such a thought. I think that raising material production and advancing production technology is of crucial im-

---

Liang's rural reconstruction has the same relationship to the traditional
Chinese emphasis on agriculture as the European Romantics' agrarianism
had to the premodern agrarian tradition of Hesiod, Cato, and St.
Augustine.

14. [38], pp. 378, 379, 183; see also pp. 180–185.   15. [38], p. 444.

portance. . . . I consider economic development quite essential. Only through it can we make our life more reasonable."[16]

Liang acknowledged that the Soviet model of industrialization had averted many of the problems inherent in capitalistic industrialization, but he was not happy with its overly centralized planning, its urban concentration of industry, and the generally "mechanistic" quality that it shared with capitalism. To avoid these undesirable characteristics—and, of course, to be "practical"—he advocated diffused, small- and medium-scale industries that would be rural-based and run by the peasants themselves in primary and direct response to the actual needs of agriculture. The only exception he made in his general emphasis on decentralization and local initiative were for certain nationalized industries in such fields as national defense, transportation, energy resource development, and highly technological industries. According to Liang's vision, electrification and agricultural mechanization would raise rural labor productivity. Then, unlike free-enterprise development, a collectivized and technologically advanced agricultural sector would bring about industries that really served the masses. Agriculture and industry would thus form a "cycle" of mutual stimulation: agriculture's need for fertilizer would eventually lead to a chemical industry; farm implements would require a machine industry; agricultural-product processing would give rise to a host of other small industries. "In turn, industrial production will push agricultural production ahead, so that they will mutually help each other and both increase their production. This is true self-reliance [tzu-li keng-sheng]. Our environment compels us to be self-reliant in this way." To accomplish this goal, "the peasant must simultaneously be a worker."[17]

Also from this stance as a realistic analyst of the objective facts, Liang dismissed rival designs for China's future as the illusions of subjective idealists.[18] He accused his old foes, the Westernized liberals such as Hu Shih and Ting Wen-chiang, of substituting their own "wishful thinking" for a systematic study of actual conditions and an analysis of the historical forces that had created them. "Although they are of the 'science' school," Liang taunted, "all they

16. [47], pp. 88–89.
17. [38], pp. 389, 390; see also pp. 388–394, 409–414, 432–438, 443–444.
18. [38], pp. 178–179, 219–220, 321, 264–265, 395; [11d], pp. 158, 176; [14g], pp. 69–70.

have are subjective demands and hopes. None of them have observed the objective situation, understood the social changes, or sought solutions through study of objective conditions." Liang pronounced the liberals' programs "truly silly and laughable" and asked "these gentlemen to wise up right away!"[19] He also twitted Hu Shih for not admitting the "objective reality" of imperialism, feudalism, and warlordism.[20] In the same fashion, Liang criticized the KMT neotraditionalists (and the Marxists) for ignoring the concrete Chinese situation, while they constructed grand theories of no relevance to reality.[21]

This seemingly incongruous strain in Liang's thought is important. True, subjective idealists, who brand everyone else as subjective idealists, are often messianic. Yet Liang's attitude harkens back to Liang Chi's "striving for reality," his disgust with the hollow war cries of the *ch'ing-liu* and with the phony paper reforms of the late Ch'ing. It fits with Liang Shu-ming's own early aversion to "empty verbiage," his profound reaction to the failure of the 1911 revolution to realize its ideals *in practice*, his personal demand for absolute unity of theory and practice, and his emphasis upon China's actual social structures and historical background. Perhaps this aspect of Liang accounts for some of his similarities with Mao.

The *Shih* and the Peasantry

China had actually had another series of self-salvation movements, Liang revealed, and they had been initiated by the uneducated peasants of the interior who were out of touch with conditions of the littoral.

> During the Kuang-hsu and Hsuan-t'ung periods [between 1862 and 1908], there had been countless missionary cases [attacks on foreign missionaries] and the 1900 Boxer movement. . . . More recently, the Red Spears and Heavenly Gate

19. [14b]. On this basis Liang opposed—or qualified to an extent that amounted to opposition—the liberals' constitutionalist movements before, during, and after World War II.
20. [11k], p. 335. This was Liang's reaction to Hu's widely read and discussed antirevolutionary article, "Which road shall we follow?," in which Hu dismissed the importance of warlordism, imperialism, and feudalism. "Our real enemies," Hu asserted, "are poverty, disease, ignorance, greed, and disorder." See [309e]; [98].
21. [47], p. 122.

societies in North China, the Spirit Soldiers in Szechwan, etc., are all examples . . . . Viewing these two forces [the separate self-salvation movements of the peasants and the intellectuals] historically, we can see that the great difficulty is that they have gone off in different directions; the upper and lower forces have not been in communication. The lower-level forces [peasants] take action blindly and so do not have any effect. The upper-level forces [intellectuals] are separated from the places where the problems are and take action on the basis of [their own] imaginings. The result has been that either they have not scratched where it has itched, or they have betrayed the masses.[22]

Therefore, Liang concluded, the key to the Chinese revolution was to:

Combine the [peasants'] motive force with that [of the in-tellectuals] to form one united force. . . . In other words, the revolutionary intellectuals must go down to the countryside and merge with the inhabitants. . . . Each side will transform the other. . . . All that needs to be done is for the peasants to train and transform the revolutionary intellectuals and for the revolutionary intellectuals to shift the direction of and transform the peasants. Ultimately, there will be no differ-ence between the two; then the problem of China can be considered solved.[23]

If the peasants would constitute the "major force" of the revolu-tion, and rural reconstruction would be a movement of the peas-ants themselves, then why would the intellectuals be needed at all? Because, although only the peasants knew their problems first-hand, they were unable to define, articulate, and analyze these empirical experiences to produce systematic solutions. "The op-pressed and maltreated are urgently seeking relief from their suf-ferings . . . [but] they lack direction."[24] The intellectuals would sys-tematize peasant demands and provide solutions.

Moreover, Liang acknowledged, "all intellectuals live off the blood and sweat of the peasantry," and they should make good the debt by going to the countryside with their modern knowledge. The crucial issue for him, however—as with his father's critique of the late Ch'ing reforms—was one of the people and their moral

22. [11e], pp. 187–188.
23. [11e], p. 191; see also pp. 189–190; [38], p. 344.
24. [11e], p. 186; see also [38], pp. 220–233.

will, and not their knowledge or training. The role Liang assigned to the intellectuals in rural reconstruction was but the final expression of that ongoing strain in both his and his father's thought: the responsibility of the Confucian moral aristocrat toward society and culture.

> The so-called intellectuals of today are the educated class [*shih*] of former times. . . . They represented rationality and maintained society. Their position was that of teacher . . . they were responsible for leading [the masses] and for their ethical transformation. . . . If today [the intellectuals] cannot fulfill their natural duty, [if they] only care about easy living and crave a comfortable life, then they will be thieves of society. Will today's intellectuals be teachers or thieves? There must be a choice between these two roads. This is a moral question, there is no guarantee that [the intellectuals] will be one or the other.[25]

Explicit in both Liang's and his father's ideas on the proper role of the educated elite in society was their vehement reaction to the Western bourgeois influence that had turned the *chün-tzu* into such mean-spirited, luxury-loving merchants of expertise. In the 1920s, Liang had attacked the Westernized educational system for creating a privileged class that had lost the tradition of the *chün-tzu*. In the 1930s, he sent out his urgent call for the intellectuals to go to the countryside, but not as little dictators in their realms of expertise. The peasants also needed emotional and mental involvement in production. If, "as under capitalism and [Soviet] communism, a minority of people control the management of property and monopolize the privilege of doing the brain work," then the masses are forced to act "mechanically" as the minority's mindless servants; consequently, they have no opportunity for self-initiative. Therefore, rather than rely upon foreign-trained experts, local rural administrators "must rely entirely upon emotional indentification with the people and the locality. . . . If we cannot awaken this sort of affection and sympathy, then our so-called reconstruction will be both constructive and destructive. Even if we do have some success, we will never know how much the people have covertly suffered" and so "we cannot rely on skill alone."[26] The *shih*'s inner spring of

25. [38], p. 360.
26. [38], pp. 422–423; [42c], p. 17; see also [38], pp. 217–218; [9d], pp. 63–67.

moral force was more essential than their expertise (somewhat similar to the politically red and professionally expert dichotomy in China today).

This theme of the primacy of correct consciousness, motivation, and morale over a person's intelligence or technical competence winds through all of Liang's thought; it often seems linked with his father's ideas. During one of his lectures, Liang quoted from the letters of Lin Tse-hsu (Wen-chung; 1785–1850), one of Liang Chi's special heros. The gist of the passage was that, without a sense of duty to and sympathy with the people, an intellectual's talent and ability were worthless.[27]

Stress upon the primacy of the moral-political factor over technical expertise (and faith in the power of a unified, galvanized peasantry) was also evident in Liang's thoughts about national defense. He shared Mao's belief that "the human factor is more important than weapons," because, after all, "it is people who must employ them." The most important people, Liang opined, were the rank and file, and more important than their technical skill or physical strength was their spirit. Of course, both Mao and Liang might simply have taken a page from the ancient military strategist Sun Tzu (fourth century B.C.), who said that, of the five basic factors of strategy, the first was moral influence. Liang accurately predicted that, should Tokyo launch its highly mechanized juggernaut, China's regular armies stood no chance of withstanding it; only an organized and motivated peasantry fighting a protracted defensive war could prevail. Successful resistance depended upon a "spontaneous voluntary force. Who? You must rely upon the people . . . upon the peasants militarily. Only then can we have [effective] self-defense." The only way to mobilize this rural resistance, Liang insisted, was his rural reconstruction.[28]

In fact, Liang believed war presented a golden opportunity for rural reconstruction:

> After a Sino-Japanese war begins, there will be many areas from which our regular troops will withdraw. Lacking sufficient military manpower, the enemy will not be able to occupy these areas either. There will also be a lot of places from which our government administrative organs will withdraw; yet the enemy will not have time to establish their own administrative organs. In all these areas, the peasants will need the

27. [42c], p. 17.   28. [42n].

aid and guidance of the intellectuals . . . [and] rural work will surely be easy to do. Although ordinarily we are thinking of the peasants' best interests in our work, we are, after all, innovative while they are conservative; we are full of enthusiasm and action while they are bound by inertia. Unavoidably, we end up standing on the side of the government, and they seem like governed masses, even to the point that an antagonism seems to exist between us. Now, with the arrival of enemy oppression, we and the peasantry will be forced to deal with [this new] environment together. Then [our relations] will be transformed from antagonism to unity in dealing with the external [enemy]. At the same time, [the peasantry] will be forced to organize and unify to deal with this environment . . . [and] will spontaneously walk the road of collective life. All of this will be the gift of the enemy.[29]

As it turned out, Liang's notions were perfectly accurate, but the Communists, not his rural reconstructors, would reap the rewards from this unsolicited Nipponese benefaction.

Collective Organizational Forms and Politics

According to Liang's cultural theory, traditional China's major weaknesses—and the West's two great strengths—were organization and science. Rural reconstruction's basic task, then, was to create collective organizational forms for China, through which the people could carry out all other specific programs for economic development, technological diffusion, education, and political reform. This unification of the disorganized Chinese countryside into activist, collective organizations, Liang stressed, must be based upon *li-hsing* and ethical relationships. Through improving and strengthening ethical bonds on a small scale and "adjusting social relationships," the new collectives would take shape and China could have modernization without the Western defects:

[This] concrete actual blending of China and the West . . . might be described as based upon China's original spirit. . . . Its organizational principles derive from Chinese ethical thought; it is as though all we have to do is add another relationship to the five [Confucian] relationships [*wu lun*] . . . a relationship between member and group. This collective or-

29. [51], no. 32.

ganization is an ethical organization that takes as its goal the advancement of human morality.[30]

"Each member," Liang insisted, "must vigorously participate in the life of the group organizations," which would be of a "spontaneous, voluntary" nature and would be "controlled by the majority." Could this "democratic" regard for the majority be combined with China's undemocratic tradition of a moral aristocracy? The solution, he suggested, might lie in the eventual adoption of one-party rule, a form he believed would avoid the faults of a "mechanistic," liberal-democratic constitutional system (which he repeatedly predicted would never work in China) and yet still be capable of galvanizing the masses for voluntary action. Liang concluded that such a system could reconcile the contradiction between mass participation and the Chinese respect for the virtuous and wise, which he equated with the old conflict between Western rule by law and Chinese rule by men. He dubbed it "majority government through rule by men" and found it "extremely compatible with the spirit of the Chinese and the ideals of the ancients." It was democratic because "the successful leader is supported by the majority and relies on [their] backing," but in effect, it was still "the old Confucian ideal of a minority rule through education."[31]

Although this political party thing is a Western trinket and discordant with China ['s traditions], idolizing the party leader is similar to the [original] Chinese respect for teachers. The party leader's words and teachings are supreme above all. This too is congruent with the concept of "respecting the virtuous and esteeming the wise." A party's success, its programs and theories, are often created singlehandedly by [the party leader] . . . whom the party members naturally want to respect and the majority of the people want to obey. . . . The majority [thus] obeys and is led by a single person, the party leader, and so it seems as though the majority are passive. But because they understand the programs of the party leader and want to obey the party leader, they want to do it [voluntarily]. If a person wants to do something, can you call it passive? The personal character of the party leaders [of one-party governments] are all special. [They] are looked up to by the masses, and the majority willingly obey. These several points suggest that within a collective body [the two systems

30. [38], p. 175.   31. [38], p. 158; see also pp. 157–160.

of] of a minority leadership of virtuous, wise people and the initiative of the majority can be brought into agreement and are not at all in conflict.[32]

Liang's simultaneous demands for spontaneous, mass self-initiative and active participation, as well as an authoritarian spirit of "respecting the virtuous and esteeming teachers" does preshadow the system that seems to have evolved under the Communists. His concept of the supreme, charismatic party leader certainly seems to foreshadow the role Mao actually played in the Chinese revolution.

If Liang was so enthusiastic about the virtues of one-party rule and a supreme leader, should not the aspiring dictatorship of Chiang Kai-shek and the KMT—a self-proclaimed "neotraditional" one to boot—have attracted his support? In fact, the opposite was true; Liang heaped scorn upon both Chiang and the KMT regime. He regarded Chiang as merely an ambitious and relatively successful militarist, the KMT as a confused hodgepodge of discordant factions, and its ideology, based on Sun Yat-sen's "San-min chu-i" (Three Principles of the People), as a "big chop-suey" of incongruous elements with no relevance to reality.[33] The regime was "unsound" and "corrupt." The party had "lost its ideals," and its leaders had become "good-for-nothings, who enjoy an easy life and . . . are comfortable with the status quo." As they had neither any understanding of Chinese society nor any "power of judgment," they had failed to provide any direction for the Chinese revolution. Although they talked about socialism, in reality they walked the capitalist road. The KMT had "failed" in every way: it had not unified the nation politically; it had not carried out its original plan of land equalization; it was incapable of eliminating warlordism. Its reforms had only added to the peasants' burden. In a word, it was "divorced from the masses and had betrayed the masses."[34]

Since the KMT government had obviously already played out its historical role in the Chinese revolution, Liang urged it now to perform the suitably subordinate function of logistic support for

32. [38], pp. 156–157; see also pp. 146–147, 175–176. It seems particularly relevant that Mao wanted to be remembered in history as a "teacher." See [490], p. 169.

33. [11n], p. 351; [11d], pp. 167–170; [11a], pp. 25–26; [38], pp. 315–316, 338.

34. [38], pp. 140, 316, 319–320, 363, 372–373, 414, 432–433; [11d], p. 176; [11e], pp. 177–189; [14a], p. 20; [39], pp. 7–8; [51], no. 15.

the revolution of the future: rural reconstruction. Therefore, rather than openly calling for a strengthening of one-party government, Liang demanded that the KMT allow all parties and political groups, including the Communists, access to governmental power.[35]

Rural reconstruction, however, had to be a cultural rather than a political movement because, Liang claimed, China's various problems—political, social economic, moral—were merely distinct manifestations of the underlying cultural crisis.[36] Unless the cultural crisis was solved first, any new seizure of political power would result in nothing more than another period of destructive chaos, violence, and civil war. In fact, there was no political power to seize. Liang saw that—the KMT's pretensions notwithstanding—China had no legitimized national government. The political situation of the 1930s was actually not so dissimilar from that of the 1920s; political power still corresponded to military strength, and warlords in one guise or another still controlled everything. Therefore, "since the rural movement people must have military power to take political power, the day that they take military power, they will become warlords." (As in the two preceding decades, Liang's first practical political concern was to eliminate internal use of military force.) Government power was inherently inimical to true cultural revolution. "As soon as you take power you are separated from society. . . . No matter if even a sage took power, it still would not work." From this, Liang drew a conclusion that was as prophetic as it was paradoxical: "Rural reconstruction itself must never take power and it must never allow itself to be controlled by the government."[37]

Although Liang's nonpolitical solution to China's modern crisis might appear fundamentally different from Mao's revolution, the theme of alienation between society and government does underlie much of Mao's thought. Mao also realized that seizure of power was not a final solution. Indeed, reliance upon the masses themselves, aversion to bureaucratic commandism, and suspicion of civil routinization and even institutionalization are significant aspects of

35. [36], p. 8.
36. [38], pp. 11–24, 205–207, 293–294, 443; [14g], p. 69; [14h], pp. 74–75; [47], pp. 120–121; [11b], p. 98; [11e], pp. 182–183.
37. [38], pp. 315, 319, 364–365; see also pp. 213–214, 263, 301, 310–314, 373–374, 399–400, 410; [39], pp. 4–9; [11c], pp. 63–65; [20], pp. 301–302.

Mao's thought. Mao's Cultural Revolution was, after all, a mobilization of society against the government.

Liang never had to come to grips in practice with the unavoidable needs of a modern state for unavoidable impersonal bureaucracies. Unlike Gandhi, whom he resembles in other ways, Liang did not envision a future society composed of thousands of independent village republics; he hoped that somehow the separate "cultural" system might overcome the evils inherent in modern government. Mao had to deal with the problem in practice, but it is far from clear that he found a true solution.

Hsiang-yueh

What basic organizational form could Liang adopt for his rural reconstruction? If Western institutions were inherently productive of (and produced by) moral inferiority, how could they provide for China's needs? Conversely, if a Chinese weakness was its lack of collective organizational forms, what could be found in its own culture to serve the purpose? Liang did find a traditional Chinese institution that conformed to his ideals in the hsiang-yueh (village covenant)—an institution he believed "the Westerners were incapable of even imagining." Hsiang-yueh provided the final expression of Liang's cardinal concept of small-group moral reinforcement-renewal. With it he expected to realize the goal he had ardently cherished since his conversion to Confucianism: to "make society and chiang-hsueh form an indivisible whole."[38]

The hsiang-yueh was a kind of rural community-action and mutual-aid institution created by Lü Ho-shu (Ta-chün) of the Northern Sung dynasty (eleventh century) who derived his inspiration from the Classics—the Rites of Chou (Chou li) and the Book of Rites (Li chi). The two giants of Neo-Confucian thought, Chu Hsi (1130–1200) and Wang Yang-ming, had been much attracted to the idea and had constructed their own versions.[39] The Ch'ing dynasty revived the hsiang-yueh, but it functioned—if at all—as a thoroughly bureaucratic control device, completely losing the original ideal of a local, autonomous, mutual-aid collective. In the Ch'ing version,

38. [38], p. 189; [47], p. 1.
39. See the biography of Lü Ta-fang in [496], chüan 340; [201]; [567], "Tsou i," chüan 9, pp. 58–62. For a general treatment of the historical development of hsiang-yueh, see [596].

active villager involvement in mutual exhortation to moral improvement, confession of wrongdoing, and application of community public opinion had atrophied into *pro forma* public reading of hortatory imperial sacred edicts (*sheng-yü*).

Liang, of course, latched onto the Lü version precisely because of its anti-bureaucratic, voluntary nature. He completely disassociated his own concept of *hsiang-yueh* from any Ming or Ch'ing form because the latter had been promoted and controlled by the government—by its very nature the enemy of an active, galvanized peasantry. The "iron hook" of bureaucratic power must be kept out of the villages. Liang's *hsiang-yueh* would be formed not by bureaucratic fiat but by moral suasion and local initiative.[40] Through "positive, activist" organization of enthusiastic mass participation, it would "build up the power of the peasantry" so essential to the rest of Liang's program.

> The *hsiang-yueh* depends upon [the people] making up [their] minds to pursue it and [their] vowing to achieve it. . . . Compulsion leads to passivity. Spontaneity and passivity are mutually incompatible. If [people are] acting under compulsion, they cannot bring their own will into play. If [*hsiang-yueh*] depends upon official power, then it becomes merely a sham and a bureaucratic formality.[41]

Thus, modern *hsiang-yueh* would be a spontaneously generated and voluntarily maintained social group through which the villagers would cooperate to meet their common economic, educational, and military needs outside of the official governmental structure. At the same time, they would scrutinize and perfect each other's moral character. Some of its functions would be in the traditional mold: mutual criticism and self-criticism of faults, mediation of disputes, and identification of specific individuals as positive or negative models for the community. As in Lü's *hsiang-yueh*, the central focus would be morality; it would be an organization "aimed at making *chün-tzu* of the masses."[42]

40. [38], pp. 187–197, 202–204, 302; [25], pp. 127–128. Hsiao Kungch'uan accentuates the same contrasts between the "unprecedented" Lü version of *hsiang-yueh* and those analogous institutions that existed both before and after it. [276], IV, 532, 552.

41. [38], p. 204.

42. Liang quoted Lü's original words. See [38], pp. 188–191, 197–198, 207–208, 214–215; [11b], pp. 53–63.

Although Liang acknowledged that the aims of his *hsiang-yueh* were similar to those in Lü Ho-shu's original, he felt that certain modifications were necessary to adapt it to conditions in modern society and his own ideals. "Today's world is different from that of antiquity. In addition to imitating the ancients' method of encouraging one another to do good, we must put the pursuit of progress uppermost in our minds."[43] Untraditional progress included, of course, economic development and all that it implied, as well as other new organizational forms. Liang was attempting to synthesize modernization (mass mobilization, political participation, and economic development) with the retention of the paternalistic heart of traditional Chinese social organization (the small intimate group and human feelings).

Another salient difference between Liang's *hsiang-yueh* and that of tradition echoes Liang's relativization of the formal Confucian ethical codes (*li-chiao*) in *Eastern and Western Cultures*: "In the *hsiang-yueh* of the ancients, it can be seen that they seemed to have standard mores and customs in mind, and that if this standard was met, then it would work. In reality, goodness is limitless and is continually in a process of development. . . . We must take the [concept of goodness] to be in perpetual development."[44]

If no governmental sanctions or legal standards would be allowed, what would define Liang's grass-roots organization? The peasants themselves, Liang explained, would create new "customs and mores," which in turn would gradually produce a new activist Confucian man. In Liang's theory, as in Mao's, the masses were the final arbiter of the commonweal. And both Liang and Mao predicated their cultural revolutions upon the assumption that a new kind of humanity might be produced, often by similar methods.

Liang emphasized that this seemingly paradoxical effort to create a cake of custom overnight, as it were, was the only way to avoid the West's (and the KMT's) impersonal legalistic bureaucratism, which turned people into mean-spirited schemers and stifled human ethical potential. According to Liang's program, community values would not be articulated by statute and enforced by mechanical law, but by ethically based propriety and decorum (*li*) and internalized moral standards. No rigid, detailed organiza-

43. [38], pp. 258–259, 307; [12], p. 4; see also [38], pp. 187–215; [25], pp. 127–129.
44. [38], p. 201.

tional statutes would be set; specifics of the form would spring up "naturally" in the newly heated moral atmosphere. The ethos itself would advance on its own momentum so that formal law, bureaucratic regulations, and physical force would be forever unnecessary. In direct contrast to the West, and in keeping with Confucius' faith in humanity's moral potential, the individual (reinforced by community public opinion) would make moral, not calculatingly self-interested, decisions.

> As long as all the people [in the community] understand [the principles] in their hearts, then if you do something unethical, you yourself will naturally know, and the others will also know. . . . The rural reconstruction organization must rely upon the people themselves and not become a mechanistic organization that depends upon an external force to maintain itself. Each member of the organization must be made self-consciously aware of the needs of the group, its [the group's] necessity, and its direct personal relationship with the individual and the individual's own interests.[45]

(Liang apparently never recognized the contradiction in relying upon the "individual's own interests" while simultaneously hoping to cultivate his "disinterested" moral capacity of li-hsing. Mao at least recognized the contradiction but his concept of "class struggle" hardly solves it.)

Anyone familiar with Chinese Communist society will immediately see the parallels between aspects of Liangs's long-treasured chiang-hsueh ideal and Maoist forms of small-group organization and practices, both as they functioned during the War of Resistance period and after Liberation (especially in the ways they differ from comparable Western and Russian forms). In both Liang's Confucian and Mao's Marxist models, the small group serves as a primary instrument in horizontal and vertical reintegration of the political (and underlying moral) community as well as in mass mobilization for various specific economic and social reform plans. Both could be regarded either as a tool for social and political control (recalcitrants are smothered by zealots and a febrile enthusiasm) or as the institutionalization of a grand moral drama of perpetual progress toward perfection. The aim in both is to organize and shape social interaction to generate social pressures for the values and goals of the movement; praise and blame of the

45. [38], pp. 252–254.

immediate primary group can act as a mechanism of ideological indoctrination (either Confucian or Marxist) as well as a brake on undesirable behavior such as philandering or drunkenness. Liang hoped that active peasant participation in *hsiang-yueh* types of organization would train them to be more reflective, analytical, and independent-minded, and thus enable them to break with their traditional passive acceptance of the existing habits or status quo. He also envisioned that education together with community meeting practices could lead, for instance, to peasant emotional and intellectual involvement in national and world affairs—a hope realized by the CCP.

Liang and Mao differed radically, however, both in their attitudes about conflict within the small group and in their approaches to the basic contradiction of reform: how to get to the good society of the future using people conditioned by the bad society of the present. What if the masses, with values and behavior patterns still shaped by the present bad society, sincerely and unanimously desired something that was obviously undesirable? Some villages, for example, still unquestioningly favored footbinding. How should such a situation be dealt with? Moreover, the agents of change themselves—be they rural workers or party cadre—could always regress or even fail in really achieving the new consciousness. Mao characteristically recognized the dilemma. He expected the small groups to bring conflicts out into the open so the group could deal with them and eliminate them. Liang's optimistic Confucian predilections turned him away from squarely confronting conflict and contradiction. He insisted that things should never be allowed to come to even a hint of actual coercion. Rather, "the masses must be thoroughly persuaded to submit voluntarily." The only method is "appeal to human feeling and logical explanation. After the new habits are formed, the problem will no longer exist" and the character of some agents will no longer matter. Mao knew that there would have to be "many cultural revolutions," some even waged against the agents of change.

The peasant school. Liang's basic *hsiang-yueh* institution—the organ of self-government and the managing body for the other community enterprises—was not a town hall, but a peasant school (*hsiang-nung hsueh-hsiao*). Each community would elect a "wise and virtuous" person from among its numbers to serve as the school director (*hsiao-chang*). He or she would not have the position or identity of an elected official, but of a "teacher" whose most important function was mediation.

This mediator role—both between the community and the outside world and among members of the community—was crucial to Liang's scheme and his ideal of harmony. He designed the peasant schools so the masses could not criticize or attack rural reconstruction cadre directly, but would have to go first to the school director, who would then represent them and their desires to the cadre. If a clash of opinion should arise within the community, the school director was to "investigate with intensive personal attention to determine the desires of the masses" and then articulate, in systematic and "suitable" form, their scattered inchoate demands. As with Mao's mass line, the effectiveness of the director naturally depended upon his talent, sincerity, and ability to inspire the masses' "respect and trust." Liang admitted that, at the beginning, really virtuous and wise individuals would be needed as school directors, but after the emergence of the new ethos, that is, after morality had become mores, it "would make no difference what kind of person became the school director."[46]

Rites and music (li yueh), which figured so prominently in Liang's 1921 book, would also play an important role in the new society, especially in the conduct of community meetings. Liang stressed ceremony and decorum during the meetings to avoid any open display of dissension. Music, he believed, was needed to offset "the creeping overintellectualization and selfish calculation that comes with civilization," and "to increase the peasants' vitality. . . . We can create a kind of simple, economical opera and teach [the peasants] to sing; gradually this will make the peasants start operas on their own. . . . We must propagate among the people music and songs suited to the peasants' environment and sentiments."[47] Liang the sage would never allow himself to do such frivolous work, but his ideas on the subject constitute an intriguing link between his father's attempts to use folk opera as a vehicle for his moralizing and the products that did follow after Liberation.

Although a cardinal tenet of Liang's plan was maximum local autonomy, he realized that grass-roots movements without inter-

46. [38], pp. 143, 180, 189–193, 200–204, 252–260, 312–314, 373–374; [12], pp. 1–2; [11e], pp. 191–192; [11f], pp. 201–206; [11g], pp. 207–216; [11h], pp. 217–220; [21].

47. See [47], pp. 137, 139–140; [38], pp. 256–257.

communication and central organization would lead nowhere. Therefore, he planned that all peasant schools would be organizationally linked at the village, *hsiang*, hsien, and provincial levels to form one great nationwide social-educational-cultural system (separate from any governmental structure). Once rural reconstruction had built up its strength, society would eventually replace government. For the time being, most existing systems currently managed by the government—such as the school systems—should be abolished and re-created from the ground up on the basis of the peasant's true needs and desires.[48]

The actual plans Liang made for education within his rural reconstruction scheme were extensions of his earlier educational experiments and his critique of China's Westernized educational system. Again there are parallels with what would come later with Mao. Liang insisted that "the new Chinese education must above all be practical—of real use in raising production, with less classroom work and more practice; it should emphasize social education, especially for adults." Primary education should eventually be universalized, but under the control of the local peasantry; only they know what "is really useful to themselves. We must let the people [of the locality] manage it. . . . That is to say, before you can reform [primary education], you must become a peasant." He decried the existing university education as "utterly irrelevant to actual society. . . because the people it trains are not useful to society." The students must stop studying foreign books that have nothing to say about actual Chinese conditions. Moreover, academic research should emphasize those applied sciences that would meet the practical needs of Chinese society, such as in rural public health and rural engineering.[49]

Confucian socialism. Even Liang could not trust to naked moral power alone to create and maintain the new collective institutions. Unless the peasants could perceive that the organizations were benefiting them and solving their problems (such as protecting them against bandits, increasing their standard of living, and improving their health), the new peasant schools had no

48. See [38], pp. 205–207, 213–214, 262–263, 296–297, 312–314, 319, 364–365, 398–399, 400–410; [14f], pp. 63–65; [39], pp. 1–2, 8; [11h], pp. 233–237, 245–248; [20], pp. 301–302.
49. [42k].

hope. The economic arm of his *hsiang-yueh* was the cooperative society, an organization that would function to rationalize and increase production as well as equalize distribution. Like his sage predecessor Mencius, Liang saw virtue inextricably connected with economic conditions. He added, moreover, that economic inequality was an obstacle to the realization of true Confucian values. "Private property must be abolished. . . . The present social order creates sin and evil and inhibits bringing the virtues of humanity into play. . . . [It] really does make people mean and selfish . . . and does not allow for ideals or individuality. . . . The reason that [my] ideal society can reach the sphere of perfection lies in its removing the oppression of the struggle for survival."

The Confucian revival would also receive unintended help from the imperialists' economic aggression. "Under this pressure, the peasants, who are now disorganized, will naturally seek to collectivize in the future so they can make use of the advanced production technology." The cooperatives would gradually increase their capital so that eventually all would be publicly owned. The general direction of rural reconstruction in all spheres was "from private (*szu*) to public (*kung*)."[50]

Cooperatives also provided a key link in Liang's solution to the land question—a problem he broke down into three fundamental difficulties: unequal landholdings, inefficient land utilization, and overall insufficiency of arable land. In rough outline, his program approximates the way Chinese agricultural reform and reorganization *actually did proceed* after 1949, but minus, of course, the crucial element of violent anti-landlord struggle. The first step was to see that the cultivator got his own land, and then to promote cooperative utilization of the land.

> We should not tolerate the slightest delay in vigorously implementing these two points. After they have been actually carried out, public ownership of land is but a short time away. . . . If the cultivators own their own land, it will be of enormous help in raising agricultural production. Still, each family operating its own farm independently is not the most efficient utilization of the land. We must go further and em-

50. [38], pp. 288–289, 169–171, 416, 293, 432; see also pp. 172–175, 189–190, 227, 285–294, 300–306, 386–394, 415–432; [11g], p. 207; [9r], p. 275; [485], pp. 258–259. Liang did not have in mind the kinds of cooperatives that had previously been established in China; he thought they had been failures.

ploy cooperative utilization (one way is to operate cooperative
societies) in order to rationalize land utilization and agricultural management.[51]

China's general shortage of arable land could be solved, Liang
contended, through creating collectives to develop sparsely popu-
lated regions. He was confident that, "for the most part, all these
problems can be eliminated through our rural organizations and
cooperative societies." The cooperative collectives, he repeatedly
emphasized, "should arise through [the stimulus of] ideals [among
the peasantry], not through compulsion." The only effective solution to the land problem was "formation of a political force through
readjustment of social relationships," not government-managed
programs.[52] Neither bureaucrats nor soldiery—even a "people's
army"—should have a hand in the process. No matter how anxious
he was about the agrarian problem, Liang always stopped short of
(and censured the Communists, particularly during the Kiangsi
period, for) forcible land confiscation.

Liang's Confucianist socialism did not go so far as, let us say, the
Slavophiles in their idealization of the *mir*, but he did hint (as his
father had) that because there had been no individual property
rights within the traditional Chinese family or clan, Chinese ethical
relationships nurtured a tendency toward public property:

> Property was never considered the possession of an individual
> but rather of the whole family, and the boundaries of this
> family group were flexible. . . . Communism did not exist in
> Chinese society before only because the techniques and
> means of production were limited, backward, and simple;
> therefore, the scope of the productive unit was small. It was
> not because there was some element in Chinese tradition that
> was antagonistic to socialism.[53]

Liang's attitude toward the Soviet Union's experience in agricultural collectivization was similar to his assessment of the Soviet
model for industrialization. "China must copy the Soviet Union in
collectivization of agriculture," but of course, unlike the "mechanistic" Russians, China's collectivization must rely primarily upon the
initiative and desires of the peasantry rather than on compulsory
laws enforced by a centralized bureaucracy. As with the peasant

51. [38], p. 414.   52. [38], pp. 411–414, 304–307.
53. [38], pp. 168–169.

schools, the main contours of his plan were shaped by the ideals of local initiative and self-sufficiency ("there is always a gulf between the nation and the local community"), but nationwide coordination would be necessary to serve the interests of China as a whole. "All peasants will be part of a nationwide cooperative organization. This way, the peasants unconsciously become economic warriors in a central network."[54]

Confucianism and Maoism

If the parallels between certain aspects of Liang's plans for a new rural civilization and Mao's revolution are so evident, why was Liang so anti-Communist before 1937? For one thing, of course, he was also anti-KMT, anti-liberal, anti-warlord, and anti everything else that was not in absolute agreement with his version of the ancient sages' message to mankind. Second, the popular image of the CCP in China at the time (spread by KMT-controlled journalism and government reports) was one of bandit-vagabonds who "burn and kill"—an image that Liang naturally picked up.[55] Third, the nature of the Kiangsi Soviet period CCP (1931–1934) was, in fact, quite different from that of the Yenan period. Mao was not yet in command of the party and had not yet settled into the enterprise of creating "Maoism." Later, in his specific criticisms of the pre-Yenan period Communists, Liang often hit upon the differences between the Kiangsi Soviet methods, which failed, and those of the war-period border regions, which succeeded spectacularly.[56]

Suggestions of ambivalence in Liang's attitude toward the CCP increased as time went on. In comparison with the past self-salvation movements and the KMT, Liang came to acknowledge,

54. [38], pp. 416, 293, 432; see also pp. 26, 168–169, 303–304; [86], p. 197; [32].

55. A statement Liang made in the 1930s (and naturally quoted *ad nauseam* during the 1955–1956 criticism campaign against him) reflects the popular image of the CCP at the time: "The Communist Party kills and burns, and the harm it causes is not that different from that of bandits." See [38], p. 279. See also [302], p. 78; [609], p. 62; [351], p. 131; [202], pp. 156–157; [260], p. 196; [342], p. 177; [414], p. 282.

56. See, for example, [51], no. 17. To an extent Mao's own comments on the Kiangsi period admitted some mistakes in the direction Liang criticized. For instance, in "On Correcting Mistaken Ideas in the Party," he mentioned "the purely military point of view," "a vagabond outlook," "the search for material satisfaction," lack of discipline, and so on. [424e].

the CCP was at least on the right track: it was working with the peasantry. (This was due, of course, more to Mao than to Marxism.) The Communists even shared certain goals with his rural reconstruction movement: both "want to raise the peasants' consciousness, want the peasants to get organized and get power to solve the problems that affect them directly."[57] Such admissions, of course, were partial and conditional; Liang naturally remained committed to his own vision for the salvation of China and intensely critical of those aspects of the Communists' work that he perceived as departures from his own scheme.

Liang did not, however, draw the revolution-reform distinction between the CCP's efforts and rural reconstruction that one might expect from him. Liang allowed that "rural reconstruction smacks of reformism," but "in all aspects it also discloses revolutionary connotations. I say positively that the form of the solution to the problems of China should be 'revolution.'" China's problem was "how successfully to create a new order," and rural reconstruction "ultimately is a kind of revolution: creating from the bottom up a completely new democratic-socialist order out of the old order of political despotism and free-enterprise economy. If you do not call that revolution, what can you call it?"[58]

The distinction Liang drew instead was that "the work we do is positive, creative, and constructive. Theirs [the CCP's] is negative and destructive." At a time the countryside needed positive unity and construction, the CCP "first applies a kind of divisive effort to rural society and creates a situation of disassociation and mutual antagonism within the village [so that] struggle comes about."[59] Liang attributed this "mistake" to the fact that the CCP—like the KMT, the liberals, and every other self-salvation movement that had preceded rural reconstruction—blindly followed foreign theories that were not valid for or relevant to China. "I have . . . been in sympathy with the CCP's social reform spirit. But I also deeply oppose the CCP's misunderstanding of Chinese society and their adopting foreign methods for use in China." At one point Liang concluded his argument against the CCP's use of struggle and violence with a droll plea: "Buddy, how about just acknowledging that this bit of artistry handed down by your revered ancestors Marx and Lenin is useless here."[60] Mao had yet to apply creatively

57. [12], p. 63.   58. [11e], pp. 191–192.
59. [12], pp. 64, 63–64; [363], p. 1; [38], pp. 197, 282; [42a]; [39], p. 8.
60. [51], no. 15; [11d], p. 158; see also [39], p. 6.

"the universal truths of Marxism-Leninism" to the Chinese situation and so Sinify them. Some years later, after the lessons of Kiangsi and the appearance of the Japanese on the scene, Mao would begin to add a bit of his own artistry to his esteemed predecessors' original creation and manage to iron out some of the difficulties.

On the most fundamental level, however, this struggle-harmony dichotomy between Mao and Liang was a difference that would always remain. Not surprisingly, it reflects an unequivocal and antipodian dissimilarity between the Marxian and Confucian modes. A connective thread that runs through all Mao's thought—as well as the practices and processes that follow from it—is the positive value of contradiction and conflict. Mao glorified struggle. Equally pervasive in Liang's Confucianism (and in most traditional Confucian thought) is the core value of harmony. Liang's concept of transformation and unity substituted a harmonious pan-moralism for struggle, as struggle was the diametric opposite of *li-hsing*. In solving internal contradictions [among the people], Liang pleaded, "we must avoid struggle at all costs . . . we must use *li-hsing* to solve the problems."[61] The mass spiritual resurrection that had been brewing in Liang's mind since his recovery from his early emotional crisis was based on a revitalization of the harmonious Confucian relationships.

Thus, at the heart of Liang's opposition to the Communists' "divisive work," was the fear that it would "destroy good relations and damage friendships. . . . Friendly feeling is the thing most capable of energizing vital activity. Talk about benefits! This is fundamentally the most precious of all. If it is destroyed, then imperceptibly there is incalculable loss." A "psychology of mutual suspicion, envy, and enmity" would thrust Chinese rural society—that last fragile refuge of *li-hsing*—down into the same subhuman depths as the morally squalid bourgeois West; the Chinese peasant—that hope for salvation of all humanity—would degenerate into *Homo economicus*. Giving the peasants something "ready-made—land, rent, money"—would create a "windfall psychology" of "getting more money for less work."[62]

As usual, there was a pragmatic edge to Liang's argument:

I am not saying that economics is not important, or that it is not possible for us to move the peasants through self-interest.

61. [38], p. 282.   62. [38], pp. 283–284.

I am just saying that if you move them *only* in this way, you will of course immediately move them a little, but in the long run they will not be able to be moved! . . . If everybody does not have concern for each other, and they just look out for themselves, then nobody will be able to solve their problems. . . . We do not want to seduce the peasants with petty advantages. Rather, we want to restore the peasants' spirits fundamentally and galvanize them into action. Only then will it work.[63]

Liang could never have considered the possibility that if the peasantry believed that the "ready-made" was rightfully theirs anyway, and if they personally struggled for it, then they would not necessarily contract "the psychology of looking for windfalls."

Be that as it may, the realization of Mao's Good Society was not ultimately based on a pandering to the "natural" petit bourgeois instincts of the peasantry either. Redistribution of material goods does not, to say the least, diminish calculated individual selfishness. Mao's revolution—like Liang's construction of a new Confucian society—was posited upon the "irrational" self-sacrifice of the individual; it appealed not to his own private material interest, but to the collective's. Liang's selfless Confucian peasant was no more idealized than Mao's Marxian proletarian or his peasant possessed of "proletarian consciousness."

What Liang ultimately wished to deny, of course, was the possibility and desirability (pragmatic and prescriptive) of genuine class struggle in China's villages. He conceded that the villages did have internal "contradictions," "problems," and "inequalities," but insisted that these paled in comparison to the contradiction between rural and urban society. "In present Chinese society, the only clearly visible differences between rich and poor, between the comfortable and the miserable, exist between city and village." (Here we can see the roots of Liang's confrontation with Mao twenty years later.) Not only did a gap exist between consumption levels but also between degrees of "freedom of person and property. In recent years both warlords and bandits have flourished, but they dare not carry out their depredations and oppressions in the city; they are all concentrated in the countryside. After they have robbed to satisfaction, only then do they fly off to the cities." The rural inhabitants who could and did join the warlords in their cozy oppidan ease "are

63. [38], pp. 298–299.

all landlords and rural gentry." This led Liang to conclude: "The truly oppressed and exploited are the 80 percent of Chinese society—the laboring producers who constitute the peasantry. . . . The most genuinely oppressed people are the ignorant peasants in China's isolated villages."[64]

Moreover, Liang warned, attempts to rank villagers into classes were bound to be impractical, labyrinthine, and unfair: "If 'property' refers to the means of production, then a poor peasant with two *mou* of land and someone who works a handicraft operation are both propertied. If property refers to cash, it becomes even more difficult to distinguish among the people."[65] As Liang described the process:

> I saw Mao Tse-tung analyze Kwangtung rural society into eight classes, and only the lower three or four classes were allowed to join the peasant associations. . . . The borders [between classes] were drawn very strictly. The peasants armed and formed peasant militias which came into conflict with the gentry-controlled militia. In the area around Hua hsien [where Liang had lived in his student Huang Ken-yung's house] there were large-scale battles. Here I am only speaking of the differences [between Mao and me]. I am not commenting upon whether it was right or wrong, good or bad. It is because our interpretations and evaluations of the problem of China are different.[66]

Liang himself summarized three conscious points of difference with CCP interpretations and evaluations:

> (1) They do not understand the special characteristics of disorganization and pacifism in [rural] Chinese society. Because it is dispersed, there are no unified bases on which to conduct struggle. Even if struggle can be started, it cannot produce results. At the same time . . . [society] has a revulsion to and dislike of struggle and destruction, so they [the CCP] will not be accepted by society. More importantly, the central purpose of the peasant movement lies in building up the power of the peasants themselves; I believe that the Chinese peasants have always lacked collective life, and so we must use positive,

64. [11e], pp. 188–189; [38], pp. 304–376; [12], pp. 63–64.
65. [11e], p. 188. Although not expressing it well, Liang was getting at a serious difficulty that later Communist-led land reform would also encounter.
66. [12], p. 64.

gradual efforts to get results. . . . (2) They [the CCP] do not understand the special character of the Chinese revolution . . . (The old order is already destroyed; there is no order at all right now, and so neither is there an unequal order.) At present the need is for construction to complete the revolution, to use progress to reach equality. On the other hand, struggle and destruction can only throw China into chaos and stop progress, and the revolution will, contrary to their purpose, not be able to be completed. (3) They do not understand that the revolutionary regime that they hope to establish—and which will complete the revolution by carrying out construction—has no possibility of being realized at this time in China.[67]

Liang's argument on the impracticality of a class-struggle revolution—based ultimately upon his philosophical theories of Chinese culture and society—derives also from his interpretation of Republican period politics and society. China had undergone complete social, economic, and political disintegration. There was no surviving legal-social superstructure, built upon the modes and relations of production, to overthrow.

If the old order still existed, we would have need of some destructive effort. In other words, if we had a strong object of revolution which could serve as a point of convergence for the revolutionary forces, things would be easy to handle. But at present there is no one object of revolution, the [revolutionary] demands are not the same, and it is impossible to talk about just who we should go all out to fight with.[68]

Who, Liang asked, were the power-holders? The warlords? The KMT? The local village bullies? None could be said to really constitute, or genuinely represent, a true economic class.

That archetypical oppressor, the warlord, was a good example. Did he have any commitment to or support from any specific class? No. Was he committed to any specific type of political or social program or policy reflecting the interests of a certain class? No. Were the warlords themselves of the same class background? No. (Liang did make a valid point. Depending on time, place, and circumstances, Republican period militarists had allied themselves with *or* against imperialist powers, the KMT, the CCP, the USSR, urban bourgeoisie, labor unions, landlords, tenants, and local bul-

67. [38], p. 282.   68. [39], p. 6.

lies.) Were they supported by some legal superstructure? No. "They do not depend on any legal system. Everyone detests them. Society is full of an atmosphere of opposition [to them] and yet they exist." Why *do* they hold power? Because they hold the gun. "All rule [today] is rule by the gun. . . . Warlords are quite the same as bandits. They simply take advantage of disorder to grasp and maintain power." Like everyone else in positions of power at whatever level, they were simply astute opportunists without any class loyalties or affiliations.

If a warlord was "simply an opportunist who can see the way things are going and can cope well with his environment," so too were all political parties: "Their struggles are just for their own selfish advantage and their party organizations are bogus. . . . The contestants have no fixed social base of support." The Communists, Liang quipped, "will not like to hear this . . . there are a lot of university students in Peiping, but far more rickshaw coolies. Yet most Communist party members are university students [not coolies]. The students who want to become Communists are exactly the same [in social background] as their classmates who want to be missionaries, or compradores, or bureaucrats."[69]

What about the local rural elite—the local bullies and evil gentry (*t'u-hao lieh-shen*)? Liang claimed that this group had been virtually created by the recently established Western-style local government and local defense organs, which have given "a minority of sly cunning people" a "chance to freely bully and terrorize the others" and "become local despots." But these opportunistic "parasitic thieves" could not be considered an economic class. In short, "in China, whoever has the gun today oppresses people. If he loses his gun tomorrow, then he becomes one of the oppressed."[70]

69. [38], p. 326; [11d], pp. 164–165; [38], pp. 362, 338; [11e], p. 186; see also [38], pp. 74–75, 82–94, 304, 317–318, 324–325, 338–339, 366–367; [11d], pp. 163–165; [42a]; [39], pp. 6–8.

70. [38], pp. 278, 276; see also pp. 274–278; [11d], p. 157; [11f], pp. 194–200. Liang claimed (and there is considerable historical evidence to support him) that the bureaucratic local government organs established since the late Ch'ing and early Republic had given a new class of unscrupulous lower gentry and criminals an opportunity to control and exploit the villages. Through seizing control of the Western-style bureaus and offices, they had come to monopolize complete power in the countryside. Not only did such a local self-government system give birth to the *t'u-hao lieh-shen*, Liang held, it also increased the power of the landlords. Local militia, for instance, "inevitably fall into the hands of the landlords"

Therefore, Liang protested that the CCP's "shallow" methods would also end up just temporarily substituting one group of oppressors for another. "As soon as an individual achieves power and position, [that person] soon becomes attached to the status quo and ends up following a nonrevolutionary or counterrevolutionary path."[71] Mao himself was not unmindful of the insidious potential in the entrenchment of a "new class," but the key difference between his solution and Liang's was in *means*, not ends. For Liang, the will of history was not embodied in a revolutionary vanguard or a single oppressed class; the peasant masses themselves were his protagonists. And he insisted that the Communists' violent measures were "no way to create a new society. Our ultimate goal is to make the peasantry economically and politically equal. We forge forward toward this objective through continuous readjustment of social relationships . . . [which require] strengthening and bolstering the power of the peasants themselves and bringing about the new society in systematic steps."[72] Mao's cultural revolution would proceed in leaps and spurts, not "in systematic steps," and through open struggle, not by "readjusting social relationships." Yet it would be a process not unlike what Liang had in mind, especially in those aspects in which it differed from Western models.

The phrase "continuous readjustment of social relationships" recurs repeatedly throughout Liang's writings and approximates Gandhi's solution to social contradictions: "the transformation of social relationships." Satyagraha is a far cry from cooperatives and Confucian *chiang-hsueh*, yet in certain respects Liang does appear very much the Chinese version of the Mahatma; the moral man is essentially a nonviolent man. Liang could never accept violence and internal use of armed force as a revolutionary necessity. He was quite aware that political power grew out of the barrel of a gun, but political power was precisely what he wanted rural reconstruction to avoid. Although Liang's opposition to armed violence naturally reflects his Confucian urge to harmony, it also evinces the indelible impression made by the chaos and destruction he witnessed during his 1917 trip through Mao's native district.

Liang was not shy about pointing out to Mao the consequences

---

and so "become nothing more than an aid to the landlords in monopolizing power and enriching themselves at the expense of [the people of] their locale." [38], pp. 274–276; see also pp. 196–197, 274–280; [11f], pp. 193–200; [42c], p. 170.

71. [38], p. 284.   72. [11e], p. 185.

he perceived in reliance upon armed force. In 1938 at Yenan, Liang told Mao that the CCP had failed in Kiangsi precisely because they had relied too much upon military force and not enough on the people's political support. "The fact that in the past ten years the Communist revolution has failed almost to the point where the party itself was exterminated testifies to its political defeat and the mistakes of its political line," Liang chided.[73] On balance, Mao probably agreed. Clearly the CCP of the Kiangsi Soviet period and of the wartime period differed in the degree to which it relied upon armed force.

Despite Liang's profound aversion to the use of armed force and his Confucian gravitation toward harmony, murky ambivalences still cloud his thought on the question. Could he have suspected, as his later critics did, that even with the emphasis on "continuous readjustment of social relationships," a new rural civilization, born without the harsh midwifery of bloody class struggle, would end up dominated by rich peasants and landlords? It often appears that Liang would have liked to reap the benefits of struggle without the destruction of harmonious human relations, much in the same way that he would have liked to reap the material benefits of modernization without its inevitable attendant evils. For instance, although Liang categorically denied that rural China had classes in the usual sense, he did admit: "It does have inequalities of wealth and class exploitation, such as tenants being exploited by landlords. . . . And the tenancy problem is extremely serious." Despite his insistence on the absolute necessity of hamlet harmony, he paradoxically allowed that "there are locales where the internal contradictions [within the village] would make unity impossible." Not just tenancy, but even unequal landholdings, Liang declared, "were very serious problems in some places. This fault is due to the private-tenure land system, which inevitably results in unequal distribution."[74]

Perhaps Liang did feel, however vaguely, a tormenting twinge of self-contradiction, for he was more than a little defensive about his nonviolent, gradualist road to communes and socialism.

[What the Communists and leftists] talk about most is just what I talk about least. This by no means indicates any definite predisposition on my part [against solving the land problem immediately]. Probably it is just [because] my emotions are a trifle too serene; [I] lack the heightened mood of excited

73. [80].   74. [38], p. 304; also p. 282.

indignation that [you] gentlemen possess [and so I] . . . talk
less [about it than you do]. Even more important, because I
am thinking only in terms of [practical] methods of solving
[the problem], if [I] do not have a [practical] method, then [I]
put it aside temporarily and do not talk about it. Actually,
though, how can I not recognize [the problem]? How could it
be that we people who talk about peasants all day long are not
anxious to solve the land problem? But a regime capable of
solving this problem does not exist. The methods of the
Communist party are indeed quite straightforward and satisfying; it is just that for the nation as a whole, they are useless.
If they were able to establish a regime, then the methods would
be useful.[75]

So, the pragmatic (as distinguished from the prescriptive of harmony and nonviolence) side of Liang's argument against class
struggle and immediate redistribution of land was a conditional
one. "Although the methods of the Communist party are not good,
still there are some places where they are useful. If it were *really
possible* to overthrow the local tyrants and bad gentry and redis-
tribute the land equally, short and sweet just like that, it would be
pretty good too." The problem was that "to solve the land problem
requires a political force, and this political force has not yet taken
shape." The only thing that would make it "really possible," Liang
implied, was a unified and unifying revolutionary regime. Such a
regime would have to be truly "revolutionary." "Unless it was a
revolutionary regime, it would only represent inertia and nonpro-
gressiveness." Only a regime like that in the Soviet Union could
"carry out the revolution." In the end, Liang said, "methods of
solving the land problem are easy enough to think up; the crucial
thing is: who will carry them out?"[76]

Part of the reason it was impossible for Liang to conceive of the
establishment of a revolutionary regime might have been his lack of
dialectical thinking (because of his own "realistic" insistence upon
viewing only the current "facts"?). Yet his inability to imagine the
possibility of such a regime was also manifestly due to those facts—
the concrete historical situation in the early and mid-1930s. The
Communists, having obviously failed to ride the original "revolutionary wave" to success, were literally on the verge of extinction. The KMT had shown itself incapable of uniting itself, much
less the nation. Foreign imperialist dominions aside, the rest of

75. [38], pp. 440–441 (emphasis mine).
76. [38], pp. 197 (emphasis mine), [38], pp. 304, 401; [39], p. 2.

China was actually controlled by independent or semi-independent militarists who, although they might sometimes share KMT affiliation, would go to war with each other almost annually. Given the situation, Liang's dismissal of any idea that a revolutionary regime might emerge in the near future was far more realistic than anticipating what actually happened in 1949. Despite Mao's skill in dialectics, he was doubtless as surprised as Liang by the turn of events only a few years later. Therefore, we cannot dismiss Liang's proposed solution at the time—a unified and unifying movement of "society itself" to carry out the reforms—as simply a crackpot idea of a religious megalomaniac.

We must quickly add, however, that Liang never seemed to grasp the other side of the coin: what about the current power-holders—the KMT and the various militarists—that *did* exist? Here we come to the nub of the question of Liang's ultimate failure and, perhaps, his ultimate irrelevance to the unfolding drama of Republican period history. Liang hoped to have the rural movement use (*li-yung*) the various power-holders for its own ends by "controlling" and "directing" them through the power of *li-hsing*. He was not unaware that the rural movement existed only at the sufferance of and financial support from the present power-holders (and thus, it could not avoid being "on the side of the government"). He also understood that the only way to be free of such dependence was violent revolution—the "destructive type of work" he had criticized the Communists for. Yet because his ultimate concern was Chinese culture, he could never draw the logical conclusion that, in order to succeed, rural reconstruction had to be an independent, armed, political movement. *Li-hsing*, the essence of that culture, would, like Gandhi's "truth," have to do the job somehow. His insistence that rural reconstruction "must use *li-hsing* to solve the problem" had its inevitable result.

Nevertheless, Liang's ambivalences do foreshadow his eventual acceptance of the Communist regime. "We do not definitely oppose communism," he said. "If the external realities develop to the point where they are suitable, then we will talk about it. If the external realities demand communism, who wants to be stubborn about it? . . . Our path and that of communism are in the same direction. There is only a slight difference in degree, and the measures [we adopt] are different."[77]

77. [39], p. 8; [38], pp. 282, 307–308, 378.

CHAPTER X

Rural Reconstruction
During the Nanking Decade:
A Political and Social Analysis

> Recently, amid clamor and cries of "rural bankruptcy" and "rural collapse," the slogans "rural reconstruction" and "rural revival" reverberate through the entire nation; this is really a kind of sudden awakening of government and people.[1]

Thus, the major chronicler of Republican period rural reform movements began his 1934 compendium. Another reporter counted almost seven hundred distinct organizations devoted to rural work of various kinds.[2] The pens of the intelligentsia churned out hundreds of monographs and specialized periodicals and thousands of articles on the rural problem and the rural reconstruction solution. The powerholders—the Nanking regime itself, the provincial governments under its control, and the semi-independent militarist provincial governments—were concurrently formulating policies, instituting measures, establishing agencies, reorganizing local government structures, and generally manifesting great concern for the giant rural sector of Chinese society they had previously ignored.

This plethora of projects and programs ranged in scope from a single village to the entire nation. Some limited themselves to one specific activity such as cooperatives, self-defense organization, or irrigation; others expanded into broad programs that simultaneously attacked all rural problems and sought to transform the entire environment within a designated area. An idea usually associated with rural reform was local self-government (*ti-fang tzu-chih*) or rural self-government (*hsiang-ts'un tzu-chih*), which implied political organization on the village level.

1. [366], p. 1.   2. [259].

1927

Although the 1930s were the heyday for rural reconstruction, the "sudden awakening" for many actually came in 1927. That was the year in which Liang Shu-ming finally dared believe in the potential for a rural movement, and Wang Hung-i's Village Government Group first began to attract widespread attention and important new converts. In March of that year, Mao Tse-tung proclaimed his own "awakening" to the possibility that rural dissatisfaction could serve as the motive force for a Chinese "proletarian" revolution.[3] Also in 1927, Feng Yü-hsiang began to support rural projects, P'eng Yü-t'ing's group got started, and T'ao Hsing-chih established his Hsiao-chuang Normal School. Moreover, the National Education Improvement Society (Chung-hua chiao-yü kai-tsao she), which had hitherto shown no particular interest in rural reform, sponsored T'ao's pioneering work.[4] At about the same time, Shen Ting-i—the man whose personality and programs "most resembled P'eng's—began his rural reform and local self-government work in his home area of Tung hsiang in northern Chekiang.[5] Several other reform organizations and intellectuals simultaneously and independently ("as though arranged by heaven," Liang Shu-ming said) shifted their urban-oriented line of vision to the rural areas. Most notably, James Y.C. Yen's China Association for the Promotion of Mass Education moved its base of operations to the countryside,[6] and the China Vocational Education Society began to focus on rural work.[7]

3. Mao's famous "Report on an Investigation of the Agrarian Movement in Hunan" was first published in *Hsiang-tao chou-pao* (Guide weekly), no. 191 (Mar. 20, 1927).
   4. [366], pp. 282–283; [494]; [339], p. 27; [562], p. 1.
   5. [366], pp. 330–331; [396], p. 65; [629].
   6. The mass education movement had already been established in Chai-ch'eng in 1926, but it did not expand operations and become a major rural reform experimental center until Y. C. Yen returned from a fundraising trip abroad in 1929. See [366], pp. 67–75; [241]; [120], p. 38; [562].
   7. The experimental district was originally founded in conjunction with Southeastern University and the Association for Promotion of Mass Education, both of which had to drop out after a year. After April, 1928, Huang's organization continued on alone. The next year the association started another project at Huang-hsu in Chiang-ning hsien. Thereafter, the association continued to increase the number of its sites throughout Kiangsu and Chekiang. See [366], pp. 140–157; [329], pp. 38–39; [449a]; [400], p. 21; [562], p. 2.

Contemporary observers noted this striking "simultaneous convergence of different people and organizations" into a rural movement.[8] One journalist compared the concomitant appearance of projects after 1926 to "bamboo shoots after spring rain, a violent gale and roaring tide" and the "tumultuous flowing of water as if coming to lift up the heavens and cover the earth."[9] A leftist observer concluded that the "spring rain" responsible for this luxuriant sprouting was the Communist-led peasant movement of 1925–26: "It is only that after 1927, after various kinds of changes had taken place, a part of this movement was obliterated. But as far as it reached, it made an indelible mark politically, socially, and intellectually. The reformist rural movement is a reaction to this peasant movement."[10]

The hypothesis is tempting. Conversely, we could also argue that the path the CCP eventually took (away from the Marxist orthodoxies) might in itself reflect the urgency of the rural problem in China and the intense concern it was generating among reform-minded Chinese. Certainly several factors seemed to merge at the time and provoke a tremendous increase in the attention paid to China's rural areas. Many viewed with growing distress such negative phenomena as the social and political consequences of warlord rule and rapine; the *embourgeoisement* of the hsien-seat "higher" gentry—the traditional rural leaders—and their subsequent desertion of the countryside; and the expansion of urban areas to the detriment and neglect of the vast rural areas. Moreover, the spread of schools and education and the increase in nationwide communications raised the general awareness of these problems.[11] More debatable, but still relevant, were the effects of imperialism on the rural economy, and the decline in the rural standard of living.

Although these conditions undoubtedly contributed to the spread of the rural reconstruction idea, none can fully explain the sudden blossoming of interest and work in rural reconstruction in 1927 and 1928. All were ongoing trends that had existed at least

8. [562], p. 5.   9. [297].   10. [400], p. 3.
11. Ramon Myers, for instance, noted the special significance of 1927 when he asked: "Why was an interest in agriculture not prompted until after 1927?" The factors listed in his answer, however, were all either trends already evident before the 1920s or factors, such as the effects of the world economic depression, which were not present until after 1931. [444], pp. 13–14.

since 1900. Moreover, they had already given rise to scattered rural reconstruction theories, proponents, and small-scale organizations, but none of the earlier efforts had attracted significant attention or support before 1927. The crucial difference in 1927 might indeed have been the existence (or threat) of the successful Communist example for mobilizing rural society. In Liang's case, the success of the peasant associations does seem to have been at least one factor in erasing his doubts (partially inspired by the more "orthodox" urban-oriented Marxist Ch'en Tu-hsiu) regarding the feasibility of his ideas on a peasant-based mass movement. Certainly Feng Yü-hsiang's projects were specifically and unambiguously in reaction to the CCP. The evidence for the other rural reformers is more circumstantial, but it does seem to be more than mere coincidence that so many different kinds of rural reform projects should emerge or take on new vigor within a year after the CCP had demonstrated the spectacular potential of peasant associations. Even some leaders in the KMT were intrigued for a time with the possibility of using rural reconstruction for their own purposes.

The Local Rural Elites

The usual assumption of a "natural" alliance between the KMT and local elites is at odds with evidence that the two were in direct competition for rural economic and political resources. The difficulty lies in the vague category of "local elite," which also raises problems for identifying the natural constituency for rural reconstruction. Because of the enormous regional variation, generalizations about rural social classes are almost impossible, but by the late 1920s there were certain identifiable trends.

First, there was a "big landlord" rentier class, whose interests, capital, and sometimes residences were in the cities (or at least the hsien seats, or larger urban areas). With their money in coastal city banks and their Western-educated sons in urban occupations, these rentier-capitalists might be interested in rural law and order (and the efficient collection of rents) and, to an extent, higher agricultural production, but they obviously were not the socio-economic base for rural reconstruction and village self-government schemes. These were, perhaps, the remnants and descendants of the "upper" gentry of imperial times, but by the end of the Northern Expedition, they were well launched into economic, social, and cultural *embourgeoisement* and cut loose from the deteriorating fabric of traditional rural society. The KMT's local elite confederates might be found among their numbers.

For rural reconstruction's class base we might look further down the scale of wealth and power to the "lower" gentry of the imperial era (the *sheng-yuan*, *chien-sheng*, and their descendants). This group, with smaller landholdings and wealth, lived in the towns and villages. Most important, they had neither the city connections nor the urban cultural coloration of the upper gentry. (Much of the rhetoric of the rural reconstruction movement was intensely anti-urban and put all manner of rural ills at the city's doorstep.) The lower gentry and small landlords were the most common leaders of spontaneous mass movements and peasant protest below the hsien level.[12]

Could this lower-gentry small landlord class be identical with the bad gentry (*lieh-shen*), who, in collusion with local bullies (*t'u-hao*), dominated the Republican period local rural scene? Was the constituency for the rural reconstruction and local government movements composed of the famed local bullies and bad gentry?[13] Investigation of the most noted rural reconstruction projects does not give a clear-cut answer. In both Ting hsien and Tsou-p'ing there was continuous conflict between the reformers and at least some segments of the lower gentry, as well as numerous references to the difficulties with local bullies and bad gentry.[14] The tension, moreover, was not limited to those projects run by idealistic urban-bred "outsiders." P'eng Yü-t'ing and his associates were lower-gentry natives of the area in which they operated; yet one of their first acts was to kick out of office all sub-hsien-level administrative officials (village managers—*ts'un li-shih*—and district heads—*ch'ü-chang*) and revise election procedures so the "bad gentry" could not continue to control the posts.[15] Liang Shu-ming

12. This assertion is based upon a conversation with Professor Lucien Bianco in the fall of 1973, concerning his recent research on "Spontaneous Peasant Uprisings in the 1920s and 1930s." Although it was not his major thesis, he did emphasize that small landlords often organized and led anti-hsien-government, anti-tax, and other kinds of uprisings during the period he studied.

13. See [362].   14. See, for example, [258], p. 208.

15. P'eng and his associates, such as Pieh T'ing-fang, are termed "local tyrants" or "local despots" (*e pa*), a designation similar to *lieh-shen*. See [173], pp. 49–50; [225]. P'eng himself openly admitted that, in its early stages, his program was plainly "rule by gentry" (*shen chih*). See [336], p. 28; also pp. 8–12.

blamed the very existence of the *t'u-hao lieh-shen* on the bureaucratic local government reforms of the late Ch'ing and early Republic, which he believed had merely produced tools for further governmental oppression and extortion. He specifically designed his
own movement as a nonbureaucratic, voluntary association, initiated and maintained by the peasants themselves, to avoid the evils
he perceived in all existing self-government institutions.[16]

The rural reconstruction and village self-government reformers
themselves distinguished two kinds of lower gentry, just as the
Yenan-period Communists did: the "bad gentry" and the "enlightened gentry" (*k'ai-ming shen-shih*). For both reformers and revolutionaries, the distinction was not based on socio-economic
grounds, but on the gentry's attitude and actions. This similarity
between the rural reconstructionists and the Communists is not
irrelevant; rural reconstruction was fundamentally a reformist version of Mao's peasant movement. But rural reconstruction sought
to transform bad gentry into enlightened gentry through education, moral influence, and occasional application of hsien government power; the Communists, with their poorer peasantry base,
were able to take more direct measures. As one contemporary
pundit had it, the goals of the rural reconstructionists and the
Communists were the same, but their methods could be clearly
distinguished with Buddhist terminology: rural reconstruction's
method was one of "gradual enlightenment" while the Communists
advocated "sudden enlightenment."[17] When the CCP, during the
Yenan period, abandoned the latter faith for the former, it was a
conversion that was important to the Party's astonishing success.

KMT Ambivalence toward Rural Reconstruction

Chinese political theorists from Ku Yen-wu (1613–1682) to Mao
Tse-tung have been attracted to the idea of releasing the latent
energies and initiative of the local community through programs of
local autonomy. Ku had argued that the net result of harnessing
the selfish but energetic and efficient local elite would be an increase of national power (somewhat along the lines of Adam

16. [38], pp. 146–148, 187–188, 196–197, 221, 234–235, 273–280; [11f],
pp. 193–203.
17. [178], pp. 8–10.

Smith's "invisible hand" effect). With later intellectuals, who were both influenced by Western ideas and confronted with the imperialist threat, a totally untraditional concept of mass mobilization almost imperceptibly entered into their intellectual discourse. With the rise of the May Thirtieth movement (1925–26), newer Marxist-influenced concepts of popular mobilization became widespread.

Rural reconstruction would seem to be the natural solution for Nanking's two chief rural concerns: security and economic development. Sun Yat-sen himself, in *Outline of National Reconstruction*, envisioned a process of democratization "from the bottom up," whereby mass political participation would be gradually introduced on the hsien level. Rural reconstructionists were forever quoting appropriate passages from the *Outline* to legitimize their activities in the eyes of the Nanking government.

Nanking, however, was in a double dilemma. It was the heir (however much dispossessed) of the Peking Imperial government and, as such, was faced with the tricky operation of manipulating the nonofficial rural elite into fulfilling their traditional role as the enforcers of political control and economic exploitation of local society on behalf of the capital. Yet, since the nineteenth-century rebellions, the local elite had become an increasingly more independent and less reliable governmental instrument.

Nanking was, moreover, not just a central government, but one bent upon creating a modernized nation-state; the Kuomintang (quite in accord with the principles of developmental political science) equated modernization with bureaucratization. To this end of modernization, rural reconstruction (and its instrumentality, local self-government) was a double-edged sword. The potential it possessed for control and economic development in the local community derived primarily from its ability to involve and mobilize the local, nonofficial elite. Its success, therefore, no matter how desirable, economically productive, or socially beneficial, threatened the interests and bureaucracy of the central government.

The second side of the Nationalist government's problem was the Communist movement, which instilled Nanking with an overwhelming obsession with security. Nanking's concern for control reinforced and compounded its constitutional antagonism with nonbureaucratized grass-roots organization. With its anti-Communist purges in the late 1920s, the Kuomintang had actually burned all its bridges to mass movements. The lower echelons of the party had learned the lesson of 1927 only too well; the subsequent two decades are replete with examples of their heavy-handed (and often independently initiated) efforts to squelch mass organizations.

This two-way pull of the rural reconstruction idea resulted in a brief period of ambivalence in the KMT attitude toward rural reform and reformers. Chiang Kai-shek himself visited T'ao Hsing-chih's project at Hsiao-chuang in 1930. In March 1931, he and Mme. Chiang met with Y.C. Yen to discuss the Ting hsien program and arrange for the establishment of a reform program in Chi-kou, Chekiang—Chiang's birthplace. They also arranged to have some Central Military Academy cadets trained at Ting hsien.[18] The next year, Chiang invited Liang Shu-ming south to discuss his program of rural government "so that measures can be adopted in the various provinces, such as Hupei, Hunan, and Kiangsi." Liang, wary of governments in general and the KMT's in particular, refused to go. The motive for looking at Yen's and Liang's programs was obvious. Chiang had asked to talk with Liang, for instance, because "recently he had been looking very hard for ways of governing the areas recently cleared of [Communist] bandits"[19]

The experimental hsien regulations. Vice-minister of the Interior Kan Nai-kuang—a Wang Ching-wei man of the Left-KMT—was especially active in seeking to tame rural reconstruction to serve Nanking's purposes. Immediately after his appointment in June 1932, Kan set about forming a nine-man commission on local self-government for the nine provinces of North and Central China. The ministry appointed the leading rural reconstruction figure of each province to the commission (including Liang Shu-ming in Shantung, Y.C. Yen in Hopei, and Kao Chien-szu in Kiangsu). Liang hesitated over accepting the post because of his objections, on general principles, to the idea of local self-government and rural reform carried out by the "government," and his specific disapproval of Nanking's 1927–1929 regulations for local government.[20]

The Ministry of Interior also planned a conference in December 1932 and invited leading nongovernment rural reconstruction

18. [495], pp. 5–6; [606], pp. 28–30; [258], pp. 215–218.
19. [272f]. A similar statement on the Kuomintang's purpose in investigating rural reconstruction experimental projects is in [426], p. 1.
20. [272c].

figures. In October, Kan made a tour of North China rural reconstruction projects and stopped for long discussions with both Liang
and Y.C. Yen. Liang questioned Kan on the significance of his trip
and pressed him on the matter of bureaucratization of local administrative organizations. "Previously the Ministry of Interior has set
down all self-government legal regulations. Actually, though, many
of them are not suitable for use. What about that?" Liang asked.
Kan replied that the ministry was presently planning to allow each
province to carry on certain rural experimental work without central government regulation. This promise of greater freedom for
rural experimentation must have reassured Liang, for he overcame
his hesitation and agreed to attend the conference.[21]

The conference did indeed pass an important proposal (later
approved by the Central Political Council), which required each
province to establish an experimental social and political reform
district (*hsien-cheng chien-she shih-yen ch'ü*) of one to four hsien.
These districts would be free from any national or provincial government regulations so they could experiment with methods "to
reform the people's lives" as well as search for new political forms
and organizational techniques at the hsien level and below. Each
province was also instructed to establish a school for training local
self-government personnel.[22] Once approved, the new regulations
provided the basis for provincial designation as experimental hsien
of Tsou-p'ing and Ho-tse in Shantung, Ting hsien in Hopei, and a
few other hsien throughout the country. That the KMT government should actually implement such regulations reflected both its
increasing concern with rural problems as well as its continuing
ambivalence toward rural mobilization.

KMT repression of rural reconstruction. In the final
analysis, however, the natural antagonisms between the central
government and rural reconstruction ideals outweighed the attrac-
tions. When Chiang's men took Honan in the fall of 1930, one of
their first acts was to close down the Honan Village Government

21. [272e]; [272i].
22. For the text of the proposals, see [519], pp. 223–226. See also [561];
[272j]. Another major proposal passed by the conference called for abolition of the independent sub-hsien bureaus (*chü*) and establishment of departments (*k'o*) in their place. See [519], pp. 212–231; also [399], pp. 178–
181; [562], p. 3.

Academy.[23] Although Chiang had personally visited T'ao Hsing-chih's experimental districts around Hsiao-chuang in 1930, he later personally ordered T'ao's arrest, abolished the Hsiao-chuang Normal School, and had troops occupy the entire area. Many students, however, refused to go home; they remained in the area living secretly with peasant families.[24] In Chekiang, Shen Ting-i was mysteriously cut down by a hail of bullets (a common KMT form of assassination) while returning from a meeting with high KMT leaders, and his experimental work stopped within a year.[25]

Shen's Honanese counterpart, P'eng Yü-t'ing, who had remained in Honan after the closing of Tao's school, continued to work at organizing his own self-defense self-government system in several hsien around Nan-yang. When his organization protested the various new tax burdens (fu-shui and tsa-shui) and flatly refused to pay the KMT "special tax" (the opium tax), the provincial government ordered P'eng's arrest. Since P'eng, however, could literally mobilize his entire area within an hour, nothing could be done against him at the time. (Some compared the military impregnability of P'eng's realm to the Communist-controlled areas, which lay just across the railway line.)[26] This confrontation between rural reconstruction and the KMT bureaucracy suggests a classic meeting of forces contending over local resources. In 1933, the KMT launched a major campaign in Honan to extend its bureaucratic system downward and unseat the local gentry who had monopolized local administrative positions. It happened that P'eng, too, was gunned down by anonymous "bandits" that year.[27] Thereafter, the KMT dropped any pretense of encouraging local self-government. It opted instead for the less threatening plan of at-

23. As soon as Chiang's troops had entered the Honan capital of Kaifeng, the acting chairman of the provincial government Chang Fang (made commissioner of the civil government a few months later) issued orders abolishing the academy. The teachers and students formed an alumni association before disbanding, and through this organization P'eng built up his influence. See [533c].

24. Chiang's motive for closing T'ao's school was actually very complicated. Probably the most important single factor was T'ao's personal connection with Chiang's rival, Feng Yü-hsiang. Other contributing factors were the students' radicalism (refusing to pay trolley fares in Nanking while preaching socialization of the facility) and T'ao's own criticism of Chiang. See [495], pp. 5–6; [504], pp. 41–48; [366], p. 283.

25. [366], p. 339; [272d], p. 1.   26. [178].

27. [396], p. 65; [562], p. 2; [588], pp. 22, 35, 65.

tempting to fly rural China into the modern world on the wings of bureaucracy.

Yen Hsi-shan's rural reconstruction—the form the KMT tentatively adopted for a time—went the same path as the KMT. After 1927, the Shansi self-government system degenerated into a control-oriented bureaucracy, which simply lowered official power to the local levels. As such, Yen's programs were disclaimed and discredited by the rural reconstruction movement.[28]

The CC Clique experimental hsien. The two CC Clique-controlled experimental hsien projects reflected the KMT's shift to bureaucratic "control" and bureaucratically imposed rural economic development. Ch'en Kuo-fu, supported by Chiang Kai-shek, originally suggested establishing an experimental hsien at Chiang-ning, Kiangsu. Formally established in 1933 and under the direct supervision of the Nanking government, the Chiang-ning experimental hsien was staffed by students and teachers of the Central Political Academy (Chung-yang cheng-chih hsueh-yuan, a CC Clique institution). The magistrate, Mei Szu-p'ing, was a professor of political science from the academy. As director, the KMT central committee appointed its specialist in local government, Li Tsung-huang. Lan-hsi hsien in Chekiang was also a CC-Clique-run project.[29]

The general line of these two experimental hsien was "from the top down" agricultural development and rural security. As far as Mei Szu-p'ing was concerned, the goal of rural reconstruction was to see to it that directives from the top got implemented at the bottom.[30] Thus, the initiative for all programs rested with the hsien government; lower administrative levels functioned only as extensions of the hsien government. Paralleling Nanking's policy in China as a whole, these two hsien stressed transport (especially

---

28. The KMT government used a version of the Shansi local-government scheme as the basis for its 1927–1929 national regulations. See [399], pp. 118–139; also [297]; [142], p. 2. Liang Shu-ming noted the tendency toward bureaucratization and increased hsien government control when he visited Yen-Hsi-shan and toured the Shansi village government system in early 1929. [9q], pp. 244–252.

29. [397], pp. 84–85; [399], p. 184.

30. [274], II, 29. In the experimental hsien, as in the rest of China, the breaking of *t'u-hao lieh-shen* power was the basic principle of KMT rural administration. See [400], p. 27.

motor roads—another reflection of Nanking's obsession with security) and improved agricultural technology.[31] Although the CC Clique seemed to be looking for a method by which they could both mobilize and control the local rural communities, the implications of mass mobilization on the local level were too threatening to the fundamental interests of the central government. Thus, the natural antagonisms between centralized control and the real goals of rural reconstruction forced them to concentrate instead on merely extending their bureaucratic control downward.

Contemporary observers quickly noted the differences between Chiang-ning and the non-KMT rural projects. The KMT effort was a government movement, while the non-KMT rural reconstruction was (ideally) a purely civilian movement.[32] Liang Shu-ming's own ideas were the diametric opposite of the KMT's; indeed, his eventual goal was the destruction of the sub-hsien-level administration in which the KMT had placed its hopes.

31. [629].   32. [297]; [562]; [383].

CHAPTER XI

Rural Reconstruction
in Shantung

In June 1931, Han Fu-ch'ü's provincial government officially opened the Shantung Rural Reconstruction Institute (Shan-tung hsiang-ts'un chien-she yen-chiu yuan) in the town of Tsou-p'ing and designated the surrounding Tsou-p'ing hsien as an experimental district (shih-yen ch'ü).[1] Under the special regulations passed by the national government in July 1933, the area also became an experimental hsien (shih-yen hsien), which permitted the institute to expand its research and training activities to include governmental administrative reforms as well. Due to Liang Shuming's position as one of the central figures involved in the Tsou-p'ing effort and his widespread reputation and prestige, Tsou-p'ing quickly became one of the main intellectual and spiritual centers of the rural reconstruction movement. The other center was the site run by James Y.C. Yen at Ting hsien in Hopei.[2]

In the eyes of contemporary observers, Tsou-p'ing and Ting hsien symbolized the "old" and "new" schools of rural reconstruction. One contemporary critic remarked: "the main difference [between the old and new schools] is that the new school relies on 'international' material and human aid, while the old school is comparatively conservative and, up to now at least, has not welcomed foreign influence or foreign participation in its rural-reconstruction movement."[3] Other observers noted that Ting hsien

1. The following description of the institute is based primarily on [472], [473], the periodicals [533], [272], and numerous interviews with Hu Ying-han (Liang's correspondence secretary at Tsou-p'ing in 1934–1935), Chou Shao-hsien (a graduate of the institute training department and later a rural worker at Ch'ü-fu hsien, Shantung), and Ch'en Wen-chung (a student of Liang's).

2. [401], p. 150; [400], p. 11; [239]; [204], p. 63.

3. [400], p. 21. Y. C. Yen originally had hoped the experiment at Ting hsien would become "self-operating, self-supporting, and self-propagating," but he never achieved this objective. See [605].

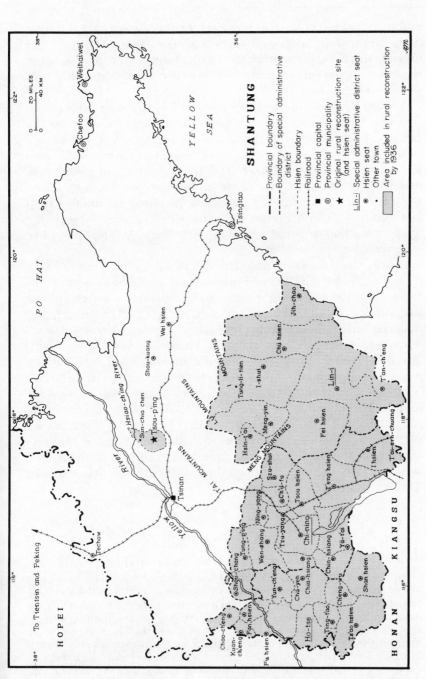

SHANTUNG

- –·–·– Provincial boundary
- –––––– Boundary of special administrative
  district
- ·········· Hsien boundary
- +++++++ Railroad
- ■ Provincial capital
- ⊚ Provincial municipality
- ★ Original rural reconstruction site
  (and hsien seat)
- **Lin-i** Special administrative district seat
- ⊙ Hsien seat
- · Other town

  Area included in rural reconstruction
  by 1936

MAP 2

and similar projects, such as those run by the Vocational Education
Association, were conceived of as a kind of philanthropic relief
movement to "save others" (chiu-jen). Tsou-p'ing, on the other
hand, was based on the premise that only the peasants could save
themselves (tzu-chiu).[4]

Above all else, Tsou-p'ing represented Chinese-style rural reconstruction.[5] The "fundamental spirit" of the institute was "to use the
power of character reformation to solve practical problems."
"Tsou-p'ing had," as one disdainful, modern-minded KMT man
put it, "a decidedly Confucian smell to it." Even visiting American
educators commented that of the places they visited, only Tsou-
p'ing had "the spirit of the Chinese people, the education of Eastern culture." Another visitor remarked: "I've already seen the
Russian method of getting close to the masses. At Tsou-p'ing I've
seen the Chinese method."[6]

In contrast, observers noted that Yale-educated "Jimmy" Y.C.
Yen considered "the five thousand years of Chinese history, its
habits and customs, as the enemy. So he worships Western culture
unconditionally and wants to use Western spiritual, technical, and
material aid to help create 'modern,' 'scientific' rural villages."
Thanks to American "material aid," Ting hsien had "ample financial and human resources."[7] Material standards—at least for the
personnel of the two hsien projects—were decidedly different.
Ting hsien worker Li Ching-han found a salary of 150 yuan a
month "barely enough to live on"; the salary scale at Tsou-p'ing
ranged from 15 to 50 yuan a month.[8] Because of Ting hsien's
glamorous affluence, its proximity to Peking, and most of all, Yen's
contacts in the missionary and American academic communities,
Westerners most often identified the rural reconstruction idea with
Ting hsien rather than Tsou-p'ing.

4. [562].
5. [472], pp. 4–6; [562], pp. 11–15; [401], p. 161; [170], pp. 133–134;
[142]; [143], p. 17; [429].
6. [11g], pp. 207–208; [618]; [560].   7. [400]; [142].
8. [258], p. 105. The salary scale at Tsou-p'ing depended on the wealth
of the particular village. Teachers or managers of the village center-
schools were paid from 15 to 30 yuan a month. [430], pp. 81–83. Only the
three top-level administrators of the institute (such as the training department director) received a salary of 80 yuan a month. The only funds the
institute received from the outside came from the provincial government
(through the department of civil government—Min-cheng t'ing) and varied from 107,000 yuan in 1931–32 to 116,000 yuan in 1934–35. [473], pp.
24–26; [472], pp. 14–17; [623]; [621].

Yet it was the Shantung institute that had the broadest influence and directly touched the lives of the most people. By 1937, over 70 of the 107 hsien in Shantung had been designated as experimental rural reconstruction districts and were directly or indirectly influenced by Liang's organization or its personnel: former Tsou-p'ing workers and students filled hsien government posts or worked implementing one or another of the programs they had learned about at the institute. If the Japanese had not occupied Shantung, every hsien in the province would have become part of the Tsou-p'ing network by 1938. In addition, about a fifth of the personnel trained by the institute were from provinces other than Shantung. Most returned to their home areas to work in local projects or to set up their own programs.[9]

Finally, the Tsou-p'ing effort distinguished itself from all the other rural work agencies by its grandiose and audacious ultimate goal—creation of a whole new Chinese culture and society with implications for the entire world. Through a simultaneous revival and reform of traditional culture, the workers at the Tsou-p'ing research institute would evolve—through experimentation based on the principles of Liang's "true" understanding of the wisdom of the sages—new and unique social and economic forms of organization. These new forms would enable China to reap the benefits of modernization while avoiding the spiritual and physical evils of the overly urbanized, excessively industrialized West. But Liang was not content with just the vision of how his project would remold the Chinese countryside; he saw it producing the forms that would ultimately replace the present "abnormal" "distorted" civilization of the West with an agrarian "new world civilization" generated by the Chinese.[10]

The Shantung Rural
Reconstruction Institute

According to Liang's scheme, the institute would perform three basic functions. First, it would be the center for research on rural problems and experimentation with the new organizational forms

9. [472], pp. 14–15, 19–23, 31–38; [473], pp. 27–30, 40, 48, 52; [449a], p. 272; [533e], p. 1; [13], pp. 34–35; [20], pp. 294–295; [42d], pp. 22–23; [42h], pp. 46–47; [613].

10. [472], pp. 3–7; [274], III, 59–62; [473], p. 3; [11g], pp. 208–210; [9r], pp. 281–282; [9m], p. 150; [562], p. 2.

(and thus "become a factory for the manufacture of plans, programs, and policies"). Second, it would train rural reconstruction cadre and direct their work. Third, it would promote interest in rural problems among the young intelligentsia so they would return to the countryside they had deserted.[11] Roughly parallel to these functions, the institute had three main sections: the research department (*yen-chiu pu*); the rural service personnel training department (*hsiang-ts'un fu-wu jen-yuan hsun-lien pu*); and the experimental farm (*nung-ch'ang*). Other institutions and organizations affiliated with the institute included a hospital, library, social-survey department, and the Tsou-p'ing Normal School.

The research and training departments.[12] The research department trained groups of eighteen to thirty college graduates as high-level rural-work administrators, planners, and researchers. Their year-long program included required courses (primarily indoctrination in Liang's thought), courses in their own fields (such as agriculture, cooperatives, or self-defense), as well as practical work around Tsou-p'ing and independent research on some rural problem. On completion of their training, about half usually remained associated with the institute. The others moved into high-level administrative posts throughout Shantung or similar positions in their home provinces. In addition to its educational role, this department was the institute's policy-making and planning organ.[13]

The training department prepared lower-level cadre to man grass-roots programs. Each year about three hundred students (mostly from rich peasant or landlord families) enrolled in the program, which covered rural political problems, military matters, economic problems, and technical specialities such as forestry, animal husbandry, and irrigation. Upon graduation, they were expected to return to their home districts, where they would turn their intimate knowledge of local conditions and their family con-

11. [11g], pp. 207–208; [13], p. 33.
12. Although there were several minor alterations between 1931 and 1937 in such areas as entrance requirements, subsidies, and length of training, the following discussion gives a general outline of the various training programs run by the institute. See [472], pp. 8–9, 27–34; [473], pp. 51–52; [47], p. 2; [13], p. 34; [20], p. 295; [132], pp. 256–258; [449a], p. 272; [620]; [623]; [625]; [617].
13. [13], p. 34; [366], pp. 14–16; [472], pp. 18–21; [473], pp. 36–40, 47–50.

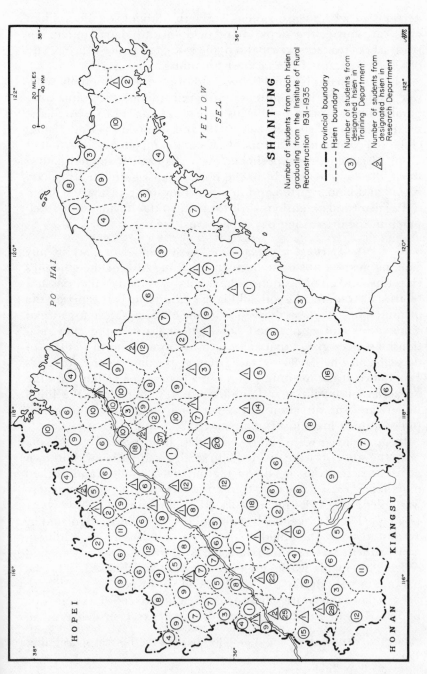

SHANTUNG

Number of students from each hsien graduating from the Institute of Rural Reconstruction 1931–1935

— ‧ — Provincial boundary

— — — Hsien boundary

③ Number of students from designated hsien in Training Department

⟨2⟩ Number of students from designated hsien in Research Department

HOPEI

PO HAI

YELLOW SEA

KIANGSU

HONAN

20 MILES
40 KM

MAP 3

nections to advantage in their work. In addition to this regular one-year course, the department held various short courses for rural school teachers, normal-school graduates, police officers, and other such groups from all over Shantung.

The Tsou-p'ing Normal School, although organizationally separate from the institute, also administered training programs comparable to those run by the institute's training and research departments. Established in July 1933, and manned by T'ao Hsing-chih's old colleagues and students, it was a complete resurrection of T'ao's Hsiao-chuang experiment. Aside from their regular course work, the students taught in the normal-school-affiliated primary school and kindergarten and in other Tsou-p'ing primary schools, did agricultural extension work for the institute farm, and participated in the organizing of cooperatives.[14]

Spiritual training. The most important part of any training at the institute—which claimed one fifth of the student's class time and all of his out-of-class time—was Liang's theories and "spiritual" training. As with all Liang's educational enterprises, the institute's program was derived from the old Sung-Ming practice of *chiang-hsueh* and emphasized close, personal student-teacher relationships, peer-group dynamics, and continuous moral scrutiny of oneself and one's fellows. The primary purpose of the student's experience at the institute was not really to acquaint him with the mysteries of fertilizer and firearms, but rather "to make [him] understand the direction of the rural movement and change his philosophy of life and his daily habits."[15]

In accordance with Liang's old "class-head system" (*pan-chang chih*), the students were divided into small groups, each with its own adviser-teacher (class head). Each group lived, studied, and worked together as a self-governing community. Of playing together there was little; Liang's Confucian work ethic allowed for no Sundays or holidays. The average day began at 5:30 A.M. and was regulated by an austere monastic schedule of purposeful activity. In addition, each student was required to keep a diary of observations and reflections on his work, his environment, and himself. This he handed in periodically to the class head for inspection.

Each dawn the entire school assembled in the semi-darkness for a period of silent meditation. Liang or another teacher delivered an

14. T'ao's student, Chang Tsung-lin, headed the normal school after 1935.
15. [472], p. 28.

inspirational talk (*chao-hua*), which provided further meditation material. Through this type of experience, Liang hoped the students would be forged into suitably tempered spearheads for the institute's assault on the problems of the Shantung countryside. They would be inured to physical hardship, awakened to the profound significance of their work, aflame with Confucian enthusiasm for the exercise of moral influence, and habituated to living and working in a nonkin collective.

The rural service guidance office (hsiang-ts'un fu-wu chih-tao ch'u). Even after the students' graduation, the institute kept them locked into its network of supervision and mutual encouragement and criticism through its rural service guidance office.[16] Founded in 1932 when the first training department class of students went off to their home districts, the office administered several activities and programs designed to perpetuate a sense of common mission and struggle among the graduates. It sent teachers and advanced students from the institute into the Shantung countryside on regular inspection circuits; advised on how to deal with problems encountered in the founding and managing of peasant schools; provided teaching materials specifically prepared for the peasant schools on agriculture, general science, local history, and spiritual training; and circulated an alumni newsletter. The graduates also sent the office monthly reports on their personal moral and intellectual development and the progress of their work. Sometimes these reports were published in the newsletter to keep the graduates informed on each other's activities. As it had primary responsibility for holding the institute's ever-growing rural Shantung empire together, Liang took the guidance office seriously. He personally presided over it and went on inspection trips. An alumni association (*t'ung-hsueh hui*), which the graduates managed themselves, also helped maintain a sense of community and affiliation with the institute.[17]

The institute farm. The technological arm of institute operations was the experimental farm, which did agricultural extension work and carried out experiments with seed strains and

16. The name was changed in 1934 to the Shantung Provincial People's Educational Advisory Committee (Shan-tung sheng min-chung chiao-yü fu-tao wei-yuan-hui), which operated jointly with the provincial department of education.

17. [472], pp. 34–40; [473], pp. 67–68; [272b]; [13], p. 35; [132], p. 253; [366], p. 17; [272g].

livestock breeding. It also cooperated with the peasant schools and the rural credit bureau in the promotion and establishment of agricultural cooperatives. As a first step toward the realization of Liang's plan for the development of local industries to free rural society from its dependence on the urban industrial centers, the farm ran a soy sauce and soybean cake factory. Its basic extension and research methods and even its director were imported directly from Ting hsien.[18]

The institute farm made the first direct contact with Tsou-p'ing's peasant populace in November 1931. Six months after the institute opened, it held an agricultural fair complete with prizes, games, opera, and movies. The fair provided the opportunity for introducing new agricultural technology, seed strains, and equipment, as well as the institute itself. About fifty thousand people attended, including some from neighboring hsien. The event was so successful that another fair was held the next fall for the twenty-seven hsien of the old Tsinan circuit.[19]

A few days after the 1931 fair, the training department's first class of students and their teachers—availing themselves of the goodwill and recognition created by the fair—went into the countryside for their first period of practical work. Their specific task was to found peasant schools, the fundamental institution informed by Liang's theories. Peasant schools—and their later transformation, the school-centers—were organizations unique to Liang's rural reconstruction movement and its main grass-roots agency.[20]

Governmental reorganization. The 1933 carte blanche from the national government to experiment with administrative structures enabled Liang to move his rural reconstruction work a step closer to the realization of his ideals.[21] Although he had always intended for the institute to function as an upper-level quasi gov-

18. The farm director, Yü Lu-hsi, had two technical assistants and a few dozen workers. The farm managed several branch plots, the largest of which was at Hsin Chuang near Tsinan. This plot was managed jointly with the International Famine Relief Fund and Ginling University Agricultural College. [472], pp. 42–49; [132], pp. 261–262; [430], pp. 99–105; [449a], pp. 275–279; [608].

19. [272h], pp. 10–14; [132], pp. 254–260; [449a], p. 278; [473], p. 54.

20. A detailed report on the schools in each part of Tsou-p'ing during this initial period is found in [272a]. See also [533e], pp. 1–6; [449a], p. 272; [473], p. 27.

21. [473], pp. 54–62; [473], pp. 70–80; [366], pp. 17–18.

ernment for the experimental reconstruction districts, it did not have the necessary control over governmental functions until after the National Regulations for Experimental Hsien went into effect in July 1933. Even then, its jurisdiction was limited to the two hsien of Tsou-p'ing and Ho-tse. Under the regulations, however, these two hsien governments became independent of the provincial departments (*t'ing*) and instead reported directly to the provincial government committee. Although the hsien governments remained organizationally distinct from the institute, all their staff, including the magistrates, were in effect appointed by the institute.

Once the hsien governments could function autonomously from national and provincial government regulation, the institute set out to alter governmental structure under its jurisdiction in ways that would make it both more efficient and more amenable to the overall purposes of rural reconstruction. On the hsien level, the institute abolished all the bureaus (*chü*)—the separate offices dealing with specific matters such as taxation and security—and replaced them with sections (*k'o*) within the government yamen itself. Because this arrangement permitted the section heads in a locality to meet together and reach immediate decisions, it eliminated the shuffling of documents from one bureau to the other and up and down the administrative ladder and, thus, greatly increased administrative efficiency.[22] A year later in July 1934, the Nanking government ordered nationwide adoption of the system.[23]

Liang's vision for governmental reorganization below the hsien level came closest to realization in Tsou-p'ing. Prior to 1933, the hsien in Shantung, as in most of China, had been organized into sub-districts (*ch'ü*), which were in turn divided into rural districts (*hsiang*) and townships (*chen*), each with its own administrative office (*kung-so*). Below this level were the neighborhood sub-units *lü* and *lin*. In July 1933, Liang abolished all eight *ch'ü* and 158 *hsiang* and *chen* in Tsou-p'ing. Basing himself upon a survey taken by the institute's students, he redivided the hsien into fourteen *hsiang*, which conformed to "natural" customary and economic divisions (apparently market areas). Below that level he incorporated 366 "natural" villages as the lowest administrative unit. Most important, school-centers—*hsiang-hsueh* (rural district school-centers) on the *hsiang* level and *ts'un-hsueh* (lower-level village school-centers) on

22. [472], p. 2; [533f]; [272k]; [561]; [430], pp. 72–75; [20], pp. 297–298; and [42d], pp. 21–22.
23. [160], p. 170.

the village level—replaced all the former government administrative offices.[24] A school manager ran the actual business of the school and was responsible to the hsien government.

The School-Center as People's Yamen: The Essence of the Tsou-p'ing Program

Through the school-centers Liang hoped to do away with that scourge of the peasantry, bureaucratic government; instead, the government would relate to the peasants through the organizational form of a school and the rural-reconstruction cadre would relate to them as teachers. This "schoolification of government" would in turn effect the "schoolification of society" (she-hui hsueh-hsiao-hua), which would then transform the countryside into one great school of Confucian collectivist thought.[25] The approach was designed to avoid the traditional peasant suspicion and hostility toward government and public enterprises, but engender instead a very untraditional peasant political and social activism. Through village-level participatory democracy, political power would rise from the organic local community upward toward the state, rather than flowing down from a distant official issuing commands from the top of a vast bureaucratic structure.

In Liang's rural reconstruction vision, the school-center was the instrument by which Gemeinschaft would vanquish Gesellschaft. Thus, the details of their organizational structure were to be determined by the local community; the school-centers would at once create and be created. "The significance of these schools," wrote Liang, "lies in organizing the countryside, but we nevertheless do not want to form organizational relationships by hard legal orders. Rather, we want to form new customs and mores [li-su] and to form the organizational relationships by soft habits. So the plan's regulations are very vague and flexible."[26]

The school-center was the final form of Liang's attempt to adapt the "village covenant" (hsiang-yueh) of the Northern Sung period to serve both his own vision and contemporary needs. As the vehicle by which Liang hoped to combine mass mobilization, political participation, and economic development with the traditional Chinese ideals of human feelings and moral encouragement in small inti-

24. [12], p. 2; [472], pp. 61–62; [396], pp. 77–83.
25. [14p], p. 125.   26. [12].

mate groups, it was the actual institutionalization of Liang's abstruse cultural philosophy. These school-centers, particularly on the village level, were actually established only in Tsou-p'ing; the peasant school remained the basic rural reconstruction institution in Ho-tse and the other experimental hsien areas. Three elements made up the school-center: the cadre, the "local notables," and everyone else in the village or *hsiang*.

The cadre's role. The spark Liang hoped would set off the grass-roots prairie fire of spontaneous local political and social organizing was the trained rural worker. Indoctrinated first in the small, intimate group, Liang's Confucian cadre would merge with the masses on the model of their own training. Both Confucian and expert, they would cultivate the masses' inherent goodness through the example of their personal character and moral leadership, while drawing on their technical expertise to help guide the modernization of economic production and social organization. These rural reconstruction cadre would serve as the school managers and, together with the teachers (*chiao-yuan*) and guides (*fu-tao-yuan*), manage the many enterprises that the school-center promoted.

Before setting out for the countryside, Liang's newly forged *chün-tzu* agreed to a pact, which reads much like the Red Army's "three great disciplines and eight points of attention." It prohibited drinking or smoking, borrowing from the peasants, and being "disrespectful" toward them or "licentious" with their daughters; in general, it enjoined avoidance of those attitudes and practices that did not endear government personnel, bandits, or soldiers to Chinese villagers. The Tsou-p'ing cadre were also required to dismount when going through any village and forbidden to enter a strange village without a local introduction.[27]

Liang realized that generations of official oppression and exploitation had bred in the peasantry an inveterate suspicion of any involvement in collective action. To counteract this attitude, the cadre would not set out initially to press any reform programs or new organizational forms on the villagers; they would not "issue orders" of any kind. Instead, they would strive at the outset only to gain the villagers' confidence and to integrate themselves into village life. As Liang wanted the whole society to serve as a school, the cadre would not limit their function as teachers to just the school-center building.

27. [272a.1], p. 1.

The first step of the cadre's task was to make the school-center a kind of town hall *cum* teahouse where "the villagers would gather, whether or not there is business to attend to." At these gatherings, the cadre would discuss village problems with the peasants, suggest possible solutions, and "cultivate in the villagers a new mentality" that they could solve their problems by their own collective actions. The cadre, however, would wait patiently until the villagers demanded a program on their own initiative, or actively press a program only when the villagers seemed receptive. For instance, they might promote public health measures during an epidemic or launch a well-digging campaign during a drought.

The local community and the school-center. The second element—the local notables—were individuals of "reputation, character, and influence." Five to ten of them constituted a board of trustees (*tung-shih-hui*). This body invited an especially virtuous and respected person to be the school director (*hsiao-chang*), who would have final authority over school (and, by extension, community) affairs, as well as the honorific position as teacher.

Everyone else in the village—men, women, and children—were the students (*hsueh-chung*), who must "respect the school director. . . . Since the position is that of an elder and a father, all must act as sons and younger brothers." The students also "must cherish the managers; that is to say, not let them lapse into unrighteousness," but "come forth with any reproofs with friendliness and avoid open and direct conflict."

The first principle the students needed to grasp was "the importance of the village group." They had to realize the need for "attending meetings and thinking over all matters [brought up]." They had to learn to think: "Any affair of the village is my affair. . . . I must express my opinions at meetings. Good people must be courageous in taking responsibility. Previously, to be a good person meant simply to avoid doing evil things. [Now] to be positively good, I must take positive action."[28]

The school-center educational programs. The formal classroom education dispensed by the schools was divided into three departments: adult education, women's education, and children's education. In conscious reaction to the current fashion of Western-style urbanized curricula, the children's department

28. [12].

stressed "useful" education: basic literacy, agriculture, general science, hygiene, and civics. "We must look at the problem from the viewpoint of the fathers and elders of the village, and make it so that they want to send their children to school."[29] The needs of the locality determined the specific curriculum (for example, sericulture was not taught in a wheat-growing area), but the schools universally stressed character-building and spiritual training. The children's department held classes daily, except during the busy farming seasons.

The adult education department held classes from seven to nine every evening, during the leisure period of the farmer's day. These regular classes were optional, but after 1935, a short ten-week course during the slack farming season was made compulsory for all males between ages sixteen and thirty. The adult education curriculum consisted of civics (which included such items as storytelling, current events, Liang Shu-ming thought, and spiritual training), basic literacy, basic knowledge (about cooperative societies, agriculture, and public health), music, and martial arts. The classes held for women in the afternoons were similar, but also included instruction on child care and home economics.

The *hsiang* school-center was run on the same pattern as the village school-center, but in addition, provided more specialized higher-level vocational training and formal education through junior high school. It also acted as an administrative-logistical center for the village schools within the *hsiang*.[30]

An assessment of the school-centers. The centers were not, even in the institute's and Liang's own estimate, an unqualified success. The cadre-teachers, having had only one year of training, obviously had not been so easily transformed into the technically proficient teachers and managers Liang's program required them to be. They were often inexpert in handling teaching materials and methods and sometimes lacked basic knowledge, such as how to use

29. [22], p. 1.
30. This description of the village and *hsiang* school-center would also apply to the peasant school (*hsiang-nung hsueh-hsiao*), which was the institution founded and managed by the institute-trained personnel in hsien other than Tsou-p'ing. Before 1933, the school-centers within Tsou-p'ing were also called *hsiang-nung hsueh-hsiao*. My sketch of the school-center is based primarily upon the following of Liang's works: [19]; [14p]; [23f]; [23g]; [21]; also [472], pp. 78–90; [200]; [430], pp. 76–80; [132], pp. 253–254; and interviews with people who worked in the school-centers: [621]; [623]; [619]; [617]; [625].

the Chinese phonetic symbol system (*kuo-yin fu-hao*). The schools themselves, supported by an increasingly poverty-stricken Shantung countryside (hit in this period by the world economic depression, loss of markets, catastrophic floods and droughts), sometimes lacked essential physical equipment, such as sports equipment, playgrounds, abacuses, and even desks.[31]

What bothered Liang most, however, was his cadre's insufficient grasp of his own basic principles. They, along with the top administrators in the hsien government, could not shake off two thousand years of bureaucratic commandism so easily. In June 1935, Liang personally took the post of hsien magistrate in order to rectify the situation. Admitting that in the past "the *ts'un* schools consistently failed to achieve good results," he ordered all the village school teachers back to the institute and selected a number of them for concentrated training. Henceforth, Liang declared, the emphasis must be on the village rather than the *hsiang* schools. Further, all local enterprises run by the schools (cooperatives, health measures, well-digging, and so on) would "rely upon the self-initiative of the village school, and no orders or compulsion should be used." In the past, the hsien government had been using too much force in dealing with these problems. At the same time, Liang concentrated his cadre in several *hsiang*; schools in the other *hsiang* temporarily ceased operation.[32]

Group study centers. A further problem was finances. Although the hsien government aided the educational programs of the village school-centers financially, the bulk of the funds was raised locally, and some areas remained too poor to support such a luxury. Even where primary education existed, poorer families often did not send their children, so thousands of children remained untutored. In 1935, the institute and the normal school put into operation their own version of T'ao Hsing-chih's "little teacher system," which they called the "group study center" (*kung-hsueh-ch'u*). To make scarce educational resources go as far as possible, the teachers and normal school students organized the best students of the regular schools to tutor the unlettered "wild" children of the hsien.

These gatherings, ranging from ten to one hundred youngsters, met daily at designated temples, empty houses, groves, and even on

31. [200], p. 4; [20], p. 300.   32. Ibid.

street corners. The groups held literacy classes and used singing and storytelling to inculcate some rudimentary knowledge in subjects such as hygiene and current events. They held character-recognition bees and singing contests and soon developed a great enthusiasm among the students for their "classes." Through them the poorest youngsters of the hsien were drawn into the institute's network. When the regular schools met for an "emulation meeting" (*kuan-mo-hui*), the study center children also participated. By 1937, there were almost five hundred such centers. There were also almost three hundred village primary schools, so, through a kind of patchwork system, Tsou-p'ing was on the brink of achieving universal education.[33]

Cooperative Societies

The economic structure upon which Liang's plan for a new China rested was the cooperative, which would both help raise production and gradually socialize distribution. The aim of the cooperative movement was "utilizing the cooperative form to increase rural production . . . and establish an economic system in which the capital is controlled, enjoyed, and owned in common." This ultimate goal would be accomplished through a gradual increase in the cooperatives' accumulated profits until finally all capital was publicly owned. In the meantime, the accumulated capital would be used to build small-scale industry, primarily for manufacturing capital goods needed in agricultural production and for processing agricultural products. The institute drafted a five-year plan for the gradual extension of cooperatives to all enterprises. By the fifth year, there were to be cooperatives in every village, and higher-level cooperative agencies at the *hsiang* and hsien level.[34]

Although the Sino-Japanese War interrupted implementation of the full plan, the initial efforts met with considerable success. By 1934, there were hundreds of cooperative societies in weaving, sericulture, forestry, cotton, and credit. All, with the exception of the forestry cooperatives, provided members with loans for needed improvements or to tide them over periods when prices for their products were low. Thus, members could escape the usurious clutches of the village moneylenders (usually landlords or mer-

33. [200], pp. 1–2; [199]; [281]; [20], p. 300.
34. [472], p. 111; see also pp. 112–118; [147], p. 259.

chants). The capital lent out by the cooperatives came from large banks, such as the Bank of China.

Credit cooperatives. There were two types of cooperatives organized specifically to provide credit. First, the village granary societies (*chuang-ts'ang ho-tso-she*), along with storing grain, lent money on receipt of grain so members could wait for grain prices to rise before selling. In 1935, there were 145 societies with 9,465 members. Second, credit societies (*hsin-yung ho-tso-she*) were financed by the rural banking center (*nung-ts'un chin-jung liu-t'ung-ch'u*), which managed a fund of tax moneys from the hsien government. Since the banking center acted as the hsien government's bank, it kept the tax money in continuous circulation within the hsien. The rest of the funds for the various credit societies came from urban banks and from members' savings. Credit societies sprang up quickly but generally seemed controlled by a small minority of gentry. In 1933, there was only one society with fifteen members, which lent out three hundred yuan; by 1935, the number had grown to thirty-three societies, which lent out 9,486 yuan, but the total membership was still only 589.[35]

The Tsou-p'ing credit cooperatives initially suffered from many of the same problems that plagued rural credit cooperatives elsewhere in China. They were controlled by a minority of landlords and rich peasants, who hastily organized cooperatives in a slipshod fashion to gain access to the funds the hsien government had borrowed from the city banks. Many societies had no charter and no effective accounting and auditing procedures. Their loans tended to be large and granted without checking into the purpose. Often gentry borrowed large amounts from the cooperative and then lent it out at higher interest to poorer farmers.

In June 1935, Liang ordered the formation of a supervisory committee on cooperative enterprises, which he himself headed in his capacity as hsien magistrate (a post he twice held temporarily), and which included the staff of the institute farm and the head of the rural banking center. The committee called for the dissolution and reformation of all existing credit cooperatives and sent out personnel to supervise the process. It also designed auditing and accounting procedures, model charters, and handbooks for the newly reformed societies. Hsien government personnel supervised

35. [472], pp. 102–103, 108–110, 118–124; [385a], pp. 58–62.

the founding meetings to insure that the new societies would be free of the old faults. Limits were placed on the size of loans and their purposes were taken into consideration before they were granted. The hsien government launched a major campaign to impress upon the masses the true significance of the cooperatives so that they would initiate and maintain the reformed societies themselves.[36]

Forestry and sericulture cooperatives. Forestry cooperatives were quite successful in the mountainous areas of Tsou-p'ing. In 1935, there were twenty-five societies with about two thousand members who had already planted over thirty thousand trees. The home weaving and sericulture cooperatives were even more impressive. The weaving cooperative purchased modern looms and collectivized production. Thanks to the farm's extension work carried on through the school-centers, the insects and mulberry tree blight that had troubled the silk areas were eliminated and new types of mulberry trees and cocoons were introduced. Productivity increased dramatically. By 1935, there were over five hundred families in the sericulture cooperatives. Yet within the year the new looms were idle and the new mulberry trees were uprooted. Japanese dumping of textiles had destroyed the market for both native cloth and silk.[37]

Cotton-marketing cooperatives. The Tsou-p'ing American Cotton Marketing Cooperative (Liang Tsou Mei-mien yun-hsiao ho-tso-she) was Tsou-p'ing's most outstanding and unqualified cooperative success. Liang and his followers always pointed to it when critics charged that rural reconstruction, for all its activity, had yet to help put more food on the average peasant's table. The introduction of Trice American cotton seeds, and other technological improvements, as well as cooperative production and marketing, dramatically raised farm income in the traditional cotton-growing northern section of Tsou-p'ing.[38]

36. [385a], pp. 1–13; [485], pp. 259–260; [272p.4]; [272p.5]. For examples of these problems in Chinese cooperatives during the 1930s, see [100], pp. 208, 216.
37. [472], pp. 103–104; [272p.6]; [430], p. 102.
38. [315], p. 15. The institute was not the first to introduce Trice seeds to Shantung. Already in 1904, the Peking Ministry of Agriculture and Commerce had started spreading Trice seeds through cotton-growing

In 1931, the institute farm designated Sun-chia chen—the important Tsou-p'ing cotton collection depot—as a demonstration
area and selected several middle-peasant families as "demonstration farmers." These families planted the new Trice seeds and
encouraged their neighbors to come and see the results. The
schools pressed the campaign with lectures and other propaganda
on the merits of a cotton-marketing cooperative and the Trice
seeds. The cotton-growing peasants responded quickly and enthusiastically; the number of cooperative members went from 458
in 1932 to 15,000 in 1935.

The cotton cooperative's success is easily explained; it was
specifically designed to correct the abuses of the old broker system
(which had been in the hands of the lower gentry). The cooperative
ran all grading, baling, storing, and marketing operations, so
members avoided the numerous and excessive fees of the cotton
brokers. The cooperative also guaranteed its members an honest
deal. Bookkeeping and auditing were strict and clear. Care was
taken that the scales operator was free of favoritism, and the scales
free of defect, but members could still challenge the weighing.
Members could also borrow from the cooperative during the
spring to buy seeds and fertilizer, and during the fall, when they
were short of cash. The loans, at only 1 percent interest per month,
had an upper limit to prevent rich peasants and landlords from
taking advantage of them.

The cooperative required all members to grow only Trice cotton.
The advantages to the cotton farmer were obvious and overwhelming. Not only did production leap 30 percent, but also, because of
the quality of Trice and the cooperative's rigidly maintained quality
control, this product sold at a price almost a third above other
products. The Tsou-p'ing cooperative's cotton soon had a reputation as the best in China.

Organizationally, the cotton cooperative came closest to Liang's
ideals. Education was the main means of expansion, lower-level
organizations were emphasized, and the leading elements were
middle peasants. The village branches continually held meetings to
raise standards and to further train members in cooperative management and organization. More than any other cooperative the

---

areas. Again in 1918, the Peking warlord government distributed American cotton seeds in Shantung. In 1930, there were efforts to promote
American cotton, but apparently the peasants were unable to preserve the
strain, for the old native cotton continued instead of Trice. See [498]; [499].

cotton cooperative's activities revolved around the village school-center.[39]

Although the cotton cooperative was Tsou-p'ing's best, it still failed to fulfill Liang's expectations completely. As in all the Tsou-p'ing cooperatives, there was a continuous struggle for control between the hsien government (representing the interests of the poor and middle peasants) and the local gentry. Because of the rapid increase in the number of cotton cooperatives, the quality of the cadre and their supervision and guidance slipped a bit, allowing the tendency toward rich-peasant control to manifest itself. Second, efforts to educate the peasants on the significance of cooperative enterprise were not altogether successful; the cooperatives had to rely heavily on their ability to grant loans to maintain themselves. Originally the fall-harvest lending program was meant only to help the poor peasants over the crucial fiscal hump, but the average member considered the receipt of a fall loan as a precondition for selling his cotton to the cooperative. Although the cooperative's retention of a certain percentage of profits as publicly owned capital did represent a beginning toward socialization, in practice, the old peasant individualism (or, more precisely, familialism) asserted itself. In the beginning, the cotton cooperative retained 20 percent of gross profits, used another 10 percent for cooperative operating costs, and returned 70 percent to the members. In October 1935, however, it reduced the amount of retained capital to 15 percent and the operating capital to 5 percent, and returned 80 percent to members. The general direction was obviously not toward the communistic society Liang envisioned.[40]

Self-Defense Forces

The militia was an important and highly successful reform program. Banditry, always a problem in the Chinese countryside, reached unprecedented proportions in Shantung during the

39. A former Tsou-p'ing worker claimed that even the cotton cooperatives were dominated by landlords and rich peasants, who in their positions as school-center directors and trustees controlled all cooperative operations. See [497]. Taking all the evidence into account, however (including the fact that this claim was made during the 1955–56 criticism campaign against Liang), it seems that the cotton cooperatives were comparatively popularly based organizations in which middle peasants were the dominant class. See [272p], especially [272p.1–3]; also [449a], pp. 273–274; [430], p. 102; [42d], p. 25.

40. [272p.2], pp. 4–5; [497].

1920s, thanks to the incompetent governorship of that archetype of the evil warlord, Chang Tsung-ch'ang, who allowed the decay of local governmental services, especially rural security. The many wars fought in Shantung before 1931 aggravated the problem, as the marching armies left behind a trail of deserting or disbanded soldiery who turned to banditry. Before the Tsou-p'ing institute opened in 1931, Tsou-p'ing had, as did the rest of Shantung, three kinds of police: the security bureau (an ch'üan-chü), paid militia, and privately raised, local police forces, which were under the control of local gentry. All were ineffective; they often collaborated with the bandits, but were paid by taxes levied on the people. In 1930, for instance, the Tsou-p'ing government spent 28,372 yuan (over 25 percent of its total expenditures) for the security bureau and the militia.[41]

The institute created a civilian militia, which performed all peace-keeping functions and simultaneously provided an organizational network for implementing other programs. In 1933, the hsien government gradually began to disband the professional police forces and started organizing the new civilian self-defense force. To provide an officers' corps, each hsiang was ordered to select two or three young men of some education for four months training at a militia cadre training station (min-t'uan kan-pu hsun-lien-so). After training, they then returned to their hsiang's school-center where they became the directors of military affairs.

At the same time, each lü (a group of twenty-five households) was told to select one youth from a "middle peasant or above" family between the ages of eighteen and twenty-seven. Those selected underwent a similar four-month training and returned to their villages to organize village militia groups (ts'un tsu). The school-center military officer, acting as hsiang militia captain (hsiang tui-chang), then organized the village branches into one hsiang unit. An additional, ongoing program of periodic retraining for all members included general education, rural reconstruction theory, and more "spiritual training." The people's militia was to be a great school for citizenship.

Similar to the other programs, the movement for militia initially encountered wide resistance. Rumors of all kinds—that the militia was a recruiting device for Han Fu-ch'ü's army or would be sent to fight the Japanese—gained currency. Many chosen militiamen fled

41. [472], p. 70.

the hsien in panic. Others feigned illness, pleaded poverty, or hired substitutes. Since this was the one Tsou-p'ing program with the force of law, it was put into operation despite popular suspicion and resistance. Once, however, the self-defense training was actually started, the peasants became enthusiastic and even looked forward to the periodic drilling. As one institute leader put it, they had become "addicted."[42]

No "Learn from the people's militia" campaign was launched, and the institute effected no dramatic reversal in the traditional Chinese attitude toward arms and the man, but the village militiaman did become a respected local figure. Each *hsiang* unit held a monthly drill and target match presided over by the hsien magistrate who scrupulously followed the hoary rituals prescribed by the *Rites of Chou* (*Chou li*) for the village archery meet (*hsiang she*). After the ceremony, the magistrate awarded prizes, and the members held a festive picnic around the drill field.[43]

By 1935, there were no paid police or provincial troops anywhere in Tsou-p'ing;[44] the militia, composed of 2,500 relatively well-trained personnel had taken over all peace-keeping functions. Moreover, since the people made up the militia, it had the full cooperation of friends, neighbors, and relatives, and its crime-fighting zeal and capability far outstripped that of the former professional police force. Not only did they eliminate roving bandit gangs from the area, but even petty criminals—thieves, opium peddlers, and local hoodlums—became a rarity. In the beginning, some in the militia lost their lives in shootouts with bandits, but word of their bravery and skill soon spread through Shantung banditdom and the bandits avoided Tsou-p'ing, Ho-tse, and the other experimental areas.

The militia did not confine its operations to professional bandits; they also went after gamblers, vagrants, "singers of lewd operas," and "those who propagandized for the destruction of good traditional customs and teachings." They policed themselves too, and reported any militia member who used his position to extort or bully people. The Kuomintang rural reconstructor, Hu Tz'u-wei, although he sniffed at the Tsou-p'ing amateurs' lack of proper

42. [384], pp. 2–3, 9–10; [430], p. 92.
43. [384], pp. 1–10; [430], pp. 87–90; [20], p. 298; [472], pp. 90–98.
44. There was a small body of professional police in the town of Tsou-p'ing itself, but it primarily served to direct and train the civilian militia.

uniforms and modern weapons (which his own experimental militia had), expressed envious admiration for their spirit.[45]

In the 1950s, Communist critics charged that the Tsou-p'ing institute-designed militia system was a conscious "arming of the landlord class" to keep down popular "revolutionary forces." A former rural reconstruction cadre claimed that the militiamen often took advantage of their position to blackmail "the people," specifically, opium addicts and families who continued to bind their women's feet. (These charges were made against the "Ho-tse-style" militia rather than Tsou-p'ing's.) Although the critics' description of Shantung bandits and local hoodlums (often in the pocket of local gentry) as "revolutionary forces" might be dismissed as rhetoric, it is true that the institute consciously sought to build a militia composed mainly of the youth from "middle peasant or above" families, specifically excluding the déclassé "chiang-hu" underworld stratum and poor peasants. The motive, however, seems not to have been a fear of arming "naturally revolutionary" poor peasants, but rather that militia service, although it afforded some prestige, still represented an economic loss, which the poor families were least able to bear. The lumpen elements were precisely those who had composed the old paid police forces that had proven themselves given to various forms of corruption and inefficiency.[46]

The militia system was administered by the hsien government's second section, which also had jurisdiction over justice and the prison. The prison, like other institutions in the hsien, was based on the principle of perfectibility through moral influence. It gave inmates a relatively decent environment, taught them trades (such as printing and the making of soybean cake), and allowed them to work for pay.

The second section also ran a reformatory for rehabilitation of drug addicts, vagrants, and gamblers, where labor and moral exhortation were dealt out in equal measure. The magistrate, who was in charge of the court, was well aware that the ordinary peasant had neither the knowledge nor the money to make use of the regular court to redress grievances, so he made every effort to simplify procedures so that all could have the protection of the law.[47]

45. [384], pp. 2–12; [430], p. 93; [621].   46. [342], p. 178.
47. The jail had thirty inmates in late 1934. [621]; [625]; [623]; see also [20], p. 103; [430], pp. 110–111.

Local Associations for Moral Improvement

The law court and prison did not, however, perform a significant role in maintaining social order. The school-centers, because they were designed to mobilize (as well as mold) community opinion, acted as mediators in local disputes and as disciplinarians for any youth who exhibited signs of waywardness. The school-centers also encouraged the villagers to establish their own local organizations informed by the *hsiang-yueh* of mutual exhortation and supervision. Bearing names like the Rural Reform Association (Hsiang-ts'un kai-chin hui) or the Faithfulness and Virtuousness Society (Chung i she), they were based upon a community covenant (*kung-yueh*), drawn up and agreed to voluntarily by members in a public meeting. Some aimed at eliminating a specific "evil and backward practice" especially prevalent in the particular village or *hsiang*, such as opium smoking or foot-binding. Others sought to raise the community's general moral tone.

The Szu-chuang (a village in the northern part of Tsou-p'ing) Rural Reform Association's covenant, for example, had five positive exhortations: respect elders, be friendly, aid one another, be hard-working and frugal, and give ear to the criticisms of others. It also had five negative prohibitions against: cursing and fighting, being luxury-loving and lazy, becoming addicted to bad habits and hobbies, bullying the weak, and violating the covenant. The association had another covenant against smoking, drinking, and gambling, which fined members between fifty cents and two yuan for each violation. Under the terms of a third covenant, the members organized a fire-fighting brigade.[48]

Some of these associations daily assembled the entire village for a morning rally (*tsao-hui*), a kind of spiritual setting-up exercise. The villagers sang, shouted slogans, and heard hortatory harangues or informative reports from the school director or a teacher. The "morning song" of Hsu-chia tao-k'ou village, for instance, went:

The dark night is over; dawn is breaking.
The sun ascends and the people rise.
Be diligent and frugal, filial, and friendly.
Be kind to the young and respect the old.[49]

48. [479], pp. 68–70; [294], pp. 228–229; [366], pp. 25–26; [621]; [619]; [617].
49. [479], p. 70; [366], p. 26; [618].

The school-center and hsien government supplemented these enterprises with such agencies as the "foot-inspection committee," which hunted down the mothers who were clandestinely making "golden lotuses" of their daughters' underpinnings. But Tsoup'ing's most prevalent and difficult to eradicate evil custom was early marriage. Because of the scarcity of females, the brides' families were able to demand large "gifts" (between two hundred and five hundred yuan), which in effect amounted to selling their daughters. In order to gain another pair of working female hands, the groom's family would often marry off a very young son (sometimes only eight years old). In particularly desperate times, the evils of the system might be compounded by gangsters who would buy up several girls in a famine-stricken region and market them for a profit in a more prosperous area. Since early marriage was an old custom based on economic self-interest, the local *hsiang-yueh* organizations seldom agreed to a covenant forbidding it. The best the rural cadre could accomplish was a plea that the male should be at least the legal marriageable age, but even this was not easily ascertained or enforced. The institute, however, also had a social-survey department, which administered a hsien census and household registration campaign. By 1936, every person in the hsien was registered, and a registration system run by the school-centers kept the vital statistics current.[50]

Agricultural Technology

Aside from its extension work with the cooperatives, the institute farm carried out several other extension programs through the school-center system. Here, too, the reconstruction workers relied on the demonstration-farmer method to spread information on new livestock breeds and other innovations.

One of the most dramatically successful projects was hog-raising. In 1931, the farm bought three pure-bred Poland-China boars (a breed that had been developed in Ohio and had nothing to do with either China or Poland) to crossbreed with local hogs. Two of the boars made the rounds of the *hsiang* school-centers, where they were available for breeding with local sows. The issue of this international union—dubbed the Poland-Tsou pig—weighed an aver-

50. [385b], pp. 1–19; [385c], pp. 1–6; [20], pp. 299–301; [42d], p. 24; [384], p. 13; [472], pp. 124–128.

age of fifty *chin* more than the native pig, and its meat was more tender. This single generation of improved hogs increased Tsou-p'ing hog-raisers' income by 144,914 yuan. The results were so good that the farm established breeding stations in several other provinces.[51]

The farm also crossbred Leghorn cocks with hens from Shan-tung's Shou-kuang hsien and produced a chicken with twice the egg yield of the local variety. Similar programs involved research and extension work with Holstein cattle, bees, and rabbits. There was also a plan to distribute Swiss milch goats to enrich the peas-ant's protein-poor diet.

In addition, the farm operated scattered experimental plots, where it developed improved cereal strains to produce maximum yield for the climate and soil of the particular area. Occasionally a minor application of technology yielded a major increase in pro-duction. Copper carbonate was found to prevent a *kao-liang* blight which had plagued Tsou-p'ing's farmers for generations. The chemical was then sold by the school-centers.

In all its technological innovations, the farm attempted to pro-mote only those practical measures that the peasants themselves wanted and that were within their present economic and in-tellectual capabilities. It designed and promoted, for example, a simple well-drilling apparatus of bamboo and an efficient but sim-ple animal-powered water pump. These two inexpensive innova-tions (along with 20,000 yuan in interest-free loans from the hsien government) resulted in a highly successful well-digging campaign in 1935. The institute had been promoting well-digging since 1931, but typically, it took a drought in 1935 to create peasant enthusiasm for the idea.[52]

In addition to these more modern schemes for economic devel-opment, the rural reconstruction workers performed the tradi-tional gentry role of directing public waterworks during the slack farming seasons. Wherever possible, they introduced modern sci-ence and technology into the work. In flood prevention, for in-stance, the institute's engineers determined that by dredging Tsou-p'ing's main river channel at a certain point, floods could be

51. [472], pp. 47–48; [449a], pp. 272–278; [430], p. 104.
52. This was the same famous water pump used at Ting hsien. Liang invited its inventor, Li Tsu-t'ang, to come to teach well-digging technology at Tsou-p'ing in the winter of 1931. [20], p. 300; [430], pp. 105–106; [449a], p. 279.

reduced by almost 90 percent. In 1935 and 1936, the institute mobilized ten thousand peasants during the two-month agricultural slack period to complete the project.[53]

Public Health Work

Since Tsou-p'ing, like most of the Chinese countryside, lacked modern medical facilities, Liang personally beat the bushes for personnel and funds to open a clinic. Finally, through a combination of provincial and hsien government funds and grants from the Cheeloo University Medical School in Tsinan and the National Economic Committee, he managed to open a small hospital at the institute in 1935. The institute's health policy stressed preventive medicine and public health education.

The hospital, which charged only nominal fees, was the center of a hsien-wide health education network. It trained paramedical personnel and established a health station in each *hsiang*. These stations in turn trained paramedics for work in the villages. Equipped with bicycles and simple medical kits, the young men and women they trained went into the villages with rudimentary medical skills and general knowledge about health care. The institute's training department and the normal school also trained their students in basic preventive medicine and some curative skills. As part of their training, they worked in the hospital under the doctor's supervision.

Much of the hospital's health care and educational work was in obstetrics. The *hsiang* health stations had a special part-time program in midwifery for local women and further provided their trainees with kits of inexpensive native equipment. The hospital also established a system of mother-and-infant health-care clubs, through which a trained nurse, local midwives, and other interested women provided examinations and basic medical information for local mothers and mothers-to-be. Within a year, these programs cut the infant mortality rate by 80 percent.[54]

Ho-tse and the "Ho-tse Style"

Ho-tse hsien, located in southwestern Shantung near the point where the Shantung, Hopei, and Honan borders meet, was the

53. [20], p. 299.   54. Ibid.; [42d], p. 24; [472], pp. 130–144.

other area under the jurisdiction of Liang's project designated as an experimental hsien in January 1933. In July 1934, a branch of the institute was established there, and the training department's students were divided between the two institutes.

The general Tsou-p'ing organization and reform programs were duplicated at Ho-tse, but with certain modifications and reductions dictated by the resources at the institute's command and the differences in conditions at Ho-tse. For example, Ho-tse was almost three times as large in area and population as Tsou-p'ing, had a higher ratio of landless peasants, and, because of its position near the three provincial borders, was a traditional bandit hangout. Its location, in fact, was near the middle of the old *Water Margin* (*Shui hu chuan*) territory.[55] Moreover, large-scale floods had struck the area in 1933 and again in 1936. As a result, although Ho-tse had hsiang-level school-centers similar to the multifunctional administrative-economic-educational centers that existed in Tsou-p'ing, it had no village-level school-centers at all. Instead, it had only "village managers" (*ts'un li-shih*) to look after the common affairs of the village. Nor was there any major reorganization of administrative areas along "natural" lines, as in Tsou-p'ing; the old *ch'ü* were simply renamed *hsiang*. Because of the bandit problem, the self-defense system was emphasized at the expense of other programs.

Ho-tse's major divergence with Tsou-p'ing, however, lay in its fundamental spirit, perhaps because the institute's Honan contingent (and the Shantung bureaucrats it absorbed into its rural reconstruction system) had a greater influence on the development of the program there. Most of these workers had never had much confidence in Liang's visionary conception of rural reconstruction as a moral-educational force that would arouse the masses' innate capacity for self-initiative, self-reliance, and self-government. They shared neither Liang's Confucian faith in the efficacy of naked moral power nor his belief in man's potential perfectibility. Confucian they were, but their Confucianism, like that of their bureaucrat ancestors in Chinese history, was heavily streaked with Le-

55. The natives of the general area—the old Ho-tse (Ts'ao-chou) circuit and the rest of Southeast Shantung—were famous for their bellicose temper and many peasant rebellions (the rebellion of Huang Ch'ao in the T'ang [A.D. 874], for example). Secret societies have always flourished in the region—the turn-of-the-century Boxers and the Red Spears being the most famous.

galism. Liang's feudal utopianism was too "revolutionary" for their more "traditional" bureaucratic mentality.

Thus, there were said to be two "styles" of rural reconstruction in Shantung: the "Tsou-p'ing style," which relied on moral influence, educational methods, and community self-initiative to carry out its reforms, and the "Ho-tse style," which tempered Liang's idealism with hardheaded administrative practices and relied somewhat more on hsien government legal orders and political force. As a consequence, peasant resistance to and cynicism toward rural reconstruction measures appeared in Ho-tse, as they did in other provinces, and less in Tsou-p'ing.[56] Liang himself disapproved of the Ho-tse style because it departed so far from his original ideas, but Governor Han apparently found it quite impressive. It was, after all, successful in several very visible ways. The rural reconstructionists had driven out bandits quickly and permanently and restored law and order. Moreover, they had established cooperatives, credit organizations, schools, and above all, the militia system.[57]

Expansion of Rural Reconstruction in Shantung

On New Year's day, 1935, the Shantung government designated Chi-ning and the thirteen other hsien of the southwest part of the province as a "hsien political and reconstruction experimental area," thus expanding the institute's area of jurisdiction sevenfold with a stroke of the pen. This group of hsien was administered by an administrative supervisor (hsing-cheng chuan-yuan) who, together with the hsien magistrates under him, was chosen by the institute in consultation with Governor Han. Han had decided to adopt the "Ho-tse style" reconstruction for this larger area because, as even Liang admitted, it "produced faster results."[58] The institute concentrated its workers in the area to establish and man the new peasant schools. Work was progressing well when, on July 8, the

56. During the 1955–56 criticism of Liang, some of his former students who had worked at both Ho-tse and Tsou-p'ing mentioned popular resistance only in connection with Ho-tse, tacitly suggesting that the "Tsou-p'ing style" was far less oppressive and more popular than the "Ho-tse style." See [342], pp. 177–178; [341], pp. 40–41; [466], p. 10; also [42h], p. 47; [621]; [619]; [617]; [630]; [625].

57. [561]; [396], pp. 95–108; [272m]; [20], pp. 293–295.

58. [42h], p. 47.

Yellow River broke its dikes at Chen-ch'eng and flooded ten of the fourteen hsien, temporarily stopping much of the work.

The July floods might have halted further expansion of rural reconstruction altogether if the Japanese had not intervened a few months later. Throughout 1935, Japan attempted to compel the governors of the five northern provinces to form a "North China Autonomous Region." In August, the Japanese ambassador dropped in on Governor Han and demanded that he agree to Japan's demands. In the last two months of the year the Japanese intensified their pressure on Han. The chief-of-staff of the Kuantung Army flew to Tsinan several times to bring Han to Peiping for a conference at which the Japanese hoped to force the issue. Han refused to go, but he was forced to consider the possibility of Japanese military action against him. He called Liang to Tsinan for consultation.

Liang believed that, faced with the superior firepower of the enemy, China had no chance at positional warfare. The only way to meet an invasion was protracted guerrilla struggle, which could succeed only if the government had the active support of the peasant masses and if the masses had a grass-roots organization. Both of these prerequisites, Liang believed, could come only through his rural reconstruction movement. If the government benefited the people, then the people would support the government and China would be invincible.[59]

Whether because of Liang's Mencius-like proposition or because of the institute's manifest effectiveness in organizing militia, Han immediately agreed to a three-year plan for the gradual expansion of rural reconstruction over the entire province. (The gradual expansion program was to allow for training sufficient numbers of rural reconstruction cadre.) In 1936, two more administrative supervisory districts were established: one made up of the nine hsien around Lin-i, and the other of ten hsien around Ho-tse. In March 1937, forty more hsien were added, making a total of over seventy. The plan provided for incorporation of the remaining hsien in the province in 1938.

Even with this gradual expansion, the institute alone could not train all the required rural cadre by itself. Therefore, the provincial government established an institute at Tsinan for the training of high-level specialists in agriculture, economics, and education. In

59. What Liang said to Han on the occasion is not recorded, but it is likely that Liang presented his usual formula on how to deal with a Japanese war, which is best expressed in [42n], pp. 61–66, and [41].

1937, the Tsou-p'ing institute established a branch training center at Chi-ning for all provincial normal school graduates (about twelve hundred). After a period of intensive training (six months instruction and two months field practice), the graduates would found peasant schools throughout the province.[60]

The Japanese invasion and the collapse of Shantung rural reconstruction. As the Japanese were responsible for the rapid expansion of Liang's work, it seems consonant that they also brought about its final demise. With the Japanese occupation of Shantung, the rural reconstruction projects collapsed; some cadre left the province, some joined the Communist guerrillas, and others joined the Kuomintang guerrillas.[61]

Han Fu-ch'ü also had a two-sided effect on the fate of Liang's work in Shantung. It was a decision of Han's that gave Liang his opportunity in Shantung in the first place, and it was another decision of Han's that brought Liang's work to an ironic finale. There are many reasons why the infrastructure the institute created did not survive (or indeed why it did not flourish) under the Japanese occupation, but it was at least partially due to the treachery of Han Fu-ch'ü. When in the fall of 1937 the Japanese armies rolled into Shantung, the militia of about forty hsien were mobilized. While Han and his regular army retreated in the face of the advancing

---

60. [472], pp. 2–3; [20], pp. 293–295; [42d], pp. 22–23; [42h], p. 47; [613].

61. The story is far too convoluted to unravel completely here. Liang did make one attempt to organize his cadre into a political and military force against the Japanese, but KMT elements, long jealous and fearful of Liang's influence, refused to support him at a crucial point, so the organization was shattered by the Japanese. Rural Shantung quickly became a complex tangle of local groups moving in and out of alliance; both Kuomintang and Communist groups were fighting the Japanese and each other. When Liang got back to Ho-tse in February, 1939, for instance, there were three functioning hsien governments: one appointed by the Japanese, one created by the Communists, and one controlled by the Kuomintang. Liang's only surviving organizations (called the Political Department's No. 3 Political Corps—Cheng-chih-pu ti san cheng-chih ta-tui—and the 32nd Central Independent Regiment—Chung-yang tu-li san-shih-erh lü) were destroyed early in the war. Most rural reconstruction elements remaining in Shantung joined the Kuomintang, Communist, or local independent forces. Both the Kuomintang and the Communists assassinated some of Liang's disciples who had remained. See [215], p. 100; also [219], p. 160; [521], p. 38; [51], no. 32 (Oct. 19, 1941); [621].

Japanese, Han ordered Sun Tse-jang, the administrative supervisor of the second district (a dozen hsien around Ho-tse), to lead
the protesting militia into Honan (at Hankow they were eventually
turned over to the nationalist general, Ho Ying-ch'in). The peasantry, seeing themselves despoiled of both their sons and their
guns and left defenseless against the Japanese, felt themselves betrayed by the rural reconstructors. In some places the enraged
populace killed the rural cadre and school directors and burned
down the schools. When Liang returned to the Ho-tse area in 1939
to inspect guerrilla operations (significantly, he could travel there
only with the aid of the Eighth Route Army), there were still mur-
murings against him.[62] Thus, Liang's movement—and his dream
of building a new Chinese civilization—went up in the smoke of his
peasant schools, set to the torch by the same peasant masses who
were to be the creators of the new society.

Contemporary Criticism of Liang's
Rural Reconstruction

Although Liang's work at Tsou-p'ing did not represent the entire
spectrum of the rural reconstruction movement, he was the
movement's only real philosopher, and only he had provided a

---

62. [173], pp. 53–55; [225]; [342], p. 178; [621]; [619]; [639]; [617]; [626].
Keenly aware that Han's betrayal had forever destroyed peasant trust
and support (as well as any hope for large-scale resurrection and guerrilla
activity), Liang was bitter. He wept that, because of the warlord's cynical
double cross, his rural reconstruction had ended up committing precisely
the kind of villainy it had sought to combat.
"The peasant schools were the primary focus of the enmity aroused in
the people by all the authorities' actions; this is especially because they [the
peasant schools] were training organs for the masses and the usual gathering places for training and mobilization. [Thus] the militia and guns were
just sitting there for the taking [by the authorities]. So the whole batch was
taken away. If there had been no mass training or training agencies, then,
although the authorities wanted the militia and the guns, it would not have
been so convenient [for them]. . . . And so the peasants thought the peasant schools had executed the deception. [Their] anger and hatred reached
great proportions, even to the point of destroying the peasant schools and
killing the school directors. A rural reconstruction agency was used as a
tool for rural destruction. . . . Our work was truly utterly destroyed without a trace! Our colleagues and students can hardly establish a foothold in
society or look people in the eye! When I speak and think of this [incident],
I truly weep bitterly!" [44].

systematic, all-encompassing theory. Consequently, he attracted
more than his share of criticism. Since Liang himself considered his
rural work a revival of Chinese culture, not a few critics labeled him
a self-confessed restorationist (*fu-ku* or *fu-chiu*), who was using new
terms for old ideas.[63] Even many Western-educated rural reconstructionists, although they universally professed great admiration
and respect for Liang's personal character and intellect, tended to
think of him as an "unscientific," old-fashioned Confucian who did
not quite understand the modern world. Many of these people
conceived of rural reconstruction as simply a Western-oriented
modernization program for the sole purpose of raising rural productivity and educational levels, and naturally thought Liang's talk
about self-government and "a new social order" was visionary
prattle.[64]

Many "liberal" intellectuals found the very emphasis on rural
development and agrarian problems wrong; they advocated instead building up large urban industries, which, as in the West,
would bring about better economic conditions in the countryside.
Liang's attempt to create an agrarian China was national suicide in
their estimation, for agrarian nations are, by their very nature,
poor, weak, and in economic bondage to the industrialized nations.[65]

One of rural reconstruction's most caustic critics was Ch'en Hsu-
ching, a graduate of the University of Illinois and leading advocate
of "wholesale Westernization." Ch'en delighted in pointing out that
Liang's rural reconstruction was, after all, a Western import; it
copied organizational methods and scientific technology, and had
hardly anything purely Chinese. Poking fun at Liang's messianic
pretensions and his ignorance of the West, Ch'en jibed that "only
those who have not been abroad, who do not understand what the
West's rural areas are like, could exaggerate [the claims for] this
[rural reconstruction] movement as something we ourselves invented, and [that by it] we ourselves will open up a new path [for
the world]." Ch'en compared Liang's work to Robert Owen's: utopian and a failure.[66]

    63. [170], pp. 129–134, 142–143; [400], pp. 18–19; [143], pp. 13–14;
[401], pp. 161, 165–169; [115].
    64. Chang Fu-liang, letter to the author, dated July 17, 1969; [612];
[615]; [618]; [629].
    65. [581]; [268]; [143], pp. 15–17.   66. [140], p. 18; [143], p. 18.

Ch'en's main point seemed to be that since rural reconstruction had not eradicated rural poverty and backwardness, it had been proven a complete failure. An archetypical Westernized urban intellectual, Ch'en returned from his visit to Tsou-p'ing with the less-than-startling conclusion that Liang had still not transformed rural Shantung into Shanghai. With almost a victorious air, he pointed out that the Tsou-p'ing hospital was poorly equipped and backward, the peasant houses were dirty and stinking, and in all of Tsou-p'ing there was not one good motor road. "By this, rural reconstruction may be known!" he quipped. As far as he could see, the only people who truly benefited from rural reconstruction were the intellectuals who made their living at it.[67]

The KMT critics also took up Ch'en's refrain about Tsou-p'ing's roads. In their own model hsien they had been building modern motor roads with a grand passion. Such roads, which appeared to serve as their major index of rural modernity, were excellent for moving troops and officials, both of whom had motor transport. Since peasant oxcarts, however, damaged the shiny new (and expensive) roads, they were not permitted on them. It was in answer to the Kuomintang as much as to Ch'en that a student of Liang's queried: "If oxcarts are not permitted, then aside from providing a small minority of people with roads on which to run their autos or rickshas, what meaning [do motor roads] have?"[68]

The Kuomintang critics further faulted Liang as an unrealistic Confucian moralist who did not understand the modern need for bureaucracy and political force. Their own CC-Clique-style rural work was rooted in a faith in official force; its aim was to extend political power down into the villages so that directives from the top would be put into effect on the local level. The Kuomintang remained suspicious of Liang's efforts to reverse this flow of power. The KMT Central Committee local-government specialist, Li Tsung-huang, visited Tsou-p'ing and came away fretting that he hoped Liang and his men "do not go beyond the Kuomintang's ideology or the central government's legal orders." He was also more than a bit irritated at Liang's use of his own terms, such as "village school-center" and "students." There seems to have been a lingering fear in KMT rural-reconstruction circles that Liang's projects were suspiciously similar to the Communists' style of peas-

67. [140], pp. 16–17.   68. [204], p. 15.

ant organization, and even the rumor that Tsou-p'ing had been infiltrated by the Communists.[69]

Marxists found Liang at once the most reactionary and the most progressive of rural reconstructionists, because Liang, unlike the Ting hsien leaders, recognized that imperialism and the warlords were the real causes of rural poverty.[70] Yet they were quick to point out that as long as imperialism held China in its economic grip, Liang's local cooperative path to agrarianist socialism was a chimera: "The villages, including their cooperatives, are under the control of foreign and Chinese capitalists and financiers . . . the villages are already under the complete control of the cities of London, New York, and Osaka. So Liang's cooperative Oriental third road is an illusion."[71] This criticism had some factual foundation: city-bank capital did provide the backing for Tsou-p'ing's cooperatives, and the imperialist powers' dumping of their machine-made textiles was the direct cause of the dramatic collapse of Tsou-p'ing's weaving and sericulture cooperatives. In the final analysis, however, the nature and extent of the treaty ports' economic impact upon the countryside is open to debate.

The Marxist critics came to the heart of rural reconstruction's difference from their own ideal of a rural movement when they claimed that Liang's emphasis upon the village unity was aimed at obliterating the class contradictions in rural society. Peasant interests are not identical with those of their more privileged neighbors, the Marxists insisted, and Liang's programs were designed to consolidate the rule of the landlords and rich peasants. Were not the school-center directors and trustees mostly landlords and rich peasants? Many leftist intellectuals concluded that the thrust of rural reconstruction was the same as the KMT's—to preserve the status quo. "The only difference between Liang and the others who wish to preserve the present order is that he wishes to use soft methods. The others use hard methods to deal with the masses." Another critic called for a rural movement that acknowledged class differences and represented the masses of poor peasants against the landlords (and hinted that such a movement was already afoot, but prudently refrained from naming names).[72]

69. [429]; [274], II, 29; [397], p. 86; [616]; [618].
70. In 1930, Liang accused Hu Shih of being "soft" on imperialism, and not recognizing its role in bringing about China's ruin. See [11k]; [171], pp. 91–92.
71. [401], p. 164.   72. [170], p. 143; [400], pp. 27–29.

A Critique of Liang's
Rural Reconstruction: Theory and Practice

Liang's movement, conceived of as it was in reaction to the Communists, affords some interesting points of comparison with certain aspects of Maoism. He seemed to share with Mao a peculiarly Confucian faith in the influence of the human environment and the efficacy of intimate group contact in moral and intellectual improvement. They both conceived of internal virtue (be it a rectified heart or proletarian consciousness) as linked with external political, military, and economic success. To both, the good society would be achieved by continuous spiritual transformation of the whole society, a never-ending moral drama, which would solve China's economic and political backwardness and, at the same time, avoid the dehumanization of urban bourgeois society. Both were apprehensive that selfish, mundane desires might extinguish the spirit of self-sacrifice. But for Mao, the nationalist, the purpose of sacrifice was the nation-state and the masses. For Liang, self-sacrifice was an end in itself, an expression of the true nature of man and not a means to an external end. Self-abnegation was an expression of the *tao*, and only secondarily for the material benefit of the collective.

Both Mao and Liang had broadly conceived programs based upon their synthesis and systematization of the inchoate demands and inherent wisdom of the rural masses. Both relied on small-group education and discussion to stimulate mass participation and to forge a *gemeinschaftlich* unity of leader and led. Both men hoped that from continuous moral scrutiny and struggle in small groups, a new elite of selfless moral paragons would emerge to maintain unrelenting revivalist fervor. Both movements had an earnest populist dedication to "serving the people."

In the end, it was the Communists who realized Liang's ultimate goal: the revival and reintegration of China based upon an impassioned mass commitment to a common ethic—a "religion that was not a religion," as Liang often described Confucianism. The style and methods of Mao's revival bear certain resemblances to Liang's vision: its emphasis on small rural industry and local self-reliance, its basic approach to agricultural development, small-group dynamics, rustication campaigns, and study sessions. Perhaps these resemblances are due more to the objective historico-geographic legacy of a large, poor, and disjointed agricultural society

than to any shared, subjective, cultural inheritance, but resemblances there are. Of course, China's revival under the Communists has not been based upon the traditional values that were
Liang's central concern.

Liang's failure may be explained in numerous ways, all of which
indicate an incompatibility between his traditionalism and the requirements of modernization and political success. One lapsed
Confucian in Taiwan, for instance, dismissed Liang's work as "sharing the same faults of traditional Confucians. His rural reconstruction efforts failed because he overestimated the goodness of human
nature and put too much faith in the moral power of the cadres."[73]
Similarly, Liang's idealist Confucian *Weltanschauung* seems to have
precluded his understanding the nature of political power. He
thought and expressed himself in the images and categories of a
Confucius or Mencius, a sage with a vision. He perceived modern
Chinese political disintegration in terms of the Spring and Autumn
period and believed, like Mencius, that his reform program would
attract the people of the whole nation once one of the local power-
holders put it into practice. Like the philosophers of old, Liang
spent his reformist career wandering from one local power-holder
to another, trying to convince them that his idealistic programs
would rebound to their ultimate benefit. First, he went to Shantung
on the promise of support from Wang Hung-i's group, then to the
South to solicit the Kwangsi generals' support. Finally, he went into
Han Fu-ch'ü's camp. Even his decision, against friends' advice, to
remain on the mainland after 1949 was based on his hope that he
might influence Mao Tse-tung.[74]

Liang's movement—like his philosophical theories—rested on a
contradiction, which lay at the core of several layers of inconsisten-
cies. The most obvious was rural reconstruction's political ambiguity; it was neither revolutionary nor conservative nor, indeed,
even liberal, but "revolutionarily conservative." Liang's own workers occasionally became conscious of the unanswered questions.
After the peasants were organized, one cadre was moved to ask:
"Where should they be led? To uphold the status quo? To reform
the status quo? To overthrow the status quo?"[75] Rural reconstruction walked a tightrope avoiding all three alternatives.

Liang's movement looked both to the past and to the future, and

73. [569], pp. 176–177; [638].
74. At least that is what he told friends. [634]; [633]; [635].
75. [384], p. 13.

so faced the present status quo with a Janus-like ambiguity. Liang
envisioned a movement of *Volkstum* against *Staatstum*. Government
by its very nature, he felt, was a hindrance to rural reconstruction.
Collusion with the political status quo compromised rural reconstruction from the start, forcing it "to take the side of the government against the people." At the same time, Liang realized that
rural reconstruction's only alternative to association with government was to become an independent, armed political movement
and seize power itself.[76] Yet by taking power, the movement would
metamorphose into *Staatstum* and so incorporate into itself all the
evils of impersonal bureaucracy, mechanistic law, and dehumanizing relationships that the movement originally set out to fight.
Liang never faced this contradiction squarely. Rather he hoped for
a vague, undefined process whereby society would gradually absorb the state, transform it into the image of society, and so realize
the ancient Confucian ideal of the "familization of government."

Because Liang's rural reconstruction contained within itself the
contradictory possibilities for both politico-cultural revolution and
conservative control, it managed to arouse both the suspicions of
the Kuomintang and the support of a regional power-holder, Han
Fu-ch'ü. This ambiguity even led Han's immediate successor in
Shantung, the Japanese, to view it as a device for conservative
control. One Japanese, at least, looked into Liang's theories for this
reason:

> It is said that since the [Marco Polo Bridge] incident, the con-
> structive stage of the [new order in East Asia] plan has been
> reached. The two matters that are not at present completed
> are the security of the [North China] countryside and eco-
> nomic reconstruction, and so these two things are basic obsta-
> cles to the realization of the new order. When we look at the
> phenomena of the Communists moving into those areas from
> which we have driven Chiang [Kai-shek's] army and the ir-
> regulars, we feel that this is even more important. Naturally,
> the first step is clearing the countryside militarily . . . but mili-
> tary action cannot be continued indefinitely. . . . In this re-
> spect, I am presenting Liang Shu-ming's theory of rural gov-
> ernment for consideration as something that might serve this
> purpose.[77]

The contradiction manifests itself on another level in rural reconstruction's relationship with the local rural elite. The movement

76. [39], p. 10; see also [11e], p. 177; [11i—m]; [38], pp. 314–320.
77. [346], p. 501.

sought to transform the present bad organic rural community into a future good one by partial reliance on the "natural leaders." This method was practical because local elite participation was absolutely necessary if the masses were to commit themselves; it was also prescriptive because the organic *Volkstum* would be destroyed if internal village contradictions were emphasized. But, as evidenced by the continuous struggle between the institute and the village elite over control and direction of programs, Liang never solved the obvious, if not universal, antagonism between gentry and nongentry interests. Liang again put his faith in a vague process of education, which would alter both gentry and nongentry present consciousness formed by the existing bad rural society.

Liang considered himself a sage whose knowledge of the eternal Thusness transcended history (and, of course, the conditioning of the bad society of the present). In his own mind at least, he solved the paradox confronting any advocate of social change: whence comes knowledge of the future perfect society if all men's consciousnesses are determined by their present imperfect social existence? Yet since Liang's knowledge was not of the objective intellectual kind (not "scientific" as, let us say, Marxism claims to be) then transmission of this knowledge to the agents of social transformation—his cadre—was entirely subjective. It was impossible to be sure that they had completely sloughed off the mentality, attitudes, and habits inculcated by the bad society in which they lived. The great majority quite obviously had not. The clearest example was the "Ho-tse style" of rural reconstruction. The general failure of the cadre to share Liang's commitment to the unity of theory and practice is another. Most cadre were still acting and thinking in a world of a "government of literati," where an essay or report written was a task accomplished and where there was an unbridgeable gap between the labor of the mind and the labor of muscle.

Shantung rural reconstructors—like those elsewhere—remained prone to other faults of the traditional scholar class, such as bureaucratism, petty factionalism, and above all, careerism. Liang himself later admitted that the fusion of peasant and intellectual, upon which his whole movement was based, was never realized: "The intellectuals stayed intellectuals and the peasants stayed peasants."[78] One contemporary observer of rural reconstruction

78. [88]. Several interviewees volunteered the opinion that some of

painted a vivid picture of its hypocrisy and the persistent gap between ideal and reality:

> The average rural reconstruction worker today is seldom able to effect an integration with the masses. Although they advocate going back to the villages, they still want their own wives to enjoy an urban life. Although they go on about the ruralization of education, they want their own children to enjoy privileged education. Or, what is worse, they themselves stay the entire year living in semi-urban style at the hsien town or township and seldom go down into the countryside. Most of the leaders are busy all day entertaining visiting guests, administrating and taking care of personnel matters. A lot of rank-and-file workers consider this work as just a career. The upshot is that now the countryside supports a new class that lives off rural reconstruction.[79]

Because the movement was compromised by its associations with the government, and because its cadre failed to truly unite with the peasantry, the peasants remained apathetic and passive. In summing up what he had learned from his own failure and the Communists' success, Liang concluded that "the key to success in mass movements seems to be to transform oneself into one of the masses."[80]

At yet a more fundamental level, the contradiction manifests itself in rural reconstruction's ultimate philosophical basis. Liang proclaimed that the aim of his movement was to revive the essence of Chinese culture—"reason" (li-hsing)—which was the opposite of Western "selfishness" and "utilitarianism." Because of historical circumstances and Western influence, this essence had all but vanished; only slight traces survived in China's villages.[81] Liang took his movement to the countryside both to utilize the vestigial li-hsing he saw there and, at the same time, to nurture li-hsing as the means to the ultimate salvation of China and the world. Thus, li-hsing was both the means and the end to his rural reconstruction.

In Liang's theory, people distinguished themselves from animals (and Chinese from Westerners) by their ability to act against material self-interest for moral reasons. This was the attitude that had kept China from modernizing before. Now Liang believed that its

---

Liang's subordinates and associates were simply careerists or bureaucrats who did not understand or believe in Liang's theories: [640]; [626]; [618].
   79. [142].   80. [88]; [39].   81. [38], p. 184.

revival among the masses was the *sine qua non* for China's economic
and political reconstruction.

Such a proposition contradicted itself in logic and in fact. Although rural reconstruction's aim was a society free from urban
political and economic domination, Liang still had to turn to urban
banks for capital. Moreover, the very programs carried out in
Shantung depended not upon peasant unselfishness, but on their
selfishness. The success of Tsou-p'ing's cooperatives, for instance,
rested upon the peasants' awareness of their own self-interest, not
their *li-hsing*. Even in Liang's basic design, rural reconstruction
programs and village self-government would attract peasant participation by appealing to their selfish interests, not their altruistic
impulses.

Theoretically, rural reconstruction was to allow China to preserve that priceless gift of its sages—*li-hsing*—and still acquire
wealth and power sufficient to provide material well-being and
protection against the morally inferior foreign aggressors. Yet if
the essence of Chinese culture was directly responsible for China's
material inferiority in the first place, how could renaissance of that
essence solve the problem of material inferiority? *Li-hsing* had kept
the Chinese from wealth and power; how could *li-hsing* now abruptly enable them to achieve it? Moreover, those elements in
Western culture that Liang considered the antithesis of Chinese
culture, were precisely the ones he identified as responsible for
Western material success and necessary for rural reconstruction.
For example, the reason for China's material production failure
was its inability—due to its superior *li-hsing* culture—to change to
an externally directed (*hsiang wai*) attitude. Yet the Western attitude of outward struggle destroyed *li-hsing* and made it difficult to
pay attention to human relationships and human emotions.

Ch'en Hsu-ching, Liang's redoubtable critic, sensed the same
contradiction in a slightly different form: "Our nation has been
working on spiritual reconstruction for several thousand years and,
because of it, material construction has had no results. How can
spiritual reconstruction have results now?"[82] The ultimate resolution of the question turns upon the nature of human beings and
modernization. Many—Marxists and liberals—would claim that
Mao himself shared Liang's contradiction.

82. [143], p. 17.

CHAPTER XII

The War Years and After: Politics and Polemics

The year 1937 was the peak of Liang's reformist career. The remainder of his life is a protracted postscript to his role in the rural reconstruction movement. He continued to believe he was a sage-messiah, but was once again a messiah without a movement, or at least without a movement that would lead to his vision of the new China. Nevertheless, he still had several important roles to play throughout the succeeding four decades.

During the decade 1937–1947, Liang emerged as a leader of Chinese "liberals"; through his initiative and organizational activities, the minor parties and unattached intelligentsia became an important factor in the wartime and postwar Chinese power equations. That Liang should become a paladin of democracy is not without irony. He had labored long and hard to construct a theory of culture by which to demonstrate that Western-style democracy was incompatible with Chinese spiritual and material conditions. Both before and after the war, he publicly argued that the much disputed question of constitutional government was irrelevant.[1] Yet in his actual political career he ended up fighting for some of the very forms of representative government, multiparty politics, and other Western-style institutions he had opposed in his cultural theories. Of course, some of his wartime political causes—guarantees of minimal civil rights and the separation of the military from politics—had been consistent themes since 1917.

Liang's actual decision to participate in politics of any kind repre-

---

1. Liang argued that until the customs, habits, and attitudes of the masses changed, Western-style constitutional government would be only a superficial copying of foreign institutions completely unrelated to Chinese realities and would definitely fail. [14d]; [76]. Before the war, he had repeatedly emphasized the need to steer clear of politics. See [39], p. 3; [20], pp. 301–302.

sented a major shift in attitude. Heretofore, he had considered politicians and all their political movements and methods morally inferior. His rural reconstruction movement and the various causes that had preceded it were all consciously designed to be nonpartisan, and he had steadfastly tried to keep them free from any form of political coloration or ambition. His own temperament—as all who knew him unanimously judged—was totally unsuited to politics, and he himself approached any political role with enormous reluctance.[2] Yet that same Confucian *noblesse oblige* that drove him from the quiet groves of academe in 1924 now prompted him to reenter the treacherous swamp of political bargaining and maneuvering that had so repelled him in 1912.

On the theoretical level, Liang continued to preach that China's crisis was primarily cultural, not political. With the reconstruction and reintegration of China's moral community and belief system, the reintegration of the political community would come about naturally. The new social and economic structures of cultural reconstruction (such as cooperatives and village covenants) would eventually determine the forms of the political superstructure. In the long run, he maintained, it was the culturally oriented rural movement, not the transient political figures, groups, and power struggles, that would determine China's future and resolve its problems.

Prelude to the Democratic Third Force: 1937–1939

The Japanese invasion and occupation, however, fundamentally altered Liang's estimation of what constituted the *present* urgent need; the very existence of China was threatened. Unless the Japanese were driven out, there would be no China at all, Confucian, Communist, or Nationalist; and unless the question of political parties and democracy was settled, Liang reasoned, the nation could not rally to drive out its conquerors. Thus, he began to conceive of the rural reconstruction movement as a foundation for a specifically political organization with political goals.[3]

---

2. The people who spoke with me about Liang invariably mentioned his political naiveté. See also [423], pp. 127–129.

3. See [44]; [527]; [620]. Liang first adumbrated his ideas on the political potential in rural reconstruction right after the war broke out. See [41].

During the first two years after the war broke out, however, Liang had little time for formulating any political programs of his own; he was on the road almost continually, as an official representative of the central government, inspecting local resistance capabilities and organizations throughout China.[4] His relations with Chiang Kai-shek and the KMT, moreover, were in a honeymoon period brought on by patriotic fervor and common opposition to the enemy. Liang's early commitment to working for change within the existing framework of the KMT's one-party dictatorship and his later transition to a position openly antagonistic to the KMT were symptomatic of a general trend among the liberal and unattached Chinese intellectuals.

For its own part, the KMT initially went scrambling after nonparty support for the war effort by extending a symbolic advisory role in the governing process to certain elements outside the party. Immediately after the outbreak of the war, Nanking's Supreme National Defense Council (headed by Chiang Kai-shek) appointed Liang and twenty-three other non-KMT national figures to a National Defense Advisory Council (Kuo-fang ts'an-i-hui). This first organ was soon superseded by the People's Political Council (Kuo-min ts'an-cheng-hui; the PPC), a larger body of two hundred, which also included some KMT members. Liang was elected to its standing committee.[5] As Liang and the noncommitted "democratic" elements became increasingly disillusioned over the prospects for working within the KMT power monopoly, the PPC provided them with a forum for building their own organization.

Liang had been in Peiping just a few days before the July 7 Marco Polo Bridge Incident. When the Japanese garrison at Feng-t'ai made their move toward the old walled town of Wan-p'ing and set off the frantic negotiations to stave off war, he had already returned to Shantung. On July 17 at Ku-ling, Chiang Kai-shek issued his tensely awaited answer to the Japanese: the central government would resist with force any further Japanese incursions in North China. The war that all knew was coming moved a step closer. While negotiations continued, the Japanese proceeded to move troops from Japan, Korea, and Manchuria into the Peiping area. Chiang invited Liang and other non-KMT national figures to

---

4. [51], nos. 10–14.

5. [501], July 13, 1938; [51], nos. 12, 13; [373], Record of the first session.

come to Nanking immediately for an emergency conference. When Liang's train stopped en route during the night of August 13 at the station of Wu-hsi, Kiangsu, Liang found the entire station filled with troops in full field gear; the Japanese had attacked Shanghai. This, Liang judged, meant full-scale war to the end. Therefore, he did not continue on to the conference, but rushed back to Shantung to make preparations. Upon arrival, he found telegrams from Chiang calling him to Nanking for a meeting of the newly created National Defense Advisory Council. After stopping at Tsou-p'ing to leave instructions, he again set off to the south. At this time, the Generalissimo even directed Liang to draft a program of wartime rural reconstruction, but, as with most overtures the KMT made to the liberal elements, nothing concrete ever materialized from the plan.[6] At the end of August, Chiang commissioned Liang to return to Shantung to inspect defense preparations (and perhaps privately to urge Governor Han—with whom Chiang's relations had never been good—to resist the expected Japanese drive into Shantung).

In the meantime, Nipponese troops were pouring into Hopei through the Great Wall and striking west into Shansi. In early November, General Ku Chu-t'ung's men abandoned their hopelessly heroic three-month defense of Shanghai, and the Japanese rolled inland toward Nanking and Hankow. Yet all had been relatively quiet on the Shantung front.

When confronted with a choice between the Japanese and Chiang Kai-shek, Governor Han in Shantung, it seems, felt compelled to choose the former. As he retreated with only token resistance (at the same time ordering his entire civil administration to withdraw as well), two Japanese armies cut into his province, by land from the north at Techow and by sea from the southeast; they took Tsinan and the principal port of Tsingtao on Christmas day. Liang had left the province just a few days ahead of the advancing Japanese. After arriving in the new temporary national capital at Hankow, he personally and in tears reported to Chiang what had transpired in Shantung, but Chiang had merely smiled, saying, "I already know about everything."[7] A month later, Han was arrested and shot for his unpatriotic perfidy.

6. [51], nos. 14, 46.
7. [44]. Liang had apparently tried hard to persuade Han to resist. One source reported that "Liang spent three days and nights arguing with Han and urging him to fight." [626].

Visit to Yenan and Talks with Mao

In his capacity as a member of the National Defense Advisory Council, Liang was now commissioned to inspect defense preparations in Honan and Shensi. His going to the Shensi capital of Sian that same month, however, was merely a pretext "for my real destination"—the Communist stronghold of Yenan. Liang now saw the changes in CCP policy as a "great turning point" in national life. After a two-week bout with illness in late December (brought on, no doubt, by his six months of continuous harried travel and the Shantung debacle), he crossed the broad, muddy Wei River on January 5, 1938, and began the winding two-hundred-mile trek north across the eroded hills of the Yellow Dragon. The poverty and desolation of northern Shensi impressed him deeply as he traveled the icy, mountainous road; this impression was not altered after he arrived in the small county seat on the Yen River which was to become the Valley Forge of the Chinese revolution.

Liang spent over two weeks in Yenan conferring with Party leaders and touring Party and government institutions.[8] On the whole, the wartime CCP impressed him very favorably. What pleased him most were the perspicuous changes from the days of the Kiangsi Soviet: the abandonment of the old policy of land confiscation by force; the opening up of the peasant associations to all villagers including rich peasants and small landlords; and the new local-government system. Mao and others now admitted to him that the Kiangsi land policy "had been mistaken" and that further study of the problem was necessary before they could decide upon a future course. "This is an important shift!" Liang exclaimed.

The Yenan educational system—curriculum, teaching methods, and the student life style—excited Liang greatly. Although he found some aspects "crude," "superficial and laughable," such faults "are unavoidable at this time of courageous innovation." He concluded that "the facts prove that they have been successful." Despite their unaccustomedly hard new life, the students were in excellent health and they were enthusiastic and spirited. "Does this not prove their success?" Liang remarked.

Liang was aware that his hosts "naturally showed what I wanted to see and said what I wanted to hear," but he still concluded from

---

8. The following description of Liang's visit is drawn primarily from [51], nos. 15–20.

his many interviews and from "observing the facts" that "the CCP is in the midst of transformation. I believe that this change is not false." Surveying the cumulative changes that distinguished the new border regions from the Kiangsi period, Liang judged that the CCP program was now "quite close to our rural reconstruction"— similarities that would increase and become even more apparent after Liang's visit. Yet he was also quite conscious that the CCP had not become real rural reconstructionists. "Although their transformation is not false, it is not very deep either. . . . They still see China in terms of classes and still seek to solve China's problems through class struggle." Nevertheless, Liang observed, "the external realities and their environment have made them change."

Liang's characteristic bluntness and the embarrassing questions he would ask during the interviews probably did not endear him to CCP leaders. He asked Chang Wen-t'ien, the Party secretary-general, if, after all, the old reasons for the 1927 split with the KMT were still extant. What had now changed so that the CCP was again willing to cooperate in a second united front? (Many old Party veterans were wondering the same thing at the time.) Was not the CCP's goal to take national power? No, Chang answered, not at this stage. Well, Liang persisted, "the revolutionary party must first control government power to carry out its plan of national construction. Then, is it not necessary for the CCP to struggle for power from now on? If you say, 'we do not necessarily have to control the government ourselves,' then I would really like to know just how you can carry out a Communist revolution." Chang mumbled that the CCP "did not necessarily have to control the government" and that it was "going to help the KMT carry out the revolution." As to just how to carry out a Communist revolution in that case, Liang quipped, "it seems he did not answer clearly." Liang's motive behind many of these questions, of course, was to force the CCP to admit that orthodox Marxist theory was unsuited to Chinese reality and to demonstrate the superiority of his own ideas. Strangely enough, Liang's disquisitions can almost be taken as criticism of "rightist-opportunist tendencies," which soon provoked Mao's ire as well.

Liang talked most during his visit with the peasant's son he had met almost twenty years before in Peking, Mao Tse-tung. Aside from the inevitable formal occasions at dinner and on leaving, Liang met privately with Mao six times in Mao's yellow beaten-earth house at the foot of bald Phoenix Mountain.[9] These discussions usually began after dinner and sometimes ran through the evening and night to the dawn of the next day. If Mao's irregular hours raised Liang's austere eyebrows, the chairman's heroic consumption of tobacco and alcohol during their nocturnal tête-à-têtes left him stunned. (Apparently, Mao's usual habits were not affected by Liang's visiting-pastor aura.) Mao did not even follow the usual practice of diluting the fiery white *kao-liang* whiskey with food! Astonished, Liang was moved to inquire about his health. Mao replied that although someone once told him that he had tuberculosis, he had been examined by a doctor who denied it. He did admit, however, to occasional nervous exhaustion (neurasthenia).

Between his own more potent draughts, Mao poured tea for Liang. Whatever the effect of the spirits on Mao (Liang found him "relaxed, natural, and warm"), their interviews could not have been much like convivial bull-sessions, the art of which Liang seems to have lost at age sixteen. Actually, judging from what we know of Liang's usual "conversational style," he probably sat rigidly upright, looked grave, and proceeded to lecture. Mao himself probably strengthened this tendency in Liang by addressing him as "Teacher Liang" (Liang lao-shih).[10] "[Mao] liked to take notes when I talked to him. . . . When I finished, he would point to the important points he had written, answering them one by one. He was very systematic and clear, and each sentence addressed itself to the point at hand." So, with Mao sitting on one side of the small table, a homemade cigarette in one hand and his "coarse ink" and "well-worn writing brush . . . writing as though flying" in the other, and Liang sitting stolidly sagelike on the other side, Marx and Confucius debated China's future.

This confrontation between Mao and Liang and its symbolic contrasts do not reflect the differences between their respective Marxist and Confucian ideologies as much as the differences between their two quite distinct life experiences in Chinese society— exemplified by Mao's peasant stock and Liang's scholar-official

9. This was the first of four residences Mao occupied in Yenan. He abandoned it soon afterwards because of Japanese bombings. The content of Liang's discussions with Mao is in [51], nos. 18–20.

10. Although Liang never referred to Mao's use of this honorific term in print, he did mention it in private to friends. [633]; [634]; [621].

background. Although the "big and little traditions" were more integrated in China than in other premodern societies, there is still a palpable distinction in concrete life styles and experiences. On one side of that small table, Mao smoked, drank, and probably laced his naturally salty speech with earthy aphorisms. On the other side, Liang—with the demeanor of a contemplative monk—intoned, in solemn accents, his message of the sages. Liang always insisted on wearing the long scholar's gown regardless of the work he was doing or the heat; Mao could casually remove his pants in hot weather even during a formal conference.[11] Mao laughed and joked easily; Liang always scrupulously observed the old injunction that "the superior man has no frivolous words" (chün-tzu wu hsi-yen). Mao loved to read the old adventure novels such as Water Margin and Romance of the Three Kingdoms; Liang felt that such puerile perusings constituted a frittering away of a chün-tzu's valuable time. The folk traditions embodied in such stories as the Water Margin—the world of bandits, secret societies, and itinerant bully boys—represented values, standards of conduct, and ideals that seldom found their way into the more orthodox Chinese literature. Yet they were often a more vital part of peasant life than the Confucian Classics.

At the same time, the two men shared a bone-deep Chineseness, which, in the end, made them closer to each other than to many Westernized Chinese liberals and members of either the KMT or CCP. Perhaps the Chineseness of both the Confucian sage and the Marxist revolutionary is more important than the contrasts.

In some areas there was actually little disagreement. Liang reported: "In speaking of our proposals on various current problems, we mostly agreed; nowhere did we contradict each other." For example, Liang himself agreed heartily with Mao's often repeated phrase that "war changes everything." Their one slight divergence was over the relative importance of social reform, even as China was fighting the Japanese. As Liang recorded their conversations on the subject:

> In my view China's problem has two aspects: one is the external—national liberation; and one is internal—the carrying out of social reform (that is, the construction of a new China). I asked him, "Am I right?" He answered, "I agree completely."

11. [489], p. 79.

I asked him, "Should these two problems be solved separately or simultaneously without being separated?" He answered, "These [two] affairs are basically related and should
not be talked about separately. But [they are] not, after all,
one single matter. In carrying out solutions, at times one must
be emphasized over the other. For example, at present all
should be subordinated to the War of Resistance, and the
second problem can only be solved as an adjunct to the first."

I said, "I also have no doubts about that, but I nevertheless
demand—prior to national liberation—a decision on the matter of reform of society itself. I think that this decision [of
internal reform] is exactly what is needed [to effectively carry
out] the external War of Resistance. Unity is a prerequisite. . . . If unity is not strong, then the War of Resistance
will not be strong. . . . Unity will be genuine only if the
fundamental question of carrying out social reform for our
people is thoroughly solved together with this problem [of
resistance], and [the two problems] are inseparable. Otherwise, [if we] gloss over it and cover it up [now], the lurking
dangers will certainly manifest themselves later. . . ." He
thought that what I said was quite right.

I thereupon put forth my own advocacy—to determine
national goals and specific policies now . . . that is, [to decide
beforehand] the two great questions of social reform and national liberation, and their details of implementation. . . . Especially important is the ideal goal of national construction
and the steps and line to be taken for its realization. . . . He
[too] felt that unity solely on the basis of resistance to Japan
was really just a temporary expedient. But he also was concerned because the question of social reform was very grave
and far-reaching in its implications, and that it would not be
easy for the various parties to come together on it. If their
opinions cannot be unified, would that not [unfavorably] influence the present resistance to Japan? I said, "These various
concerns of yours are valid, and [you cannot be] considered
overly cautious. But we should conquer these difficulties
through enthusiasm (enthusiasm for thorough, complete unity) and confidence (confidence that we can mutually com-
municate) and so endeavor to seek an ultimate solution."

He said, "Your intentions are good. It would be best [how-
ever] for the KMT to carry it out, or for another party to
promote and push it. The CCP and KMT have just started to
promote the War of Resistance. [If] after just six months, [the
CCP] again stirred up the question of social reform, it would
seem that it would not be convenient. Now if the KMT or

someone else wanted to have basic discussions on this, then
the CCP naturally would be extremely receptive. . . . Right at
this moment (January 1938), they [the CCP] are soliciting the
KMT's agreement on a draft of a common program by the
two parties. In Wuhan there are eight people . . . drafting it
under Mr. Chiang [Kai-shek's] leadership. This common program is quite similar to the national goals and policies you
speak of. . . . Why do you not hurry back to Wuhan and push
it?"·

   Mr. Mao repeatedly said to me that although China is already united, it still needs to be further united. I then would
say, "If you want greater unity, what other way is there except
this method of mine?"[12]

In a way, Liang had come out on the "left" side of the question.
Shortly thereafter, Mao—in an attack on Wang Ming's "rightist
opportunism"—would reverse himself somewhat and emphasize
the other side of the coin. Liang was similarly "leftist"—or just
simply naive—on the question of socialism, too. Mao adumbrated
to him what he would elaborate two years later in his "On New
Democracy": that China's revolution was to have two consecutive
stages: democratic and socialist. Liang opposed this three-stage
theory (with the addition of the final Communist stage) with his
own one-stage theory. "I hold that China's progress toward political
democratization and economic socialization are simultaneous. . . .
Both [processes] mutually push the other forward, so that they
advance together to completion. They cannot be separated, so their
[the CCP's] first two stages are one stage in my theory."

About the war itself, Liang was downcast and pessimistic. The
first six months of the struggle had seen Japan move almost at will
to seize most of China's important cities and railways. The Chinese
had yet to win a significant battle. This was one question on which
Mao actually changed Liang's mind—a feat of no mean proportions. "He analyzed [the situation] for me from the angles of the
international situation, the enemy, and us, and changed my pessimistic opinions quite a bit."

Most of the Liang-Mao discussions, however, were not on
current affairs at all, but on philosophical questions. Liang rather
presumptuously (if a sage can be presumptuous) presented Mao
with several of his books to serve as a basis for these more theoretical discussions. Sure enough, the next evening Mao would appear

12. [51], no. 19.

with a sheaf of papers on which he had neatly summarized each book's important points. He also systematically excerpted the parts he liked. Not satisfied with this show of disciplelike diligence, Liang was a bit annoyed because Mao could not find the time in the hours between their meetings to read through every book to the bitter end, especially his recently completed, 472-page *Theory of Rural Reconstruction*.

As was to be expected, some fundamental disagreements did arise between Mao and Liang when their conversation turned to the nature of Chinese society. One discussion on rural reconstruction was precipitately cut short when Mao asked Liang what problems he had encountered. Liang responded that his greatest problem was that "the peasants preferred passivity to action." Mao cut him off by blurting out: "You are wrong! The peasants want action. How can you say they prefer to be passive?"[13]

Liang, of course, held that China was qualitatively different from the West that had given birth to Marxism-Leninism. As a Marxist, Mao argued that all societies shared certain minimal qualities. After listening to Liang expound his rural reconstruction and cultural theories for a week, Mao summed up their differences: "Chinese society also has its qualities in common [with other societies]. China's problems also have common qualities. You overemphasize its special nature and neglect its universal nature." Liang answered: "The reason China is China lies precisely in these special features. You overemphasize its common qualities and neglect its special qualities. How can that be right? My debate with Mr. Mao ended here."

Such a conclusion was no doubt inevitable. Yet for the most part Mao *did* go along with Liang's particularist emphasis. He even, according to Liang anyway, accepted the validity of Liang's two basic points: that "traditional Chinese society had its unique structure, which was a different entity from both medieval and modern Europe," and that "the Chinese revolution was set off from the outside and not internally generated." These statements could be interpreted, as Liang did, as denying the validity of a Marxist revolution in China, for they implied that China was so unique that the "universal truths" of Marxism were not quite so true there. (Certainly Mao never would have seemed to accede to such points if another Party leader had been present.) Whatever was in Mao's mind, he apparently conceded some ground regarding Liang's ar-

13. [88].

guments on the general unsuitability of a foreign theory to the particular Chinese reality and his emphasis on China's special characteristics.

Liang left full of admiration and friendship for Mao. "He left me with a very good impression. In ancient times Chu-ko Liang praised Kuan the Beautifully Bearded [Kuan Yü, the god of war] as 'truly matchless, head and shoulders above others.' I also have the same feeling [about Mao]. . . . He is above the vulgar but without affectations. Although there were disagreements between us, there was no uncomfortable feeling in my heart." His main feeling on leaving Yenan was regret that he could not have stayed longer (he was supposed to have been in Kaifeng on his official business), especially because he would have liked to "become close with" the local peasantry and to ascertain their own feelings.

We can only speculate about Mao's reactions to Liang. That he spent so much time with him (far more than with any other such visitor to Yenan) and that he took their discussions so *seriously* would suggest that he was extremely interested in Liang and his ideas.[14] Just a few months after Liang's departure, Mao would launch a major attack against "foreign formalism" and "foreign dogmatism"—a theme that would then become an integral part of Maoism. Indeed, the Mao of 1937—a man in the midst of intensive study of Soviet works on Marxism—was quite different from the Mao of a short time later; the "Sinification" of Marxism was yet to come. Given the vision that Liang took with him to Mao's house in 1938 (his rural reconstruction theory and its resemblance to certain aspects of later Maoism), it is not inconceivable (but also not verifiable) that the chairman was influenced to a degree—consciously or unconsciously—by Liang. Determining "influence" is a slippery, evasive business, but we can say with some confidence, however, that at least Liang did strengthen and reinforce certain tendencies

---

14. Purely political motivation cannot be entirely discounted, for Mao did urge Liang to become politically involved. Yet, at that time, Liang had no political organization behind him, not even the miniscule Rural Reconstruction Group. He had also just lost whatever power-base he had had in Shantung. Other political independents with far more real political swat were never accorded the same treatment by Mao. Mao never mentioned Liang in any of his pre-1949 official writings, but perhaps that fact itself is significant: he personally attacked other cultural conservatives, such as Chang Chün-mai and Chou Tso-jen, but never Liang until their famous 1953 clash.

of Mao's that eventually shaped China's Marxist revolution into a peculiarly Sinified form.

How much of a role the visit with Mao played in Liang's own politicization and his concept of a third force is not clear. The CCP did consciously and shrewdly encourage Liang and other minor party heads to become politically active. And Liang did, after all, follow Mao's urging and hurry back to Wuhan. Reviewing the domestic situation in terms of realpolitik, any liberal demands, movements, or party organizations were unfavorable to the KMT and beneficial to the Communists, providing them with political allies and legitimacy. Any minor party demands for democratization, constitutionalism, or non-KMT political participation could only strengthen the Communists' position vis-à-vis the KMT, especially after the American involvement in the Chinese war effort.

For these reasons, many in both KMT and non-KMT political and intellectual circles have held that Mao "duped" Liang into mobilizing the liberal minor party elements into what amounted to an anti-KMT force. Some of Liang's own friends suggest that Liang was tricked into believing that the Communists respected him and his opinions.[15] Yet in his conversations with Mao, Liang had already adumbrated a plan for a quasi-coalition government in which input from non-KMT political elements would help determine national goals and the specific policies for reaching those goals.

My own understanding of Liang's passage into politics is that it is consistent with his continuing belief that he was a man of destiny, the savior of China. His general vision of the future good society did not change because of the war and his new political role. Rather, his past messianic role now became more a role of a national unifier and, thus, of a national savior. Once the war had started, national salvation required national unity above all. It gradually became apparent to Liang that the only means to such a goal was to organize the uncommitted intellectuals into a mediating third force, which would—through its independence—perform a unique and crucial function in keeping the united front from breaking down. Later, the third-force idea was transformed into a purely political organization with its own political interests, which, as time went on, pushed it into closer cooperation with the CCP.

15. [633]; [634]; [623]; [621]. One KMT intelligence source attributed Liang's politicalization in 1939 to the influence of the liberal journalist and PPC member Tsou T'ao-fen, who had accompanied Liang to Yenan. See [219], p. 161.

Liang, however, continued to maintain that the primary objective
of the organization was "to avoid civil war."[16]

Work for Social Reform
and National Liberation

Upon leaving Yenan, Liang went first to Kaifeng to fulfill his
inspection mission for the central government. A few days later, he
set off eastward again, following the course of the Yellow River. On
February 2, 1938, he crossed into Ho-tse, Shantung, where he met
with some of his rural reconstruction followers and tried to pull
them together into some kind of resistance force. Two days later,
he headed south to the strategic defense point in the Chinese lines,
Hsuchow. Its defense was in the capable hands of the diminutive
but pugnacious Kwangsi general, Li Tsung-jen, who had previously asked Liang to join him there for consultation on mass
mobilization techniques. During his month-long stay, Liang divided his time between Li, who was feverishly preparing for what
many thought would be the decisive battle of the war, and some of
his rural reconstruction followers who had gathered there.[17]

Liang also penned two pamphlets outlining a wartime course of
action and addressed to those rural workers left in Shantung and
Honan. The general thrust of his instructions was not unlike what
was evolving at the time in the expanding CCP base areas in North
China. The war, Liang said, would succeed only with a mass

16. [437a], p. 146.
17. Of Liang's 4,000 or so lower-level rural-reconstruction cadre, about
three-fourths remained in their home areas where they were soon dispersed and lost in the kaleidoscopic political-military maze of wartime
rural Shantung. About 800 cadre and militia men from the Chi-ning area,
however, had retreated as a unit in December, 1937, to the Nan-yang/
Chen-ping area in southern Honan where they were officially organized
into the Third Political Corps (also called the Thirty-second Political Regiment by the KMT) and trained for military and political warfare against
the Japanese. The Liaison Office was in Hsuchow at the time Liang was
there. In September 1938, the Third Political Corps, completely outfitted
and armed, crossed the Yellow River back into Shantung (one smaller
group—the Fifth Detachment—remained to fight in northern Honan).
For a time, Liang kept in contact with them by radio, but soon this link was
also broken. Liang would only see them once more before they were completely broken up by the CCP-KMT rivalry in 1940. See [51], no. 32; also
nos. 21–23; [215], p. 100; [521], p. 38.

mobilization of the peasantry through education and social reform. Liang, moreover, instructed his followers to cooperate with any elements—including the Communists—in resistance against the Japanese. The slogan "social reform internally and national liberation externally" now replaced his old maxim, "cultural reform and the people's self-salvation." He also announced a major change in his attitude toward China's problems. The urgent problem now was not purely cultural, but more political. Solution to the question of political democracy and parties was of paramount importance, a precondition for thorough national unity in its struggle with Japan. Accordingly, he formally founded his own political organization— the Rural Reconstruction Group (Hsiang chien p'ai). As he told his followers: "When we were in Shantung, we were a group of friends working for rural reconstruction. Now the nation needs a political organization. At the same time, we can use this organization to fight for our nation."[18]

In March 1938, Liang went to Wuhan to consult privately with the members of the eight-man committee (four members each from the KMT and CCP) who were working on the draft of the common program. He found that the talks had bogged down, and he made little progress himself in trying to urge the committee to action. In April, he went south through Hunan inspecting defense preparations. In the meantime, the long-awaited battle of Hsuchow had started (inauspiciously with the Japanese taking the small walled town to the northeast, T'ai-erh-chuang).

General Li, however, had laid a well-oiled trap and sprang it in a ferocious counterattack, which pulverized two of Japan's finest divisions, and scored the first (and only) clear Chinese victory of the early war. By May, unfortunately, the Japanese had put Li into a trap of their own by surrounding him with a column sent around his flank. The Japanese now started a large-scale move into Honan, and Liang rushed back to the south of that province to the old stronghold of P'eng Yü-t'ing (the Nan-yang and Chen-p'ing area) for a last meeting with his rural-worker-guerrilla outfit, the Third Political Corps. The Japanese, for their part, now had their original plans thrown awry by the mysteriously opened dikes of the Yellow

18. [619]; see also [44]; [51], nos. 21, 32, 33, 46; [527]; [138]; [215], p. 100; [521], p. 38. Liang did not openly publish his group's political platform until 1940, when his "Program of Rural Reconstruction" (Hsiang-ts'un chien-she kang-ling) was published in [326]. [215], p. 99; [279], p. 60.

River (which resulted in a colossal flooding of the North China Plain), and so changed their advance to a westward course along the Yangtze.

By the time the Japanese took the important river town of Anking in June, Liang was already in the far-western province of Szechwan, to which the Nationalist government had withdrawn and where the PPC then was meeting. He had left the front lines with great reluctance because he feared losing contact with his rural workers, and thus, he had earnestly tried to resign from his position on the PPC's standing committee. After arriving in Szechwan, however, and actually being cut off from his men in Honan and Shantung, Liang decided to apply his energies to what he considered the urgent problems of the war effort, and so stayed to attend the summer sessions of the PPC.

Rural reform. Although Liang was no longer personally engaged in rural work, he continued to see himself as a kind of national spokesman for the peasant. On arriving at the PPC meetings, he submitted several programs for rural reform based on his Tsou-p'ing model. Only in this way could the rural population be mobilized against the enemy, he argued. One article of his program called for (a) a wartime rural problems conference and (b) a coordinating agency for rural self-government and reform measures. "The content of my proposal was quite tame," Liang noted, "and by no means just for the benefit of the peasants. Rather, it was just as much for the benefit of the nation and the government itself." Yet the KMT was both suspicious and indifferent. Ultimately nothing concrete came of the proposal. After watching his proposal's year-long wanderings through the maze of KMT departments, councils, and ministries, Liang bitterly observed that "aside from the document's repeated comings and goings, my actions produced no [concrete] results at all. From 1938 to 1939, and again through 1940 and on to today, 1941, this conference [which I proposed] has yet to be convened."[19]

Conscription reform. The targets of Liang's other major effort on behalf of the peasantry when he got to Szechwan were the military conscription and service systems. With the war barely begun, the KMT's system was already notorious for its abuses and

19. [51], nos. 21–24.

inequalities. The American General Wedemeyer, in China later during the war, summed up the situation succinctly: "Conscription comes to the Chinese peasant like famine or flood, only more regularly—every year, twice—and claims more victims. Famine, flood, and drought compare with conscription like chicken pox with the plague."[20] Liang himself observed:

> The first order of business in the southwest rear area naturally was troop replacement, recruitment, and training. And yet military conscription was precisely what was being badly handled. Everything about it makes one utterly enraged and furious. [It causes] the villagers unbearable suffering and pain; and the nation does not get good recruits either. I have been a rural worker, and cannot sit by idly watching this, the greatest of the villagers' suffering. I cannot be timid [about taking actions].[21]

In Chungking Liang happened to meet three other like-minded men, two of whom were high-ranking KMT military men whose influence and reputations Liang hoped to use to further the cause of conscription reform. The four formed a discussion association, which soon attracted several government officials from organs that dealt with military service. On arriving in Szechwan, Liang also visited Chengtu, the provincial capital that lay two hundred miles to the northwest across the Szechwan basin. Quite by chance, the special administrative commissioners of the province and the security bureau were holding a meeting to discuss the recruitment problem. Szechwan governor Wang Tsuan-hsu invited Liang to chair the meeting. Perhaps Wang later regretted his decision, for Liang launched into a cutting critique of the entire government conscription system. The government had mobilized enormous numbers of peasants, a fourth of whom had died of privation or disease before they even reached their assigned units. The usual recruits arrived bound with ropes to prevent their escape. Basic-level recruitment authority was in the hands of the gentry, who invariably chose the poorest and weakest peasants. Liang pointed out that the worst aspect of the government conscription system was that it literally did not exist as a system. The phony national conscription laws and regulations, the various orders and directives that the government issued, and the actual village-level management were completely separate with no relationship to each other.

20. [254], p. 303.   21. [51], no. 23.

If conditions were such, then all Liang demanded was that the actual village recruitment process be in accord with the national regulations. After the Szechwan provincial meeting, Liang went on to the then director of Chiang Kai-shek's provisional headquarters in Chungking, Chang Ch'ün.

Liang soon found, however, that the greatest problems in the recruitment system were not at the top of the administrative order, but at the lower levels, and set about drafting a concrete plan modeled on the rural-reconstruction militia-recruitment techniques used in Tsou-p'ing and Chen-p'ing. He also contacted Chang Lan, a former governor of Szechwan and an influential educator. By early October, Liang had set up a meeting with Chang Lan, Chang Ch'ün, and several other provincial officials and educators, and the first steps were taken.

Liang's plan emphasized three points. Most important, he argued, the masses must be emotionally committed to and enthusiastic about the war effort. This would require periods of education and propaganda *before* recruitment. Second, "to create an atmosphere of operating [the recruitment process] according to the law, the masses must understand the content and the important points of the law [so they can protect [enforcement of] it and demand [enforcement of] it." Third, "especially important" is that the local figures involved are those whom the masses trust, and who will work together with them to guarantee good maintenance of a draftee's dependents. "Only with the enthusiasm and understanding of the masses . . . can it be managed conscientiously, fairly, and smoothly." Liang's formal proposal also provided for better treatment of draftees and for punishment of corrupt practices by officials and officers. (All of these conditions already existed in the CCP's system.)

Throughout the summer and fall of 1938, Liang's efforts seemed to be leading to actual results both in the province of Szechwan itself and nationally. In October 1938, he formally founded the Compulsory Military Service Implementation Association (Ping-i shih-shih hsieh-chin hui) in Chungking and soon completed his formal proposal for the PPC. Yet, in early 1939, his progress was stopped in its tracks, apparently because of some mysterious inner-KMT rivalry or because the reforms threatened certain vested interests. In early 1940, again because of some unexplained "rumors" reaching the Generalissimo, Chiang personally ordered Liang's association disbanded. Liang continued to work undauntedly for conscription reform throughout the war, but always in the teeth of KMT opposition.[22] Finally in 1944, the government established a Ministry of Conscription, but it did little to alleviate the worst abuses.

Theory of political democracy, 1938. Liang's own concept of political democracy, which he formulated in late 1938, resembled both the pre-1945 Communist position and the Western-oriented liberals' position on constitutional democracy. Yet Liang's program was informed by his own explicitly anti-liberal, anti-Marxist theory of China's unique culture. Liang's thesis was that since Chinese society lacked the prerequisites for constitutional democracy, it was an illusion to think that a paper document would really change anything. For the foreseeable future, he flatly predicted, Western-style constitutional democracy simply "will not [in reality] be implemented." He admitted that China—although it did not have classes in the Western sense—did have diverse groups of people (such as workers, peasants, and racial and religious groups), each of which had its own needs and interests. He further recognized that the ultimate ideals of political groups were also different. Effective mobilization and construction required provision for some kind of political representation of the interests of all people and the ideals of all political groups as well as for the active participation of their representatives. At the present time, moreover, all Chinese faced a threat from a common enemy and shared a common need for economic and social reconstruction. To defeat the external enemy and carry out coordinated internal reconstruction they had to have national unity.

Liang put his program on paper in December 1938 and sent it off to *L'Impartiale* (*Ta kung pao*). The KMT censors of the Ministry of Propaganda, who made no pretense at impartiality, refused to allow its publication because it was "very close to" the Communist position. Liang protested to the minister that "the Communist party did not copy me and I did not copy them either . . . there are still differences in fine points. Moreover, both [of us have our] own sources." Unintimidated, Liang sent off hand-written copies to the leaders of the various political parties. He called his formula a system for "two kinds of organization" (*erh-chung tsu-chih*). "In sum, this form is neither a multiparty system nor is it a one-party system. Rather it is a 'harmonization of the one and many' (*i to hsiang-jung*), or one containing many, or one on the basis of many."

22. [51], nos. 22–27; also [373b].

298 THE LAST CONFUCIAN

Liang's "two kinds of organization" seem to refer merely to a division between the executive and legislative organizations. The KMT, Liang allowed, would constitute the "system of synthesis" (*tsung-ho chih*), the "party above other parties," which would provide unified command in the war effort and maintain national unity. The non-KMT parties and the various cliques within the KMT would then have their own organization, a deliberative representative body. This plan would allow for nominal KMT rule because, Liang said, the ideology of the Three People's Principles was so vague that it could embrace all other ideologies and parties, and because the KMT itself contained a broad spectrum of political persuasions.[23] The principal difference between Liang's plan and Mao's "New Democracy" lies in Liang's stress on synthesis and harmony.

Liang's disappointment with the KMT government's wartime performance and its temporizing insincerity on the issue of democratization seems to have been at least as important as any possible encouragement from Mao in motivating him to advocate a proto-coalition government. The PPC itself had changed in nature during 1938. What had begun as the small, effective, non-KMT National Defense Advisory Committee in 1937 became the larger PPC in 1938 and included an increasingly larger proportion of delegates who were KMT members. Liang was quickly disabused of his hopes that this quasi-representative body would be transformed into the democratic forum he felt was needed to fully mobilize and unify all groups for the war. As the KMT appointed more of its own to the PPC, the chances for the non-KMT groups to have any real voice in national affairs naturally became smaller.[24]

Behind the Lines in 1939: A Bitter Valedictory to Shantung

The quiet fog of stalemate that characterized the China front until near the end of the war had already settled in by January 1939. In the west, the Nationalist regime had dug itself securely in and had begun the long wait for Japanese overambition to bring about Japanese defeat. In the east, the Japanese, having occupied almost all of China's cities and railways, were wondering what to do next. The recently installed Chinese ambassador to Washington, Dr. Hu Shih, was warming to his task of dramatizing to the Ameri-

23. [51], nos. 29–31.   24. [176], pp. 280–282.

can public the desperate, heroic resistance of the democratic Chinese Nationalists to Nipponese fascism. Back in Chinese reality, however, the Nationalist regime's top priority was maintaining its monopoly on political power; its resistance was no longer desperate or heroic.

With the censors refusing to allow publication of his political program, and his reforms for the conscription system frustrated, Liang decided there was little reason for him to stay in the Southwest rear area. Instead, he wanted to go to the North China war zone to see for himself what the actual conditions were behind enemy lines, to reestablish contact with his followers in Shantung, and to find out how the Third Political Corps was doing. Could he also have harbored some secret hope of resurrecting his rural reconstruction now that the favorable circumstances he had envisioned had actually come about? As it turned out, the decisions Mao and his commanders were in the midst of making at that time would eventually seal the fate of Shantung; the young CCP cadre and peasant armies Liang ended up traveling with during much of his eight-month expedition would succeed in accomplishing many of the objectives that had eluded Liang and his rural movement.[25]

Although the second PPC had just reelected Liang to its executive standing committee, he managed, with some effort, to resign. Then he requested and received Chiang Kai-shek's approval and support for the trip. Equipped with an official commission from the National Military Affairs Committee and an entourage of six, he set out from Chungking on February 1, 1939, not to return to Szechwan until October.[26] In April, he finally crossed into Shantung. After traveling through the old rural reconstruction areas in the southwest (around P'u, Fan, Shou-chang, and Yun-ch'eng hsiens) and meeting with former colleagues still in the area, he moved into the mountains of central Shantung for a month. On August 23, he left Shantung and passed through southern Hopei into Honan, where he conferred with a small guerrilla detachment composed of former rural workers from Shantung. Finally, he went into the Taihang mountains of Shansi and arrived in the Chinese-held city of Loyang on September 18.

25. At the time Liang was crossing Hopei and Kiangsi into Shantung, a detachment from Lin Piao's 115th division under the command of Ch'en Kuang was moving into the old rural reconstruction hsiens around Ho-tse and absorbing the scattered remnants of self-defense forces.
26. [51], nos. 31–32. Liang discusses his trip in detail in [51], nos. 33–40.

Initially Liang intended to move east from Szechwan in the company of troops under Yü Hsueh-chung, the Nationalist commander of the Shantung-Kiangsu war zone, but he quickly grew impatient with the delays involved in traveling with a large army. Therefore, he and his party ended up going alone or with small detachments of the CCP's New Fourth and Eighth Route armies, which were also moving into Shantung at the time. Once behind the enemy line, Liang continued to rely on Communist guerrillas for protection, especially when crossing the Japanese-held railway lines; Communist units throughout North China had been alerted to the possibility of his passage through their areas and had been instructed to provide help and protection. After a New Fourth Army unit helped him cross into Shantung, the Eighth Route, 115th Division, took over as his escort. Twice the timely intervention of New Fourth and Eighth Route troops rescued Liang and his party from the Japanese.

Always traveling by night and resting by day, Liang and his party made their way either on horseback with a guerrilla escort (he could then wear his long scholar's gown), or without escort, on foot, and wearing peasant clothing. The conditions they found along the way heightened Liang's customary indignation over the plight of the peasantry. Even he—for all his familiarity with rural life and his championing of the long-suffering peasantry—was not prepared for the poverty and isolation of some of the villages they put up in. They saw whole areas that were slowly dying of starvation, which, moreover, were also being forced to sustain several armies and governments. Liang returned from the trip saying what he had always said, but with greater urgency.

> I have . . . two particularly deep impressions. The first is that the Chinese peasants are really wonderful. Despite all they suffer because of the War of Resistance, . . . they still do not hate the nation or the central government. . . . The divisions among groups of guerrillas, troops, and governments [referring to CCP-KMT rivalry] are letting the common people down. . . . My second impression is that . . . [during this trip] I saw more clearly [than before] the backward practices and customs and the extreme poverty of the peasantry. Women in the interior of Shansi, for instance, have their feet bound almost to the point where no foot at all shows. . . . In the poor valleys on the right bank of the Yangtze the women's costumes are the same as in Peking opera, probably the old Ming

style. As to poverty, it is so bad I cannot begin to describe it. . . . These kinds of people and society cannot continue to exist in the modern world. . . . Yet the one essential enterprise [social progress] has not yet been undertaken in the thirty years of the Republic. . . . After another thirty years, will it not still be the same? . . . To speak more clearly, I oppose civil war and all things that hinder national construction and social progress even more than I did before. At the same time, I also oppose unplanned, undirected construction, which would follow in the path of capitalism, whereby all human and economic resources flow into industry and commerce, making the broad mass of the countryside backward. These impressions have strengthened my confidence in my original advocation [for rural reconstruction].[27]

Physically, the expedition was a grueling experience for Liang, who was then almost fifty. More excruciating for him, however, was what he witnessed while in Shantung: the finishing blow to the remnants of his rural reconstruction organization. In early June 1939, he happened to be meeting with various parties in the vicinity of Tung-li-tien, in Meng-yin hsien (near an Eighth Route Army first column headquarters), when the Japanese launched a "mopping up" campaign in the area.[28] During the confusion, Liang and his party were separated from the main body of rural reconstruction cadre and their commander, Ch'in I-wen. By the time they finally reestablished contact at North Tai Mesa, forty miles to the north, another Japanese attack was expected at daybreak. Thus, without rest and in the pouring rain, they prepared to evacuate again. Before setting out, Ch'in assigned Secretary Kung Chu-ch'uan and a sixty-man escort to Liang in case it became necessary for him to split off from the main party.

The further we went, the harder [the rain] fell, and the more slippery the mountain path became. We were traveling a rough, precipitous hill trail in pitch blackness (torches would attract the enemy's attention) . . . holding on to each other's

27. [51], no. 40.
28. Having discovered that seizure of China's cities and railroads did not mean control of China, Tokyo ordered a general offensive against Chinese guerrillas for 1939. During the summer of that year the North China Area Army launched a series of guerrilla-hunting forays into "unpacified" regions throughout Shansi, Hopei, and Shantung. Liang was caught in one of these campaigns.

clothing and not . . . speaking. As said in ancient times, [the troops] "marched swiftly with a gag in their mouths." . . . Twice people slipped and fell into the crevasses, and we had no way of knowing if they survived or not. . . . [Wet, cold], hungry, and tired, we marched on . . . to daybreak. . . .

Everybody was anxious to rest, but the village there [Tui-ching-yü] could not accommodate the whole corps . . . [so] Ch'in and the main body proceeded further to . . . Shih-jen-p'o. [When my escort and I] entered the village, no one was there, yet clothing and food were left in the houses. . . . Obviously the [peasants] had fled in panic . . . so enemy troops were sure to be close by. We should have cleared out immediately . . . but were so hungry and cold. . . . As we were wringing the rain from our clothes, we heard a burst of gunfire. . . . We learned later that an enemy unit had . . . spotted the main body of our troops . . . and set up heavy machine guns at all points around [Shih-jen-p'o]. Some of our men fought their way out, some were killed, some were captured, and some hid in the houses . . . [and] were burnt to death when the enemy set torches to the village. Afterwards, I sent Huang [Ken-yung] and Kung [Chu-ch'uan] there to investigate, bury the dead, care for the wounded, and get details on losses.

While the enemy was attacking . . . [my party and escort] made its escape. I spurred my horse onto a mountaintop completely without trails. . . . But it was still raining hard, and . . . very windy, so I could not stay there long. Slowly I found my way down the mountainside and met up with two or three others. We went in search of a place to dry off and eat. . . . [When] one of the staff reported that the enemy was approaching . . . we ran for cover . . . [and eventually] hid together with [some peasants] in a big cave. . . . Because our traveling clothes could be easily spotted, the peasants gave us other clothing with which to disguise ourselves. The two armies joined in battle. We heard rifle and artillery fire, and toward the end, airplanes joined the fray. . . . At dusk, the firing died down, and by night had stopped altogether. . . .

The next morning the battle resumed as furiously as the day before. [The peasants had left during the night, and only Liang and his party remained.] From the mouth of the cave we could see the enemy lines on the hilltop . . . right down to the flags, officers, binoculars, and swords. In the afternoon, the firing died down. An enemy patrol . . . came down right outside our cave. . . . All of us readied our pistols. If they looked . . . we would fight to the death. . . .

About three in the afternoon . . . both armies withdrew, and we all breathed easier. . . . Half the Third Political Corps was lost in these two engagements. The remnants went to western Shantung and linked up with the Second Political Corps, [which] endured until late 1940. . . . When I left the cave, I could not find the escort. Fortunately Secretary Kung was still with me. He was from Meng-yin hsien, and in that hsien families surnamed Kung are everywhere. . . . So we went with him from one Kung family home to another . . . from the northern to the southern end of Meng-yin hsien. He escorted us to a relatively safe place and then returned. . . . A short time later he was killed by the Eighth Route Army. His body was found decapitated.[29]

Kung's assassination was one miniscule, indirect by-product in the larger drama that was unfolding in the villages and hamlets of North and Central China,[30] but it emotionally heightened Liang's response to the obvious and ubiquitous political rivalry and military conflict between the CCP and the KMT. By mid-1939, it was hardly a secret that the united front was crumbling. Even while the Japanese were chasing Liang through the mountains of central Shantung, Nationalist troops were disbanding the New Fourth Army's office and depot in P'ing-chiang, Hunan, and killing members of the CCP. At the same time, the Nationalist government was establishing its blockade of the CCP's Shen-Kan-Ning Border Re-

---

29. [51], no. 38.

30. In the early years of the war, much of rural Shantung seems to have fragmented into myriad independent or semi-independent local military and political forces. Secret societies—most importantly, the Red Spears—again sprang to life; central government troops of one stripe or another entered; the Eighth Route Army—which eventually controlled most of the area—arrived. They—together with local militia, hsien-level *pao-an tui*, small gentry-organized bands, remnants of Han's troops and his administrative network, traditional bandits, the new KMT-controlled administrative network, puppet forces, and the Japanese themselves—merged in kaleidoscopic patterns of alliance, vendetta, accommodation, and rivalry on the local level. None of the categories, except of course the Japanese, seemed mutually exclusive. The result was all manner of jurisdictional disputes, petty jealousies, and village-level intrigues. Several of Liang's students and colleagues in Shantung seem to have fallen victim to such conflicts. The specific nature of Kung's collision with the Eighth Route Army is not known, but it is clear that in expanding their control throughout wartime China, CCP units often either liquidated or absorbed local autonomous resistance units. [564], pp. 41–42; [621]; [626]; [619].

gion, and seizing five of its hsien. It also was reinforcing an old government organ—the secret police—to root out hidden Communists.

Liang's conclusions, however, were based not on these larger events, but on his personal discovery of a hidden civil war raging throughout the countryside of the war zone. Whatever influences Liang and Mao may have had on each other during Liang's trip to Yenan, this second trip of Liang's through North China probably predisposed him to be more favorable toward the CCP and more adamant in his opposition to the KMT dictatorship. He was still wary of and reproachful toward the CCP, but grudgingly admitted that perhaps only they could eventually work out a solution to China's problem.

> China's immediate problem is completely political, but a political solution for the future is not yet at hand. Because the political problem has a profoundly complex cultural background, it is not your usual kind of struggle between feudalism and democracy. [The reason the Chinese cannot organize themselves well enough to defeat the Japanese] is a political problem that involves the old cultural background. The depth of peasant suffering in the guerrilla areas, too, is due more to what the Chinese themselves create than to what the enemy creates. This is also a political problem and again involves the old cultural background. But the Communist party and many young people do not understand this level of things. . . . The Communist party and those working under its leadership must study and understand China. These words spring from a well intentioned hope, because those who are today doing the most important work on a solution to the political problem are precisely these people.[31]

Mao and his followers could almost have been reading Liang's thoughts; in the days that followed, the Chinese Communists—especially the younger cadre—applied themselves more rigorously to the study of the concrete particulars in China, and somewhat less dogmatically to the study of the formal generalities of Marx's Europe.

The Emergence of the Third Force

As Liang wended his way back westward in the early fall of 1939, one problem dominated his thoughts: how to solve "the problem of

31. [51], no. 40.

parties and groups."[32] Even before his plane from Sian touched down in Chengtu on October 3, he had a specific plan in mind. Upon arriving in the Szechwanese provincial capital and learning that Chiang Kai-shek happened to be in town, Liang decided to report to him immediately on the trip and his newly formulated plan for national unity. The recently designated Chinese Duce (Tsung-ts'ai) received Liang cordially, and then asked in detail about the Eighth Route Army, a group Chiang knew did not completely accept him as the supreme leader of all China. Consequently, Liang had no opportunity to raise what he considered the more burning issues of the trip, but did elicit a promise from Chiang to meet again about the matter in Chungking.

Liang found a more sympathetic audience at his next stop. His old rural-work colleagues Jimmy Yen and Huang Yen-p'ei, as well as the Youth Party leader Li Huang, happened to be in Chengtu. Liang summoned them for a discussion, at which he submitted his conclusions from the trip:

> [The problem of KMT-CCP partisanship] in the immediate future, will hamper the war effort, and in the distant future, will end in renewed civil war. The third parties cannot escape their responsibility. Yet, as long as they are dispersed, no party, however much it tries, can have effect. Therefore, the immediate task before us is to unite the third parties to work in common. Messrs. Yen, Huang, and Li approved of my idea 100 percent; we made plans to seek out other friends and to proceed with further discussions in Chungking.[33]

Thus, in early October 1939, the third force in Chinese politics was born. It was destined for an exciting but foredoomed life of eight years.

Liang arrived in Chungking on October 23. The Generalissimo, away in Kwangsi and Hunan, could not keep his appointment with Liang, but Liang, in any case, had other matters to attend to. The CCP representatives to the PPC—including Tung Pi-wu, Ch'en Shao-yü, Ch'in Pang-hsien, and other party members of some consequence—were still in town. On the evening of October 26, Liang paid a formal call on the entire contingent. Naturally his first order of business was the assassination of his student in Shantung. Ch'in Pang-hsien took notes, but the delegation seemed reluctant to express any opinion on the matter. "Their drift seemed to be, 'Since you have personally observed things that we have no way of

32. [51], nos. 36, 37, 40, 41, 42.   33. [51], no. 41.

knowing about, and since we have no other reports, we cannot judge the right and wrong of the case. We can neither deny it nor accept responsibility.' "

Liang then went on to present his plan for solving the national unity problem via political democracy. The CCP representatives all responded that "your theory and ours have their differences, but our conclusions are rather in accord." This provided the basic foundation for a relationship between the CCP and the liberal party organization, which eventually would result in a KMT ban against the third force.[34]

The Association of Comrades for National Unity and Construction. Encouraged by the reception his plan had met thus far, Liang proceeded to contact other minor political party leaders in Chungking (ironically at the same time refusing to join other "liberal" elements in an emerging movement for constitutional government). He wrote a basic program for the proposed organization, which he called the Association of Comrades for National Unity and Construction (T'ung-i chien-kuo t'ung-chih-hui). He then sent a copy to Chiang, who responded immediately with objections. Liang revised his draft and finally, on the evening of November 29, had a formal audience with Chiang to request official permission to establish such an organization. Although Chiang was less than pleased, he did give the Comrades Association his public blessing. That evening when Wang Shih-chieh, a high-ranking KMT "liberal," escorted Liang back to his lodgings at the Chungking Y, he questioned Liang, in the privacy of the car, about the political aspirations of this new organization. Liang responded that the Comrades Association was not a political party, but an ad hoc organization designed to meet the national emergency brought on by continued CCP-KMT conflict. A genuine political party, Liang hinted, would "take more time" to organize.[35]

The core of Liang's program was the democratization of the government (which implied that the KMT would have to end its period of "tutelage") and the nationalization of all armed forces (which implied that the CCP would have to place its military units under national government control). The Communists had answered Liang's program with approval, if the KMT would first institute a real democratic government. Chiang had responded to

34. Ibid.; also [134], p. 186; [614].
35. [51], nos. 31, 41, 43; [76], 3.5:9; [168a]; [134], p. 186.

Liang's program with suspicion and hostility; he believed Liang was playing into the hands of the Communists. The members of Liang's group saw themselves as patriots devoted to avoiding civil war through their independent promotion of democratic government and considered their organization as the agent of mediation. The crucial issue remained: which would come first, political democratization or military nationalization? The Communists maintained that the former should, while the KMT insisted on the latter. Liang's association (and its two successors) attempted to reconcile the two. These basic positions of the KMT, the CCP, and the minor parties in 1939, however, remained essentially unchanged until 1948, when the issue was settled on the battlefield and the minor party organization was outlawed.

For the first three months of 1940, as reports of KMT-CCP friction in the war zone flowed into the capital, Liang continued to meet with the members of his new organization and draft the results of their discussions into formal proposals for the PPC. When word came in March of a serious, large-scale clash in Hopei, Liang immediately proposed that his Comrades Association mediate the dispute. Both Chiang Kai-shek and the CCP initially responded positively, but in the end, nothing came of the proposition. As incidents of partisan conflict continued unabated throughout 1940, the Comrades Association offered another proposal, which would have given it authority to make binding final decision on disputes between the KMT and CCP. Again, there were no results.[36]

The League of Democratic Political Groups: 1941. By the end of the year, Liang had come to the conclusion that only an independent, democratic political *party* could save the deteriorating situation. In December, he drafted a party program and discussed it with other liberal political leaders. Possibly some were reluctant to go so far in provoking the KMT, for there was no immediate public announcement. Events near the small south Anhwei town of Wu-hu in early January 1941, however, probably impressed upon them the urgency of the situation and confirmed Liang's judgment that China was on its way to full-scale civil war. On January 6—under circumstances that will be forever disputed—the Nationalist Fortieth Division surrounded and attacked the New Fourth Army's headquarters detachment of about ten thousand men. The ten-day battle resulted in thousands of casualties, the obliteration

36. [373c]; [344], p. 140; [229], pp. 101–105; [51], nos. 43–44.

of the detachment, the arrest of Communist commander Yeh
T'ing, and (on January 17) a Nationalist government edict that the
New Fourth Army was thereby disbanded. Yenan flamed forth
with violent denunciations of the action and diatribes against pro-
Japanese capitulationists in the KMT. Chungking responded with
counteraccusations, and the crumbling united front threatened to
collapse altogether. The Comrades Association again offered to
mediate, but this time, it also publicly announced its intention to
reorganize into a political party to "act as a kind of buffer . . . to
constitute a real third force in Chinese politics."[37]

Liang himself hoped that a third political party would signal the
beginning of an entirely new political system. To prepare the way,
he spent much of the month prior to its formal establishment trying to enlist the agreement and cooperation of both the Nationalist
government and the CCP. Almost daily meetings with Chou En-lai
and Chang Ch'ün, Chiang Kai-shek's confidant, however, produced few results. Chiang remained completely hostile to the idea,
while Chou demurred, saying that the CCP's participation would
compromise the independent character of the party. Nevertheless,
the League of Chinese Democratic Political Groups (Chung-kuo
min-chu cheng-t'uan ta-t'ung-meng) finally proclaimed its existence
on March 25, 1941. It brought together into one organization
Liang's Rural Reconstruction Group, the Chinese Youth Party (led
by Li Huang and Tso Shun-sheng), the National Socialist Party (led
by Chang Chün-mai and Chang Tung-sun), the Third Party (led by
Chang Po-chün and P'eng Tse-min), the Vocational Education
Group (led by Huang Yen-p'ei), and the National Salvation Association (led by Chang Sung-nien [Shen-fu] and Shen Chün-ju). Although the members disagreed among themselves over how far to
go in courting KMT reprisals, they did agree that Liang should
decamp to the foreign sanctuary of Hong Kong and create an
official voice for the organization away from the clutches of the
KMT. Four days after the formal announcement, Liang left
Chungking and arrived in Hong Kong in late May.[38] On Sep-

37. [549], pp. 170–171; [51], no. 43; [63]; [76]; [168a].
38. On his way, Liang stopped off for almost two months in Kweilin.
There he talked publicly about his trip to North China. He also delivered a
series of lectures on Chinese culture which he eventually published in his
last book, *The Essence of Chinese Culture*. Probably these lecture engagements provided his official pretext for leaving Chungking. [51], nos. 2–10,
41–46; [64]; [86a]; [76]; [386], Apr. 12, May 12, 1941.

tember 18, 1941, the tenth anniversary of the Mukden Incident, he published the first issue of the league's newspaper, the *Kuang-ming pao*. Three weeks later, on the thirtieth anniversary of the Republican Revolution, he published the league's political program:

1. To resist Japan to the end; to recover all lost territory and sovereignty; to oppose all compromise [with the Japanese].

2. To put the democratic spirit into practice by ending one-party rule; to establish an [interim] organ, representative of all parties and groups, for the discussion of national affairs until a constitution is implemented.

3. To strengthen internal unity by fundamentally settling all current points of disagreement in order to normalize their [the diverse parties and groups] relations.

4. To supervise and help the KMT in thoroughly carrying out the "Outline of National Resistance and Reconstruction."

5. To establish actual national unity, and oppose local separatism, but also to define suitably the jurisdiction of the central and local governments.

6. To oppose all party organizations within the armed forces and the use of armed force in interparty struggles. The army belongs to the nation and military personnel should be loyal to the nation.

7. To enforce rule by law, and to protect the lives, property, and persons of citizens; to oppose all illegal special punishments [or arrests].

8. To respect academic and intellectual freedom, and to protect freedom of lawful speech, publication, assembly, and association.

9. [To] pay attention to the following points after the abolition of one-party rule: (a) that no party or group use the power of the government to promote its interests in schools or other cultural organizations; (b) that all government agencies carry out the principle of selecting the best and most able, and strictly avoid [a situation in which] one party [can] monopolize and utilize government power to recruit members; (c) that no national or local government funds be used to meet party expenses; and (d) that the regulations for election of local government representatives be abolished.

10. To emphasize the following points in the present political situation: (a) carry out strictly the frugality movement in the rear areas, and genuinely reform the treatment of the soldiers at the front; (b) correct the various kinds of administrative measures that hinder production in order to relieve the people's poverty, and also vigorously seek to improve the

economic circumstances of the people; and (c) strengthen
supervisory agencies in order to clean up the various kinds of
corruption present in government administration.[39]

This document, as one scholar has put it, was "as much a condemnation as a program."[40] It called upon the KMT to both reform itself and relinquish its monopoly on political power. In political design, it was basically the same as Liang had outlined in 1938
and 1939; points 5, 6, 8, 9d, and 10a specifically reflected his previous causes and concerns.

KMT reaction was quick and hostile: just two days later, Sun
Fo—son of Sun Yat-sen and president of the legislative yuan—was
in Hong Kong making speeches against the league program; the
pro-KMT Hong Kong newspaper, *Liang-hsin-hua*, opened a bar-
rage of vitriolic attacks on Liang and the league; at the request of
the KMT, the British searched Liang's house; and some league
members were dismissed from the PPC. The debate over one-party
rule versus democracy was once more out in the open—at least in
Hong Kong. Liang carried on the debate there, still maintaining his
curious stance of demanding democratic representation without
constitutionalization.[41]

Kweilin, 1942–1944

The dictatorship-democracy debate, the *Kuang-ming pao*, and the
league's momentum all quickly collapsed when the Japanese, on
their way to overrunning Southeast Asia, stormed into Hong Kong
on Christmas Day, 1941. After a narrow escape from the invaders,
Liang made his way by boat up the West River into Kwangsi.[42]
Upon safely reaching Chinese-held territory, he wrote his famous
letter to his sons, which was later published in Kweilin. It was a
strange document indeed, for in it Liang allowed his usually covert
pretensions to being a man of destiny to burst forth publicly with
echoes from the Confucian *Analects* in his declaration that the fate

---

39. [360], Oct. 10, 1941.   40. [549], p. 176.
41. [408], Oct. 30, Nov. 11, 20, 30, Dec. 10, 20, 1941; [292], Nov. 4,
1941. [549], p. 176; [52]; [54]; [56]; [58]; [60]; [61]; [62]; [63]; [64]; [68]; [86];
[373a].
42. [463]; pp. 4, 25–30, 35, 54, 60, 98; [220], Jan. 27, 1942; [386], Jan.
28, Feb. 1, 6, May 5, 24, 1942.

of China and the world was tied to his personal fate.[43] It would seem that he had in mind his role as sage-transmitter of the "true" culture of China—the eternal *tao*—rather than his political role. Immediately after this outburst, he moved to Ching-shan ts'un outside of Kweilin, and settled down to write his last and longest book, *The Essence of Chinese Culture* (Chung-kuo wen-hua yao-i).[44]

During his sojourn in his ancestral home, Liang had a most uncharacteristic *affaire de coeur*, which resulted in a second marriage and a great change in his personality. Liang's first wife had died in 1934 at Tsou-p'ing. At the time, he had publicly vowed never to marry again. He had written a poem, which, although strangely haunting and sad, recognized that their relationship had always been devoid of warmth and intimacy; indeed, he seems to have felt that this had been a great boon to a dedicated sage such as himself:

> I was married to her for more than a decade.
> [Yet] I did not know her; she did not know me.
> I had more time to ponder problems and more time to work.
> Now she has died; that she has died is all right too.
> [As I] am in this kind of country and this kind of society
>   [which needs me],
> Her dying gives me more time to ponder problems, more
>   time to work.[45]

In the late summer of 1943, however, Liang chanced to meet Ch'en Shu-fen, a Kweilin school teacher six years his junior, and fell genuinely and deeply in love. Their romance became a cause célèbre for the whole of Kwangsi province. It also provided the Kweilin newspapers with a source for numerous waggish causeries and their readers with material for months of jocular tea-table talk. The journalists had a great time joshing the notoriously unromantic fifty-year-old; stories appeared entitled "A Widower's Life Is Just Too Dreary" and "Never Having Heard Sweet Talk, She Suc-

43. [311]; [220], Jan. 27, 1942; [386], Jan. 28, Feb. 1, 6, May 5, 1942; [330], p. 24.
44. Liang worked on his ideas and on sections of the book off and on throughout the war and after; as he completed each segment of it, he published them in various periodicals. See [45]; [48]; [55]. The bulk of the book was worked out during his two-year stay in Kweilin, 1942–1944. [86a].
45. [564], pp. 43–44.

cumbed within Six Months." Astoundingly, Liang went along with the fun.[46]

Just who had pursued whom was a major topic of public discussion. Reporters scurried back and forth between Ms. Ch'en and Liang. Upon being congratulated on her conquest, Ms. Ch'en replied that it was (he who swept me off my feet) and "captured the open city of my heart." (This exchange inspired the headline "A New Tale of Two Cities?") A rumor floated around town that Liang was growing a beard in order to present a more virile appearance to his beloved. Liang denied this and added that "An elderly bridegroom always shaves before his nuptials." Friends joined in the general jollity. Liang, quipped one, "has won much glory for us middle-aged fellows."

These goings on reached a climax on January 23, 1944. In the morning, the couple performed a traditional marriage ceremony at the home of a friend. That afternoon, all of Kweilin's literary and scholarly lights gathered in a chrysanthemum-bedecked reception hall of a downtown hotel. By two o'clock the room was so crammed that latecomers had to stand in the doorway. Heralded by the crackling accents of exploding fireworks, the groom arrived, an unfamiliarly broad grin dominating his freshly shaved face and pate. The new Madame Liang, smiling just enough for her dimples to show and "looking at least ten years younger than she was," followed; she wore a brocade ch'i-p'ao, no make-up, and her hair swept severely on the back of her head. ("Simple, plain, and natural," a reporter commented.)

There was still enough of the old Liang left to start off the festivities by solemnly intoning: "Marriage is an important affair in life. We first request one who has had abundant life experience, the venerable Mr. Lung Chi-chih, to instruct us." The venerable Mr. Lung then proceeded (while stroking his long gray beard) with a long and lofty discourse on the significance of marriage, interlarded with hefty excerpts from the Spring and Autumn Annals and the Book of Changes. Mr. Lung's instructions completed, General Li Chi-shen, his voice trembling with sincerity, wished the couple a happy union. Then, in his capacity as chairman of the reception, he turned over the program to the guests. First to gain the rostrum

46. The following description of Liang's courtship and marriage is drawn from [486a—b]; [169], Jan. 16, Feb. 9, 1944; [309].

was the famous writer Pai P'eng-fei, who immediately set a lighter tone for the rest of the proceedings:

> Mr. Liang is a Kweilin man, but . . . only after the war started did he return, that is, return home. But he had no household in Kweilin. Now it just does not make sense to come home when you do not have a household, so the only proper thing to do really was to create a household. Because of this, the open city of his heart was easily occupied. Now Ms. Ch'en has been so late in marrying because she had her heart set on wedding a . . . great philosopher. So when this position became available, she naturally got selected.

High wit this was not, but Pai had the whole room howling in minutes.

Liu Ya-tzu, the poet and friend to whom Mao would dedicate his most famous poem a year and a half later, presented some verse:

> Oh felicitous nuptials and fortunate pair
> How like the renowned Meng Kuang and Ch'ing Te they are.[47]
> He marshals the country's forces of the New Democracy.[48]
> Oh, that they would struggle for it hand in hand!

The next poetaster at bat was cute:

> I have heard that he has studied the *Book of Changes*
> Then he must have known that Heaven had fated him for the Ch'en of the South.

China's foremost playwright, T'ien Han, wrote the longest poem, and the most humorous.

> A determined widower for ten years, he returned from afar to his home.
> In the midst of danger he was calm and resolute.
> Although he is old and has seen through this illusionary existence

---

47. The Chinese exemplar of a happily married couple. They appear in the *History of the Later Han Dynasty*.

48. As with other poems presented, Liu's piece is loaded with allusions, puns, and double entendres that defy English translation. Most intriguing is his use of the term *new* democracy. (Surely he knew of Mao's *On the New Democracy* published four years earlier.) Was Liu identifying Liang's own third force political ideals with Mao's newly invented political category?

His faith in democracy is unwavering . . .
Anxious that the thread of Eastern Learning would snap
[He thinks] if it were not for me, who would there be?
To wed is quite fitting for an old warrior of youthful élan.
How handsome a bridegroom, fully as well favored as P'an.[49]
If life starts at seventy, then fifty is still spry.
[You, Liang,] do not have to do as Liu [Pei] who, when he
Crossed the Yangtze to be a bridegroom, spent a fortune on
    hair dye.[50]

And so on it went for hours, the guests vying with one another to
make the wittiest speech or to present the cleverest poem. The
crowning moment—and the first public appearance of the new
Liang—came at the end of the affair. The guests were gleefully
clamoring for Liang to "report" on his courtship. He finally ac-
ceded to popular demand, even coloring his narration with
whimsical—and totally uncharacteristic—humor.

Now I heard that romance costs a lot of money—for things
like going out to restaurants, the movies, the opera, and so
forth. Well, I did not spend a penny. I am ashamed to admit
it, but I did not even take her for a walk and that is a fact.
Once I did write her a letter inviting her to come out to
Ching-shan ts'un for a walk along the river, if the weather was
nice. The day turned out to be cloudy and at the appointed
time, it suddenly started to drizzle. Would she come or not? I
dithered around for a while, uncertain what to do, and then
on a hunch, I went out with an umbrella. As I suspected, I
met up with her halfway down the road [to Kweilin]. As it was
raining, we still could not go for our walk. So all we ended up
doing was sitting together for a while in a small roadside
pavilion!

Then, to prove that he was full of "the spirit of robust youth,"
Liang burst forth with an aria of Huang T'ien-pa (the fire-eating
condottiere in the Peking opera *Lien-huan-t'ao*). This must certainly

    49. P'an An—the Chinese Adonis. A man of the Western Chin Dynasty
(A.D. 265–317), he is said to have been so handsome that when he walked
down a street, women would throw him fruit from their houses.
    50. The emperor of the Shu Han, one of the states of the Epoch of the
Three Kingdoms (A.D. 220–263). Taking a wife of the state of Wu (across
the Yangtze) in his old age, he is said to have spent large sums to dye his
white hair black in order to look more youthful to his bride. Liang, of
course, was bald.

have had the same effect on the public as the Pope treating the crowds at St. Peter's Square to a pontifical rendition of "La Donna è Mobile." Still imitating the devil-may-care *beau sabreur*, Liang finished off his improbable performance by booming out, "We now take our leave," and then darted out the door with bride in hand. He had become the schoolboy he never was.

Affectionate, attentive, and tender, the new Madame Liang was quite unlike her predecessor. A highly cultured intellectual, she added a new dimension to the marital relationship that Liang had sorely missed before. This truly happy marriage seems to have metamorphosed the stern, forbiddingly serious Liang into a mellower, more light-hearted man. He actually smiled and laughed in public on occasion.[51] Mao, who had also just taken a new wife (without, however, the convenience of his former one's demise), seems to have undergone no parallel transformation.

Return to Politics: Peace Negotiations, and Civil War

Neither the Japanese nor his third-force comrades allowed Liang to remain in wedded and scholarly bliss in the city of his forebears for long. Liang had maintained his odd relationship with the constitutionalist movement; he simultaneously worked for it politically while disapproving of it philosophically.[52] In September 1944, the leading members of the old League of Democratic Groups met in Chungking to form a new organization—the Chinese Democratic League (Chung-kuo min-chu t'ung-meng). Quite naturally, they elected Liang to the standing committee of the executive council, and he grudgingly resumed his role in active politics.[53]

That same month, the massive Japanese sweep south—Operation Ichi-Go—came pouring through the mountain pass at Ch'üan-chou, the strategic bottleneck between Kwangsi and Hunan. The invaders were afforded this convenience by the Nationalist Ninety-third Army, which, after having positioned themselves for a fight to the last man, took flight to the last man without firing a shot. In the next few weeks, the Japanese rolled

51. Acquaintances of Liang's did allow that Liang laughed and joked before this—but only with his children. [619]; [623]; [628]; [634].
52. [76]; [386], Oct. 20, Dec. 11, 1943; [207], Jan. 14, 1944; [67]; [418].
53. [279], p. 62; [420]; [215], pp. 1–2, 99–100; [219], pp. 160–161.

down the railroad to take Kweilin and Liuchow, end the threat of the American airfields, and open the land corridor to their empire in Southeast Asia. The Liangs repaired to the Kwangsi countryside, first to Chao-p'ing and later to Pa-pu, still in the enemy's rear.

Operation Ichi-Go proved to be the end of the Nipponese rope in China. But when Emperor Hirohito bowed to the threat of nuclear holocaust and commanded his legions to lay down their arms in August 1945, China's real peril—at least the one Liang had been apprehensive of throughout the war—had just arrived. The CCP-KMT race for occupied China began immediately. Yet that same month, Mao, wearing a pith-helmet and the look of a man who had just taken his first airplane ride, arrived in Chungking for negotiations with Chiang on a postwar political *modus vivendi*. For a month or so, despite the open warfare flaring on the Hopei railroads, it appeared that the long-dreaded civil conflict might be avoided after all. Liang at least chose to think so and took the opportunity presented by the seemingly successful negotiations to resign once more from politics and go back to his book and his wife. They had moved to the pleasant borough of Pei-p'ei, near Chungking, a very early rural reconstruction site where Liang had friends.[54] He had established a small school there and looked forward to devoting himself once more to the tranquil pursuits of sagely scholarship.

Two months later, the Democratic League held its second general congress and once again persuaded Liang to take a place on the standing committee. In November, as civil war again loomed large on the horizon, Liang rushed to Chungking to devote himself to full-time mediation work.[55]

On Christmas Day, 1945, the Marshall Mission arrived in the midst of increasingly severe conflict between KMT and CCP troops in North China. To work out a permanent political solution, a Political Consultative Conference (Cheng-chih hsieh-shang hui-i; the PCC) was convened in January 1946. For three weeks the representatives of the KMT, CCP, Democratic League, and other independents hammered away at an agreement to serve as the basis for a democratic postwar China. During the conference, the polarization of the league into KMT and CCP factions began to emerge, a development that greatly distressed Liang. He himself remained resolutely nonpartisan in his own actions at the conference.[56]

54. [76]; [83]; [418].   55. [306]; [501], Nov. 3, 1945.
56. Liang also spoke more than any other delegate at the conference. A

Once again it appeared that lasting peace was at hand. It seemed that the Marshall Mission had succeeded. The day the conference ended, Liang publicly proclaimed his duty done and his intention to withdraw *once more* from politics. By February 1946, however, it was already clear that Chiang Kai-shek's policy toward Manchuria had cracked the seemingly solid cornerstone laid by the conference. Thereafter, the entire structure of Marshall's peace arrangement collapsed rapidly. At first, Liang balked at returning to the politics of mediation. As the KMT was the party that had violated the January agreement, Liang wrote a personal letter to Mao explaining his reasons for retiring from politics.[57]

Events, and Liang's own sense of duty, would not allow him to remain at peace in Pei-p'ei. By March, both the KMT and the CCP had de facto abandoned the PCC truce agreement. Once more Liang rushed into the breach. He flew to Peking in early March to determine the Manchurian situation, and then went to Yenan to talk with Mao. For the rest of the year he frantically rushed around China from meeting to meeting in what proved to be a vain attempt to avert full-scale war between Yenan and Nanking.[58] In April 1946, he reluctantly accepted the post of secretary-general of the league. Ironically, some pro-KMT rural reconstructionists now condemned him for abandoning his rural work in favor of politics and for "creating factions," criticism Liang had meted out to others in the 1930s.[59]

In the summer of 1946, while Liang was involved in a heavy schedule of KMT, CCP, and Marshall Mission meetings, two Democratic League members—the famous poet, Wen I-to, and Li Kung-p'u—were assassinated on the streets of Kunming. In his capacity as league secretary-general, Liang flew to Kunming and conducted an on-the-spot investigation, which the KMT hampered

---

detailed account of the conference and the activities of the delegates is found in [156], p. 101. See also the January issues of [221]; [501]; [168].

57. [68]; [215], pp. 99–100; [219], p. 161.

58. [168], Mar. 14, 16, 22, 1946; [83], p. 4; [501], Nov. 11, 1945. According to the newspaper reports, Liang spent the eight months between March and October, 1946, on the move continuously throughout China's major cities meeting with representatives of the CCP, the KMT, the Democratic League, and the Marshall Mission. Sometimes he attended two and three meetings in a single day. He was also active as a member of the PPC during the same period.

59. See [134], p. 187; [528], pp. 100, 102; [215]; [219], p. 6; [372].

at every turn. His public report clearly implied that the KMT—at least its Kunming branch—was responsible for the murders.[60] Feeling that he had fulfilled his duty with this report, Liang announced his resignation as secretary-general in October and *again* proclaimed his intention to retire from politics. Both the Communists and the American amabassador, Leighton Stuart, pressured him to continue in his role as a go-between for the fast-fading negotiations for a truce.[61]

Liang played his final act in this drama in October and November of 1946. Taking another fateful step toward his own demise, Chiang Kai-shek launched an offensive on the CCP stronghold of Kalgan, the capital of Suiyuan some 180 miles northeast of Peking. The Nationalist general Fu Tso-i took the city on October 11. Encouraged by the successes in the field, Chiang abruptly announced that same day the long-awaited convention of the National Assembly for November 12. Without prior reorganization of the government—which had been the CCP's primary demand all along—convention of the Assembly would have permanently slammed shut the door to negotiations. Chou En-lai, the CCP representative in Nanking, was on the verge of returning to Yenan. In a last ditch attempt to avert outright civil war to the finish, Liang wrote a proposal that would have allowed for a truce, government reorganization *and* the National Assembly. League leaders were enthusiastic about the proposal and confident of its acceptance by both sides. On October 28, Liang presented his proposal to Chou, Chiang, and Marshall. Fully expecting success at last ("I can guarantee that Chou En-lai will gladly accept it," he had told league leaders), Liang went personally to Chou's house with the proposal. Chou, however, claimed that Liang had assured him just a few days before that he would "talk things over [with Chou] before presenting our views." When Chou ascertained that the proposal was being presented to Chiang and Marshall without prior discussion with him, he flew into a rage; stamping his feet and crying, he shouted that "You [Liang], are a hypocrite. You have deceived us." Liang was dumbfounded. "Though our friendship

60. [97]; [501], Aug. 3, 4, 6, 9, 10, 16, 24, 26, and Sept. 2, 1946; [221], Aug. 16 and 26, 1946; [168b], July 20, 1946; see also [168], Aug. 23, 25, 1946.
61. [501], Sept. 19, 1946; [221], Sept. 19, 20, Oct. 6, 7, 8, 10, 11, 1946.

has lasted twenty years [?], it is broken today," Chou stormed. Utterly befuddled, Liang left.[62]

The National Assembly did meet on November 15, after three days of last minute efforts at negotiation and arbitration. Liang struggled frantically to the last hour, but once the Assembly actually convened, Liang knew that it destroyed whatever value he and the league had as impartial negotiators. Most of the league members considered Chiang's action a direct violation of the PCC agreements. If, however, they boycotted the assembly like the Communists, their action would place them squarely on the side of the CCP, and destroy any possibility for the league to act as a third-party mediator. As it turned out, the league split up over the question of participation in the assembly. Some of the more conservative (or more opportunistic) National Socialists, led by Chang Chün-mai, bolted the league to participate in the assembly, but the majority of league members boycotted it. Convinced that even what was left of the league had been forced to compromise itself irrevocably by siding with the CCP on the issue, Liang withdrew from the league altogether, and in November 1946—for the last time—he announced his retirement. He returned to his school in Pei-p'ei, where he intended to devote the next years to studying the problem of "understanding the old China in order to build the new China."[63]

62. [333], May 19, 1977 and [114], p. 182; See also [134], pp. 206–207; [528], p. 106; [501], Oct. 23, 1946; [306].
63. [501], Nov. 6, 7, 8, 11, 24, 1946; [79]; [418].

CHAPTER XIII

Return to Peking

From his haven in Szechwan, Liang applauded Chang Tung-sun's assumption of Democratic League leadership, but he was also convinced that any further attempts at mediation were doomed to failure. Perhaps only to clear his conscience, Liang called a press conference, in mid-November 1946, to publicly suggest one last possibility for peace. The only course left at this point, he declared, was to convene an eight-man conference, the agreement of which both the KMT and CCP must accept as binding. He proposed a list of participants whom he considered as comparatively fair-minded men: Chou En-lai and Tung Pi-wu for the CCP; Chang Ch'ün and Shao Li-tzu for the KMT; Chang Tung-sun, Chang Po-chun, Li Huang, and Mo Te-hui for the third parties.[1]

His duty done, Liang remained in Pei-p'ei, where he continued teaching and working on his last major work, *The Essence of Chinese Culture*. Liang occasionally published articles on public affairs; he became a major figure in the 1947 debate over the constitution, for example. When the Communist armies were approaching the Yangtze in early 1949, however, he steadfastly refused eleventh-hour requests from Li Tsung-jen, who had become provisional president of the rapidly collapsing Nanking regime, to engage once more in peace-negotiation efforts.[2] When he did speak out on the raging civil war, it was always as a Confucian moralist, who, aloof from the actual battle, impartially meted out praise, blame, and admonition to the combatants. He blamed the KMT hard-liners for the civil war, but at the same time, sternly warned the increasingly victorious Communists to avoid that "reliance on military force,"

1. Interview with Liang in [501], Jan. 17, 1947; [221], Jan. 20, 1947. General Marshall had privately suggested a plan similar to Liang's just two weeks earlier. [189], I, 688.
2. [72]; [73]; [74]; [75]; [76]; [77]; [81]; [501], Nov. 12, 1947; [468]; [445]; [237]; [238]; [146]; [126]; [311]; [410]; [522], p. 55; [359], May 19, 1977.

which had been responsible for their failure in the early 1930s, and which was now leading to the KMT's demise.[3]

In 1949, with the Communist victory imminent, young leftists commenced prophetically ominous attacks on Liang in the public press. (Rightists had been excoriating him all along.) The leftists now criticized and parodied his role in the peace negotiations, his withdrawal from politics, his nonpartisan independence, his praise of Marshall, his "Confucian spirit," his writings on public issues since retirement, and even his marriage. What really exasperated them, though, was Liang's damnably unshakable confidence that he alone knew the truth. In a piece of satiric doggerel entitled "An Ode to Mr. Liang Shu-ming, The Great Enemy," one wag twitted, "Oh, my, Mr. Liang Shu-ming! Do you think yourself to be modern China's sage?" How could the witcracker have known that that was precisely what Liang thought in his heart of hearts? Liang probably chuckled to himself and did not even notice the demand from another assailant that "Confucianized old-style intellectuals such as Mr. Liang Shu-ming . . . must undergo a bout of 'self-reform.' "[4] He should have marked it well.

Most of Liang's time, however, was taken up with his school in Pei-p'ei, the Mien-jen Academy, where he instituted the same reforms he had first tried out in the Sixth Shantung Provincial Middle School twenty-five years earlier. Just as before, he again hopefully suggested that his school might serve as a model for Chinese higher education in the future.[5]

Return to Public Life, 1950–1955

Liang had planned to spend the rest of his days pondering Chinese culture in his small town. The new regime, however, was not willing to allow him to cultivate his Szechwan garden. He was named as a delegate to the first People's Political Consultative Conference (PPCC), the representative body in Mao's new democracy. Liang wrote to Mao trying to beg off, but in December 1949, he acquiesced and arrived in Peking on New Year's Day, 1950.[6] Over the next several years, Mao often called Liang in for private discus-

3. [80]; [81].   4. [306]; [418]; see also [522]; [523].   5. [85].
6. [87]; [359], Feb. 7, 1956; [95]; [333], Feb. 3, 1956; [415]; [501], Jan. 20, 1947; [634]; [635].

sions, which were apparently a sort of sequel to their 1938 Yenan exchanges.[7] That Mao, who after all had become the autarch of Chinese thought as well as politics, would continue to argue with Liang about his theories, strongly suggests that Mao could not easily dismiss either the man or his ideas.

Liang's return to the city of his youth, which he had left a quarter century before, was not, in any case, the triumphal return of a man of destiny. He had left it for the villages to "create a new world civilization" and had come back to it as window-dressing for Mao's new regime. For the next quarter-century Liang would watch from the sidelines as the CCP set about implementing its own design for a new culture; contrary to his original hopes, he would have no effect on the shape of that design, at least not in ways he considered correct and meaningful. The only roles left for him to play were those of approving witness and of negative example.

Almost as soon as Liang arrived in Peking, he was cast in the first role. Because of his fame as a rural reconstruction worker, Mao personally asked him to inspect the land-reform programs in various parts of the North and Northeast. The positive enthusiasm Liang found among the peasants contrasted sharply with the apathetic indifference he had met with in his own rural-reform programs. By October 1950, he was satisfied enough with the Communists and their programs to issue a public statement of approval.

Liang's report was cast in images that suggest he saw his own goals being realized by the new regime. In *Eastern and Western Cultures*, he had looked for a mass spiritual revival to "resurrect" the dead Chinese people. In 1950, he proclaimed: "I saw that many people had been revived from the dead. In the past I had seen only corpses, so-called soulless, walking corpses." The zombies of the past had now been resurrected by the Communists, whose sincerity, Liang felt, was "a source of new life opening the road to a bright future."[8] Privately, too, he expressed approval with similar images.

---

7. [501], June 21, 1977; [424f], p. 109. In 1977, Liang explained publicly (perhaps not totally without irony) that the "major" reason for the meetings was "the chairman's generous intention of wanting to reform my thought" and that he and Mao talked privately many times "from 1950 to September 1953." Whether or not they met regularly after that is not clear.

8. [87]. Liang was not, of course, the only non-Communist scholar to be sent to the countryside to observe land reform in 1950 and 1951. It was a usual thought-reform exercise for bourgeois intellectuals during those

In a letter to the Confucian philosopher, T'ang Chun-i, a friend who had fled to Hong Kong, Liang urged T'ang to return to China: "The domestic situation can be described in one sentence: 'the beginning of a new life for the Chinese people.' "[9]

The years 1950 and 1951 were the season for "bourgeois intellectuals" to make their self-criticism and confession. Pressure was probably brought to bear on Liang to follow the example set by his fellow philosophers, Fung Yu-lan and Ho Lin. In October 1951, he published a long account of his change in thought and in his attitude toward the Communists: "Only recently, when I personally observed the various achievements of the Communist party in the work of national reconstruction, did I realize that many of my former views had been mistaken. A great feeling of shame came over me and I started reviewing my mistakes and awakened to the reasons why the Chinese Communist Party is correct." Despite its hackneyed prologue, Liang's was no standard recanting of the kind other non-Communist intellectuals were raising to the level of a minor art form. Liang openly acknowledged the obvious: the CCP's methods—specifically their mass movements—worked. Yet when he discussed the Marxist interpretation of Chinese society and history, it became clear that he remained stubbornly convinced of the ultimate truth in his own vision. "Today the [ideological] distance between me and the Communist party has been greatly reduced. . . . Although I have indeed nodded my head in agreement [with their theories], there are still things that I cannot agree with. That is to say, I cannot abandon the views I have always held."[10]

Liang's refusal to disavow his implicitly anti-Marxist views set off a wave of criticism against him in the press.[11] Unintimidated, Liang issued a sharp and sarcastic reply.

---

years. They would then be expected to articulate publicly their "changes in thought" brought about by their participation in revolutionary practice. See, for example, [382]. Liang, however, reported directly to Mao on his experiences.

9. [90].

10. [88]. Liang also made it clear that he would continue to strive for understanding of his past mistakes. A few days after his article was published, he made a statement in the PPCC which proclaimed that he would continue to work on self-reform while "trusting and following the leadership of the CCP." See [89].

11. See, for example, the article by Shen Ming in [359], Nov. 10, 1951; [266].

The gentlemen, no doubt, were motivated by the best of intentions in seeking to cure an [ideologically] sick man, but I have not really benefited. Moreover, [we] have wasted both valuable newspaper space and the valuable time of the readers. This is not good. Face-to-face discussion would be better . . . [and would also] prevent [me] from further publicizing my old ideological views.[12]

Just as thirty years earlier he had scolded Hu Shih for not reading his first book, Liang now referred his critics to his last book: "My critics have not solved the problems before us because in order to correct my mistakes it is absolutely necessary to read my *The Essence of Chinese Culture*." In effect, Liang was still defending his theories on Chinese culture and society. He openly admitted that his self-criticism was merely "reconciling the newly developed realities with my old theories."[13]

This fearless display of self-confidence and independence attracted widespread praise in Taiwan and Hong Kong. "We should all voice support for Liang Shu-ming, the one who will not yield to force," read one article.[14] Astonishingly, the criticism of him also disappeared from the pages of the mainland press. He continued to hold his position on the standing committee of the PPCC and to appear at public functions.[15] Either public sympathy with Liang's ideas and respect for his person were too entrenched and widespread, or his relationship with Mao afforded him protection, for he seems to have suffered no ill effects for his open attack on the new orthodoxy.

Collision with Mao and Criticism Campaign of 1955–1956

Liang's happy state of immunity probably ended because of his public run-in with Mao in September 1953, the episode with which this story began. What, after all, had Liang said to enrage Mao so? Liang was obstinately consistent: he seems to have presented the same blueprint for China's future which he had drawn up in the early 1930s.[16] Moreover, with that unfortunate air of moral

12. [91]; [92].   13. [91].   14. [303]; see also [190]; [542]; [311].
15. [333], Feb. 5, 1952, Aug. 12, 1953.
16. This was, admittedly, *not* so consistent with the ideological "changes" he had publicly proclaimed just a short time before, but once the sage's

superiority that often characterized his pronouncements, Liang seemed to expect the government to adopt his program. Ever the self-styled champion of the Chinese peasantry, he criticized the government plans for economic development based on the Soviet model. Mao, Liang implied, was betraying those who had put him on the throne. Like so many power-seekers in the past, once the party had "entered the cities," it had "forgotten the villages," which had become a "void." Now the urban workers were "in the ninth level of heaven," while the peasants were "in the ninth level of hell." The Communist party no longer represented them; indeed, they had no reliable agency at all to look out for their interests. Even the urban capitalists had a more dependable organization in the Federation of Industry and Commerce than the peasant had in the Party. After land reform, the peasants had gotten theirs; now the Party looked to their sweat and sacrifices to build the great industrial cities, the natural enemies of the peasants and rural villages.[17] Why import such a destructive model when, as Liang proclaimed, his own plan was "quite close to" Mao's New Democracy.

Superficially, this suggestion, even the whole situation, seems absurd, positively amusing. Why should the nation's most powerful revolutionary leader concern himself with this seemingly harmless, even deluded, old Confucian reactionary? But Mao was decidedly unamused. Could an unconscious defensiveness in part explain his curiously inappropriate vehemence and exaggerated denigration of Liang's rural reconstruction: "It was landlord construction, rural destruction, and national perdition!" Or could Liang's criticisms have touched the raw nerve of Mao's own secret misgivings about

---

heart had known ultimate truth, it was not apt to alter appreciably. The following description of Mao's and Liang's statements at the meeting is drawn from [424f].

17. It would appear that this was not the first time Liang had pleaded for the peasants. Just four days prior to his attack on Liang, in a speech which again touched upon the dilemma of building heavy industry and providing for peasant welfare, Mao noted that during the Korean war, "there had to be sacrifices, expenditures of money, and more agricultural tax collected. Because we collected more in agricultural tax, some people started caterwauling, and even claimed that they represented the peasantry's interests. I simply do not approve of this sort of thing." (Mao's tirade against Liang included a specific denunciation of Liang's lukewarm attitude toward the Korean war.) Whether Liang had done his caterwauling in private discussions with Mao or in public is not clear. [424], V, 104–105; [424f], p. 112.

the Soviet model?[18] Liang was, after all, correct to an extent. The gap between city and village would increase rather than decrease over the next few years. In just three years, the dependent population in the cities would grow by 70 percent as migrants poured in to enjoy urban amenities and privileges. The "consumption center" nature of the city, which Mao himself had feared and Liang had always cursed, would intensify.

Still it seems odd that Mao felt compelled to insist openly: "I repeat yet another time, we will definitely not adopt your line." Was he actually worried that there were people somewhere who expected the Communist party to follow the lead of China's chief traditionalist thinker? Who was he reassuring when he proclaimed that no matter how often Liang had come forth with his "original theories," he (Mao) had not been affected: "Can all this make me believe? It cannot!" What was the point in bringing up that once during their private discussions he had told Liang to his face: "I have never believed that line of yours"? Did anyone sense that he was protesting a bit too much? Mao showed himself surprisingly well informed on the specifics of Liang's obscurantist theories of Chinese society and history, yet he proceeded to taunt Liang that "no one except some reactionaries and fuzzy-minded types" still read his books or listened to him. "He says he is better able to represent the peasants than the Communist party. Is it possible this is not ridiculous?" Then why was it necessary to inform Liang and the audience that "nobody believes that twaddle of yours; the people all believe the Communist party"?[19]

18. My discussion is not meant to suggest "the cause" of Mao's curious outburst, either in the historical or psychological sense. As all psychological events are "overdetermined," and historical events are due to "multiple causation," I do not mean to rule out other (presently unknown) "causes," be they hidden political-ideological factors, or a spat with Chiang Ch'ing that morning.

19. During his tirade Mao inexplicably compared Liang's case twice to that of Po I-po (the first Minister of Finance of the PRC and a top finance and economic specialist throughout the 1950s and early 1960s). On August 12, 1953, Mao had criticized Po for his rightist mistakes, and in September, Po was replaced as Minister of Finance. There seems no connection at all, however, between Po's mistake of advocating the "equality of public and private enterprises" tax system and Liang's errors. Possibly the reason is simply that since Po was the only major figure Mao had attacked recently, his name just came to mind while he was hacking away at Liang. [424], V, 90–97, 113, 115.

Mao proceeded on with his *argumentum ad hominem* to a predictable finale:

You say that the workers are "in the ninth level of heaven." Well, on what level are you, Liang Shu-ming? You are on the tenth, eleventh, twelfth, or even thirteenth level, because your salary is far more than a worker's pay! Instead of first proposing that your salary be lowered, you first propose lowering the workers' pay. I think that is unfair. If you are concerned about fairness, then first of all lower your own salary because you are far higher than "the ninth level of heaven."[20]

Well, given that Liang was not exactly noted for his riotously sybaritic life-style or his rapacious greed, and that it was Mao who had induced him to accept his government position and salary in the first place, the cut seems the unkindest of them all.[21]

What of Liang's own motives? By this point in the story, his character, his past and, above all, his unshakable identity as the last Confucian sage are clear. Perhaps they are the only explanations necessary. Still, one wonders, why did he determine to play the martyr in mid-September of 1953 and not before? Was it just coincidence that he made his suicidal gesture just before his sixtieth birthday?[22]

In the end, Mao did not dismiss him from his post. Indeed, he made a point of saying that Liang could continue to serve and even that "I hope still that he will be elected to the National Committee of the PPCC at its Second Plenary Session." At the same time, however, he pointedly invited Liang to reflect upon his mistakes and make a confession of past sins. Although the meeting was Liang's last public criticism of the government, he apparently felt that he had done all the confessing he could, and so for two years

20. [424f], p. 113.
21. In an apparent dig at Liang's sage complex, Mao quipped that Confucius "was quite like Mr. Liang" in that he was "undemocratic" and "lacking the spirit of self-criticism." He then quoted from memory (with some inaccuracies) three passages from classical texts which showed Confucius to have "the style of a despot" and "a fascist stink." Two of the passages are in [500], pp. 1917, 2194. Most scholars, incidentally, believe that neither passage has much to do with the historical Confucius.
22. Liang's sixtieth birthday, in modern reckoning, was October 10, 1953, just about three weeks after the fateful meeting. Liang Chi committed suicide just prior to his traditional-style sixtieth birthday—before he reached sixty *sui*.

nothing was heard from (or against) him. In mid-1955, however, the inevitable happened: a mammoth criticism campaign against him in both the national and local presses.[23]

There were, of course, other timely factors involved in the party's decision to launch the anti-Liang Shu-ming thought-reform campaign at this juncture. There was already a campaign in progress against Hu Shih, the archetypical Western-oriented liberal. Critics had referred to Liang as the "feudal" counterpart of Hu's bourgeois thought.[24] Moreover, Liang's criticism of the industrialization plan, often mentioned by critics during the campaign, might indeed have come dangerously close to voicing what many people, both inside and outside the Party, actually felt.[25]

The campaign in the press, which seemed to aim primarily at undermining Liang's prestige, makes for uninspiring reading. Most critiques were replete with sloppily defined categories and muddled logic. They accused Liang, the rural reconstruction leader, for instance, of being the lackey of American *and* Japanese imperialists, Chiang Kai-shek, the Kuomintang, Han Fu-ch'ü, landlords, industrial capitalists, compradores, rich peasants, and local bullies. That the interests of this motley collection of villains were hardly congruent did not bother the critics. They went on to insist that absolutely everything Liang had ever done in his entire life— from his "desertion" of the Republican Revolution in 1913 to his efforts in the peace negotiations—had sprung from pure malevo-

23. The first article of the campaign was [262]. Throughout 1955 and into 1956 a flood of about a hundred similar articles was published in the national and local press. For examples, see [409] and [101].

24. [250]; [173], p. 49; [329], pp. 115, 120–122; [493], p. 133; [456], p. 12; [101], p. 4; [202], p. 145. Probably one major reason for the campaign against Liang at this time was simply that his name was added to Hu Shih's as a target in the general "struggle against idealism," which Mao thought especially prevalent among China's intellectuals. [424], V, 199.

25. Some Party members and high-ranking military people who agreed with Liang apparently persisted in their attitude through the 1950s. On January 18, 1957, Mao commented that "During the first half of 1955 [when the anti-Liang campaign was launched] there were a good many people in the Party who sang duets with Liang Shu-ming and his ilk in complaining about the suffering of the peasants; it was as if they were the only two groups of people who represented the peasants and understood their suffering. In their eyes, our Party Central Committee does not represent the peasants, nor do the provincial committees and the majority of Party members." [424], V, 336.

lence and had begot unmitigated evil. The improved agricultural technology and increased production in Tsou-p'ing, for instance, had resulted in benefits "solely for the big landlords." (There were, in fact, almost no big landlords in Tsou-p'ing.) It would seem they were out only to show that Liang had been in the service of evil, however defined. Some even resorted to the ultimate smear—that Liang and some of his colleagues had been pro-Japanese and even collaborators.[26]

The critics hardly needed to resort to such far-fetched accusations to prove the "incorrectness" of Liang's thought. He was indeed the subjective idealist that most charged him with being. The central concept in his philosophy of Chinese culture—*jen* or *li-hsing*—did, after all, "transcend time and space," and "superseded nature" as an eternal truth. And Liang had certainly asserted—as recently as 1952—that Chinese society did not have classes. It was also undeniably true that Liang had conceived of his rural movement as being in direct competition with the CCP for the allegiance of young intellectuals and peasants.[27]

On the whole, the Party must be credited with a successful campaign, for it does seem to have destroyed Liang's reputation. Every major philosopher in China—except Liang's long-time friend, the modern Confucian thinker Hsiung Shih-li—publicly criticized him. A Buddhist scholar even called into question his understanding of the Wei-shih doctrine. Old ideological and political enemies—such as Ch'en Hsu-ching and Li Tzu-hsiang—got a chance to get in a few more licks (now with purely Marxist arguments, of course). Several who had worked with Liang in rural reconstruction were prevailed

26. [172], p. 44; [590], p. 32; [183], p. 50; [402], pp. 167–168; [260], p. 190; [266], p. 200; [582], pp. 21–22; [296], pp. 38–39; [609], p. 67; [225] p. 284; [342], pp. 178–179; [497], pp. 138–139. In 1938, there had indeed been a rumor that a former worker at Tsou-p'ing—Yang Hsiao-ch'un—was a collaborator. Actually, the rumor seems to have been a weapon used by local KMT elements in Honan (where Yang had a rural work project in 1938) to break up Yang's project. See [402], p. 164; [594].

27. [250], pp. 7–8; [582], pp. 12, 19, 26–29; [296], p. 36; [173], pp. 53–54; [609], pp. 60, 61, 62, 69; [277], p. 74, 78–79; [492]; [263]; [351]; [202], pp. 147–152, 155; [531], p. 170; [331]; [456], pp. 12–13; [330], pp. 19, 20, 21–23, 25; [590], pp. 32–42; [183]; [302], pp. 76–77, 79; [583], pp. 86–87, 91–92; [559]; pp. 131–132; [402], p. 161; [469], pp. 176–186; [260], pp. 187–197; [264], p. 211; [340], pp. 221–222; [414], pp. 282–283; [212], I, 177–178; [101], pp. 63–65; [342], p. 177.

upon to expose the horrors of their former master's doings in Shantung. Some critics even denied Liang any claim to originality in formulating his pernicious cultural and philosophical theories; they claimed he had plagiarized from Western bourgeois philosophers of history, such as Toynbee and Spengler. Others dismissed his intricate Confucian intuitionism and subtle cultural theories as nothing more than a few ideas borrowed from Bergson and Russell. Finally, a few more perceptive critics rubbed Liang's nose in his messianic megalomania.[28]

The campaign against Liang touched off a larger wave of support and praise for him in anti-Communist Hong Kong and Taiwan, where he was hailed as the embodiment of the traditional scholar of moral rectitude who refused to compromise his principles for the sake of expediency.[29] In February 1956, however, Liang did bow his head and recite a formal *confiteor* before the PPCC.[30] Although a careful reading of his confession might reveal that he was still refusing to surrender, Mao pronounced himself satisfied with it.[31]

Hu Shih, secure in his New York apartment and his position as distinguished White Chinese, made no equivalent gesture of repentance after the 1954–1955 campaign against him. (Hu, in fact, had spent most of the preceding fifteen years in the U.S., where in many ways he no doubt felt more at home than in China.) Indeed, even if Hu's own son did take part in the vilification, Hu was probably pleased at least to be the center of attention once more. In 1958, he finally returned to the fatherland—or at least that province of it still in the hands of the KMT—to spend his final years in scholarly and social putterings as the head of the Academia Sinica in Taipei.[32]

28. [183]; [403]; [296], pp. 30, 31; [329], pp. 115–116, 119, 121; [493], p. 133; [202], pp. 147, 158; [331], pp. 3–4; [330], pp. 20, 27; [590], p. 34; [183], pp. 50–56; [302], pp. 68, 80; [195], pp. 108–110, 113, 121; [559], pp. 135, 136; [222], pp. 138, 139; [101], pp. 25–29.
29. [187]; [271], Mar. 9, 1956, July 28, 29, 1955; [365], May 24, 1955; [545], May 25, July 30, 1955; [487]; [188]; [511].
30. [359], Feb. 9, 1956; [333], Feb. 8, 1956. For a more detailed account of his self-reform process, see [95]. Just as the campaign was starting in early 1955, Liang made a strong statement supporting the Communist party and urging the people of Taiwan to reunite with the mainland. See [94].
31. See [165]; [425a], p. 88.   32. [253].

In the Twilight, 1975–1977

During and after his period of pillorying and purgation, Liang's life-style did not change. Perhaps inspired by Mao's swims in the Yangtze during the summer of 1956, he took up *t'ai-chi-ch'üan* (Chinese "shadow boxing") and could be seen practicing together with other elderly Pekinese in the early morning.[33] These images of the two sixty-eight-year-olds—Mao lashing and beating his way through the furrows of the mighty Ch'ang-chiang, and Liang moving with dignified tranquility through the harmoniously flowing motions of the traditional martial arts—set in sharp relief the contrasting themes of struggle and harmony that underlie the personality of each. Liang lacked utterly Mao's Faustian streak, that urge to heaven-storming combative struggle exemplified by his remarkable sexagenarian aquatics. It is also unimaginable that Liang would ever appear in public décolleté under *any* circumstances, much less for the edification of the entire nation! But then, Mao had not had Liang Chi as a father.

Despite his national reputation as a defiantly stubborn reactionary, Liang continued to be appointed to the PPCC national committee. The 1957 Anti-Rightist campaign and the Cultural Revolution of the 1960s, which brought such abuse and vilification to so many of the distinguished elder generation, passed him by without incident. He continued to live comfortably in Peking near his faithful student of four decades, Huang Ken-yung.[34] It would appear, moreover, that his sage identity and Confucian temperament remained intact. Just a year after his turn on the stool of repentance, we find some of his public remarks recorded in the *People's Daily*. Although the statement was addressed to the question of establishing an autonomous region for the Chuang people in Kwangsi (he was serving on a committee set up to study the problem), he still managed to broach the subject of Chinese culture; it obsessed him

33. [316].
34. [333], Dec. 11, 1954, Feb. 2, 1956, June 4, 1957, Apr. 12, 1959. In the middle of the campaign against him, Liang participated in the contemporaneous campaign against Hu Feng. [359], June 10, 1955; [93b]; [316]. Liang's friends in Hong Kong did hear that Huang Ken-yung was attacked during the Cultural Revolution and forced to return to his ancestral home in Kwangtung. Liang himself was probably protected by his special private relationship with Mao.

yet. "The spirit of Chinese culture," Liang proclaimed, was one of "compromise, mutual yielding, and harmony. . . . Today, our life should have precisely this spirit."[35] Had Mao failed in the end to bring his student around to abandoning Confucian harmony for Marxist struggle?

Throughout the late 1950s and the 1960s, Liang continued to appear at various ceremonial occasions, to serve on committees, and to travel about on inspection tours as a member of the PPCC. When in 1965 his old friend and fellow provincial, General Li Tsung-jen, returned from his New Jersey exile, Liang was on hand to welcome him back.[36]

Later in the 1970s, however, a high-ranking official privately attempted to wring from him an essay for the Criticize Confucius campaign. (Certainly a public denouncement of Master K'ung by the world's most distinguished living Confucianist would have been a definite contribution to the campaign.) This confrontation occasioned yet another display of his unbending integrity. Liang replied that he was "a man of independent thought" whose "internal [convictions] and external [behavior] were identical." So, he continued, because his inner self could not criticize Confucius, his outer self could not write such an essay. When his interlocutor turned to threats, Liang complacently observed that as he was already eighty-three, he "had nothing to fear." The official later remarked to a friend that Liang "is really a pigheaded old diehard."[37] (His image had not changed much in sixty years.)

By this time, most of Liang's generation had passed from the scene; all his friends and adversaries—Hu Shih, Chou En-lai, Li Chi-shen, Li Tsung-jen and even his second wife—were dead. Until September 9, 1976, there had been one notable exception: the country boy with scholarly aspirations whom he had first met in Peking over half a century before. It was Mao, not Liang, who had become the sage of a revitalized China. Ironically, Liang lived on to see China take the first steps back from the dead leader's vision, a retreat brought about ultimately by the very historical forces

35. [333], Apr. 20, 1957. He happened to make the statement right at the highpoint of the "Hundred Flowers" period of ideological relaxation; otherwise, it probably never would have been published.

36. [333], June 4, 1957, April 12, 1959, Sept. 22, 1962, Dec. 14, 1964, Aug. 7, 1965.

37. [395]; [587].

against which Liang had vainly struggled.[38] As for Liang himself, he found that he had become just a vague memory to most Chinese, a final ghostly symbol of the old Confucian scholar. But he did have grandsons, good health and self-respect[39]—not a bad old age. Perhaps he would occasionally take a solitary walk on the shores of Pure Dharma Lake. Perhaps he would contemplate the broken stone upon which his father's monument once rested. And when he turned his gaze to the spot where his father's body had been found, now a swimming area for children, what could have been his thoughts?

38. After the arrest of the radical Maoist "Gang of Four" in 1976, it became increasingly obvious that the dominant leaders of the Party were committing themselves to "modernization" at the expense of some basic "Maoist" values. In a strange, convoluted way, Liang might be said to have a small part in this reshaping of the Maoist legacy. In March 1977, the new regime published a fifth volume of Mao's Selected Works, the first such addition in seventeen years. Covering the period 1949–1957, it included the official record of Mao's 1953 speech attacking Liang. Even after editing, the piece is disjointed, confusing, and in general is lacking in any real theses, contributions to theory or even well-articulated ideas; it is more than anything else, one long emotional tirade. Moreover, its shrill vindictive tone and sheer vehemence makes Mao look quite undignified. Why did the leadership choose to include such an anomaly in this volume of "immortal monuments of Marxism-Leninism" which have "great and deep world significance"? Merging with the fanfare and publicity that naturally accompanied the volume's publication and the continuing campaign against the Gang of Four, several essays on the anti-Liang piece appeared in the national press. (See, for example, [333], May 10, 19, 25, 1977; [359], April 14, 15, 26, May 19, June 7, 12, July 7, 1977; [323], No. 6 (June 2, 1977), pp. 69–72.) What purpose could all of this have served? One possibility is that, at one level, resurrecting Liang as a target for criticism is itself a covert attack on Mao's own "anti-modern" aspects. Mao shared much with the Confucian reactionary, certainly more than he did with those "Westernizer/modernizer" advocates, be they liberals like Hu Shih, or Marxists. By making Mao's attack on Liang widely known (it had not been public knowledge up to this time), the present leadership might have been seeking to deemphasize those anti-modern aspects of Mao that he shares with Liang. It would have suited their purposes, in the delicate operation of transforming the Maoist heritage, to play up Mao's violent condemnation of Liang's "line."

39. [316]. When Liang appeared at a public occasion for the first time in a dozen years in June 1977, a reporter observed that "at age eighty-four, his health is fine, his walk sprightly and his mind clear." [501], June 21, 1977.

CHAPTER XIV

Epilogue 1986

When I wrote the concluding paragraph of the previous chapter in 1976, little did I suspect that I would actually have the opportunity to ask Liang Shu-ming personally what his thoughts were while he strolled the lake.[1] This epilogue relates how I came to be able to ask him and what his answers were.

Naturally, I had spent years before the book was published trying to see Liang, but without success. In any case, in those days of the nefarious "Gang of Four," any meeting with him would have been at most a formal exchange of meaningless pleasantries in the company of myriad official witnesses. Thus, the book was written, as most historical biographies are, without any hope of ever meeting its subject. Although I had no record of his demise, Liang was simply a historical figure to me, not that different in my mind from those who had died in the distant past.

The book was published in January 1979. During the period that the book was in press, Teng Hsiao-p'ing launched a second "liberation" of China with a series of far reaching reforms. As the political atmosphere became increasingly relaxed, the possibility of seeing even such an outspoken figure as Liang increased. Nevertheless, the book "had been put to bed," and my research turned in other directions. I was then teaching at the University of Akron in Ohio, where a Chinese colleague in the Physics Department had recently been reunited with his family from Peking. By chance, one of his daughters was enrolled in one of my classes. Late in 1979, this young woman phoned to tell me that "Elder Uncle Liang" had heard about the book and hoped that I would visit him, because he had some new writings to show me. It seemed that the girl's maternal grandmother was an old friend and neighbor of Liang's and had, apparently at Liang's request, instructed her granddaughter to make this circuitous overture. I then mailed to Laing, in care of the grandmother, a letter together with copies of the book. A month later I received a phone call from an elderly Chinese engineer in California who had been a student of Liang's at Peking University. This gentleman, after repeated attempts, had finally been able to visit Liang in the past year, and was charged with letting me know that my letter and books had arrived. Finally, after another month, I received a letter from Liang himself. Liang was then eighty-eight. The letter, however, was written in exquisitely brushed "grass-style" calligraphy and in elegant classical style. It was obviously the product of someone with a lucid mind and in vigorous health. Liang formally thanked me for having written the biography and noted that he had heard that I was coming to China. "I very much hope for it," was his comment.

With these indications of good health and a warm welcome, I immediately made arrangements to go to Peking. After spending years of my life studying Liang's, I was naturally elated at the prospect of meeting him. At the same time, however, I also approached the meetings with some apprehension. Had my attempt to paint a portrait of a man I had never met produced a poor likeness to the flesh and blood man I would soon meet? Liang would no longer be just another historical figure, a mental abstraction that would remain silent to his biographer's analysing, criticizing and theorizing. I had imputed complex motives to him, pointed out paradoxes in his thought and actions, and generally made free and easy with his innermost self. He was now going to talk back, to judge me as much as I had judged him. In principle, of course, personal acquaintance does not necessarily enhance the biographer's power to capture his subject. Indeed, such "contamination" harms the delicate distance of scholarly judgment and so might even diminish the truth of a portrait. Yet one suspects that the historical biographer wonders continually what relationship his intellectual creation bears to his subject in more prosaic human terms.

This also appeared to be the first occasion for any non-Chinese historian of China to discuss a published biography with the subject of that work. Thus, the meetings had some significance for many of my academic colleagues in Chinese history, as well as for myself. Probably they have shared some of my anxieties at one time or another. In relying on decaying paper pages to understand a life lived in a culture foreign to our own, how close can we hope to come to the rich reality of that life? Had my necessarily Western concepts and categories distorted the Chinese reality?

The Interviews

I conducted two series of interviews with Liang, the first in 1980 and the second in 1984. We would meet alone in Liang's study for several hours daily. I taped all of these conversations and later transcribed them. Liang also lent me several personal documents, such as various diaries he had kept and some correspondence. We have also maintained a correspondence ever since our initial contact.

As I knew that Liang's knowledge of English was limited, I asked him, as casually as I could manage, if he had actually read the book. He replied that he had, with the help of friends and his sons, who have a good command of English. Some time later, I noticed lying on a table in his study an obviously well-thumbed copy bristling with dozens of slips of paper sticking out of the pages. Each slip seemed to have notes written on it. When I asked Liang directly for criticism and comments of the book, he replied that he had none. Moreover, he insisted that he did not want to influence a historian's judgment or impression of him. Nevertheless, I surmise that since he went through the book with such care, the interviews were as much a reply to the book as to my questions.

For the most part, the interviews confirmed the major theses in the book. Certainly the fundamental portrait of the man in this book was confirmed by the experience. Moreover, they produced a wealth of information that, had I had access to it ten years ago, would have greatly enhanced the book in many ways. The interviews conflicted with the book quite dramatically on two issues, Liang's marriages and, *horribile dictu*, the title itself.

The Last Confucian a Buddhist? During the very first interview, Liang proclaimed that he was still a Buddhist! In almost the same words he used with Ts'ai Yuan-p'ei upon arriving at Peking University in 1917,[2] he began by saying that he hoped that through these interviews I would be able to carry the true meaning of Confucianism *and* Buddhism to the West. When I pointed out that, in 1921, he had publicly and quite dramatically announced his abandonment of Buddhism for Confucianism, Liang blandly replied: "That does not matter. I abandoned Buddhism and yet at the same time I did not really abandon it. Ever since the age of sixteen or seventeen, I have longed to become a monk, but at age twenty-nine I married and so gave up the idea." All of China, including his close friends and students, had always considered Liang a Confucian, and, moreover, a very self-conscious and celebrated one. Is there any way to reconcile this obvious contradiction? Was Liang reporting his present honest conviction that he was a Buddhist, something that he had not felt comfortable telling others until his old age? Was he projecting his private mythology?

In the first place, of course, doctrinal exclusivity of the sort that emerged early in the monotheistic civilizations of the world has never existed in China. Most Chinese of the past two thousand years probably felt themselves to be both Buddhist and Confucian, and never perceived any contradiction in doing so. I believe that Liang undoubtedly did maintain his Buddhist beliefs on one level of consciousness throughout his life, as many historical Neo-Confucian figures had done before him. As I have noted,[3] he had clearly stated in *Eastern and Western Cultures* that even while he was announcing himself to the world as a Confucian convert, his belief that ultimate human salvation was possible only through Buddhism would never change. He had stressed that Buddhism would do harm to China only at this time in the evolution of humanity. Confucianism, however, could save it, and all of humanity as well. So, until the 1950s at least, he vigorously participated in the mundane world playing a self-consciously Confucian role. He had hierarchized Confucianism and Buddhism, so that while the need of the age was for the former, the latter was, on a higher, timeless level, still valid.

Yet, as we discover from our own lives, a person's conscious past is in continuous transformation. We tend to project present feelings and beliefs backwards through time, or re-order the past with them. The semi-retirement of Liang's old age, in contrast to his busy and strenuous life before the 1950s, probably intensified his earlier philosophical commitment to Buddhism. The older he became, the closer to the ultimate and final human reality, the more Buddhism—a wisdom of ultimates—came to the fore in his consciousness. We might say that in 1980 he was relatively more Buddhist than in 1930. Otherwise, what had prevented him all these years, as he said to me was his constant desire, from "retiring to live the life of a monk on a hilltop monastery"? Liang had always been famous for his unity of thought and action, after all. He had had opportunities throughout his life, but had never gone off to that hilltop. Finally, Liang did tell me outright that he could accept the "Last Confucian" title.

Marriages. As there was almost nothing written about Liang's two marriages, I had relied primarily on interviewees for information.[4] Many of these informants, quite independently, had contrasted Liang's two marriages in exactly the same way. The first marriage, they said, was a bad one for Liang. The woman was an uneducated Manchu aristocrat, so not only did she fail to provide him with the intellectual companionship he needed, but she could not cook or keep house either. Moreover, the interviewees claimed in one voice, their relationship seemed cold and distant. (One of Liang's own writings had suggested the same thing).[5] The second marriage, all interviewees agreed, was a far better, warmer, more intimate relationship, because it was with an educated woman who was able to share Liang's intellectual life.

In 1980, however, Liang's own version was the diametric opposite. It was the first marriage which had been golden. The woman had been a veritable saint, absolutely devoted to him. If anything had even upset him in his life (the implication being that nothing really had, at least since his youthful emotional crisis), it had been his first wife's death. The passing of his second wife, which had taken place the year before I first talked to him, elicited no like response. It was clear that Liang himself considered the second marriage the mistake. His second wife's individuality was too strong, and since she married so late, she was permanently set in her ways. "So when the wife's personality is so strong, the result is . . . ha ha ha," he commented. I even had the second wife's age wrong, Liang pointed out: "She was forty-seven when she married me, three years younger than I." (Alitto): "The newspaper accounts of the wedding gave her age as forty." (Liang): "She told that to the newspapers because she was embarrassed about it! She concealed her true age not just from the newspapers, but also from the marriage go-betweens and me."

Can the contradiction be resolved between Liang's 1980 assessment and the impressions of the interviewees? It is probable that interviewees, who had not known Liang's first wife, but who did know his second wife well, would be biased toward the second marriage. Moreover, Liang would never have allowed his negative feelings about his second wife to become known to any of them. As a committed Confucian, he probably appeared consistently as a loving and respectful husband. After all, who was better equipped than Liang to comment on his own personal life?

Yet I cannot help but wonder if, as in the matter of his Buddhist identity, the Liang of the 1980s had unconsciously changed somewhat from the Liang of the 1940s. Liang's first wife had been the companion of his glorious youth and had borne him three children during the decade of their marriage. She was part of the now distant and forever golden past, and had been dead for over forty years. Liang's second wife, on the other hand, had been with him during the most difficult and discouraging periods of his life. She was his companion for over forty years into his advanced old age. She was part of the non-romanticizable present. How else can we explain the unanimity of the interviewees?

Apart from these two questions, the interviews corrected or clarified several minor details.

The Cultural Revolution. Although everyone in Hong Kong said that the Cultural Revolution had "passed him by without incident,"[6] the upheaval actually struck Liang almost immediately. On August 24, 1966, a group of Red Guards (that is, junior high school students from nearby No. 123 Middle School) carried out an "assault" ("*ch'ung-chi*" in the language of the time) on Liang's house, the same house from which his father had departed the world. The students threw the Liangs into a small room and warned them not to try to get out. For the next several weeks the students made the house their "headquarters." The first day they threw most items of value—furniture, books, paintings, heirlooms—into the alley, where they were later burned. "It took many cartloads over several days to carry away the ashes," Liang recalled. "They even ripped up all of my reference books—dictionaries and so on, books that had no ideological content." The Red Guards also plastered the house with big character posters reviling Liang. For a time there were other similar posters pasted on the meeting hall of the Chinese People's Political Consultative Conference (PPCC). Liang's wife was dragged outside several times where she was "struggled against"—cursed, criticized and generally abused. During one of these public struggles against her, the seventy-year-old woman was beaten so severely that "the blood soaked through to the outside of her clothes." Yet, for reasons that Liang himself could not explain, the children never harmed him physically, or even verbally assaulted him. It might have been his personal relationship with Mao that protected him, as I originally had assumed. Yet at the beginning of the Cultural Revolution, one doubts if Mao could have gotten in touch with this particular group of rampaging Red Guards even if he had wanted to. (Liang said that he wrote to both Mao and Chou En-lai, but received no reply from either.) Perhaps Liang's personal aura was sufficient to give the teenagers second thoughts.

The Criticize Lin Piao and Confucius Campaign. The incident of Liang's refusal to write an essay for the Criticize Confucius campaign is garbled a bit.[7] Liang clarified his role in the incident. During the campaign, Liang continued to attend the sessions of his particular PPCC subgroup. Both privately and during the public meetings, Liang's colleagues in the group persistently urged him to make a statement or write an essay criticizing Confucius, which he steadfastly refused to do. For several days in succession, his fellows pounced on Liang for his maddening reticence and sternly demanded that he respond in some way. Finally Liang did agree to respond publicly, but he spoke only one single sentence, from the *Analects* of Confucius: "You can carry off the commander of the armed forces of a large state, but you cannot change the will of even the humblest person." (*San chün k'o to shih yeh, p'i-fu pu k'o to chih yeh.*)

The original description of the incident was not really inaccurate because his colleagues could be considered "high-ranking officials," and it is even probable that one or more of them had remarked on Liang's pigheadedness when he refused to comment. According to Liang, however, he was never threatened physically, nor did he observe to anyone that he was "already eighty-three, so had nothing to fear."

Liang's First Meeting with Mao. Liang's friendship with Yang Ch'ang-chi, Mao's teacher and father-in-law (and so Liang's first acquaintance with Mao in 1919), was not because they were colleagues in the Peking University Philosophy Department,[8] but because of a Hunanese second-cousin, Liang Huan-k'uei,[9] who was both Yang's benefactor/teacher and from Mao's home county. When Liang Huan-k'uei was in Peking, he stayed in Liang Shu-ming's house, and Yang often called on him there.

Liang Chi's Stone Monument. The stone monument on Pure Dharma erected by the neighborhood to commemorate Liang Chi's suicide was destroyed during the Cultural Revolution, not, as

I had guessed, during the 1950s.[10] With hindsight I know now that I had actually seen the monument, at least for a short moment and in an unrecognizable form. When I located the pedestal in 1973, some young children led me into a neighbor's courtyard where, hidden under a covering, there was a neat pile of cut stone blocks stored for future use. (This had been a harvest from the Cultural Revolution, I was told.) Just as I had managed to see a few of the characters carved on some of these blocks, the present owner came out of the house and angrily hustled me out of his courtyard. As I did not actually have sufficient time to read the characters and confirm my original impression, I made the cautious but erroneous guess that what I had seen was not Liang Chi's monument. After talking to Liang, however, I now surmise that what I saw was indeed the disassembled stone monument.

Han Fu-ch'ü and the Village Government Academy. Feng Yü-hsiang and Han Fu-ch'ü actually gave only "permission," rather than a "commission" to set up the Honan Village Government Academy.[11] The provincial government provided no funds for it, nor did it have control over it. The money for the academy came from one of the village government group, Wang I-k'o[12] who had managed a fund for the teachers of Hopei province in the early 1920s. Wang was a talented investor. Not only did he succeed in making a handsome return for the teachers, but also accumulated a surplus which was used to found the school.

Alfred Westharp.[13] The interviews revealed such fascinating details on the subject of Liang's only close foreign friend, Alfred Westharp, that I cannot resist elaborating a bit here. Westharp was a Prussian aristocrat, the son of the director of the national bank of Germany. He went through university courses in both medicine and philosophy before he settled upon music as a career. Before coming to the United States and becoming a U.S. citizen, he studied with both Ravel and Montessori. His music was apparently resoundingly rejected in both Europe and America, which impelled him to go East with it. The Indians and Japanese liked his music no more than the Westerners, so he finally went to Shanghai, where his music was again resoundingly rejected by the Westernized musical community.

To make matters worse, the First World War had cut off Westharp's money from home. In despair, he was on the verge of suicide when he wrote to the famous (and by then the culturally conservative) translator, Yen Fu, pleading for help. Yen aided him financially and translated one of his articles.[14] Later he attracted the attention of and became a life-long friend and advisor to Yen Hsi-shan, which is how he happened to run a school in Taiyuan.[15] I imagine that this was the first Montessorian school in China. He later became friends with some of the Kwangsi Clique leaders as well.

Detained by the Japanese during the war as an enemy national, he was sent to Japan as a prisoner. Apparently depressed by his captive condition, he attempted suicide by jumping into the sea. The abbot of a Zen monastery near the spot happened to see this and saved him. Fantastic as it may seem, the abbot had studied in Germany. The two hit it off and so Westharp lived out his days as a Zen monk.

The Kuang-ming Pao.[16] One other rather startling example of an error of omission concerns the funding of Liang's Hong Kong newspaper, *Kuang-ming-pao*. I had no idea where the funds to start the paper came from and so didn't bring up the matter at all. As it turns out, much of the money came from some unknown overseas Chinese organization which, Liang suspected at the time, was a CCP front, or at least communist-affiliated. That the organ of the Chinese "Third-Force" political organization was funded by one of the major parties is of considerable significance.

Jen *in* Eastern and Western Cultures. It would seem fitting that Liang himself have his opportunity to add his own *errata*. I asked Liang if he now thought any parts of his works were out of date, or, upon reflection, in error. He thought for a long time, and then replied that his interpretation of the Confucian virtue, *Jen* (Benevolence), as expounded in *Eastern and Western Cultures*, was slightly in error, or at least misleading.

"I said that Confucius' *Jen* is a kind of extremely sensitive, acute intuition. Didn't Mencius use terms like "intuitive understanding of the good"? That is what is called "instinct" nowadays. *Chih-chueh* is called "intuition" in English. *Pen-neng* is called "instinct" in English. So, in this way, I used these modern terms to explain the thought of Confucius and Mencius. Now I see that I was wrong. These modern terms are quite similar in meaning [to *Jen*] but they are not exact equivalents and are not really correct. But they aren't totally incorrect either."

[Alitto]: Any other mistakes?

[Liang]: No, not that I can think of.

This, of course, is exactly how the Liang of *The Last Confucian* would have answered such a question, and so confirms the book's delineation of his character and personality. I should add that Liang, as befits a sage, was exceedingly modest throughout the interviews, and often disclaimed having any wisdom or historical significance.

Liang and the Chinese Communists. In the areas of interpretation, however, the interviews turned out to corroborate more than they corrected. The motivations the book imputes to Liang and conjectures made to cover lacunae were in general borne out by this opportunity to talk over his life with him, and especially by reading some of his diaries.

The book demonstrates (to my own satisfaction at least) that Liang's blueprint for China's solution to the dilemma of modernity and Mao's were strikingly similar, even though Liang is usually considered an arch conservative and Mao *the* arch radical. The book also shows the areas in which Chinese communism and Confucian conservatism overlap. The more I talked to Liang, the more justified I felt in making this case. Liang himself felt strongly that the programs and goals of his rural reconstruction movement had in fact been carried out by the CCP. The resemblances were especially close in the CCP's programs as they were in fact implemented during the war with Japan. Liang felt that even CCP land reform as it was carried out in the late 1940s and early 1950s accomplished essentially the same goals as his rural reconstruction had striven for. "The peasantry needed organization and science. This was the purpose of rural reconstruction and this is what the CCP accomplished." Liang saw the question of struggle as the major difference between his rural program and that of the CCP. He was still not convinced that class struggle and violence had been absolutely necessary for success and he still argued that the nature of "class" in Chinese society was fundamentally different from that of Western society. He thought that the CCP's success in mobilizing the peasantry during the war had relied on using essentially the same techniques and organizations that he had been preparing to use in Shantung (had Han Fu-ch'ü not betrayed him) and that he had tried to propagate nationwide before and during the war. As to whether or not he had directly influenced Mao's sinification of Marxism (page 290), he replied with the masterly equivocal statement "*wo pu-kan chemma shuo*" ("I don't dare say that" or "I should not say that"). He said no more on that matter.

Psychological Analysis and Motives. Liang said that he did not fully understand much of the psychological analyses in the book, but felt that insofar as he understood them, they were reasonable. When I put some of the book's more subtle analyses of his motives or subjective state into Chinese, he would often ponder perplexedly for a few moments and then agree hesitantly that "Yes, you could put it that way."

On the other hand, the book's observations of the paradoxical or ironic in his life seemed to puzzle Liang. He felt no irony or saw no paradoxes. For example, Liang consistently argued against the efficacy of liberalism, democracy, constitutionalism and political activity itself as solutions to China's problems. Yet during and after the war he emerged as a "liberal democratic political leader" (even while he continued to oppose the constitutionalism movement of his liberal-democratic colleagues). Liang remained completely insensible to any incongruity in this. His own political activities were simply a continuation of his previous activities, adjusted to the circumstances created by the war. His analysis of China's underlying problems, his own proposed solution, and his goals had not changed at all. His work during and after the war was completely consistent with and based on the same principles as what he had been doing all along (*i kuan hsia lai te*).

How would the book have been different if I had interviewed Liang before I wrote it, instead of after? Of course, it would have avoided such factual errors as mentioned above and the wealth of detail on all aspects of Liang's life would have made it a far more lively and vivid, as well as much longer, work. It would also have been better-constructed because, with that much more material, there would have been no need to create awkward bridges over those great abysses of ignorance engendered by a lack of written material. Yet at the same time, because of the "contamination" of knowing the subject personally before the fundamental judgments were made and basic concepts were formed, I think the book might have been less "true" or less accurate in some ultimate sense.

I would add one final reflection on history. I came away from my meetings with Liang all the more certain that the exercise of "intuition" or "sympathetic imagination" is at least as important to the historian as his sureness of touch in documentary interpretation. The interviews reinforced my fundamental image of Liang that integrated the biography. This image came not so much from any particular sources as from the net influence of all sources (including those of interviewees) on my own imagination and intuition.

Liang's Final Years

Liang's last years are being spent in a "modern" style apartment house in one of Peking's more pleasant neighborhoods, into which he moved in 1979.[17] The other residents all appear to be noted figures in cultural fields and high ranking members of the PPCC. His neighbor across the hall, for instance, is the famous woman writer Ting Ling.

Liang still remains devoted to duty, which for the past decades has been his work in the Standing Committee of the PPCC, and in several sub-committees. He attends these meetings religiously. On several occasions, he postponed my appointment because a committee meeting had been called.

During those decades after 1957 when Liang disappeared almost completely from the news, he had been doing more than taking walks around Pure Dharma Lake. He has continued to think, and write. The Cultural Revolution, as mentioned above, destroyed his library and his personal freedom. The Four Modernizations brought Liang the opportunity to return to serious work. By the time I met him in 1980, Liang had already finished two book manuscripts—a smaller one called "An Introduction to Eastern Thought" (*Tung-fang hsueh-shu kai-lun*), and a massive statement of summation entitled "The Human Heart/Mind and Life" (*Jen-hsin yü jen-sheng*).[18] He considers this his conclusive and best work. I was only able to skim through it because he had only one copy and so was reluctant to allow me to remove it from his apartment for a thorough study. It appears to be a further development and final statement of the ideas in his previous books *Eastern and Western Cultures* and *The Essence of Chinese Culture*. When asked what he thought he might be remembered for in history, he replied that if remembered at all, it would be only for this book.

This does not mean, however, that all has gone smoothly for him under the Four Modernizations. Although a respected elder "democratic personage," what he has to say philosophically does not fit well with the new order of things, which in some respects appears to be, if not "wholesale Westernization," at least "retail Westernization." In certain respects, Liang found himself in a situation similar to that in his days at Peking University, when the pro-Western *New Youth* group dominated. In 1979 he submitted his smaller book manuscript, "An Introduction to Eastern Thought," for publication. As his work unit was the PPCC, he gave it to the chairman of that body, who at the time was Teng Hsiao-p'ing. Teng replied that he was too busy to read it himself, and turned the matter over to his secretary. The secretary did not get to it for a while, and when pressed on the matter, replied that he had lost the manuscript.

After this experience, Liang did not dare to submit the only copy of the larger work, *The Mind/Heart and Life*, to the same process, lest the secretary lose that too. When I first met Liang in 1980, I offered to translate the book into English and have it published in the U.S., or to have it published in Chinese in Hong Kong. Liang refused immediately, saying that as he was a Chinese, the book should first be published in China. In the first years of the 1980s, Liang sought to publish his *magnum opus* through regular channels but without success. Finally, he gave the book to a Shanghai press which asked a very large fee for publishing it. Liang paid. (I didn't ask where the money came from.) When I last saw him in late 1984, he was awaiting copies.

He has continued to write short pieces for publication by the PPCC. He wrote, for instance, a short biography of his uncle Chang Yao-tseng, for the biography section of the new *History of the Chinese Republic*, and another biography of his relative Liang Huan-k'uei, for the new *Hunan Provincial Gazetteer*. He had also written several historical essays on the Democratic League and its two predecessors.

Although he has been a slight, frail person all his life, he has remained remarkably fit into his nineties. He moves with relative ease and speed. In 1980, he took his family and me out to dinner at a second-floor restaurant (vegetarian, of course) and climbed the stairs with no difficulty. However, he does seem to have deteriorated somewhat in the years since I first met him. By 1984, for example, he could no longer do large-sized characters for decorative scrolls, although his smaller calligraphy is still, as before, universally recognized as superb. His mental faculties, however, seemed unimpaired.

He rises around 5 a.m., and goes through a routine of simple exercises. He works all day, either attending meetings or doing serious reading and writing in his study. He takes a short nap in the middle of the day. He lives alone in his apartment, except for a housekeeper. His two sons, daughters-in-law and grandchildren stay with him when their work allows. His study, where the interviews were conducted, is sparsely furnished with a few bookshelves for Liang's now diminished library, a writing table, a simple wooden straightback chair and two upholstered chairs with a tea table between them (for conversation with guests). The next room is Liang's bedroom, in which he stores more books and papers, and a simple wooden-plank bed. The apartment also has a small dining room, where a television is kept. Liang occasionally watches it.

When I asked him if he had any pastimes or hobbies, he chuckled and replied that once a friend of his asked him that, and he had to answer that it was thinking. It is still his favorite pastime. He attributes his long life and relatively good health to his psychological immunity to the slings and arrows that tend to upset the rest of us. It was frustrating for me, however, to ask for his reactions to this or that buffet of fate (his break-up with Mao, the criticism campaign against him, the Red Guards, and so on) only to have him reply over and over that "It was nothing to me." Of course, he is still a vegetarian, and drinks only plain water.

Since moving into the apartment (and into the freer atmosphere), Liang has regularly received visitors of various backgrounds. During those times I was with him, for instance, many different types of people called: several colleagues from the PPCC, a young student, a daughter of an old friend soliciting an essay from him on her father, a *New China News* reporter from Hong Kong, and an old student from the days of the Honan Village Government Academy who had journeyed from far Szechwan specifically to read Liang's book manuscript. He estimates that he has had four thousand students over the years.

Both of Liang's sons, P'ei-k'uan and P'ei-shu, live in Peking. They have been quite successful in their careers. Both joined the CCP in the early 1950s. The older, P'ei-k'uan, is a scientist in the Chinese Academy of Sciences. The younger, P'ei-shu, worked at *People's Daily* for a time, and is now at the Soviet Studies Institute of the party central committee. Liang has three grandsons. The two older boys, Ch'in-yuan and Ch'in-ning, are college graduates. The youngest, Ch'in-tung, entered Peking University as a law student in the fall of 1984.

Liang seems, overall, a happy, contented man whom mere worldly events do not affect in any way. Some might consider him to have come out on the losing side in the great game of history. He said to me, however, that he has had "no disappointments," and "no regrets." "I have accomplished what I wanted in this life."

1. I learned that such walks were, in fact, one of his favorite pastimes.
2. See page 74.
3. See page 84.
4. Liang's two marriages are compared on pages 311–313.
5. See page 311.
6. See pages 331–332.
7. See page 332.
8. See page 70.
9. Although much older than Liang Shu-ming, Liang Huan-k'uei was of the same formal generation in the Liang clan, so the first character in his given name, Huan, was the same as that of Liang and his brother. Liang referred to Liang Huan-k'uei as his "elder brother" (*ko-ko*). He was of a branch of the Liang family that had moved to Hunan from Kweilin at about the same time Liang Shu-ming's grandfather left for Peking. The son of a minor clerk in Mao's home county of Hsiang-t'an, he attended the *chü-jen* degree in the old examination system. He was one of the young reform-minded Hunanese who clustered around Liang Ch'i-ch'ao's Academy of Current Affairs (*Shih-wu hsueh-t'ang*). For a time he was the official supervisor of Hunanese students in Japan, and it was in this position that, in traditional Chinese usage, he became Yang Ch'ang-chi's "teacher," and was addressed by him as such. Apparently Yang's study in Japan was made possible because of his help. Liang Huan-k'uei returned to China in 1903 to lead his three brothers into the mining business and became one of the most successful early Chinese entrepreneurs.
10. See page 65, n72.
11. See page 73.
12. Wang was mentioned as a member of the Village Government Group on page 173.
13. Westharp is discussed on pages 56, 144–145, 152, 163.
14. As mentioned in note 22, page 145.

15. See page 144.

16. *Kuang-ming Pao* is discussed on pages 308–310.

17. Liang still owns his father's house on what was Tassle Lane, although the present occupants pay him no rent. Situated near the lake in which Liang Chi drowned himself, it was this house that was occupied by Red Guards in 1966.

18. Liang had actually published the preface for the projected work in 1926 (see [9j]), so in every sense the book is his lifework.

Glossary

This glossary does not include proper names which appear in Arthur W. Hummel, ed., *Eminent Chinese of the Ch'ing Period*; Howard L. Boorman, ed., *Biographical Dictionary of Republican China*; Donald W. Klein, ed., *Biographic Dictionary of Chinese Communism, 1921–1965*; or the names of people or works cited in the bibliography to this volume. Names of well-known places and people in Chinese history as well as common, readily identifiable Chinese terms are also omitted.

an-ch'üan-chü 安全局
Ao 傲
Chai-ch'eng (Hopei) 翟城
Chang Ch'un-i 張春漪
Chang Nan-hsien 張難先
Chang Sung-nien (Shen-fu) 張松年
　(申府)
Chang Shu-chih 張俶知
Ch'ang-p'ing (Hopei) 昌平
Chao-ch'eng (Shantung) 朝城
chao-hua 朝話
Chao Ping-chün 趙秉鈞
Chao-p'ing (Kwangsi) 朝平
Chao Tai-wen 趙戴文
ch'ao-i ta-fu 朝議大夫
chen 鎮
Chen-p'ing (Honan) 鎮平
Chen Yuan-hsi 甄元熙
Ch'en Chi-lung 陳冀龍
Ch'en Shu-fen 陳淑芬
cheng 政
Cheng-chih hsieh-shang hui-i 政治
　協商會議
Cheng-chih-pu ti-san cheng-chih ta-
　tui 政治部第三政治大隊
Ch'eng Ting-kuo 程定國
Ch'eng-wu (Shantung) 城武
Ch'i-k'ou (Chekiang) 溪口
Ch'i-meng hua-pao 啟蒙畫報
Chia-hsiang (Shantung) 嘉祥
chiang-hsueh 講學

chiang-hu 江湖
Chiang-ning (Kiangsu) 江寧
chiao 教
chiao-hua 教化
chiao-yuan 教員
chieh 節
chien-she 建設
chien-sheng 監生
Ch'ien-men 前門
chih-yeh fen-t'u 職業分途
ch'ih, ho, wan, le 吃喝玩樂
Chin-hsiang (Shantung) 金鄉
Chin-pu tang 進步黨
Chin Yun-p'eng 靳雲鵬
Ch'in I-wen 秦亦文
Ch'in Pang-hsien 秦邦憲
ch'in shih ch'ü yu 親師取友
ching 靜
Ching-hua jih-pao 京話日報
Ching-hua pao 京話報
Ching-shan-ts'un 經山村
Ching-shih i hsueh-kuan 京師譯學館
Ching-shih shih-yeh hsueh-t'ang
　京師實業學堂
Ching-yeh 淨業
ch'ing-liu 清流
Ch'ing Te 清德
chiu-jen 救人
Chou li 周禮
Chu I-hsin 朱一新
Ch'u Ch'eng-po 褚成博

ch'u-shih 出世
ch'uan-hsien cheng-t'i 傳賢政体
chuang-ts'ang ho-tso-she 莊倉合作社
chung 忠
Chung-ho yuan 中和園
Chung Hsi hsiao-hsueh-t'ang 中西小
　學堂
chung, hsiao, chieh, i 忠孝節義
Chung-hsueh wei t'i; Hsi-hsueh wei
　yung 中學爲体西學爲用
Chung-hua chiao-yü kai-chin she
　中華教育改進社
Chung-hua chih-yeh chiao-yü she
　中華職業教育社
Chung-hua p'ing-min chiao-yü ts'u-
　chin hui 中華平民教育促進會
Chung-hua wen-hua fu-hsing yun-
　tung 中華文化復興運動
Chung i she 忠義社
Chung-kuo min-chu cheng-t'uan ta-
　t'ung-meng 中國民主政團大同盟
Chung-kuo min-chu t'ung-meng
　中國民主同盟
Chung-kuo pen-wei chih wen-hua
　chien-she 中國本位之文化建設
Chung-yang cheng-chih hsueh-yuan
　中央政治學院
Chung-yang tu-li san-shih-erh lü
　中央獨立三十二旅
chung-yung 中庸
Ch'ung-hua shu-yuan 重華書院
chü 局
Chü hsien (Shantung) 莒縣
Chü-yeh (Shantung) 鉅野
ch'ü 區
ch'ü-chang 區長
Ch'ü-fu (Shantung) 曲阜
Ch'üan-chou (Kwangsi) 全州
ch'üan-p'an ch'eng-shou erh ken-pen
　kai-kuo 全盤承受而根本改過
ch'üan-p'an Hsi-hua 全盤西化
chün-hsien 郡縣
chün-tzu 君子
chün-tzu wu hsi-yen 君子無戲言
e pa 惡霸
erh-chung tsu-chih 二種組織

Fa-hsiang 法相
Fan hsien (Shantung) 范縣
fan-nao 煩惱
feng-chien 封建
Feng-t'ai (Hopei) 豐臺
fu-chiu 復舊
fu-ku 復古
fu-shui 附稅
fu-tao-yuan 輔導員
han-jung 含融
han-ts'un 含存
hao-jen 好人
ho-shang 和尚
Ho-tse (Ts'ao-chou; Shantung)
　菏澤（曹州）
hou-pu chih-fu 候補知府
Hsi hsien (Honan) 息縣
Hsi-shih 西施
hsiang 鄉
Hsiang chien p'ai 鄉建派
hsiang-hsueh 鄉學
hsiang-jang 相讓
hsiang-nei yung-li 向內用力
hsiang-nung hsueh-hsiao 鄉農學校
hsiang-she 鄉射
hsiang-ts'un fu-wu chih-tao ch'u
　鄉村服務指導處
hsiang-ts'un fu-wu jen-yuan hsun-lien
　pu 鄉村服務人員訓練部
hsiang-ts'un kai-chin hui 鄉村改進會
hsiang-ts'un tsu-chih 鄉村組織
hsiang tui-chang 鄉隊長
hsiang-wai yung-li 向外用力
Hsiang-yang (Hupei) 襄陽
hsiang-yueh 鄉約
hsiao 孝
hsiao-chang 校長
Hsiao-chuang shih-yen hsiang-ts'un
　shih-fan hsueh-hsiao (Kiangsu)
　曉莊實驗鄉村師範學校
Hsiao wu 肖吾
hsien-cheng chien-she shih-yen ch'ü
　縣政建設實驗區
hsin chü 新劇
hsin-hai 辛亥
Hsin hsiao-shuo pao 新小說報

Hsin-min ts'ung-pao 新民叢報
hsin p'ai 新派
Hsin-t'ai (Shantung) 新泰
hsin-yung ho-tso-she 信用合作社
hsing-cheng chuan-yuan 行政專員
hsing-shih tsou-jou 行屍走肉
Hsu Chia-chü 徐家菊
Hsu-chia tao-k'ou (Shantung)
　　許家道口
Hsu-kung ch'iao, K'un-shan hsien
　　(Kiangsu) 徐公橋崑山縣
Hsu Ming-hung 徐名鴻
hsuan-chiang so 宣講所
hsueh chih chu-i 學治主義
hsueh-chung 學案
hsueh-hsi 學習
hsun 殉
Hu Tz'u-wei 胡次威
Hua hsien (Kwangtung) 花縣
Huan-hao (Hsin-ming) 煥誥(新銘)
Huan-shen (Chin-ming) 煥紳(謹銘)
Huang T'ien-pa 黃天霸
i 義
I Ching 易經
i kuan chih 一貫之
I-shui (Shantung) 沂水
i to hsiang-jung 一多相融
jang 讓
jen 仁
jen-ch'ing 人情
Jen-hsueh 仁學
jen-lei pen-hsing 人類本性
jen-sheng t'ai-tu 人生態度
Jih-chao (Shantung) 日照
Jui-chin (Kiangsi) 瑞金
k'ai-ming shen-shih 開明紳士
kan-ch'ing 感情
kang 剛
Kao Chien-szu 高踐四
kao-liang 高梁
ko-hsing ti fa-chan 個性的發展
ko-hsing ti shen-chan 個性的伸展
k'o 科
k'o-chi 克己
kua 卦
Kuan-ch'eng (Shantung) 觀城

kuan-chih chu-i 官治主義
kuan-mo-hui 觀摩會
Kuang-te lou 廣德樓
kung 公
Kung Chu-ch'uan 公竹川
kung-ho chien-she t'ao-lun-hui
　　共和建設討論會
kung-hsueh-ch'u 共學處
kung so 公所
kung-yueh 公約
Kuo-fang ts'an-i-hui 國防參議會
Kuo feng pao 國風報
Kuo Hsiao-feng 郭曉峯
kuo-ku 國故
Kuominchün 國民軍
kuo-min ts'an-cheng-hui 國民參政會
kuo-ts'ui (kokushi) 國粹
kuo-yin fu-hao 國音符號
Lan-hsi (Chekiang) 蘭谿
li 禮
Li chi 禮記
li-chiao 禮教
li-chiao ming-chiao 禮教名教
li-chih 立志
li-chih (intellect) 理智
Li Ching-han 李景漢
li fa 禮法
li-hsing 理性
Li Kung-p'u 李公樸
li-shih 理事
li-su 禮俗
li yueh 禮樂
li-yung 利用
Liang Ch'eng-kuang 梁承光
Liang Chung-hua 梁仲華
Liang hsien-jen, Kuo sheng-jen
　　梁賢人，郭聖人
Liang Tsou Mei-mien yun-hsiao ho-
　　tso-she 梁鄒美棉運銷合作社
lien-chuang 聯莊
Lien-huan-t'ao 連環套
lin 鄰
Lin-i (Shantung) 臨沂
Liu-chou (Kwangsi) 柳州
Liu Jen-hang 劉仁航
Liu Shih-p'ei 劉師培

Luan-ch'ing 鑾慶
lun-li-hua 倫理化
lun-li pen-wei she-hui 倫理本位社會
Lung Chi-chih 龍積之
lü 閭
Mei Szu-p'ing 梅思平
Meng Kuang 孟光
Meng-yin (Shantung) 蒙陰
Mi-lo 汨羅
Mi Ti-kang 米廸剛
min-chu-hua 民主化
Min-li pao 民立報
min-tsu ching-shen 民族精神
min-t'uan 民團
min-t'uan kan-pu hsun-lien-so
　民團幹部訓練所
ming-chiao 名教
Ning-yang (Shantung) 寧陽
Nan-yang (Honan) 南陽
Nü-hsueh ch'uan-hsi-so 女學傳習所
nung-ch'ang 農場
nung-ts'un chin-jung liu-t'ung-ch'u
　農村金融流通處
Pa-pu (Kwangsi) 八步
pa tao 霸道
Pai-ch'üan, Hui hsien (Honan)
　百泉，輝縣
Pai P'eng-fei 白鵬飛
pan-chang chih 班長制
pan chu-jen 班主任
P'an An 潘安
pao-an tui 保安隊
pao-chiao 保教
pao-kuo 保國
Pei-p'ei (Szechwan) 北培
P'eng I-sun 彭詒孫
P'eng Tse-min 彭澤民
P'eng Yü-t'ing 彭禹庭
p'in-ch'ing 聘請
Ping-i shih-shih hsieh-chin hui
　兵役實施協進會
P'ing-chiang (Hunan) 平江
pu hsiao yu san, wu hou wei ta
　不孝有三，無後爲大
P'u-hsien (Shantung) 濮縣
"San min chu-i" 三民主義

San niang chiao tzu 三娘教子
Shan hsien (Shantung) 單縣
Shan-tung hsiang-ts'un chien-she yen-
　chiu yuan 山東鄉村建設研究院
Shan-tung sheng min-chung chiao-yü
　fu-tao wei-yuan-hui
　山東省民衆教育輔導委員會
Shang-chuang 上莊
she-hui-hsing ti fa-chan
　社會性的發展
she-hui hsueh-hsiao-hua 社會學校化
she-hui-hua 社會化
shen-ch'a 審察
shen-chih 紳治
Shen pao 申報
Shen Ting-i (Hsuan-lu)
　沈定一（玄盧）
sheng-yuan 生員
sheng-yü 聖諭
shih 士
Shih-jen-p'o (Shantung) 石人坡
shih-shih 事實
shih mu so shih shih shou so chih
　十目所視十手所指
shih-yen ch'ü 實驗區
shih-yen hsien 實驗縣
Shou-chang (Shantung) 壽張
Shou-kuang (Shantung) 壽光
Shun-t'ien 順天
Sun-chia chen (Shantung) 孫家鎮
Sun Ch'un-chai (Fa-hsu) 孫純齋（發
　緒）
Sun Tse-jang 孫則讓
szu 私
Szu-chuang (Shantung) 四庄
Szu-shui (Shantung) 泗水
ta-i-yü 大意欲
ta-t'ung hsiao-i 大同小異
T'ai-erh-chuang (Shantung) 台兒莊
T'an-ch'eng (Shantung) 郯城
tao 道
tao-t'ung 道統
Te yü chien 德育鑑
Ti-ch'iu yun-yen 地球韻言
ti-fang tsu-chih 地方組織
Ti-kuo jih-pao 帝國日報

t'i (essence) 体
t'i (fraternal submission) 悌
t'iao-ho 調和
T'ien Han 田漢
t'ien-li 天理
Ting hsien (Hopei) 定縣
Ting-t'ao (Shantung) 定陶
t'ing 廳
tsa-shui 雜稅
Tsai Feng 載澧
tsao-hui 早會
Ts'ao-hsien (Shantung) 曹縣
Tsi-ning (Chi-ning, Shantung) 濟寧
Tsou hsien (Shantung) 鄒縣
Tsou Ying-wo 鄒應我
Ts'ui Ling-fen 崔靈芬
ts'un 村
Ts'un-chih p'ai 村治派
ts'un-hsueh 村學
ts'un-ku hsueh-t'ang 存古學堂
ts'un li-shih 村理事
ts'un tsu 村組
tsung-ho chih 綜合制
Tsung-ts'ai 總裁
tuchün 督軍
t'u-hao lieh-shen 土豪劣紳
Tui-ching-yü (Shantung) 對經峪
t'uan-t'i sheng-huo 團体生活
tung 動
Tung hsiang (Chekiang) 東鄉
Tung-li-tien (Shantung) 東理店
Tung-p'ing (Shantung) 東平
tung-shih-hui 董事會
Tung-tan erh-t'iao 東單二條
T'ung (Chuang) 僮
t'ung-hsueh hui 同學會
T'ung-i chien-kuo t'ung-chih-hui
　統一建國同志會
T'ung-meng-hui 同盟會
tzu-chi 自己
tzu-chi ken tzu chi ta chia
　自己跟自己打架

tzu-chiu 自救
tzu-li keng-sheng 自立更生
Tzu-yang (Shantung) 滋陽
Wan-p'ing (Hopei) 宛平
Wang I-k'o 王怡柯
Wang Ken (Hsin-chai) 王艮（心齋）
Wang Pi (Tung-yai) 王襞（東厓）
Wang P'ing-shu 王平叔
wang tao 王道
Wei Hsi-ch'in (Wei Chung)
　衞西琴（衞中）
Wei-shih 唯識
wei wo 爲我
Wen ch'ang 文昌
wen-hua 文化
Wen I-to 聞一多
wen-ming hsi 文明戲
Wen-ming yuan 文明園
Wen-shang (Shantung) 汶上
wo 我
Wu-chou (Kwangsi) 梧州
Wu-hsi (Kiangsu) 無錫
Wu-hu 蕪湖
wu lun 五倫
Wu Mi 吳宓
wu so wei erh wei 無所爲而爲
Wu Yung-po 伍庸伯
yang 陽
Yang Yun-fu 楊韻甫
yen-chiu pu 研究部
Yen Hui 顏回
yin 陰
yin (cause) 因
yin ming 因明
yu so wei erh wei 有所爲而爲
yuan 緣
yueh (compact) 約
yueh (music) 樂
Yun-ch'eng (Shantung) 鄆城
yung 用
Yü-t'ai (Shantung) 魚台

Bibliography of Works Cited

Works by Liang Shu-ming appear at the beginning of the bibliography—numbers [1] through [99b]—so the reader may readily identify the numerical note references to Liang's own writings. The names of people with whom I have had extensive interviews concerning the subject of this book appear together at the end of the bibliography. Works by the same author are listed chronologically by date of publication unless they are also included in a subsequently published collection.

Works by Liang Shu-ming

1. Liang Shu-ming 梁漱溟. "Fo li" 佛理 (Essence of Buddhism). [159] 1.10 (October 1915): 18–20.

2. ——— *Yin-tu che-hsueh kai-lun* 印度哲學概論 (Introduction to Indian philosophy). 1919; 3rd ed. Shanghai, 1922; Taipei reprint, 1966.
    a. "Ti-san-pan tzu-hsu" 第三版自序 (Preface to the 3rd edition). Also in [5], pp. 125–128.

3. ——— "Lun hsueh-sheng shih-chien" 論學生事件 (On the student incident). [427], May 18, 1919.

4. ——— *Tung Hsi wen-hua chi ch'i che-hsueh* 東西文化及其哲學 (Eastern and Western cultures and their philosophies). Shanghai, 1922; Taipei reprint, 1968.
    a. "Ti-san-pan tzu-hsu" 第三版自序 (Preface to the 3rd edition).

5. ——— *Shu-ming sa-ch'ien wen-lu* 漱溟卅前文錄 (Writings of Liang Shu-ming before the age of thirty). Shanghai, 1924; Taipei reprint, 1972.
    a. "Chiu-yuan chueh-i lun" 究元決疑論 (On tracing the origin and solving doubts), pp. 1–20. Also [540] 13.5–7 (May–July 1916).
    b. "Wan-Chou Han Wei wen-ch'ao tzu-hsu" 晚周漢魏文鈔自序 (Preface to anthology of writings from late Chou, Han, and Wei dynasties), pp. 21–26. Originally in [159] 1.10 (October 1915): 30–36, under the title "Kuo-wen chiao-k'o ch'ü ts'ai szu-i" 國文教科取材私議 (Personal view on adapting materials for teaching Chinese).
    c. "Yü Chang K'uan-hsi chiu-shih shu" 與張寬谿舅氏書 (Letter to Uncle Chang K'uan-hsi), pp. 27–30. Originally in [159] 1.8: 16–17, under the title "Ju shu" 儒術 (Confucianism).
    d. "Wu hsing t'an" 無性談 (On the concept that 'nothing' has an independent nature of its own), pp. 31–34. Originally in [540] 14.5 (May 15, 1917): 100–102.
    e. "*Szu-fa li-kuei* hsu" 「司法例規」序 (Preface to *Judicial handbook*

[by Chang Yao-tseng]), pp. 35–36.

f. "Chung-hua hsueh-yu-hui hsuan-yen" 中華學友會宣言 (Remarks at the China Scholars Society), pp. 37–38.

g. "Wu-ts'ao pu-ch'u ju ts'ang-sheng ho?" 吾曹不出如蒼生何? (What can the people do if we do not set out?), pp. 39–56. Originally published as a pamphlet. Also [533], n.s. 1.1 (June 1, 1930): Fu-lu, pp. 1–14.

h. "Ta Ch'en Chung-fu hsien-sheng shu" 答陳仲甫先生書 (Answer to Ch'en Chung-fu [Ch'en Tu-hsiu]), pp. 57–64. Originally in [286] 6.4 (Apr. 15, 1919):427–431.

i. "I-ko jen ti sheng-huo" 一個人的生活 (An individual's life), pp. 65–68. Originally in [476], no. 3 (March 1919).

j. "Ta Ch'en Chia-ai lun Yin-ming shu" 答陳嘉藹論因明書 (Answer to Ch'en Chia-ai's discussion on the Hetuvidyā), pp. 69–75. Originally in [283], no. 5 (1919).

k. "Li Ch'ao nü-shih chui-tao-hui yen-shuo" 李超女士追悼會演說 (Speech at the memorial service for Miss Li Chao), pp. 76–78. Also in [4], pp. 188–190.

m. "Tsung-chiao wen-t'i chiang-yen" 宗教問題講演 (Lecture on the question of religion), pp. 79–96. Originally in [476] 2.8, 2.11, 3.1 (February, May, August 1921); also [4], pp. 89–105.

n. "Wei-shih-chia yü Po-ko-sen" 唯識家與柏格森 (Wei-shih Buddhism and Bergson), pp. 97–102. Originally in [440] 3.1 (December 1921):1–6.

p. "Tui-yü Lo-su chih pu-man" 對於羅素之不滿 (My dissatisfactions with Russell), pp. 103–106. Originally in [209], 1921.

q. "Tung Hsi jen ti chiao-yü pu-t'ung" 東西人的教育不同 (Differences in the education of Easterners and Westerners), pp. 107–112. Originally in *Chiao-yü tsa-chih*, 1922; also in [23], pp. 1–5.

r. "Ho-li ti jen-sheng t'ai-tu" 合理的人生態度 (A reasonable philosophy of life), pp. 113–116.

s. "Shen chu *Chia-t'ing hsin-lun* hsu" 沈著「家庭新論」序 (Preface to Shen's *New discussion on the family*), pp. 117–124.

t. "P'ing Hsieh chu 'Yang-ming hsueh-p'ai'" 評謝著陽明學派 (Critique of Hsieh's writings on 'Wang Yang-ming's school'), pp. 129–145.

6. ———"Pa chi" 跋記 (Postscript). In [404], chüan 1.

7. ———"P'u hou chi" 譜後記 (Postscript to the biography [of Liang Chi]). In [404], chüan 1.

8. ———"Ching ta Ch'en Chia-i hsien-sheng" 敬答陳嘉異先生 (Rejoinder to Mr. Ch'en Chia-i). [533], n.s. 1.1 (June 1, 1930):1–5.

9. ———*Shu-ming sà-hou wen-lu* 漱溟卅後文錄 (Writings of Liang Shu-ming after the age of thirty). Shanghai, 1930; Taipei reprint, 1971.

a. "Huai-t'an chiang-yen chih i tuan" 槐壇講演之一段 (One lecture of the locust tree platform), pp. 1–12. Originally in [533], n.s. 1.1 (June 1, 1930): Fu-lu, pp. 14–18.

b. "Che pien shih wo-ti jen-sheng-kuan" 這便是我的人生觀 (This is my view of life), pp. 13–18.

c. "Ta Hu p'ing *Tung Hsi wen-hua chi ch'i che-hsueh*" 答胡評「東西文化及其哲學」(Answering Hu Shih's criticism of *Eastern and Western cultures and their philosophies*), pp. 19–54. Originally in [298], Nov. 13, 14, 1923.

d. "Wu-ch'ai tang ho wei?" 吾儕當何爲 (What should we do?), pp. 55–70.

e. "Pan-hsueh i-chien shu-lueh" 辦學意見述略 (Outline for education), pp. 71–86. Also in [23], pp. 96–110.

f. "Ch'ung-hua shu-yuan chien-chang" 重華書院簡章 (Regulations of Chung-hua school), pp. 87–91. Also in [23], pp. 108–110.

g. "*Kuei-lin Liang hsien-sheng i-shu* hsu-mu" 「桂林梁先生遺書」叙目 (Annotated bibliography of the *Collected writings of Mr. Liang of Kweilin*), pp. 93–96.

h. "Szu ch'in chi" 思親記 (Thoughts on my father), pp. 97–104. Also in [404], chüan 1.

i. "Wei Chung hsien-sheng tzu-shu t'i-hsu" 衞仲先生自述題序 (Preface to Mr. Westharp's autobiography), pp. 105–112.

j. "*Jen-hsin yü jen-sheng* ch'u-pan tzu-hsu" 「人心與人生」初版自序 (Preface to the 1st edition of *Psychology and life*), pp. 113–120.

k. "Chieh-shao Wei Chung hsien-sheng hsueh-shuo" 介紹衞仲先生學說 (Introducing Mr. Westharp's theories on education), pp. 121–143.

m. "Pao-ch'ien—k'u-t'ung—i-chien yu-hsing-wei ti shih" 抱歉—苦痛——件有興味的事 (Regret—sorrow—a matter of interest), pp. 145–169. Also in [23], pp. 131–154.

n. "Chin-hou i-chung kai-tsao ti fang-hsiang" 今後一中改造的方向 (The direction of the First middle school reforms from now on), pp. 171–188. Also in [23], pp. 114–130.

p. "Ju-ho ch'eng-kung chin-t'ien ti wo" 如何成功今天的我 (How my thought and personality were formed), pp. 189–214. Also in [47], app., pp. 139–152.

q. "Pei-yu so-chien chi-lueh" 北游所見紀略 (Record of what I saw during my travels to the North), pp. 215–273. Originally in [533], o.s. 1.4 (June 15, 1929). Also in [11], pp. 257–288.

r. "Ho-nan ts'un-chih hsueh-yuan chih-ch'ü-shu" 河南村治學院旨趣書 (Aims of the Honan village government academy), pp. 275–290. Originally in [533], o.s. 1.9 (Nov. 5, 1929); also in [11], pp. 289–297; [23], pp. 162–170; [534], pp. 10–19.

10. ———"Tui-yü Tung-sheng shih-chien chih kan-yen" 對於東省事件之感言 (Sincere words on the Manchurian incident). [501], Oct. 7, 1931.

11. ———*Chung-kuo min-tsu tzu-chiu yun-tung chih tsui-hou chueh-wu* 中國民族自救運動之最後覺悟 (Final awakening of the Chinese people's self-salvation movement). 3rd ed. Shanghai, 1932; Taipei reprint,

1971.

a. "Chu-pien pen-k'an chih tzu-pai" 主編本刊之自白 (Personal statement on assuming the editorship of this publication), pp. 1–2. Originally in [533], n.s. 1.1 (June 1, 1930).

b. "Chung-kuo min-tsu tzu-chiu yun-tung chih tsui-hou chueh-wu," pp. 27–100. Originally in [533], n.s. 1.2–4 (June 16, July 1, 16, 1930).

c. "Wo-men cheng-chih shang ti ti-i-ko pu-t'ung ti lu—Ou-chou chin-tai min-chu cheng-chih ti lu" 我們政治上的第一個不通的路—歐洲近代民主政治的路 (First road that will not work for us politically—the European road of modern political democracy), pp. 101–142. Originally in [533], n.s. 1.3, 1.6, 1.7 (July 1, Sept. 1, Sept. 16, 1930).

d. "Wo-men cheng-chih shang ti ti-erh-ko pu-t'ung ti-lu—E-kuo kung-ch'an-tang fa-ming ti lu" 我們政治上的第二個不通的路—俄國共產黨發明的路 (Second road that will not work for us politically—the road discovered by the Russian Communist party), pp. 143–176. Originally in [533], n.s. 2.5, 2.9/10, 2. 11/12 (Sept. 8, 1931, May 15, Sept. 5, 1932).

e. "Chung-kuo wen-t'i chih chieh-chueh" 中國問題之解決 (Solution for China's problems), pp. 177–192. Originally in [533], n.s. 1.8, 2.9/10 (Oct. 1, 1930, May 15, 1932).

f. "Kan-kao chin chih yen ti-fang tzu-chih che" 敢告今之言地方自治者 (Warning to those who now talk of local self-government), pp. 193–206. Originally in [533], n.s. 2.1, 2.2, 2.3 (Dec. 1, 1930, June 18, July 15, 1931). Also in [16].

g. "Shan-tung hsiang-ts'un chien-she yen-chiu-yuan she-li chih-ch'ü chi pan-fa kai-yao" 山東鄉村建設研究院設立旨趣及辦法概要 (Outline of purposes and methods for establishing the Shantung rural reconstruction research institute), pp. 207–216. Originally in [533], n.s. 1.11/12 (Nov. 16, 1932); also in [23], pp. 171–190; [272] 1.19/20 (Apr. 11, 1932):2–12.

h. "Tan-mai chiao-yü yü wo-men ti chiao-yü" 丹麥教育與我們的教育 (Danish education and our education), pp. 217–256. Originally in [533], n.s. 2.6, 2.8 (Oct. 31, 1931; Jan. 5, 1932); also [23], pp. 37–70.

i. "Mien-jen chai tu-shu lu" 勉仁齋讀書錄 (Notes from Mien-jen studio), pp. 299–323. Originally in [533], n.s. 1.2, 1.10 (June 16, Nov. 10, 1930).

j. "Tao Wang Hung-i hsien-sheng" 悼王鴻一先生 (Mourning Mr. Wang Hung-i), pp. 325–331. Originally in [533], n.s. 1.5 (Aug. 16, 1930).

k. "Ching i ch'ing-chiao Hu Shih-chih hsien-sheng" 敬以請教胡適之先生 (May I be enlightened by Mr. Hu Shih-chih), pp. 333–342. Originally in [533], n.s. 1.2 (June 16, 1930).

m. "'Chien-she hsin-she-hui ts'ai suan ko-ming' ta Ch'ing Chung chün" 「建設新社會才算革命」答晴中君 ("Only the construction of a new society can be considered revolution"—answer to Mr. Ch'ing Chung), pp. 343–350. Originally in [533], n.s. 1.3 (July 1, 1930).

n. "Ta Ma Ju-hsing chün lai-shu" 答馬儒行君來書 (Answer to Ma Ju-hsing's letter), pp. 351–354.

p. "Ching-ta Yen Ching-chai hsien-sheng" 敬答嚴敬齋先生 (Answer to Mr. Yen Ching-chai), pp. 363–365. Originally in [533], n.s. 2.4 (Aug. 12, 1931).

12. ———Ts'un-hsueh hsiang-hsueh hsu-chih 村學鄉學須知 (Essential knowledge about hsiang and village schools). Tsou-p'ing, 1933 (pamphlet). Also in [14], pp. 105–124; [23], pp. 221–249.

13. ———"Shan-tung hsiang-ts'un chien-she yen-chiu-yuan kung-tso pao-kao" 山東鄉村建設研究院工作報告 (Report on the work of the Shantung rural reconstruction research institute). Speech in Tsou-p'ing, July 15, 1933. Published in [274], I, 31–38.

14. ———Hsiang-ts'un chien-she lun-wen-chi, ti-i-chi 鄉村建設論文集第一集 (Collection of writings on rural reconstruction, first series). Tsou-p'ing, 1934.

a. "Tzu-shu" 自述 (Self-account) pp. 1–36.

b. "Ch'ing ta-chia yen-chiu she-hui wen-t'i" 請大家研究社會問題 (Please, everyone study the social problems), pp. 37–44. Originally in [533], n.s. 3.4 (Mar. 15, 1934).

c. "Chieh-chueh Chung-kuo ching-chi wen-t'i chih t'e-shu k'un-nan" 解決中國經濟問題之特殊困難 The unique difficulties in solving Chinese economic problems), pp. 44–47.

d. "Chung-kuo tz'u-k'o shang-pu-tao yu hsien-fa ch'eng-kung ti shih-hou" 中國此刻尚不到有憲法成功的時候 (China has not yet reached the stage where it can have a successful constitution), pp. 47–51. Also in [501] (Shanghai), Jan. 4, 1934.

e. "Yu hsiang-ts'un chien-she i fu-hsing min-tzu an" 由鄉村建設以復興民族案 (Proposal for national revival through rural reconstruction), pp. 52–62.

f. "Chien-she yü peng-k'uei" 建設與崩潰 (Construction and destruction), pp. 62–65.

g. "I-feng kung-k'ai ti hsin" 一封公開的信 (An open letter), pp. 66–70.

h. "Hsiang-ts'un chien-she shih shen-ma?" 鄉村建設是什麼？(What is rural reconstruction?), pp. 70–75.

i. "Jen-lei she-hui chien-she ying-yu ti yuan-tse" 人類社會建設應有的原則 (Necessary principles for reconstructing human society), pp. 75–79. Also in [23], pp. 33–36.

j. "Hsiang-ts'un chien-she li-lun t'i-kang" 鄉村建設理論提綱 (Outline of rural reconstruction theory), pp. 79–89.

k. "Tsai Chung-kuo ts'ung-ch'ien li-shih-shang yu wu hsiang-ts'un tzu-chih?" 在中國從前歷史上有無鄉村自治？(Has there been village self-government in Chinese history?), pp. 89–95.

m. "Hsien-cheng chien-she shih-yen ch'ü shih-yen chi-hua hsu-yen" 縣政建設實驗區實驗計劃緒言 (Statement on the experimental plan for experimental-district hsien government reconstruction), pp. 95–96.

n. "Tsou-p'ing hsien hsien-cheng chien-she shih-yen ch'ü chi-hua chai-lu" 鄒平縣縣政建設實驗區計劃摘錄 (Outline of plan for Tsou-p'ing hsien government experimental area), pp. 96–104.

p. "Hsiang-nung hsueh-hsiao ti pan-fa chi ch'i i-i" 鄉農學校的辦法及其意義 (Methods and significance of rural schools), pp. 125–134. Originally in [272] 1.16 (Jan 1, 1933); also in [23], pp. 191–200.

q. "She-hui pen-wei ti chiao-yü hsi-t'ung ts'ao-an" 社會本位的教育系統草案 (Draft proposal for social education), pp. 135–154. Also in [23], pp. 201–220.

r. "Wo ti i-tuan hsin-shih" 我的一段心事 (A personal concern), pp. 196–206. Also in [501], Aug. 31, 1934; [23f].

15. ———"Shan-tung hsiang-ts'un chien-she yen-chiu-yuan chi Tsou-p'ing shih-yen hsien kung-tso pao-kao" 山東鄉村建設研究院及鄒平實驗縣工作報告 (Work report on the Shantung rural reconstruction research institute and Tsou-p'ing experimental hsien). Speech in Ting hsien, Hopeh, Oct. 10, 1934. Published in [274], II, 177–178.

16. ———Chung-kuo chih ti-fang tzu-chih wen-t'i 中國之地方自治問題 (Problem of China's local self-government). Tsou-p'ing, 1935. Also in [14], pp. 155–196.

17. ———"Hsiang-ts'un chien-she chih-ch'ü" 鄉村建設旨趣 (Purposes and objectives of rural reconstruction). [502], no. 25 (Jan. 6, 1935).

18. ———"Tsou-p'ing nung-ts'un chin-jung liu-t'ung-ch'u ti kung-tso" 鄒平農村金融流通處的工作 (Work of Tsou-p'ing rural finance and credit centers). [502], no. 50 (June 30, 1935).

19. ———"Pan ts'un-hsueh ti mu-piao" 辦村學的目標 (Objectives in operating village schools). [272] 5.1 (Aug. 16, 1935).

20. ———"I-nien-lai ti Shan-tung kung-tso" 一年來的山東工作 (This past year's work in Shantung). Speech in Wu-hsi, Kiangsu, Oct. 10, 1935. Published in [274], III, 293–302.

21. ———"Ts'un-hsueh ti tso-fa" 村學的做法 (Methods of village schools). [272] 5.5 (Oct. 16, 1935).

22. ———"Hsu yen" 序言 (Preface). [272] 5.8/9 (Dec. 5, 1935):1–2.

23. ———Liang Shu-ming hsien-sheng chiao-yü wen-lu 梁漱溟先生教育文錄 (Mr. Liang Shu-ming's writings on education). Ed. T'ang Hsien-chih. Tsi-nan and Tsou-p'ing, 1935; Taipei reprint, 1972.

a. "Tu-wei chiao-yü che-hsueh chih ken-pen kuan-nien" 杜威教育哲學之根本觀念 (Basic idea of Dewey's philosophy of education), pp. 6–23. Also [272] 4.6 (1934).

b. "K'ung-tzu hsueh-shuo chih ch'ung-kuang" 孔子學說之重光 (Revival of the doctrines of Confucius), pp. 24–32. Also [272]

4.5 (1934).

c. "Ching-shen t'ao-lien yao-chih" 精神陶鍊要旨 (Essence of spiritual cultivation), pp. 67–95. Also [272] 4.7/8 (1934).

d. "Mu-ch'ien Chung-kuo hsiao-hsueh chiao-yü fang-chen chih shang-chueh" 目前中國小學教育方針之商榷 (Discussion on the direction of present Chinese primary education), pp. 155–161.

e. "Ts'un-hsueh hsiang-hsueh shih-i" 村學鄉學釋義 (Explanation of village and hsiang schools), pp. 241–252. Also [272] 3.25/26 (1934).

f. "Kuan-yü ts'un-hsueh hsiang-hsueh ti chiang-yen i" 關於村學鄉學的講演一 (First lecture on village and hsiang schools), pp. 253–261. Also [272] 4.3 (1934).

g. "Kuan-yü ts'un-hsueh hsiang-hsueh ti chiang-yen erh" 關於村學鄉學的講演二 (Second lecture on village and hsiang schools), pp. 262–268. Also [272] 4.4 (1934).

h. "Hsiang-ts'un ch'ing-nien ti hsun-lien wen-t'i" 鄉村青年的訓練問題 (Problems in training rural youth), pp. 269–280.

i. "Min-chung chiao-yü ho-i neng-chiu Chung-kuo?" 民眾教育何以能救中國 (How can mass education save China?), pp. 281–289.

j. "She-hui chiao-yü yü hsiang-ts'un chien-she chih ho-liu" 社會教育與鄉村建設之合流 (Convergence of social education and rural reconstruction), pp. 290–297. Also [272] 4.9 (1934).

24. ——"Hsiang-ts'un kung-tso chung i-ko tai yen-chiu tai shih-yen ti wen-t'i—ju-ho shih Chung-kuo-jen yu t'uan-t'i tsu-chih" 鄉村工作中一個待研究待試驗的問題 — 如何使中國人有團體組織 (A rural work problem awaiting research and experimentation—how to make the Chinese have group organizations). [502], no. 66 (Jan. 1, 1936).

25. ——*Hsiang-ts'un chien-she ta-i* 鄉村建設大意 (Gist of rural reconstruction). Tsou-p'ing, 1936.

26. ——"Kung szu pien—ta Wu Ching-chou chün" 公私辨—答吳景洲君 (Distinguishing between public and private—answer to Mr. Wu Ching-chou). [272] 5.13 (Mar. 1, 1936).

27. ——"Tung yu kuan-kan chi-lueh" 東遊觀感記略 (Impressions from a trip to Japan). [272] 6.1 (Aug. 16, 1936).

28. ——"Wo-men ying yu ti hsin-hsiung t'ai-tu" 我們應有的心胸態度 (The attitude we should have in our hearts). [272] 5.20 (June 16, 1936).

29. ——"Chung-kuo min-chung ti tsu-chih wen-t'i" 中國民眾的組織問題 (The problem of organizing the Chinese masses). [272] 5.20 (June 16, 1936).

30. ——"Chi ko wen-t'i ti t'ao-lun" 幾個問題的討論 (Discussion of some problems). [272] 6.1 (Aug. 16, 1936).

31. ——"Min-chung chiao-yü lu-hsien wen-t'i" 民眾教育路線問題 (The question of the general line in mass education). [272] 6.1 (Aug. 16, 1936).

32. ——"Chung-kuo she-hui kou-tsao wen-t'i" 中國社會構造問題 (The

question of China's social structures). [272] 6.3 (Sept. 16, 1936).

33. ———"Wo-men tang-ch'ien ti min-tsu wen-t'i" 我們當前的民族問題
(Our present national problem). [272] 6.4 (Oct. 1, 1936).

34. ———"Erh-shih-wu nien kuo-ch'ing chi-nien" 二十五年國慶紀念
(Commemoration of the twenty-fifth national day). [272] 6.5 (Oct.
16, 1936).

35. ———"Fei-ch'ang shih-ch'i hsiao-hsueh chiao-shih ti tse-jen" 非常時期
小學教師的責任 (Responsibilities of primary school teachers in this
extraordinary age). [272] 6.6 (Nov. 1, 1936).

36. ———"Wo-men tui shih-chü ti t'ai-tu" 我們對時局的態度 (Our
attitude toward the current situation). [272] 6.10 (Jan. 1, 1937).

37. ———"Chui-tao Wang Ping-ch'eng hsien-sheng" 追悼王柄程先生
(Memorial to Mr. Wang Ping-ch'eng). [272] 6.12 (Mar. 1, 1937).

38. ———Hsiang-ts'un chien-she li-lun 鄉村建設理論 (Theory of rural reconstruction). Tsou-p'ing, 1937.

39. ———"Wo-men ti liang ta nan-ch'u" 我們的兩大難處 (Our two great
difficulties). [272] 6.14 (Apr. 1, 1937). Also [38], appendix.

40. ———"Tsen-yang yueh-tu Hsiang-ts'un chien-she li lun" 怎樣閱讀「鄉
村建設理論」(How to read The theory of rural reconstruction). [272]
6.19 (June 16, 1937).

41. ———"Wo-men tsen-yang ying-fu tang-ch'ien ta-chan?" 我們怎樣應
付當前大戰? (How should we deal with the great war facing us?).
[501] (Shanghai), Aug. 11, 12, 1937. Also [272] 7.1 (Aug. 16, 1937).

42. ———Articles in Szu-ch'uan chiao-yü 四川教育 (Szechwan education).
1.7/8 (August 1937).

a. "Lueh-shu hsiang-ts'un chien-she yun-tung yao-chih" 略述鄉村
建設運動要旨 (Brief description of the essentials of the rural
reconstruction movement), pp. 9–11.

b. "Chung-kuo chin-jih hsu-yao na-i chung chiao-yü" 中國今日
需要那一種教育 (What kind of education does China need today), pp. 12–15.

c. "Ju-ho tso hsing-cheng yen-chiu yü ts'ung-shih ti-fang hsing-
cheng?" 如何做行政研究與從事地方行政 (How should we study
government administration and how shall we carry out local
government administration?), pp. 16–18.

d. "Wo-men tsai Shan-tung ti kung-tso" 我們在山東的工作 (Our
work in Shantung), pp. 18–25.

e. "Chung-kuo jen ti ch'ang-ch'u yü tuan-ch'u" 中國人的長處與短
處 (Strengths and weaknesses of Chinese), pp. 26–32.

f. "Chung-kuo ching-chi chien-she ti lu-hsien" 中國經濟建設的路線
(The line of Chinese economic reconstruction), pp. 33–40.

g. "Chin hsieh nien lai yin-hang-chieh tui-yü nung-ts'un t'ou-tzu ti
yu-lai" 近些年來銀行界對於農村投資的由來 (Origins of com-
mercial bank investments in rural villages in recent years), pp. 41–
44.

h. "Shan-tung hsiang-ts'un kung-tso ti chin-chan" 山東鄉村工作

的進展 (Development of Shantung rural work), pp. 45–47.

i.   "Chung-kuo chin-nien-lai she-hui-shang chi-ko ch'ü-shih" 中國
近年來社會上幾個趨勢 (Several social tendencies that have
appeared in China in the past several years), pp. 48–51.

j.   "Ch'ing-nien yü shih-tai" 青年與時代 (Youth and the age),
pp. 51–54.

k.   "Ju-ho ch'uang-tsao Chung-kuo ti hsin hsueh-shu" 如何創造中國
的新學術 (How to create a new Chinese scholarship), pp. 54–59.

m.   "Chung-kuo ho-i yao t'an hsiang-ts'un chien-she" 中國何以要談
鄉村建設 (Why must China concern itself with rural reconstruction), pp. 59–60.

n.   "Ju-ho k'ang-ti" 如何抗敵 (How to resist the enemy), pp. 61–
66. Republished as pamphlet, Wuchang, 1938.

43. ———"K'ang-ti chih-nan" 抗敵指南 (Guidebook for resistance). n.p.,
n.d. (probably March 1938). Pamphlet.

44. ———"Kao Shan-tung hsiang-ts'un kung-tso t'ung-jen t'ung-hsueh
shu" 告山東鄉村工作同仁同學書 (Letter to my Shantung rural
work colleagues and students). n.p., 1938. Pamphlet.

45. ———"Li-hsing" 理性 (Rationality). [112] 2.3 (Apr. 10, 1939).

46. ———"Ch'ing-nien hsiu-yang wen-t'i" 青年修養問題 (Question of
self-cultivation among the young). Tu-shu t'ung-hsun 讀書通訊 (Reader's correspondence), no. 3 (June 1, 1940).

47. ———Chao hua 朝話 (Morning talks). 2nd ed. Changsha, 1941. (Collection of lectures, most of which were previously published in [272],
1935–1937.)

48. ———"Chung-kuo wen-hua wen-t'i" 中國文化問題 (The question of
Chinese culture). Min-tsu wen-hua 民族文化 (National culture), no. 2
(May 31, 1941).

49. ———"K'ai-ch'ang ti hua" 開場的話 (Preamble). [360], Sept. 18,
1941.

50. ———"Ts'ung chiu-i-pa chi-nien erh yu-ti lien-hsiang" 從九一八紀念
而有的聯想 (Some thoughts on the anniversary of the September 18
incident). [360], Sept. 18, 1941.

51. ———"Wo nu-li ti shih shen-ma" 我努力的是什麼 (My endeavors),
nos. 1–46. [360], Sept. 18—Nov. 3, 1941.

52. ———"Min-chu shih shen-ma, shen-ma shih min-chu" 民主是什麼,
什麼是民主 (What is democratic). [360], Sept. 20, 1941.

53. ———"Chung-kuo min-chu yun-tung ti chang-ai chiu tsai ho ch'u?"
中國民主運動的障碍究在何處 (Where, after all, are the obstacles
to the Chinese democratic movement?). [360], Sept. 21, 1941.

54. ———"Tsai wu-jen i-sheng chung ti ch'ing-nien ch'i" 在吾人一生中
的青年期 (Time of youth in our lives). [360], Sept. 21, 1941.

55. ———"Chung-kuo wen-hua ti liang ta t'e-cheng" 中國文化的兩大特
徵 (Two special characteristics of Chinese culture). [360], Sept. 22–
Sept. 30, 1941.

56. ———"Min-chu chang-ai wen-t'i—ta Hung Su hsien-sheng" 民主障碍

問題一答洪素先生 (Obstacles to democracy—answer to Mr. Hung Su). [360], Sept. 26, 1941.

57. ———"Cheng-chih shang ti min-chu ho Chung-kuo-jen" 政治上的 民主和中國人 (Political democracy and the Chinese). [360], Sept. 30—Nov. 8, 1941.

58. ———"Ta Hu Ho-nien hsien-sheng, ta Tung Tung hsien-sheng" 答胡 鶴年先生，答冬冬先生 (Answers to Messrs. Hu Ho-nien and Tung Tung). [360], Oct. 4, 1941.

59. ———"Ta Ch'iao Tzu-ming hsien-sheng" 答喬子銘先生 (Answer to Mr. Ch'iao Tzu-ming). [360], Oct. 8, 1941.

60. ———"Ts'ung kuo-min ts'an-cheng-hui shuo-tao min-i chi-kuan" 從國民參政會說到民意機關 (Discussion of public opinion institutions in view of the political consultative council). [360], Nov. 12, Dec. 13, 1941.

61. ———"Shang nien kuo-min ta-hui chih yen-ch'i" 上年國民大會之延 期 (Last year's postponement of the national assembly). [360], Nov. 14, 1941.

62. ———"Tsai lun kuo-min ts'an-cheng hui" 再論國民參政會 (Another comment on the political consultative council). [360], Nov. 19, 1941.

63. ———"Ta kuo-hsun-she chi-che wen" 答國訊社記者問 (Answering questions from the national news service). [360], Nov. 19, 1941.

64. ———"Ching-ta Ku Fang hsien-sheng" 敬答孤芳先生 (Rejoinder to Mr. Ku Fang). [360], Nov. 19, 1941.

65. ———"Lun cheng-chih tou-cheng" 論政治鬪爭 (On political struggle). [360], Dec. 6, 7, 1941.

66. ———"Chi-nien Ts'ai hsien-sheng" 紀念蔡先生 (In memory of Mr. Ts'ai). [574] 2.1 (March 1942):4-7.

67. ———"Hsien-cheng chien-chu tsai shen-ma shang-mien?" 憲政建築 在什麼上面 (Upon what basis should constitutional government be built?). [501], May 1, 1944.

68. ———"Pa-nien nu-li hsuan-kao chieh-shu" 八年努力宣告結束 (Announcement at the end of eight years of endeavor). [501], Feb. 8, 1946.

69. ———"Wo chin-hou chih-li chih so-tsai?" 我今後致力之所在 (What shall I apply myself to from now on?). [501], Feb. 18, 1946.

70. ———"Chiu fou-chueh-ch'uan wen-t'i: fa-piao t'an-hua" 就否決權 問題：發表談話 (Opinion on the question of veto power). [221], Oct. 7, 1946.

71. ———Wo ti tzu-hsueh hsiao-shih 我的自學小史 (Short account of my self-education). Shanghai, 1947.

72. ———"Shu-li hsin-yung, li-ch'iu ho-tso" 樹立信用，力求合作 (Establish credibility, earnestly strive for cooperation). [356] 2.1 (Mar. 1, 1947):3-5.

73. ———"Kuan-yü Chung-kuo cheng-chü chih Ch'u An-p'ing hsien-sheng" 關於中國政局致儲安平先生 (Letter to Mr. Ch'u An-p'ing concerning the Chinese political situation). [356] 2.4 (Mar. 22, 1947).

74. ———"Chung-kuo wen-hua t'e-cheng chih yen-chiu" 中國文化特徵

之研究 (Study of the special characteristics of Chinese culture). [356] 2.5-7 (Mar. 29, Apr. 5, 12, 1947).

75. ———"Chung-kung lin-mo wei-ho chü-chueh ho-t'an" 中共臨末爲何拒絕和談 (Why the Chinese Communists, at the last minute, refuse to talk peace). [356] 2.15 (June 7, 1947):3-4.

76. ———"Yü-kao hsuan-tsai, chui-lun hsien-cheng" 預告選災，追論憲政 (Prophesying disaster if there is an election; resurrecting the debate on constitutional government). [356] 3.4-5 (Sept. 20, 27, 1947).

77. ———"Lueh-lun Chung-kuo cheng-chih wen-t'i—ta Chang Fei erh hsien-sheng" 略論中國政治問題 — 答張費二先生 (Brief discussion of the Chinese political question—answer to Messrs. Chang and Fei). [356] 3.14 (Nov. 29, 1947):9-11.

78. ———"Tao-nien T'ao Hsing-chih hsien-sheng" 悼念陶行知先生 (In memory of Mr. T'ao Hsing-chih). In [515], pp. 152-154.

79. ———"Kei ko-fang p'eng-yu i-feng kung-k'ai ti hsin" 給各方朋友一封公開的信 (Open letter to my friends on all sides). [501], Feb. 11, 1949.

80. ———"Ching-kao Chung-kuo kung-ch'an-tang" 敬告中國共產黨 (Advice to the Chinese Communist Party). [501], Feb. 21, 1949.

81. ———"Lun ho-t'an chung ti i-ko nan-t'i" 論和談中的一個難題 (Difficult problem in the peace talks). [501], Feb. 21, 1949.

82. ———"Chung-kuo na t'ien neng t'ai-p'ing?" 中國那天能太平？(When can China have peace?), [501]. Mar. 3, 1949.

83. ———"Mien-jen wen-hsueh-yuan ch'uang-pan yuan-ch'i chi chih-ch'ü—Tai fa-k'an-tz'u" 勉仁文學院創辦緣起及旨趣 — 代發刊詞 (Origin and purpose of the Mien-jen academy). In [432].

84. ———"Li-hsing—jen-lei ti t'e-cheng" 理性 — 人類的特徵 (Rationality—the special characteristic of humankind). In [432].

85. ———"Ta hsueh chiao-yü—hsin shih-yen—t'an Mien-jen hsueh-yuan ti li-hsiang" 大學教育 —新試驗— 談勉仁學院的理想 (University education—a new experiment—on the ideals of the Mien-jen academy). [501], May 18, 1949.

86. ———Chung-kuo wen-hua yao-i 中國文化要義 (Essence of Chinese culture). Shanghai, 1949.
    a. "Tzu-hsu" 自序 (Preface).

87. ———"Kuo-ch'ing-jih ti i-p'ien lao-shih-hua" 國慶日的一篇老實話 (Some honest talk on national day). [575], Oct. 1, 1950. Also [185].

88. ———"Liang-nien-lai wo yu-le na-hsieh chuan-pien" 兩年來我有了那些轉變 (Changes I have undergone during the past two years). [359], Oct. 5, 1951. Also [501] (Hong Kong), Oct. 6, 1951.

89. ———"Hsin-ts'ung Chung-kuo Kung-ch'an-tang ti ling-tao ping kai-tsao tzu-chi" 信從中國共產黨的領導並改造自己 (I trust and follow the leadership of the Chinese Communist Party while I am reforming myself). [333], Nov. 2, 1951. Also [501] (Hong Kong), Nov. 3, 1951.

90. ———Letter to T'ang Chun-i. Dated Dec. 31, 1951. (In Mr. T'ang's

possession.)

91. ———"Ching-ta szu-chiao ti chi-wei hsien-sheng" 敬答賜教的幾位先
      生 (Rejoinder to several gentlemen who have instructed me). [359],
      Jan. 10, 1952.

92. ———"Ho Szu-yuan hsien-sheng wen-nei chiang-tao wo ti hua pu-ho
      shih-shih" 何思源先生文內講到我的話不合事實 (What Mr. Ho
      Szu-yuan's essay said about me does not accord with the facts). [359],
      Jan. 18, 1952.

93. ———Letters to Hu Ying-han.
      a. Dated Sept. 14, 1953.
      b. Dated Dec. 30, 1956.

94. ———"Kao Tai-wan t'ung-pao" 告台灣同胞 (Letter to my fellow
      countrymen in Taiwan). [333], Feb. 3, 1955. Also [289], no. 3 (1955).

95. ———"Liang Shu-ming t'an chi-nien-lai kan-hsiang" 梁漱溟談幾年
      來感想 (Liang Shu-ming gives his impressions of the past several
      years). [359], Feb. 7, 1956. Also [333], Feb. 8, 1956; [501] (Hong
      Kong), Feb. 25, 1956.

96. ———and Ch'en Ching-tang 陳敬堂. "Ts'un-cheng wen-ta" 村政問答
      (Dialogue on village government). In [534], pt. 3, pp. 35–40.

97. ———and Chou Hsin-min 周新民. Li Wen an tiao-ch'a pao-kao shu 李聞
      案調查報告書 (Report after investigating the case of Messrs. Li
      and Wen). Nanking, 1946.

98. ———and Hu Shih. "Kuan-yü 'Wo-men tsou na i t'iao lu?'" 關於「我
      們走那一條路」(Discussion of "Which road shall we follow?"). [291b]
      3.1 (July 29, 1930). Also [533] 1.5.

99a. ———[Liang Huan-ting 梁煥鼎] and Liang Huan-nai 梁煥鼐. "Kuei-
      lin Liang hsien-sheng i-shu hsu" 桂林梁先生遺書序 (Preface to
      Collected writings of Mr. Liang of Kweilin). In [404], chüan 1.

99b. ———"Nien-p'u" 年譜 (Chronological biography [of Liang Chi]).
      In [404], chüan 1.

Works by other authors

100. Agrarian China: Selected Source Material. Chicago: University of Chicago
      Press, 1938.

101. Ai Szu-ch'i 艾思奇. P'i-p'an Liang Shu-ming ti che-hsueh szu-hsiang 批判梁漱
      溟的哲學思想 (Critique of Liang Shu-ming's philosophical thought).
      Peking, 1956.

102. Beal, John Robinson. Marshall in China. Garden City, N.Y.: Doubleday &
      Co., 1970.

102a. Benda, Julien. Sur le succes du Bergsonisme: Précédé d'un réponse aux défenseurs
      de la doctrine. Paris: Mercure de France, 1914.

103. Bergson, Henri. Matière et Memoire. Paris: F. Alcan, 1908.

104. ———L'Evolution creatrice. Paris: F. Alcan, 1909.

105. ———La perception du changement. Oxford: Clarendon Press, 1911.

106. ———La pensée et le mouvant: Essais conférences. Paris: F. Alcan, 1934.

107. Boorman, Howard, ed. Biographical Dictionary of Republican China. 4 vols.

New York: Columbia University Press, 1967–1971.

108. Briere, O., S.J. *Fifty Years of Chinese Philosophy*. Trans. Laurence G. Thompson. London: George Allen and Unwin, 1956.

109. British Foreign Office. *Tsinan Intelligence Reports*, 228/3140—228/3277. 1919–1925.

110. Carlson, Evans. "The Chinese Army, Its Organization and Military Efficiency." Mimeo. New York: International Secretariat, Institute of Pacific Relations, 1939.

111. *Chai-ch'eng ts'un-chih* 翟城村誌 (Chai-ch'eng village history). Ed. I Chung-ts'un 伊仲村. n.p., 1925; Taipei reprint, 1966.

112. *Chan-shih wen-hua* 戰時文化 (Wartime culture). Chungking, 1938–1939. Monthly.

113. Chan Wing-tsit. *Religious Trends in Modern China*. New York: Columbia University Press, 1953.

114. Chang Carsun [Chang Chün-mai]. *The Third Force in China*. New York: Bookman Associates, 1952.

115. Chang Chih-min 張志敏. "P'ing Liang Shu-ming hsien-sheng ti hsiang-ts'un chien-she li-lun chih fang-fa wen-t'i" 評梁漱溟先生的鄉村建設理論之方法問題 (Critique of the methodological problems of Mr. Liang Shu-ming's rural reconstruction theory). In [174], pp. 172–190.

116. Chang Chih-tung 張之洞. *Chang Wen-hsiang-kung ch'üan-chi* 張文襄公全集 (Complete works of Chang Chih-tung). Ed. Wang Shu-t'ung 王樹枏. Peiping, 1928.

117. Chang Chün-mai 張君勱. *Ming-jih chih Chung-kuo wen-hua* 明日之中國文化 (Chinese culture of tomorrow). Shanghai, 1936; Taipei reprint, 1966.

118. ———"Hsi-fang hsueh-shu szu-hsiang tsai wo-kuo chih yen-pien chi ch'i ch'u-lu" 西方學術思想在我國之演變及其出路 (Development and future of Western thought and scholarship in China). *Hsin Chung Hua* 新中華 (New China) 5.10 (May 25, 1937):33–37.

119. ———"Jen-sheng-kuan" 人生觀 (Philosophy of life). In [352], vol. 1.

120. Chang Fo-ch'uan 張佛泉. "Ts'ung li-hsien t'an-tao she-hui kai-tsao" 從立憲談到社會改造 (From establishing a constitution to discussing social reform). [535], no. 101 (May 20, 1934).

121. Chang Ling-kuang 張凌光. "P'i-p'an Liang Shu-ming ti fan-tung chiao-yü szu-hsiang" 批判梁漱溟的反動教育思想 (Critique of Liang Shu-ming's reactionary educational thought). [332], no. 69 (Jan. 9, 1956).

122. Chang Shih-chao 章士釗. "Nung kuo pien" 農國辯 (On agrarianism). [291a] 1.5 (Nov. 3, 1923):6.

123. ———"Nung chih i" 農制翼 (Agrarian rule). [159] 1.5:6.

124. ———"Hsin chiu" 新舊 (New and old). [159] 1.7:9.

125. Chang T'ieh-chün 張鐵君. *Wu-szu yun-tung lun-ts'ung* 五四運動論叢 (Collection of essays on the May Fourth movement). Taipei, 1961.

126. Chang Tung-sun 張東蓀. "Ching-ta Fan Hung hsien-sheng" 敬答樊弘

先生 (Rejoinder to Mr. Fan Hung). [356] 3.16 (Jan. 3, 1948).

127. Chang Yao-tseng 張耀曾. "Tu *Kuei-lin Liang hsien-sheng i-shu* hou-hsu" 讀桂林梁先生遺書後序 (Postscript to *Collected writings of Mr. Liang of Kweilin*). In [404], chüan 4.

128. Chang Yu-i 章有义, ed. *Chung-kuo chin-tai nung-yeh-shih tzu-liao* 中國近代 農業史資料 (Materials on modern Chinese agricultural history). 3 vols. Peking, 1957.

129. Chang Yuan-shan 章元善. "Nung-ts'un yun-tung chih chin-jih" 農村 運動之今日 (Present condition of the rural movement). [535], no. 128 (Nov. 25, 1935):6-7.

130. Chang Yun-ch'uan 張雲川. "Tsou-p'ing chih nung-min fu-tan" 鄒平 之農民負擔 (The peasants' burden in Tsou-p'ing). [502], nos. 27-28 (Jan. 20, 28, 1935).

131. Ch'ang Yen-sheng 常燕生. "Tung Hsi wen-ming wen-t'i chih Hu Shih-chih hsien-sheng" 東西文明問題質胡適之先生 (Questioning Mr. Hu Shih-chih on Eastern and Western civilizations). *Hsien-tai p'ing lun* 現代評論 (Contemporary critic) 4.90-91 (Aug. 28, Sept. 4, 1926).

132. Chao Ju-heng 趙如珩. *Ti-fang tzu-chih chih li-lun yü shih-chi* 地方自治之理 論與實際 (Theory and reality of local self-government). Shanghai, 1933.

133. *Che-hsueh* 哲學 (Philosophia). Peking, 1921-24. Quarterly; later monthly.

134. Ch'en Ch'i-t'ien 陳啓天. *Chi yuan hui-i lu* 寄園回憶錄 (Recollections of Ch'en Ch'i-t'ien). Taipei, 1965.

136. Ch'en Chia-ai 陳嘉藹. "Yin-ming ch'ien-shuo" 因明淺說 (Layman's explanation of hetuvidyā). [283] 1.3 (March 1919).

137. Ch'en Chia-i 陳嘉異. "Tung-fang wen-hua yü wu-jen chih ta-jen" 東方文化與吾人之大任 (Eastern culture and our major responsibility). [540] 18.1-2 (Jan. 10, 25, 1921).

138. Ch'en Ch'uan-kang 陳傳綱. "Ch'üan-kuo nung-ts'un kung-tso-che ta t'uan-chieh ti meng-ya" 全國農村工作者大團結的萌芽 (Beginnings of cohesive organization among the nation's rural workers). [218], no. 13 (Mar. 20, 1938).

139. Ch'en Heng-che 陳衡哲. "Tsai lun tzu-sha" 再論自殺 (Another discussion on suicide). In [293], pp. 159-160.

140. Ch'en Hsu-ching 陳序經. "Hsiang-ts'un wen-hua yü tu-shih wen-hua" 鄉村文化與都市文化 (Rural culture and urban culture). [535], no. 126 (Nov. 11, 1935):12-18.

141. ———*Chung-kuo wen-hua ti ch'u-lu* 中國文化的出路 (The way out for Chinese culture). Shanghai, 1934.

142. ———"Hsiang-ts'un chien-she yun-tung ti chiang-lai" 鄉村建設運動 的將來 (Future of the rural reconstruction movement). [535], no. 196 (Apr. 20, 1936):2-7.

143. ———"Hsiang-ts'un chien-she li-lun ti chien-t'ao" 鄉村建設理論的檢 討 (Review of rural reconstruction theories). [535], no. 199 (May 3, 1936):13-18.

144. ———"Tung Hsi wen-hua kuan" 東西文化觀 (Views on Eastern and Western cultures). [412] 5.1 (July 1936):90–98.

145. ———"Hsiang-ts'un chien-she yun-tung p'ing-i" 鄉村建設運動平議 (Balanced appraisal of the rural reconstruction movement). [448] 1.1 (1938).

146. ———"Hsuan-chü hsien-cheng yü Tung Hsi wen-hua" 選舉憲政與東西文化 (Elected constitutional government and Eastern and Western cultures). [478] 2.23/24, 3.1/2 (Dec. 6, 1947, Jan. 10, 1948).

147. Ch'en I 陳一. "Hsien-tai Chung-kuo chih nung-ts'un chien-she shih-yen yun-tung chi ch'i ch'ien-t'u" 現代中國之農村建設實驗運動及其前途 (Modern Chinese rural reconstruction and experimental movement and its future prospects). [211] 12.13 (1937).

148. Ch'en, Jerome. *Mao and the Chinese Revolution.* London: Oxford University Press, 1965.

149. Ch'en Shou-i 陳受頤. "Hsi-yang Han-hsueh yü Chung-kuo wen-ming" 西洋漢學與中國文明 (Sinology in the West and Chinese civilization). [535], no. 198 (April 1936):8–11.

150. Ch'en Teng-yuan 陳登原. *Chung-kuo wen-hua-shih* 中國文化史 (Cultural history of China). 2 vols. Taipei reprint, 1966.

151. Ch'en Tu-hsiu 陳獨秀. "Ching-kao ch'ing-nien" 警告青年 (Warning to youth). [286] 1.1 (Sept. 15, 1915).

152. ———"Tung Hsi min-tsu ken-pen szu-hsiang chih ch'a-i 東西民族根本思想之差異 (Basic differences in the thought of Easterners and Westerners). [286] 1.4 (December 1915).

153. ———"Tui-yü Liang Chü-ch'uan hsien-sheng tzu-sha chih kan-hsiang" 對於梁巨川先生自殺之感想 (Some thoughts on Mr. Liang Chü-ch'uan's [Liang Chi] suicide). [286] 6.1 (Jan. 15, 1919):19–20.

154. ———"T'ai-ko-erh yü Tung-fang wen-hua" 泰戈爾與東方文化 (Tagore and Oriental culture). *Chung-kuo ch'ing-nien* 中國青年 (China's youth), no. 219 (Apr. 18, 1924):1–2.

155. Ch'en Tuan-chih 陳端之. *Wu-szu yun-tung ti p'ing-chia shih* 五四運動的評價史 (Historical evaluation of the May Fourth movement). Shanghai, 1935.

156. *Cheng-chih hsieh-shang hui-i shih-mo chi* 政治協商會議始末記 (Complete record of the political consultative conference). Ed. Ch'in Huan-chang 秦綬章 and Wu Po-ch'ing 吳伯卿. Changsha, 1946.

157. *Chi-nan chih-nan* 濟南指南 (Guide to Tsinan). Tsinan, 1914.

158. Chia I-chün 賈逸君. *Wu-szu yun-tung chien-shih* 五四运动简史 (Brief history of the May Fourth movement). Peking, 1951.

159. *Chia-yin tsa-chih* 甲寅雜誌 (Tiger magazine). 1914–1916, 1922–1925.

160. Chiang Chün-chang 蔣君章. *Chung-hua min-kuo chien-kuo shih* 中華民國建國史 (History of the Chinese republic's nation-building). 1934; Taipei, 1957.

161. Chiang Fu-tsung 姜扶宗. "Chui-nien Ts'ai hsien-sheng" 追念蔡先生 (Reminiscences about Mr. Ts'ai [Yuan-p'ei]). In [526], pp. 1493–1494.

162. Chiang Heng-yuan 江恆源 . *Nung-ts'un kai-chin ti li-lun yü shih-chi* 農村改進的理論與實際 (Theory and reality of rural reform). Shanghai, 1935.

163. Chiang T'ing-fu 蔣廷黻, trans. "Chung-kuo ti chiao-yü" 中國的教育 (Chinese education [by Tawney]). [535], no. 38 (Feb. 19, 1933).

164. *Chiang tsung-t'ung chüan* 蔣總統傳 (Biography of president Chiang). 3 vols. Taipei, 1954.

165. Chiang Yü-lung 江毓龍 . "Yu kan yü Liang Shu-ming hsien-sheng ti pei-fen chih yin" 有感於梁漱溟先生的悲憤之音 (Feelings about news of Mr. Liang Shu-ming's grief and resentment). *Tsu-kuo chou-k'an* 祖國週刊 (Fatherland weekly), no. 171 (Apr. 9, 1956):11–12.

166. *Chiao-hsueh yü yen-chiu* 教學與研究 (Education and research). 1954–1955.

167. Chiao-yü shih-chiao yen-chiu-tsu pien 教育史教研究組編 (Teaching and research section of educational history). *Chung-kuo chin-tai hsien-tai chiao-yü shih* 中國近代現代教育史 (History of modern and contemporary Chinese education). Vol. 1. Peking, 1957.

168. *Chieh-fang jih-pao* 解放日報 (Liberation daily). June 1945—February 1947.
    a. "Chieh-fang jih-pao chi-che Hai Leng Liu Mo-ping fang-wen Liang Shu-ming hsien-sheng" 解放日報記者海稜劉漠冰訪問梁漱溟先生 (*Liberation daily* reporters Hai Leng and Liu Mo-ping interview Mr. Liang Shu-ming). Mar. 16, 1946.
    b. "Liang Shu-ming k'ang-i tang-chü an-sha tsui-hsing" 梁漱溟抗議當局暗殺罪行 (Liang Shu-ming protests assassinations by the authorities). July 20, 1946.

169. *Chien-kuo jih-pao* 建國日報 (National reconstruction daily). Kweilin, 1942–1944.

170. Ch'ien Chia-chü 千家駒 . "Chung-kuo ti ch'i-lu: p'ing Tsou-p'ing hsiang-ts'un chien-she yun-tung chien lun Chung-kuo kung-yeh-hua wen-t'i" 中國的歧路：評鄒平鄉村建設運動兼論中國工業化問題 (The wrong road for China: critique of the Tsou-p'ing rural reconstruction movement with discussion of China's industrialization problems). In [174], pp. 123–149.

171. ———"Chung-kuo nung-ts'un ti ch'u-lu tsai na-li?" 中國農村的出路在那裡？ (Where is the way out for China's villages?). In [174], pp. 89–95.

172. ———"P'i-p'an Liang Shu-ming chien-ch'ih Chung-kuo lo-hou fan-tui kung-yeh-hua ti miu-lun" 批判梁漱溟堅持中國落後反對工業化的謬論 (Criticism of Liang Shu-ming's erroneous views that oppose industrialization and maintain China's backwardness). In [409], I, 41–48. Also [333], Aug. 10, 1955; [289], September 1955.

173. ———"Liang Shu-ming ti hsiang-ts'un chien-she yun-tung chiu-ching wei shei fu-wu?" 梁漱溟的鄉村建設运动究竟為誰服務？ (Whom did Liang Shu-ming's rural reconstruction movement really serve?). In [409], I, 49–56. Also [323], no. 9 (1955); [299], September 1955;

[289], September 1955.

174. ———and Li Tzu-hsiang, eds. *Chung-kuo hsiang-ts'un chien-she p'i-p'an* 中國鄉村建設批判 (Critique of Chinese rural reconstruction). Shanghai, 1936.

175a. Ch'ien Mu 錢穆. *Chung-kuo wen-hua yü k'o-hsueh* 中國文化與科學 (Chinese culture and science). Taipei, 1970.

175b. ———*Chung-kuo wen-hua ts'ung-t'an* 中國文化叢談 (Talks on Chinese culture). 2 vols. Taipei, 1970.

176. Ch'ien Tuan-sheng. *The Government and Politics of China.* Cambridge, Mass.: Harvard University Press, 1950.

177. Chih Fei 知非. "P'ing Liang Shu-ming chün hsueh-sheng shih-chien lun" 評梁漱溟君學生事件論 (Critique of Mr. Liang Shu-ming's remarks on the student incident). [427], May 18, 1919.

178. Chih Sheng 芝生. "Hsiang-ts'un yun-tung chih cheng-chih ti i-i" 鄉村運動之政治的意義 (Political significance of the rural movement). [535], no. 60 (July 23, 1933):7–10.

179. *Chin-jih* 今日 (Today). 1.1—1.5 (May—July 1933). Irregular.

180. *Chin-jih p'ing-lun* 今日評論 (Today's critic). Kunming, 1.1—2.7 (1938–1940).

181. *Chin-jih shih-chieh* 今日世界 (Today's world). Hong Kong, 1952–1956. Daily.

182. *Chin-jih ta-lu* 今日大陸 (Today's mainland). Taipei, 1952–1961. Fortnightly.

183. Chin K'o-mu 金克木. "P'i-p'an Liang Shu-ming kuan-yü Yin-tu wen-hua ho che-hsueh ti miu-lun" 批判梁漱溟關於印度文化和哲學的謬論 (Critique of Liang Shu-ming's erroneous theory on Indian culture and philosophy). In [409], II, 50–66. Also [285], November 1955.

184. Chin Lun-hai 金倫海. *Nung-ts'un fu-hsing yü hsiang-chiao yun-tung* 農村復興與鄉教運動 (Rural revival and the rural education movement). Shanghai, 1934.

185. *Chin-pu jih-pao* 進步日報 (Progress daily).

186. Chin Ta-k'ai 金達凱. *Chung-kung p'i-p'an Hu Shih szu-hsiang yen-chiu* 中共批判胡適思想研究 (Study of Chinese Communist criticism of Hu Shih). Hong Kong, 1956.

187. ———"Chung-kuo wen-hua ti k'an-k'o—lun Chung-kung tui Liang Shu-ming szu-hsiang p'i-p'an 中國文化的坎坷 — 論中共對梁漱溟思想的批判 (The bad luck of Chinese culture—discussion of Chinese Communist criticism of Liang Shu-ming's thought). [436] 7.2 (Jan. 20, 1956).

188. Ch'in Ching 秦鏡. "Liang Shu-ming tsai tsao ch'ing-suan" 梁漱溟再遭清算 (Settling accounts again with Liang Shu-ming). [436] 6.11 (June 5, 1955).

189. *China White Paper, The.* Intro. Lyman P. Van Slyke. 2 vols. Stanford: Stanford University Press, 1967. Reissue of *United States Relations with China with Special Reference to the Period 1944–1949.* Dept. of State Publication 3573, Far Eastern Series 30. Washington, D.C., 1949.

190. "Chinese Scholars' Tribulations." *Far Eastern Economic Review* 13.20 (Nov. 27, 1952):679–681.

191. *Ching-shih wai-ch'eng hsun-ching tsung-t'ing ti-i-tz'u t'ung-chi shu* 京師外城巡警總廳第一次統計書 (Police department statistics for the Chinese city of Peking, first compilation). Peking, 1907.

192. *Ching-shih wai-nei-ch'eng hsun-ching tsung-t'ing t'ung-chi shu* 京師外內城巡警總廳統計書 (Police department statistics for the Chinese and Manchu cities of Peking). Peking, 1908.

193. *Ch'ing shih kao* 清史稿 (Draft history of the Ch'ing dynasty). Ed. Chao Erh-hsun 趙爾巽 et al. Mukden, 1937.

194. Chou Ching-wen 周鯨文. *Feng-pao shih-nien* 風暴十年 (Ten years of storm). Hong Kong, 1959.

195. Chou Fu-ch'eng 周輔成. "Liang Shu-ming tsen-yang hsuan-ch'uan fan-tung wen-hua che-hsueh" 梁漱溟怎樣宣傳反动文化哲学 (How Liang Shu-ming propagated a reactionary cultural philosophy). [409], II, 106–122. Also [501], Oct. 22, 1955.

196. Chou Shao-hsien 周紹賢. "Hsien-hua Liang Shu-ming hsien-sheng" 閒話梁漱溟先生 (Random talk about Mr. Liang Shu-ming). [288], no. 2 (July 1, 1969):44–48.

197. ———"T'an Liang Shu-ming hsien-sheng chih szu-hsiang" 談梁漱溟先生之思想 (On Mr. Liang Shu-ming's thought). [288], nos. 4–7, 9, 10 (October–December 1969, January, March, April 1970).

198. Chow Tse-tsung. *The May Fourth Movement: Intellectual Revolution in Modern China.* Cambridge, Mass.: Harvard University Press, 1960.

199. Chu Ch'ao-jan 祝超然. "Tsou-p'ing kung-hsueh-ch'u shih-ch'a-chi" 鄒平共學處視察記 (Record of an inspection of Tsou-p'ing's study centers). [272] 6.1 (Aug. 16, 1936).

200. [Chu] Ch'ao-jan and [?] T'ien-p'ei 天培. "Tui Tsou-p'ing chiao-yü hsien-chuang ti hsun-shih" 對鄒平教育現狀的巡視 (Inspection of present educational conditions in Tsou-p'ing). [272] 6.11 (Mar. 1, 1937).

201. Chu Hsi 朱熹. "Tseng-shan Lü shih hsiang-yueh" 增刪呂氏鄉約 (Emendation of the village covenant of Mr. Lü). In Shen Chieh-fu 沈節甫, ed. *Yu-ch'un lu* 由醇錄 (Texts by which can be gained pure simplicity). 1.1–7b.

202. Chu Po-k'un 朱伯崑. "P'i-p'an Liang Shu-ming hsien-sheng ti wen-hua-kuan" 批判梁漱溟先生的文化觀 (Critique of Mr. Liang Shu-ming's cultural viewpoint). In [409], I, 145–165. Also [289], no. 10 (1955).

203. Chu Wu-shan 朱悟禪. "Pei-ta erh-shih-wu chou-nien chi-nien-jih 'min-i ts'e-liang' chih fen-hsi" 北大二十五週年紀念日「民意測量」之分析 (Analysis of the Peking university twenty-fifth anniversary "public opinion survey"). *Hsin min-kuo* 新民國 (New republic) 1.4 (1924).

204. Chuang Tse-hsuan 莊澤宣. "Tsou-p'ing hsiang-ts'un chien-she ti chin-k'uang chi ch'i tung-hsiang" 鄒平鄉村建設的近況及其動向 (Recent situation and general direction of Tsou-p'ing's rural reconstruction). [540] 32.1 (Jan. 1, 1935).

205. Chueh t'ang 覺堂 [Liu Hsin-huang 劉心皇]. "Kuan-yü Liang Shu-ming" 關於梁漱溟 (Concerning Liang Shu-ming). *Hsin sheng-pao* 新生報 (New life; Taiwan), Nov. 11, 1970, p. 9.

206. *Chueh-wu* 覺悟 (Awakening). Shanghai, 1924. Weekly supplement to *Min-kuo jih-pao* 民國日報 (Republic daily).

207. *Chung-cheng jih-pao* 中正日報 (Chung-cheng daily). Kweilin, 1942–1944.

208. *Chung-hua chiao-yü chieh* 中華教育界 (Chinese educational community). Shanghai, 1912–1932. Monthly.
   a. "Liang Shu-ming hsien-sheng shu Shan-tung hsiang-ts'un chien-she yen-chiu-yuan chih kung-tso" 梁漱溟先生述山東鄉村建設研究院之工作 (Mr. Liang Shu-ming describes the work of the Shan-tung rural reconstruction research institute). 20.4 (October 1932).

209. *Chung-hua hsin-pao* 中華新報 (New China news). Shanghai, 1921. Daily.

210. *Chung-hua tsa-chih* 中華雜誌 (China magazine). Taipei, 1970–1977. Monthly.

211. *Chung-kuo chien-she* 中國建設 (China's reconstruction). Kweilin, 1937–1938. Monthly.

213. *Chung-kuo chin-tai shih ts'ung-shu* 中國近代史叢書 (Collection of materials on modern Chinese history). Ed. The China modern history writing and editing group. Shanghai, 1973.

214. *Chung-kuo ch'ing-nien chün-jen-she* 中國青年軍人社 (Society of young Chinese soldiers). n.p., 1934.

215. *Chung-kuo hsiao tang-p'ai hsien-k'uang* 中國小黨派現況 (Present situation of minor Chinese political parties). "Secret." n.p., 1946.

216. *Chung-kuo hsueh-pao* 中國學報 (China journal). Peiping, 1944.

217. *Chung-kuo ko tang-p'ai hsien-k'uang* 中國各黨派現況 (Present situation of China's various political parties). "Secret." n.p., 1946.

218. *Chung-kuo nung-ts'un* 中國農村 (China's villages). Nanchang, Kiangsi, 1935–1938. Fortnightly.

219. *Chung-kuo tang-p'ai* 中國黨派 (Chinese political parties). Nanking, 1948.

220. *Chung-shan jih-pao* 中山日報 (Chung-shan daily). Wuchow, Kwangsi, 1942–1944.

221. *Chung-yang jih-pao* 中央日報 (Central daily news). Nanking, 1930–1936, 1946–1947; Chungking, 1940–1947; Taipei, 1950–1960.

222. *Chung Yü-jen* 鍾宇人. "P'i-p'an Liang Shu-ming ti chu-kuan wei-hsin-lun che-hsueh szu-hsiang" 批判梁漱溟的主观唯心論哲学思想 (Critique of Liang Shu-ming's subjective idealist philosophical thought). In [409], II, 138–147. Also [359], Sept. 21, 1955; [166], no. 10 (October 1955).

223. [Ch'ü] Chü-nung [瞿] 菊農. "Chin-nien ti hsiang-ts'un chien-she yun-tung" 今年的鄉村建設運動 (Rural reconstruction movement this year). [501], Jan. 1, 1935.

224. Ch'ü Chü-nung. "Hsiang-ts'un chien-she yun-tung chih kuo-ch'ü yü chiang-lai" 鄉村建設運動之過去與將來 (Past and future of the rural reconstruction movement). [573], Jan. 21, 1944.

225. ———"Liang Shu-ming teng so-wei 'hsiang-ts'un chien-she yun-tung'

shih wei shen-ma jen fu-wu ti?" 梁漱溟等所謂鄉村建設運動是爲甚
么人服務的 (Who was served by the so-called 'rural reconstruction
movement' of Liang Shu-ming and such people?). [333], Nov. 10,
1955. Also [289], December 1955.

226. *Ch'üan-p'an hsi-hua yen-lun-chi* 全盤西化言論集 (Collection of public
statements on the question of wholesale westernization). Canton, 1934.

227. *Ch'üan-p'an hsi-hua yen-lun-chi, hsu-chi* 全盤西化言論集,續集 (Second
collection of public statements on wholesale westernization). Canton,
1935.

228. Clopton, Robert, ed. *John Dewey: Lectures in China 1919–1920.* Honolulu:
University of Hawaii Press, 1973.

229. "Democracy vs. One-Party Rule in Kuomintang China: The Little
Parties Organize." *Amerasia,* Apr. 25, 1943, pp. 97–117.

230. Dorris, Carl E. "Resistance in the Shansi-Chahar-Hopei Border Region,
1938–1945." Ph.D. dissertation, University of Kansas, 1975.

231. Durkheim, Emile. *Le Suicide. Etude de sociologie.* Paris: F. Alcan, 1897.

232. ———*Le Socialisme: sa définition, ses débuts, la doctrine Saint-Simoninenne.*
Paris: F. Alcan, 1928.

233. E Shih 惡石 (pseudonym). "Tse Liang Shu-ming" 責梁漱溟 (Repri-
mand to Liang Shu-ming). [206], Apr. 21, 1924.

234. Eliot, T.S. *Notes toward the Definition of Culture.* New York: Harcourt,
Brace and Co., 1949.

235. Erikson, Erik H. *Young Man Luther.* New York: W.W. Norton and Co.,
1962.

236. Fan Ch'ing-p'ing 范清平. "Lun wen-hua lei-hsing san fen-fa" 論文化類
型三分法 (On the trichotomy of culture types). [436] 7.20 (Oct.
16, 1956):545–552.

237. Fan Hung 樊弘. "Wo tui-yü Chung-kuo cheng-chih wen-t'i ti ken-pen
k'an-fa" 我對於中國政治問題的根本看法 (My basic viewpoint about
China's political problems). [356] 3.14 (Nov. 29, 1947).

238. ———"Yü Liang Shu-ming Chang Tung-sun liang hsien-sheng lun
Chung-kuo ti wen-hua yü cheng-chih" 與梁漱溟張東蓀兩先生論中
國的文化與政治 (Discussing China's culture and politics with Messrs.
Liang Shu-ming and Chang Tung-sun). [356] 3.18 (Dec. 27, 1947).

239. Fan Yun-ch'ien 范雲遷. "Ho-tse ch'eng-li nung-min yin-hang ch'u-i"
菏澤成立農民銀行芻議 (My opinion on establishing peasant banks
in Ho-tse). [502], nos. 40–41 (Apr. 21, 28, 1935).

240. Feng Jui 馮銳. "P'ing-min chiao-yü ti nung-yeh kai-chin" 平民教育
的農業改進 (Agricultural reforms of the popular education movement). [284a] 2.9–10 (July, September 1926).

241. ———"P'ing-chiao tsung-hui yü hsing-pan hsiang-ts'un p'ing-min
sheng-chi chiao-yü chih li-yu fang-fa chi hsien-chuang" 平教總會與興
辦鄉村平民生計教育之理由方法及現狀 (Methods and present con-
ditions of the mass education movement and its management of rural
popular economic education). *Chiao-yü tsa-chih* 教育雜誌 (Education
journal) 19.9 (September 1927).

242. ——— "Ho-nan ts'un-chih hsueh-yuan t'ui-kuang nung-yeh chi-hua" 河南村治學院推廣農業計劃 (Agricultural extension work plan of the Honan village government academy). [533], o.s. 1.19 (Feb. 15, 1929).

243. Fu Ssu-nien 傅斯年. "Chung-kuo hsueh-shu-chieh szu-hsiang-chieh chih chi-pen wu-miu" 中國學術界思想界之根本誤謬 (Basic fallacy of Chinese academic intellectual circles). [286] 4.4 (Apr. 15, 1918).

244. ——— "Yin-ming ta cheng" 因明答諍 (Rebuttal on Hetuvedyā). [283] 1.5 (May 1, 1919). Also *Fu Ssu-nien collected works*. 8 vols. Taipei, 1967. II, 333–334.

245. Fu T'ung 傅銅. "Chih-pu-k'o-erh-wei chu-i chih-pu-k'o erh-an chu-i yü chin-i an-ming chu-i" 知不可而爲主義知不可而安主義與盡義安命主義 (Philosophies that advocate acting although one knows there is no chance of success; taking a resigned attitude when one knows there is no chance of success; and acting according to one's duty but accepting whatever fate decrees). [133], no. 9 (May 1926):1–12.

246. Fung Yu-lan 馮友蘭. "Yü Yin-tu T'ai-ko-erh t'an-hua" 與印度太戈爾談話 (A chat with India's Tagore). [283] 3.1:1–2.

247. ——— "Pei-ta huai-chiu-chi" 北大懷舊記 (Reminiscences of Peking university). In [457], pp. 21–26.

248. ——— *Szu-shih-nien ti hui-ku* 四十年的回顧 (A look back at forty years). Peking, 1959.

249. ——— "Lun pi-chiao Tung Hsi" 論比較東西 (On comparing East and West). [300] 3.19:1–6.

250. ——— "P'i-p'an Liang Shu-ming hsien-sheng ti wen-hua-kuan ho 'ts'un-chih' li-lun" 批判梁漱溟先生的文化觀和村治理論 (Critique of Liang Shu-ming's view on culture and his theory of village government). In [409], I, 3–10. Also [333], May 11, 1955; [285], no. 9 (1955).

251. *Gendai Chūgoku jinmei jiten* 現代中國人物大字典 (Biographical dictionary of modern Chinese). Tokyo, 1964.

252. *Gendai Chūgoku shisō ronsō* 現代中國思想論爭 (Controversies in modern Chinese thought). Tokyo, 1957.

253. Grieder, Jerome B. *Hu Shih and the Chinese Renaissance: Liberalism in the Chinese Revolution, 1917–1937*. Cambridge, Mass.: Harvard University Press, 1970.

254. Guillermaz, Jacques. *A History of the Chinese Communist Party, 1921–1949*. Trans. Anne Destenat. New York: Random House, 1972.

255. Halbwachs, Maurice. *Les causes du suicide*. Paris: F. Alcan, 1930.

256. Hashikawa Tokio 橋村時雄. *Chūgoku bunkakai jinbutsu sōkan* 中國文化界人物總鑑 (Biographical dictionary of Chinese cultural personages). Peiping, 1940.

257. Hay, Stephen N. *Asian Ideas of East and West: Tagore and His Critics in Japan, China and India*. Cambridge, Mass.: Harvard University Press, 1970.

258. Hayford, Charles. "Rural Reconstruction in China." Ph.D. dissertation, Harvard University, 1973.

259. Ho, Franklin L. "Rural Economic Reconstruction in China." *Nankai Social and Economic Quarterly* 9.2 (July 1936).

260. Ho Ju-pi 何汝璧 . "P'i-p'an Liang Shu-ming fou-jen chieh-chi ho chieh-chi tou-cheng ti fan-tung kuan-tien" 批判梁漱溟否認階級和階級鬪爭的反動觀點 (Critique of Liang Shu-ming's reactionary view of denying class and class struggle). In [409], II, 187–197. Also [359], Oct. 19, 1955.

261. Ho Lin 賀麟 . *Tang-tai Chung-kuo che-hsueh* 當代中國哲學 . (Chinese philosophy in the present age). Taipei reprint, 1954.

262. ———"Liang-tien p'i-p'an, i-tien fan-hsing" 兩點批判，一點反省 (Two points of criticism, one for introspection). [333], Jan. 19, 1955.

263. ———"P'i-p'an Liang Shu-ming ti chih-chueh chu-i" 批判梁漱溟的直覺主义 (Critique of Liang Shu-ming's intuitionism). In [409], I, 95–113. Also [285], August 1955; [289], September 1955.

264. Ho Ping-jan 何炳然 . "Liang Shu-ming ti fan-tung li-lun shih, wei shei fu-wu ti?" 梁漱溟的反动理論是为誰服务的？(Who did Liang Shu-ming's reactionary theory serve?). In [409], II, 210–217. Also [359], Oct. 21, 1955.

265. ———"Liang Shu-ming ho Hu Shih ti li-shih wei-shin chu-i kuan-tien i-mo hsiang-t'ung" 梁漱溟和胡適的歷史唯心主义观点一脉相通 (Liang Shu-ming's and Hu Shih's idealist historical outlooks are closely related). [359], Dec. 20, 1955.

266. Ho Szu-yuan 何思源 . "Liang Shu-ming so pan ti hsiang-ts'un chien-she yen-chiu-yuan" 梁漱溟所辦的鄉村建設研究院 (The rural reconstruction research institute run by Liang Shu-ming). [359], Jan. 10, 1952.

267. ———"Chieh-ch'uan Liang Shu-ming ti fan-tung pen-chih" 揭穿梁漱溟的反動本質 (Exposing the reactionary fundamental character of Liang Shu-ming). In [409], II, 198–209. Also [501], Oct. 19, 1955; [289], no. 11 (1955).

268. Ho Yü-sheng 何育生 . "Chieh-chueh Chung-kuo ching-chi wen-t'i ying tsou ti lu" 解決中國經濟問題應走的路 (The road to be taken to solve China's economic problems). [535], no. 131.

269. Holcombe, Arthur N. *The Chinese Revolution*. Cambridge, Mass.: Harvard University Press, 1930.

270. ———*The Spirit of the Chinese Revolution*. New York: Alfred A. Knopf, 1930.

271. *Hsiang-kang shih-pao* 香港時報 (Hong Kong times). 1951–1956. Daily.

272. *Hsiang-ts'un chien-she* 鄉村建設 (Rural reconstruction). Tsou-p'ing, Shantung, 1.1—7.1 (June 1930—August 1937).
   a. *Hsiang-nung hsueh-hsiao chuan-hao* 鄉農學校專號 (Special issue on peasant schools), 1.21 (July 21, 1932).
      1. "Shan-tung hsiang-ts'un chien-she yen-chiu-yuan hsueh-sheng hsia hsiang fu-wu kung-yueh 山東鄉村建設研究院學生下鄉服務公約 (Covenants of Shantung rural reconstruction research institute students going to the villages to serve), pp. 1–2.

b. "Pen-yuan hsiang-ts'un fu-wu chih-tao ch'u ch'eng-li ching-kuo chi ch'i tsu-chih" 本院鄉村服務指導處成立經過及其組織 (Founding and organization of our institute's rural service guidance office), 2.6 (Sept. 21, 1932):3–8.

c. "Nei-cheng-pu wei-jen ti-fan tzu-chih ch'ou-pei wei-yuan" 內政部委任地方自治籌備委員 (Ministry of interior appoints preparatory committee on local self-government), 2.6 (Sept. 21, 1932):8.

d. "Shen Ting-i hsien-sheng chi ch'i chu-pan ti hsiang-ts'un tzu-chih" 沈定一先生及其主辦的鄉村自治 (Mr. Shen Ting-i and his rural self-government program), 2.7/8 (Oct. 11, 1932): 1–10.

e. "Nei-cheng-pu tz'u-chang Kan Nai-kuang yü Liang Shu-ming hsien-sheng chih t'an-hua" 內政部次長甘乃光與梁漱溟先生之談話 (Talks between Vice-minister of interior Kan Nai-kuang and Mr. Liang Shu-ming), 2.7/8 (Oct. 11, 1932):32.

f. "Chiang wei-yuan-chang yueh Liang Shu-ming hsien-sheng fu E" 蔣委員長約梁漱溟先生赴鄂 (Chairman Chiang invites Mr. Liang Shu-ming to visit Hupeh), 2.9 (Oct. 21, 1932):21.

g. "Liang Shu-ming hsien-sheng ch'u-fa hsun-hui" 梁漱溟先生出發巡廻 (Mr. Liang Shu-ming sets out on an inspection trip), 2.9 (Oct. 21, 1932):22.

h. *Ti-erh-chieh nung-p'in chan-lan-hui chuan-hao* 第二屆農品展覽會專號 (Special issue on second agricultural products fair), 2.10/11/12/13/14 (Dec. 11, 1932).

i. "Liang Shu-ming hsien-sheng ch'u-hsi nei-cheng hui-i" 梁漱溟先生出席內政會議 (Mr. Liang Shu-ming attends ministry of interior conference), 2.15 (Dec. 21, 1932):15.

j. "Liang yuan-chang yü Liang Shu-ming hsien-sheng yu ching hui-yuan" 梁院長與梁漱溟先生由京回院 (President Liang and Mr. Liang Shu-ming return to the institute from the capital), 2.16 (Jan. 1, 1933):15.

k. "Sun yuan-chang Hsu Ching-yen hsien-sheng teng fu Ho" 孫院長徐晶岩先生等赴菏 (President Sun, Mr. Hsu Ching-yen and others visit Hotse), 2.21 (Feb. 21, 1933):19.

m. "Ho-tse fen-yuan kai-k'uang" 菏澤分院概況 (General account of the Ho-tse branch institute), 5.5 (Oct. 16, 1935).

n. *Shih-fan hsueh-hsiao chuan-hao* 師範學校專號 (Special issue on the normal school), 5.8/9 (Dec. 5, 1935).

p. *Tsou-p'ing shih-yen hsien ho-tso shih-yeh pao-kao chuan-hao* 鄒平實驗縣合作事業報告專號 (Special issue reporting on the cooperative enterprise in Tsou-p'ing experimental hsien), 5.11/12 (Feb. 16, 1936).

   1. "Hsu-yen" 序言 (Preface).
   2. "Ho-tso k'uai-chi chih chih-tao chien-tu" 合作會計之指導監督 (Guidance and supervision of cooperatives and accounting).
   3. "I-nien-lai chih mien-yeh yun-hsiao ho-tso-she chih-tao kung-

tso" 一年來之棉業運銷合作社指導工作 (This past year's guidance work with cotton transport and marketing cooperatives).

4. "Hsin-yung ho-tso-she chin-k'uang" 信用合作社近況 (Recent state of credit cooperatives).

5. "Chuang-ts'ang ho-tso-she chih kuo-ch'ü yü wei-lai" 莊倉合作社之過去與未來 (Past and future of village granary cooperatives).

6. "Ts'an-yeh ho-tso-she kai-k'uang" 蠶業合作社概況 (General account of sericulture cooperatives).

273. *Hsiang-ts'un chien-she hsun-k'an hui-yao ti-i-chi* 鄉村建設旬刊彙要第一集 (Collection of writings from rural reconstruction magazine, first series). Tsou-p'ing, Shantung, 1935.

274. *Hsiang-ts'un chien-she shih-yen* 鄉村建設實驗 (Experiments in rural reconstruction). Ed. Chang Yuan-shan 章元善 and Hsu Shih-lien 許仕廉. 3 vols. Shanghai, 1936–1938.

275. *Hsiang-ts'un yun-tung chou-k'an* 鄉村運動週刊 (Rural movement weekly). Tsou-p'ing, Shantung, nos. 1–4 (April 1937).

276. Hsiao Kung-ch'uan 蕭公權. *Chung-kuo cheng-chih szu-hsiang shih* 中國政治思想史 (History of Chinese political thought). 6 vols. Taipei, 1954.

277. Hsiao Liang 曉亮. "Liang Shu-ming ho t'a ti fan-tung szu-hsiang" 梁漱溟和他的反動思想 (Liang Shu-ming and his reactionary thought). In [409], I, 72–79. Also [364], Sept. 7, 1955.

278. *Hsiao shih pao* 小時報 (Afternoon times). Shanghai, 1918–1919.

a. "Ming-shih yu kuo tzu-ch'iang" 名士憂國自戕 (Celebrated scholar commits suicide out of concern over the fate of the nation), Nov. 16, 1918.

b. "*Hsiao-shih pao* chih pien-che lun Liang Chü-ch'uan" 小時報之編者論梁巨川 (Editor of *Afternoon times* discusses Liang Chü-ch'uan), Dec. 2, 1918.

279. Hsiao Wen-che 蕭文哲. *Hsien-tai Chung-kuo cheng-tang yü cheng-chih* 現代中國政黨與政治 (Contemporary Chinese political parties and politics). Nanking, 1946.

280. Hsieh Kuo-hsin 謝國馨. "P'ing Wu Chih-hui ti jen-sheng-kuan" 評吳稚暉的人生觀 (Critique of Wu Chih-hui's philosophy of life). [482], Jan 1, 3, 5, 1924.

281. Hsieh T'eng-ying 謝騰英 and Yü Lin-yen 喩林炎. "Wo-men ti fu-tao shih-yeh" 我們的輔導事業 (Our guidance program). [272n], pp. 2–4.

282. *Hsien-tai hsin-wen* 現代新聞 (Contemporary news). 1.1—1.7 (1947).

283. *Hsin ch'ao* 新潮 (New tide). Peking, 1.1—3.2 (January 1919—March 1922). Monthly.

284. *Hsin chiao-yü* 新教育 (New education). Shanghai, 1.1—2.3 (April 1919—October 1925). Monthly.

284a. ———*Hsin chiao-yü p'ing-lun* 新教育評論 (New education critic). Weekly supplement to [284].

285. *Hsin chien-she* 新建設 (Reconstruction). Peking, 1954–1960. Monthly.

286. *Hsin ch'ing-nien* 新青年 (New youth). Shanghai, Peking, Canton, 1915–1925.

287. *Hsin-hai ko-ming* 辛亥革命 (The 1911 revolution). Ed. Chung-kuo shih-hsueh-hui 中國史學會. 8 vols. Shanghai, 1957.

288. *Hsin Hsia* 新夏 (New Cathay). Taipei, nos. 1–20 (1969–1971). Monthly.

289. *Hsin Hua* 新華 (New China). Peking, 1952–1957. Monthly.

290. *Hsin pao* 新報 (The news). Hong Kong, 1952–1957. Daily.

291a. *Hsin-wen pao* 新聞報 (News). Shanghai, 1946–1947.

291b. *Hsin-yueh* 新月 (Crescent moon). Shanghai, 1928—.

292. *Hsing-tao jih-pao* 星島日報 (Hsing-tao daily). Hong Kong, 1941.

293. Hsu Chih-mo 徐志摩. "Lun tzu-sha" 論自殺 (On suicide). In *Hsu Chih-mo ch'üan-chi* 徐志摩全集 (Works of Hsu Chih-mo). 6 vols. Taipei, 1969. III, 141–167.
    a. "Tu *Kuei-lin Liang hsien-sheng i-shu*" 讀「桂林梁先生遺書」 (On reading *Collected writings of Mr. Liang of Kweilin*), pp. 141–152.

294. Hsu Ching-yen 徐晶岩. "Ti ch'i-ch'ü hsiang-nung hsueh-hsiao kung-tso pao-kao" 第七區鄉農學校工作報告 (Work report on seventh district peasant schools). [272] 1.21 (July 21, 1932):107–135.

295. Hsu Ti-shan 許地山 [Lo Hua-sheng 落華生]. *Kuo-ts'ui yü kuo-hsueh* 國粹與國學 (National essence and national studies). Taipei, 1966.

296. Hsu Tsung-mien 徐宗勉. "Liang Shu-ming tui ti-kuo chu-i ts'ai-ch'ü shen-ma t'ai-tu" 梁漱溟对帝國主义探取甚麼态度 (What attitude Liang Shu-ming has had toward imperialism). In [409], I, 30–40. Also [333], July 18, 1955; [289], September 1955.

297. Hsu Yung-shun 徐雍舜. "Chung-kuo nung-ts'un yun-tung chih tsung-chien-t'ao" 中國農村運動之總檢討 (General review of the Chinese rural movement). [502], no. 13 (July 5, 1934).

298. *Hsueh heng* 學衡 (Critical review). Nanking, nos. 1–66 (January 1922—November 1928). Monthly.

299. *Hsueh-hsi* 學習 (Study). Peking, 1954–1956. Monthly.

300. *Hsueh-i* 學藝 ("Wissen und Wissenschaft"). Peking, 1922.

301. *Hsueh lu* 血路 (Blood road). Hankow, 1938–1939. Weekly.

302. Hu Ch'ing-chün 胡慶鈞. "Liang Shu-ming shih tsen-yang hsiang Ma-k'o-szu chu-i chin-kung ti" 梁漱溟是怎样向馬克思主義進攻的 (How Liang Shu-ming attacked Marxism). In [409], II, 67–85. Also [166], no. 10 (1955).

303. Hu Ch'iu-yuan 胡秋原. "Wo-men ying sheng-yuan pu-ch'ü pao-li ti Liang Shu-ming hsien-sheng" 我們應聲援不屈暴力的梁漱溟先生 (We should all voice support for Mr. Liang Shu-ming, one who does not yield to force). [271], Feb. 15, 1952.

304. ———"I-pai san-shih nien lai Chung-kuo szu-hsiang shih-kang" 一百三十年來中國思想史綱 (Outline of one hundred and thirty years of Chinese intellectual history). [210] 9.9 (September 1971):45–47.

305. ———"Hsin ch'uan-t'ung lun—Chung-kuo t'ai-tu chih ch'ung-hsin k'en-ting yü ts'un-chih yun-tung" 新傳統論—中國態度之重新肯定與村治運動 (On a new tradition—the affirmation of China's attitude

and the village government movement). [369], no. 303 (February 1971).

306. Hu Ming-shu 胡明樹. "Shih tseng ta-ch'ou-jen Liang Shu-ming hsien-sheng" 詩贈大仇人梁漱溟先生 (Poem for the great enemy Mr. Liang Shu-ming). [501], Feb. 13, 1949.

307. Hu Shih 胡適. "Ta Liang Shu-ming hsien-sheng shu" 答梁漱溟先生書 (Answer to Mr. Liang Shu-ming). [286] 6.4 (Apr. 15, 1919):431–432. Also included in [5], pp. 63–64.

308. ———Hu Shih wen-ts'un ti-erh-chi 胡適文存第二集 (Collected works of Hu Shih, second collection). 4 chüan. Shanghai, 1924.
    a. "I-nien-pan ti hui-ku" 一年半的回顧 (One and a half years in retrospect), chüan 1, 141–144.
    b. "Wo-men ti cheng-chih chu-chang" 我們的政治主張 (Our political proposals), chüan 3, 27–34. Also [540] 19.8 (Apr. 25, 1922); [447], no. 2 (May 14, 1922).

309. ———Hu Shih wen-ts'un, 1–4 chi 胡適文存, 1–4集 (Collected works of Hu Shih, collections 1–4). 4 vol. Taipei, 1953.
    a. "Pa" 跋 (Postscript), I, 707.
    b. "Tu Liang Shu-ming hsien-sheng chu ti Tung Hsi wen-hua chi ch'i che-hsueh" 讀梁漱溟先生著的「東西文化及其哲學」 (On reading Mr. Liang Shu-ming's Eastern and Western cultures and their philosophies), II, 158–177. Also [536], Mar. 30, 1923.
    c. Exchange of letters between Liang Shu-ming and Hu Shih, II, 177–179.
    d. "Wo-men tui-yü Hsi-yang chin-tai wen-ming ti t'ai-tu" 我們對於西洋近代文明的態度 (Our attitude toward modern Western civilization), III, 1–15.
    e. "Wo-men tsou na-i-t'iao lu?" 我們走那一條路? (Which road shall we follow?), IV, 429–444.
    f. "Shih p'ing so-wei 'Chung-kuo pen-wei ti wen-hua chien-she'" 試評所謂「中國本位的文化建設」 (Critique of so-called "cultural reconstruction on a Chinese base"), IV, 535–540. Also [535], no. 145 (Apr. 7, 1935):4–7.

310. ———Chung-kuo ku-tai che-hsueh shih 中國古代哲學史 (History of ancient Chinese philosophy). Taipei, 1958. Republication of the original Chung-kuo che-hsueh shih ta-kang, shang chuan 中國哲學史大綱，上卷 (Outline of the history of Chinese philosophy, I). Shanghai, 1919.

311. Hu [Ying]-han 胡[應]漢. "Chi Liang Shu-ming hsien-sheng" 記梁漱溟先生 (On Mr. Liang Shu-ming). [181], May 15, 1952.

312. Hu Ying-han. "Liang Shu-ming hsien-sheng nien-p'u ch'u-kao" 梁漱溟先生年譜初稿 (Draft chronology of the life of Mr. Liang Shu-ming), pts. 1–7. [334], nos. 295–301 (Feb. 10—May 1, 1963).

313. Hua Kang 華崗. Wu-szu yun-tung shih 五四運動史 (History of the May Fourth movement). Shanghai, 1952.

314. Huang Ch'iang 黃強. "Tsai Min-pien chung ti Ch'en Ming-shu yü wo" 在閩變中的陳銘樞與我 (Ch'en Ming-shu and I during the Fukien

uprising). *Ch'un-ch'iu* 春秋 (The annals; Hong Kong), no. 131 (Dec. 16, 1962).

315. Huang Hsing-min 黃省敏. "Tu 'Hsiang-ts'un chien-she yun-tung ti chiang-lai' ching-ta Ch'en Hsu-ching hsien-sheng" 讀「鄉村建設運動的將來」敬答陳序經先生 (Answer to Mr. Ch'en Hsu-ching on reading "The future of the rural reconstruction movement"). [535], no. 216 (Aug. 30, 1936).

316. Huang Ken-yung 黃艮庸. Letter to Hu Ying-han, dated Mar. 6, 1959. (In Mr. Hu's possession.)

317. Huang Tsung-hsi 黃宗羲. *Ming ju hsueh-an* 明儒學案 (Critical anthology of Ming dynasty Confucianists). Nanchang edition, 1888.

318. Huang Yen-p'ei 黃炎培. "Huang-hsu ti pei-ching ho ta Liang Shu-ming hsien-sheng" 黃墟的背景和答梁漱溟先生 (The background of Huang-hsu and an answer to Mr. Liang Shu-ming). [533], n.s. 2.2 (Nov. 16, 1930).

319. Huang Yuan-sheng 黃遠生. "Hsiang ying-lu" 想影錄 (Reflections). [540] 13.2 (Feb. 10, 1916).

320. Hucker, Charles, ed. *Chinese Government in Ming Times.* New York: Columbia University Press, 1969.

321. Hughes, H. Stuart. *Consciousness and Society.* New York: Vintage Books, 1961.

322. Hummel, Arthur W., ed. *Eminent Chinese of the Ch'ing Period.* 2 vols. Washington, D.C.: 1943–1944.

323. *Hung-ch'i* 紅旗 (Red flag). Peking, 1954–1977. Monthly.

324. Hung Huan-ch'un 洪煥春. *Wu-szu shih-ch'i ti Chung-kuo ko-ming yun-tung* 五四時期的中國革命運動 (Chinese revolutionary movement during the May Fourth period). Peking, 1956.

325. *I hui jih-pao* 藝匯日報 (I hui daily). Shanghai, 1954–1956.

326. *I shih pao* 益世報 (Public welfare). Kunming and Chungking, 1938–1945.

327. Isaacs, Harold R. *The Tragedy of the Chinese Revolution.* 2nd ed. New York: Atheneum, 1966.

328. Jefferson, Thomas. *Works of Thomas Jefferson.* Ed. Paul Leicester Ford. 11 vols. New York: C.P. Putnam's Sons, 1904. Vol. 11: 1816–1826.

329. Jen Chi-yü 任繼愈. "Chieh-ch'uan Liang Shu-ming ti wen-hua-kuan-tien ti mai-pan-hsing" 揭穿梁漱溟的文化觀點的買辦性 (Exposing the compradore nature of Liang Shu-ming's viewpoint on culture). In [409], I, 114–122. Also [333], Sept. 6, 1955.

330. ———"Hsiang Liang Shu-ming ti fan-tung szu-hsiang chan-k'ai tou-cheng" 向梁漱溟的反動思想展開斗爭 (Launch the struggle against Liang Shu-ming's reactionary thought). In [409], II, 19–29. Also [575], no. 18 (Sept. 30, 1955).

331. ———and T'ang Yung-t'ung 湯用彤. "P'i-p'an Liang Shu-ming ti sheng-ming chu-i che-hsueh" 批判梁漱溟的生命主義哲學 (Critique of Liang Shu-ming's philosophy of vitalism). In [409], II, 3–11. Also [333], Sept. 9, 1955.

332. *Jen-min chiao-yü* 人民敎育 (People's education). Peking, 1952–1956.

333. *Jen-min jih-pao* 人民日報 (People's daily). Peking, 1951–1977.

334. *Jen-sheng tsa-chih* 人生雜誌 (Human life). Hong Kong, 1960–1964. Monthly.

335. Ju Ch'un-p'u 茹春浦 . "Pien-che ti hua" 編者的話 (Editor's note). [272] 1.19/20 (Apr. 11, 1932).

336. ——— "Chieh-shao i-ko jen-min tzu-tung pan-li ti hsien tzu-chih" 介紹 一個人民自動辦理的縣自治 (Introducing a case of hsien self-government managed by the people on their own initiative). [272] 2.17/18 (Jan. 21, 1933): 1–30.

337. Jung Chao-tsu 容肇祖 . *Ming-tai szu-hsiang-shih* 明代思想史 (Intellectual history of the Ming period). Taipei, 1962.

338. *Kai tsao* 改造 (La reconstruo). Peking, September 1919—September 1922.

339. Kan Yü-yuan 甘豫源 . *Hsiang-ts'un chiao-yü* 鄉村教育 (Rural education). Shanghai, 1937.

340. Kao Fang 高放 "P'i-p'an Liang Shu-ming kuan-yü Chung-kuo ko-ming shih ts'ung wai yin-fa ti miu-lun" 批判梁漱溟關於中國革命是從外引發的謬論 (Critique of Liang Shu-ming's ridiculous theory that the Chinese revolution was touched off from the outside). In [409], II, 218–237. Also [285], no. 11 (1955), no. 2 (1956).

341. Kao Tsan-fei 高贊非 . "P'i-p'an Liang Shu-ming ti fan-tung chiao-yü szu-hsiang" 批判梁漱溟的反動教育思想 (Critique of Liang Shu-ming's reactionary educational thought). [332], no. 12 (1955).

342. ———"Ts'ung li-lun ho shih-chien shang lai k'an Liang Shu-ming ti hsiang-ts'un chien-she ti fan-tung-hsing" 從理論和實踐上來看梁漱溟的鄉村建設的反動性 (Looking at the reactionary nature of Liang Shu-ming's rural reconstruction from theory and practice). [289], no. 5 (1956).

343. Keenan, Barry C. "John Dewey in China: His Visit and the Reception of His Ideas, 1917–1927." Ph.D. dissertation, Claremont Graduate School, 1969.

344. Kennedy, Melville T., Jr. "The Chinese Democratic League." *Papers on China* (East Asian Research Center, Harvard University), no. 7 (1953).

345. Kiang Wen-han. *The Chinese Student Movement*. New York: King's Crown Press, 1948.

346. Kikuta Tarō 菊田太郎 . "Ryō Sōmei no sonchi ron" 梁漱溟の村治論 (Liang Shu-ming's theory of village government). *Keizai ronsō* 經濟論爭 (Debates in economics; Tokyo) 52.4 (April 1941): 501–508.

347. Kimura Eiichi 木村英一 . "Ryō Sōmei no shisō—*Tōzai bunka oyobi sono tetsugaku* ni suite" 梁漱溟の思想 —「東西文化及其哲學」にすいて (Thought of Liang Shu-ming—on his book *Eastern and Western cultures and their philosophies*). *Toa jimbun gakuho* 東亞人文學報 (East Asian journal of humanities; Tokyo) 3.3 (January 1944): 496–542.

348. *Kindai Chūgoku kyoiku kenkyu* 近代中国教育研究 (Research on modern Chinese education). Hayashi Tomoharu 林倫治 , ed. Tokyo, 1958.

349. "Ko hsiao tang-p'ai chien-pao" 各小黨派剪報 (Newspaper clippings

on the various minor political parties). Unpublished collection compiled by the Bureau of Investigation, Nanking.

350. Ko Kung-chen 戈公振. *Chung-kuo pao-hsueh shih* 中國報學史 (History of Chinese journalism). Hong Kong, 1964.

351. Ko Li 葛力. "Chieh-lu Liang Shu-ming ti wei-hsin chu-i ti shih-chieh-kuan" 揭露梁漱溟的唯心主義的世界觀 (Exposing the idealism of Liang Shu-ming's world view). In [409], I, 123-132. Also [359], Sept. 9, 1955.

352. *K'o-hsueh yü jen-sheng-kuan* 科學與人生觀 (Science and philosophy of life). 2 vols. Shanghai, 1923.

353. Ku Hung-ming. *The Spirit of the Chinese People.* 1915; Taipei, 1956.

354. ———"The Peace of Cathay." *Living Age,* no. 216 (Jan. 6, 1923):7-11.

355. ———"The Chinese Soul Self-interpreted." *Living Age,* no. 327 (Dec. 5, 1925):523-531.

356. *Kuan-ch'a* 觀察 (Observer). Shanghai, 1.1—3.18 (September 1946—January 1948). Weekly.

357. Kuan Ch'i-t'ung 關琪桐. "Man-t'an wen-hua chih-i—wen-hua ti ting-i" 漫談文化之一 — 文化的定義 (Random comments on culture—the definition of culture). [216] 1.1 (Mar. 25, 1944).

358. *Kuang-hsi jih-pao* 廣西日報 (Kwangsi daily). Kweilin, 1941-1945.

359. *Kuang-ming jih-pao* 光明日報 (Light daily). Peking, 1950-1977.

360. *Kuang-ming pao* 光明報 (Light). Hong Kong, Sept 18—Dec. 7, 1941.

361. *Kuang-tung min-cheng-t'ing hui-pao* 廣東民政廳彙報 (Bulletin of the Kwangtung provincial civil government commission). Canton, 1927-1931.

362. Kuhn, Phillip. "Local Self-Government under the Republic." In Frederic Wakeman, Jr. and Carolyn Grant, eds. *Conflict and Control in Late Imperial China.* Berkeley and Los Angeles: University of California Press, 1975. pp. 257-298.

363. Kung Chu-ch'uan 公竹川. "Liang-ko yen-kuang" 兩個眼光 (Two visions). [275], no. 4 (Apr. 26, 1937).

364. *Kung-jen jih-pao* 工人日報 (Workers' daily). 1954-1956.

365. *Kung-shang jih-pao* 工商日報 (Industrial commercial daily). Hong Kong, 1954-1956.

366. K'ung Hsueh-hsiung 孔雪雄. *Chung-kuo chin-jih chih nung-ts'un yun-tung* 中國今日之農村運動 (Present-day Chinese rural movement). Shanghai, 1934.

367. Kuo Chan-p'o 郭湛波. *Chin wu-shih-nien Chung-kuo szu-hsiang shih* 近五十年中國思想史 (History of the past fifty years of Chinese thought). Shanghai, 1935.

368. *Kuo feng* 國風 (National customs). Nanking, 1931-1936; Chungking, 1941-1944.

369. *Kuo hun* 國魂 (Spirit of the nation). Taipei, 1971. Monthly.

370. *Kuo ku* 國故 (National heritage). Peking, nos. 1-4 (1919).

371. *Kuo lun* 國論 (National opinion). Chengtu, 1938-1942. Weekly.

372. Kuo Min-hsueh 郭敏學. "Hsiang-ts'un wen-hua" 鄉村文化 (Rural

culture). *Nung-lin hsin-pao* 農林新報 (Agriculture and forestry news; Nanking), Apr. 21, 1946.

373. *Kuo-min ts'an-cheng hui-i shih-liao* 國民參政會議史料 (Historical records of the people's political council). Taipei, 1962.

    a. "Ti-i-chieh ts'an-cheng-hui hsun-wen ching-chi pu-chang" 第一屆參政會詢問經濟部長 (The first People's political council interpellates the economic minister). First session, July 12, 1938.

    b. "Ti-i-chieh ts'an-cheng hui 'pan-li ping-i chi-ying kai-shan ko-tien' chien-i" 第一屆參政會「辦理兵役亟應改善各點」建議 (Proposal of the first People's political council on various urgently needed draft reforms). Third session, no. 79, Feb. 18, 1939.

    c. "Ts'an-cheng-hui ti-i-chieh ti-wu-tz'u ta-hui Liang Shu-ming teng hsun wen" 參政會第一屆第五次大會梁漱溟等詢問 (Fifth session of the first People's political council interpellation by Liang Shu-ming and others). Fifth session, April 1940.

374. Kuo Mo-jo 郭沫若. "Chung-kuo wen-hua chih-ch'uan-t'ung ching-shen" 中國文化之傳統精神 (Traditional spirit in Chinese culture). *Ch'uang-tsao chou-pao* 創造週報 (Creation weekly) 1.2 (Feb. 28, 1924): 10–15.

375. *Kuo-wen chou-pao* 國聞週報 (National news weekly). Tientsin, 1931–1936.

376. Kwok, D.W.Y. *Scientism in Chinese Thought.* New Haven, Conn.: Yale University Press, 1965.

378. Legge, James, trans. *The Chinese Classics.* 2nd ed. 5 vols. Oxford: Oxford University Press, vols. 1–2 (rev.), 1893–1895; vols 3–5, 1865–1872.

379. Levenson, Joseph R. *Confucian China and Its Modern Fate.* 3 vols. Berkeley and Los Angeles: University of California Press, 1958–1965.

380. Li Chien-nung 李劍農. *Chung-kuo chin-pai-nien cheng-chih-shih* 中國近百年政治史 (Political history of China in the past hundred years). 2 vols. Shanghai, 1947.

381. Li Ch'ing-sung 李清悚. "Chan-mu-shih 'shu-shih chu-i' yü Mo-ti 'hsi-sheng chu-i'" 詹姆士「淑世主義」與墨翟「犧牲主義」 (James' "meliorism" and Mo-tzu's "sacrificism"). [541], Dec. 1, 1923.

382. Li Ch'ing-t'ien 李慶田 et al. *Wo-men ts'an-kuan t'u-ti kai-ko i-hou* 我們參觀土地改革以後 (After we have observed land reform). Peking, 1951.

383. Li K'ang-min 黎康民. "Hsiang-ts'un yun-tung yü cheng-fu nung-cheng chih fen-chi wen-t'i" 鄉村運動與政府農政之分際問題 (Question of the division between the rural movement and the governmental agricultural administration). [272] 6.7–8 (Nov. 16, Dec. 1, 1936).

384. Li Nai 李鼐. "Tsou-p'ing erh-nien-lai ti hsiang-ts'un ch'ing-nien hsun-lien chih wo chien" 鄒平二年來的鄉村青年訓練之我見 (My view of the past two years of the rural youth training program in Tsou-p'ing). [272] 5.10 (Jan. 16, 1936).

385. ———, ed. *Shan-tung Tsou-p'ing shih-yen-hsien shih-yen kuei-ch'eng hui-pien* 山東鄒平實驗縣實驗規程彙編 (Collection of experimental regulations of the Tsou-p'ing Shantung experimental hsien). Tsou-p'ing,

1936.

   a. "Ho-tso" 合作 (Cooperatives), sec. 4.

   b. "Hu chi" 戶籍 (Household registration), sec. 9.

   c. "Feng-su kai-ko" 風俗改革 (Reform of customs), sec. 10.

386. *Li pao* 力報 (Strength). Kweilin, 1940–1944. Daily.

387. *Li pao* 立報 (Li daily). Hong Kong, 1941.

388. Li P'u-sheng 李樸生. "Hao-hsi hai tsai hou-t'ou k'an-k'an" 好戲還在
後頭看看 (The best is yet to come). In *Ch'en Ping-ch'üan hui-i lu* 陳炳
權回憶錄 (Reminiscences of Ch'en Ping-ch'üan). Taipei, 1954.

389. Li Shih-ts'en 李石岑. *Li Shih-ts'en lun-wen chi yen-chiang chi* 李石岑論文
集演講集 (Collected essays and lectures of Li Shih-ts'en). 2 vols.
Shanghai, 1924.

   a. "Tzu-hsu" 自序 (Preface).

390. ——*Jen-sheng che-hsueh* 人生哲學 (Philosophy of life). Shanghai, 1926.

391. ——"P'ing *Tung Hsi wen-hua chi ch'i che-hsueh*" 評「東西文化及其哲
學」(Critique of *Eastern and Western cultures and their philosophies*). [440]
3.3 (Mar. 1, 1922):25–26.

392. *Li-shih yen-chiu* 歷史研究 (Historical research). Peking, 1954–1957.

393. Li Ta-chao 李大釗. *Li Ta-chao hsuan-chi* 李大釗選集 (Selected writings
of Li Ta-chao). Peking, 1962.

   a. "Ta ai p'ien" 大哀篇 (The great tribulation), pp. 1–3.

   b. "Ch'ing-nien yü nung-ts'un" 青年與農村 (Youth and the villages),
pp. 146–150.

   c. "'Shao-nien Chung-kuo' ti 'shao-nien yun-tung'" 「少年中國」的
「少年運動」("Young China's" youth movement), pp. 235–238.

394. ——"Tung Hsi wen-hua ken-pen chih i-tien" 東西文化根本之異點
(Fundamental differences between Eastern and Western cultures).
Yen chih 言志 (Statesman; Peking), July 1918.

395. Li Ta-san 李達三. "Liang Shu-ming hsien-sheng chin-k'uang" 梁漱溟
先生近況 (Mr. Liang Shu-ming's present situation). [210], June 1976.

396. Li Tsung-huang 李宗黃. "K'ao-ch'a shih-chi" 考察實際 (Record of an
inspection trip). n.p., n.d. Printed book length report shown to me by
the author.

397. ——"K'ao-ch'a ko-ti nung-ts'un hou chih kan-hsiang" 考察各地農村
後之感想 (Impressions after inspecting various rural areas). [449] 2.5
(Oct. 26, 1934):84–91.

398. ——*Chung-kuo ti-fang tzu-chih kai-lun* 中國地方自治概論 (General discussion of Chinese local self-government). Taipei, 1949.

399. ——*Chung-kuo ti-fang tzu-chih tsung-lun* 中國地方自治總論 (General
discussion of Chinese local self-government). Taipei, 1954.

400. Li Tzu-hsiang 李紫翔. "Chung-kuo nung-ts'un yun-tung ti li-lun yü
shih-chi" 中國農村運動的理論與實際 (Theory and reality of the
Chinese rural movement). In [174], pp. 1–30.

401. ——"Hsiang-ts'un chien-she yun-tung ti p'ing-chia" 鄉村建設運動的
評價 (Appraisal of the Chinese rural reconstruction movement). In
[174], pp. 150–171.

402.   ———"Liang Shu-ming ti szu-shih nien" 梁漱溟的四十年 (Liang Shu-
        ming's forty years). In [409], II, 156–168. Also [285], October 1955.

403.   Li Yueh-hua 李曰華. "P'i-p'an Liang Shu-ming ti tsung-chiao szu-
        hsiang" 批判梁漱溟的宗教思想 (Critique of the religious thought of
        Liang Shu-ming). [285], no. 93 (June 3, 1956).

404.   Liang Chi 梁濟. Kuei-lin Liang hsien-sheng i-shu 桂林梁先生遺書 (Col-
        lected writings of Mr. Liang of Kweilin). Ed. Liang Huan-nai and
        Liang Huan-ting [Liang Shu-ming]. 4 chüan. Shanghai, 1927.
        a. "I pi hui ts'un" 遺筆彙存 (Collection of bequeathal letters), chüan
            2.
        b. "Kan-ch'ü shan-fang jih-chi chieh-ch'ao" 感劬山房日記節鈔
            (Selections from a diary on the study of appreciating [my mother's]
            endeavors), chüan 3.
        c. "Shih-chi jih-chi" 侍疾日記 (Diary of caring for my sick [mother]),
            chüan 3.
        d. "Hsin jen lei kao" 辛壬類槀 (Notes from 1911–1912), chüan 3.
        e. "Fu luan lu" 伏卵錄 (Record of brooding over eggs), chüan 4.
        f. "Pieh chu tz'u hua chi" 別竹辭花記 (On bidding farewell to
            bamboos and flowers), chüan 4.

405.   Liang Ch'i-ch'ao 梁啓超 Yin-ping-shih ts'ung-chu 飲冰室叢著 (Collection
        of works from the Ice-drinker's studio). 4 vols. Shanghai, 1907.

406.   ———"Kuo hsing lun" 國性論 (On national character). [610] 1.1
        (December 1912):1–5.

407.   ———Ou yu hsin-ying lu chieh-lu 歐遊心影錄節錄 (Reflections on a
        European journey). Taipei reprint, 1966.

408.   Liang-hsin-hua 艮心話 (Honest talk). Hong Kong, 1941–1944.

409.   Liang Shu-ming szu-hsiang p'i-p'an 梁漱溟思想批判 (Criticism of Liang
        Shu-ming's thought). 2 vols. Peking, 1955.

410.   "Liang Shu-ming yü Ku Meng-yü" 梁漱溟與顧孟餘 (Liang Shu-ming
        and Ku Meng-yü). Cheng-wu pao 正午報 (Noontime post; Hong Kong),
        Jan. 8, 1963.

411.   Lin Cheng-fu 林徵福. "Chung-kuo che-hsueh" 中國哲學 (Chinese phi-
        losophy). [436] 14.9/10 (May 5, 1963).

412.   Ling-nan hsueh-pao 嶺南學報 (Lingnan journal). Canton, December 1929
        —September 1937. Monthly.

413.   Liu Po-ming 劉伯明. "P'ing Liang Shu-ming chu Tung Hsi wen-hua chi
        ch'i che-hsueh" 評梁漱溟著「東西文化及其哲學」(Critique of Liang
        Shu-ming's Eastern and Western cultures and their philosophies). [298] 3.3
        (March 1922):3–7.

414.   Liu Ta-nien 刘大年. "Ts'ung Chung-kuo feng-chien t'u-ti chih-tu wen-t'i
        shang k'an Liang Shu-ming szu-hsiang ti fan-tung pen-chih" 從中國
        封建土地制度問題上看梁漱溟思想的反動本質 (Looking at the re-
        actionary nature of Liang Shu-ming's thought from the question of the
        Chinese feudal land system). [289], no. 12 (1955). Also [392], no. 5
        (1955).

415.   Liu Ta-yuan 劉達源. "Chieh-fa kung-fei ti nei-wai tsai wei-chi" 揭發共

匪的內外在危機 (Revealing that the Chinese Communists have crises externally and internally). [182], no. 56 (Mar. 1, 1956).

416. Liu Ya-tzu 柳亞子. *Nan-she chi-lueh* 南社紀略 (Brief record of the Southern society). Shanghai, 1940.

417. Lo Chia-lun 羅家倫, ed. *Ko-ming wen-hsien* 革命文獻 (Documents of the revolution). Taipei, 1953.

418. Lou Ch'i 樓棲. "Liang Shu-ming yü Chiang Ching-kuo" 梁漱溟與蔣經國 (Liang Shu-ming and Chiang Ching-kuo). [501], Feb. 10, 1949.

419. Lu Hsun 魯迅. *Lu Hsun san-shih-nien-chi* 魯迅三十年集 (Thirty years of Lu Hsun's writings). 8 vols. Peking, 1970.
   a. "Pai kuang" 白光 (White light). In *Na han* 吶喊 (Call to arms). II, 165-172.

420. Lu Ping 鹿冰. "Hsiang-chien p'ai ling-hsiu—Liang Shu-ming" 鄉建派領袖—梁漱溟 (Leader of the rural reconstruction group—Liang Shu-ming). [282] 1.7 (June 1947):150-151.

421. Mai Ch'ing 麥青. *T'ao Hsing-chih* 陶行知 (T'ao Hsing-chih). Shanghai, 1949.

422. Mannheim, Karl. "Conservative Thought." In Paul Keckemeti, ed. *Essays on Sociology and Social Psychology*. New York: Oxford University Press, 1953.

423. Mao I-heng 毛以亨. "Liang Shu-ming yü Pei Sung Lü hsueh" 梁漱溟與北宋呂學 (Liang Shu-ming and the theories of Mr. Lü of the Northern Sung dynasty). *Tzu-yu wen-hsuan* 自由文選 (Selections from *Liberty magazine*), pp. 121-135. Taipei, 1954.

424. Mao Tse-tung 毛澤東. *Mao Tse-tung hsuan-chi* 毛澤東選集 (Selected works of Mao Tse-tung). 5 vols. Peking, 1969, 1977.
   a. "Hu-nan nung-min yun-tung k'ao-ch'a pao-kao" 湖南农民运动考察报告 (Report on an investigation of the peasant movement in Hunan), I, 12-44.
   b. "Chung-kuo ti hung-se cheng-ch'uan wei-shen-ma neng-kou tsung-tsai?" 中国的紅色政权为什么能夠存在 (Why is it that red power can exist in China?), I, 47-55.
   c. "Ching-kang-shan ti tou-cheng" 井冈山的斗争 (The struggle in the Chingkang Mountains), I, 56-82.
   d. "Hsing-hsing chih huo, k'o-i liao-yuan" 星星之火, 可以燎原 (A single spark can start a prairie fire), I, 94-104.
   e. "Kuan-yü chiu-cheng tang-nei ti ts'o-wu szu-hsiang" 关于纠正党内的錯误思想 (On correcting mistaken ideas in the party), I, 83-93.
   f. "P'i-p'an Liang Shu-ming ti fan-tung szu-hsiang" 批判梁漱溟的反动思想 (Criticism of Liang Shu-ming's reactionary thought), V, 107-115.

425. ——— *Mao Tse-tung szu-hsiang wan-sui* 毛泽东思想万岁 (Long live the thought of Mao Tse-tung). n.p., 1969; Taipei reproduction.
   a. "Tsai sheng shih wei-shu-chi hui-i shang ti ch'a-hua" 在省市委书记会义上的插话 (Remarks to provincial and municipal secre-

taries).

426. Mao Ying-chang 毛應章. *Ting-hsien p'ing-min chiao-yü k'ao-ch'a chi* 定縣平
      民教育考察記 (Notes on an inspection of popular education in Ting
      hsien). Nanking, 1933.

427. *Mei-chou p'ing-lun* 每週評論 (Weekly critic). Peking, nos. 1–37 (Dec. 22,
      1918—Aug. 31, 1919).

428. Meisner, Maurice. *Li Ta-chao and the Origins of Chinese Marxism.* Cam-
      bridge, Mass.: Harvard University Press, 1967.

429. Meng Fei 夢飛. "Tao-le Tsou-p'ing" 到了鄒平 (A visit to Tsou-p'ing).
      [221], Oct. 29, 1935.

430. Meng Kuang-p'eng 孟廣澎. *Tiao-ch'a hsiang-ts'un chien-she chi-yao* 調查鄉
      村建設記要 (Record of important information from an inspection of
      rural reconstruction). Wuchang, 1935.

431. Metzger, Thomas A. "Neo-Confucianism and the Political Culture of
      Late Imperial China." Paper read at the Regional Seminar, Center
      for Chinese Studies, University of California, Berkeley, May 10, 1974.

432. *Mien-jen wen-hsueh yuan yuan-k'an* 勉仁文學院院刊 (Mien-jen academy
      journal). Pei-p'ei, Szechwan, no. 1 (May 1949).

433. Mill, John Stuart. "Autobiography." In Max Lerner, ed. and intro.
      Essential Works of John Stuart Mill. New York: Bantam Books, 1961.

434. Millican, Frank R. "Liang Shou-ming sees it through." *The Chinese
      Recorder* 18.10 (October 1926):698–705.

435. *Min chien* 民間 (Among the people). Peiping, vols. 1–4 (1934–1947).
      Fortnightly.

436. *Min-chu p'ing-lun* 民主評論 (Democratic critic). Hong Kong, 1.1—17.9
      (June 16, 1946—Sept. 16, 1966). Fortnightly.

437. *Min-chu t'ung-meng wen-hsien* 民主同盟文獻 (Documents on the democ-
      ratic league). Nanking, 1946.
      a. "Liang Shu-ming hsien-sheng shuo-ming Min-meng tui Chung-
          kung ti t'ai-tu" 梁漱溟先生說明民盟對中共的態度 (Mr. Liang
          Shu-ming explains the Democratic League's attitude toward the
          Chinese Communists).

438. *Min-i* 民意 (Public opinion). Hankow, 1.1—2.123 (1937–1940). Weekly.

439. *Min-sheng chou-k'an* 民生週刊 (People's livelihood weekly). Peking, 1924.

440. *Min-to tsa-chih* 民鐸雜誌 (People's tocsin). Shanghai, 2.1—10.5. Quar-
      terly.

441. Mou Tsung-san 牟宗三. "Wo yü Hsiung Shih-li hsien-sheng" 我與熊十
      力先生 (Mr. Hsiung Shih-li and I). *Chung-kuo hsueh-jen* 中國學人
      (Chinese scholar; Hong Kong), no. 1 (1970).

442. ———*Chih ti chih-chueh yü Chung-kuo che-hsueh* 智的直覺與中國哲學 (In-
      tuitive knowledge and Chinese philosophy). Taipei, 1971.

443. Mu Feng-lin 繆鳳林. "Liu hsien-sheng lun Hsi-fang wen-hua" 劉先生論
      西方文化 (Mr. Liu discusses Western culture). [368], no. 9 (Nov. 4,
      1932).

443a. Mu Po 暮泊. "Chung-kuo wen-hua yü t'ien-hsia kuan-nien" 中國文化
      與天下觀念 (Chinese culture and the concept of all under heaven).

Chung Mei yueh-k'an 中美月刊 (Sino-American monthly; Taipei) 6.10–12, 7.2–3.

444. Myers, Ramon H. *The Chinese Peasant Economy: Agricultural Development in Hopei and Shantung, 1890–1949.* Cambridge, Mass.: Harvard University Press, 1970.

445. Ni Cheng-ho 倪正和. "Lun wen-hua shu" 論文化書 (Letter on culture). [356] 2.16 (June 14, 1947).

446. Ni Ho-sheng 倪鶴笙. "P'i-p'an Liang Shu-ming fan-kung fan-jen-min fan-ko-ming ti 'hsiang-ts'un chien-she yun-tung' "批判梁漱溟反共、反人民、反革命的「鄉村建設運動」 (Critique of Liang Shu-ming's anti-Communist, anti-people, anti-revolutionary "rural reconstruction movement"). [576], January 1956, pp. 5–41.

447. *Nu-li chou-pao* 努力週報 (Endeavor weekly). Peking, May 22, 1922—October 1924.

448. *Nung-ts'un chien-she* 農村建設 (Rural reconstruction). Kweiyang, 1938. Bi-monthly.

449. *Nung-ts'un fu-hsing yun-tung* 農村復興運動 (Rural revival movement). Nanking, 2.1—2.11 (June 1933—April 1935).
   a. "I-nien-lai fu-hsing ts'un-nung cheng-ts'e chih shih-shih chuang-k'uang" 一年來復興村農政策之實施狀況 (Situation in implementing the rural revival policy this past year), 2.3 (Aug. 26, 1934).

450. *Nung-ts'un kung-tso* 農村工作 (Rural work). Hankow, 1938. Monthly.

451. Okazaki Fumio 岡崎文夫. "Ryō Sōmei cho *Tōzai bunka oyobi sono tetsugaku*" 梁漱溟著「東西文化及其哲學」 (Mr. Liang Shu-ming's book *Eastern and Western cultures and their philosophies*). *Shinagaku* 支那學 (China studies) 2.9 (May 1922):697–701.

452. Omura Kodo 尾村神戶. "Shincho kyoiku shisō ni okeru 'sheng-yü kuang-hsun' no chii ni tsuite" 清朝教育思想に於ける聖諭廣訓の地位について (The position of the proclaiming of the sacred edicts in the history of Ch'ing dynasty educational thought). In [348].

453. Onogawa Hidemi 小野川秀美. "Ryō Sōmei ni okeru kyōson kensetsuron no seiritsu" 梁漱溟に於ける鄉村建設論の成立 (Establishment of Liang Shu-ming's theory of rural reconstruction). *Jimbun kagaku* 人文科學 (Science and humanities) 2.2 (March 1948):86–123.

454. *Pa-pu jih-pao* 八步日報 (Pa-pu daily). Pa-pu, Kwangsi, October 1943—September 1944.

455. Pa Ta 巴達. "Liang Shu-ming cheng-chih chih chu-chang ti p'i-p'an" 梁漱溟政治之主張的批判 (Critique of Liang Shu-ming's political views). [179], nos. 3–5 (June-August 1933).

456. P'an Tzu-nien 潘梓年. "Liang Shu-ming ti li-lun shih chi-tuan wei-hsin chu-i ti" 梁漱溟的理論是極端唯心主義的 (Liang Shu-ming's theories are the ultra-idealistic). [409], II, 12–18. Also [333], Sept. 24, 1955; [289], no. 10 (1955).

457. *Pei-ching ta-hsueh wu-shih chou-nien chi-nien t'e-k'an* 北京大學五十週年紀念特刊 (Commemorative volume for the fiftieth anniversary of Peking university). Peking, 1949.

458. Pusey, James R. *Wu Han: Attacking the Present through the Past.* Harvard
      East Asian Monograph 33. Cambridge, Mass.: East Asian Research
      Center, Harvard University, 1969.

459. Russell, Bertrand. *The Problem of Philosophy.* New York: Henry Holt and
      Co., 1912.

460. ———*Principles of Social Reconstruction.* London: George Allen and Unwin,
      1916.

461. ———*The Problem of China.* New York: George Allen and Unwin, 1922.

462. ———with Dora Russell. *The Prospects of Industrial Civilisation.* London:
      George Allen and Unwin, 1923.

463. Sa K'ung-liao 薩空了. *Hsiang-kang lun-hsien jih-chi* 香港淪陷日記 (Diary
      of the fall of Hong Kong). Hong Kong, 1946.

465. Schwartz, Benjamin I. *In Search of Wealth and Power: Yen Fu and the West.*
      Cambridge, Mass.: Harvard University Press, 1964.

466. ———"The Limits of 'Tradition versus Modernity' as Categories of
      Explanation: The Case of the Chinese Intellectuals." *Daedalus,* Winter
      1972, pp. 71–88.

467. Selden, Mark. *The Yenan Way in Revolutionary China.* Cambridge, Mass.:
      Harvard University Press, 1971.

468. Sha Hsueh-ling 沙學浚. "Yü Liang Shu-ming hsien-sheng lun 'kuo-t'u
      t'ai-ta' chi ch'i li-pi" 與梁漱溟先生論「國土太大」及其利弊 (Discuss-
      ing with Mr. Liang Shu-ming the question "the country is too large,"
      the advantages and disadvantages). [356] 2.13 (June 14, 1947).

469. Sha Ying 沙英. "P'i-p'an Liang Shu-ming kuan-yü chieh-chi tou-cheng
      ti fan-tung kuan-tien" 批判梁漱溟關於階級鬥爭的反動觀點 (Cri-
      tique of Liang Shu-ming's reactionary view of class struggle). In [409],
      II, 169–186. Also [333], Oct. 15, 1955; [289], no. 11 (1955).

470. *Shan-hsi ts'un-cheng hui-pien* 山西村政彙編 (Compendium of Shansi
      documents on local administration). Taiyuan, 1928.

471. *Shan-tung chin-tai-shih tzu-liao* 山東近代史資料 (Materials on the modern
      history of Shantung). 3 vols. Tsinan, 1958.

472. *Shan-tung hsiang-ts'un chien-she yen-chiu-yuan chi Tsou-p'ing shih-yen-ch'ü kai-
      k'uang* 山東鄉村建設研究院及鄒平實驗區概況 (General account of
      the Shantung rural reconstruction institute and the Tsou-p'ing ex-
      perimental district). Tsou-p'ing, 1936.

473. *Shan-tung hsiang-ts'un chien-she yen-chiu-yuan kai-lan* 山東鄉村建設研究院概
      覽 (Conspectus of the Shantung rural reconstruction institute). Tsou-
      p'ing, 1934.

474. *Shan-tung nung-k'uang-t'ing kung-pao* 山東農鑛廳公報 (Bulletin of the
      Shantung provincial commission of agriculture and mining). Tsinan,
      1.2–2.6 (September 1929—March 1931). Monthly.

475. *Shan-tung sheng-chih tzu-liao* 山東省志資料 (Shantung provincial gazetteer
      materials). 2 vols. Tsinan, 1959.

476. *Shao-nien Chung-kuo* 少年中國 (Young China). Shanghai, 1.8—3.8 (Sept.
      15, 1918—Mar. 1, 1922). Monthly.

477. Sheridan, James E. *Chinese Warlord: The Career of Feng Yü-hsiang.* Stan-

ford: Stanford University Press, 1966.

478. *Shih-chi p'ing-lun* 世紀評論 (Century critic). Shanghai, 1947–1948. Weekly.

479. Shih Chi-yun 時濟雲. "Ti-wu-ch'ü hsiang-nung hsueh-hsiao kai-k'uang" 第五區鄉農學校概況 (General account of the fifth district's peasant schools). [272a], pp. 65–87.

480. *Shih pao* 時報 (Times). Shanghai, 1918–1922. Daily.

481. *Shih-shih hsin-pao* 時事新報 (China times). Shanghai, 1907–1937.

482. ———*Hsueh-teng* 學燈 (Lamp of learning). 1918–1924. Supplement to [481].

483. *Shih yü ch'ao* 時與潮 (Times and currents). Chungking, 1938–1941. Fortnightly.

484. *Shih yü wen* 時與文 (Times and writing). Shanghai, 1948. Monthly.

485. Shou Mien-ch'eng 壽勉成 and Cheng Hou-po 鄭厚博. *Chung-kuo ho-tso yun-tung shih* 中國合作運動史 (History of the Chinese cooperative movement). Shanghai, 1947.

486. *Shu-kuang pao* 曙光報 (Dawn light journal). Kweilin, 1937–1944. Tri-weekly.
   a. "Kuan-chü sheng-huo t'ai ch'i liang" 鰥居生活太淒涼 (The bleak life of a widower), Jan. 14, 1944.
   b. "Liang Ch'en hun-li kuan-kuang chih" 梁陳婚禮觀光誌 (Record of the Liang-Ch'en wedding festivities), Feb. 6, 1944.

487. Shu Ying 樹瑩. "Liang Shu-ming ch'eng chung-shih-chih-ti" 梁漱溟成衆矢之的 (Liang Shu-ming becomes target of public attacks). *Tien-wen-t'ai pao* 天文臺報 (Observatory journal; Hong Kong), Oct. 14, 1955.

488. *Shun-t'ien shih-pao* 順天時報 (Shun-t'ien times). Peking, 1918–1930. Daily.

489. Snow, Edgar. *Red Star Over China*. New York: Random House, 1938; Grove Press edition, 1961.

490. ———*The Long Revolution*. New York: Vintage Books, 1973.

491. Su Yü 蘇輿, ed. *I-chiao ts'ung-pien* 翼教叢編 (Collected treatises on heretical doctrines). Taipei reprint, 1970.

492. Sun Ting-kuo 孫定國. "Po-ch'ih Liang Shu-ming ti chih-yeh fen-t'u ti fan-tung li-lun" 駁斥梁漱溟的職業分途的反動理論 (Refutation of Liang Shu-ming's reactionary theory on the division of labor). In [409], I, 80–94. Also [359], Sept. 16, 1955; [289], no. 10 (1955).

493. ———"P'i-p'an Liang Shu-ming ti fan-tung ti shih-chieh-kuan" 批判梁漱溟的反動的世界觀 (Critique of Liang Shu-ming's reactionary world view). In [409], I, 133–144. Also [333], Sept. 11, 1955.

494. Sung Le-yen 宋樂顏. "Kei Liang hsien-sheng shu" 給梁先生書 (Letter to Mr. Liang). [533], n.s. 1.1 (June 1, 1930).

495. ———"Chiang Che hsiang-ts'un yun-tung tiao-ch'a t'ung-hsun" 江浙鄉村運動調查通訊 (Report on investigation of the rural movement in Chekiang and Kiangsu). [533], n.s. 1.3 (July 1930).

496. *Sung shih* 宋史 (Sung dynastic history). Shanghai, 1934.

497. Sung Te-min 宋德敏. "P'i-p'an Liang Shu-ming ti fan-tung ti ho-tso-she

li-lun" 批判梁漱溟的反動的合作社理論 (Critique of Liang Shu-ming's reactionary theory of cooperatives). [501], Dec. 5, 1955. Also [285], February 1956.

498. Sung Tseng-ch'ü 宋增渠. "Hsiao-ch'ing ho-liu-yü mien sheng-ch'an tiao-ch'a pao-kao" 小清河流域棉生產調查報告 (Report of investigation of cotton production in the Hsiao Ch'ing river valley). [474] 2.6 (March 1931): 1–2.

499. ——"Shan-tung mien-yeh pao-kao" 山東棉業報告 (Report on the Shantung cotton industry). [474] 2.6 (March 1931):9–18.

500. Szu-ma Ch'ien 司馬遷. Shih chi 史記 (Historical records). 10 vols. Peking edition, 1959.

501. Ta kung pao 大公報 (L'Impartiale). Shanghai, 1930–1937, 1946–1949; Tientsin, 1930–1937; Hankow, 1937–1938; Hong Kong, 1937–1977; Chungking, 1940–1949.

502. ——Hsiang-ts'un chien-she 鄉村建設 (Rural reconstruction). Weekly supplement to [501].

503. Ta-lu tsa-chih 大陸雜誌 (Mainland magazine). Taipei, 1950–1977. Fortnightly.

504. [Tai] Po-t'ao [戴]伯韜. T'ao Hsing-chih ti sheng-p'ing chi ch'i hsueh-shuo 陶行知的生平及其學說 (T'ao Hsing-chih, his life and his doctrines). Peking, 1949.

505. T'ai Hsu 太虛. "Tung-yang wen-hua yü Hsi-yang wen-hua" 東洋文化與西洋文化 (Eastern culture and Western culture). [298], no. 32 (August 1924):1–6.

506. Tan, Chester C. Chinese Political Thought in the Twentieth Century. New York: Doubleday and Co., 1971.

507. Tang-tai p'ing-lun 當代評論 (Contemporary critic). Kunming, 1941–1942; Chungking, 1.13—4.10 (Sept. 29, 1941—Mar. 1, 1944).

508. T'ang Chün-i 唐君毅. Chung-kuo wen-hua chih ching-shen chia-chih 中國文化之精神價值 (Spiritual value of Chinese culture). Taipei, 1953. Also published in Hong Kong, 1953.

509. ——Letter to author, Dec. 7, 1974.

510. T'ang Hsien-chih 唐現之. "Pien-che chui-yen" 編者贅言 (Editor's preface). In [23].

511. T'ang Tsung 唐縱. "Liang Shu-ming tsai Kung-fei 'szu-hsiang kai-tsao' chih piao-hsien" 梁漱溟在共匪「思想改造」之表現 (Liang Shu-ming's behavior while subjected to Chinese Communist thought reform). [182], no. 22 (May 1, 1953).

512. T'ao Hsing-chih 陶行知. "Chung-kuo hsiang-ts'un chiao-yü chih ken-pen kai-tsao" 中國鄉村教育之根本改造 (Fundamental reform of Chinese rural education). [208] 16.10 (April 1927):1–5.

513. ——Chih-hsing shu-hsin 知行書信 (Letters of T'ao Hsing-chih). Shanghai, 1931.

514. ——"Sheng-huo chi chiao-yü" 生活及教育 (Life and education). In Wei chih-shih chieh-chi 僞知識階級 (The false knowledge class). Peking, 1950.

515. *T'ao Hsing-chih hsien-sheng chi-nien chi* 陶行知先生紀念集 (Collection of essays commemorating Mr. T'ao Hsing-chih). Shanghai, 1949.

516. T'ao Meng-ho 陶孟和. "Lun tzu-sha" 論自殺 (On suicide). [286] 6.1 (Jan. 15, 1919):12–18.

517. ———"Tsai lun Liang Chü-ch'uan hsien-sheng ti tzu-sha" 再論梁巨川先生的自殺 (Second comment on the suicide of Mr. Liang Chü-ch'uan). In [293], pp. 152–157.

518. Thomson, James C., Jr. *While China Faced West: American Reformers in Nationalist China, 1928–1937.* Cambridge, Mass.: Harvard University Press, 1969.

519. *Ti-erh-tz'u ch'üan-kuo nei-cheng hui-i pao-kao shu* 第二次全國內政會議報告書 (Report on the second national conference of the Ministry of Interior). Nanking, 1934.

520. *Ti-i-tz'u Chung-kuo chiao-yü nien-chien* 第一次中國教育年鑑 (First Chinese education yearbook). Nanking, 1934.

521. T'ien Sheng-nien 田聲年. *Chung-kuo tang-p'ai kai-shu* 中國黨派概述 (General account of Chinese political parties). Nanking, 1946.

522. Ts'ai Shang-szu 蔡尚思. *Chung-kuo ch'uan-t'ung szu-hsiang tsung p'i-p'an* 中國傳統思想總批判 (General critique of traditional Chinese thought). Shanghai, 1950.

523. ———"Liang Shu-ming szu-hsiang ti p'ing-chieh" 梁漱溟思想的評介 (Critical introduction to Liang Shu-ming's thought). [484] 3.1–5 (January–May 1948).

524. Ts'ai Yuan-p'ei 蔡元培. *Ts'ai Yuan-p'ei hsuan-chi, che-hsueh chiao-yü* 蔡元培選集, 哲學教育 (Selected works of Ts'ai Yuan-p'ei on philosophy of education). Taipei, 1967.
   a. "Wu-shih nien lai Chung-kuo chih che-hsueh" 五十年來中國之哲學 (Fifty years of Chinese philosophy), pp. 82–83.
   b. "Pei-ching ta-hsueh chin-te-hui chih chih-ch'ü shu" 北京大學進德會之旨趣書 (The Aims of the Society for the Promotion of Virtue of Peking University).
   c. "Wo tsai chiao-yü-chieh ti ching-yen" 我在教育界的經驗 (My experience in education).

525. ———*Ts'ai Yuan-p'ei tzu-shu* 蔡元培自述 (Ts'ai Yuan-p'ei's self account). Taipei, 1967.

526. ———*Ts'ai Yuan-p'ei hsien-sheng ch'üan-chi* 蔡元培先生全集 (Complete works of Ts'ai Yuan-p'ei). Taipei, 1968.

527. Ts'ao Yü-jen 曹欲仁. "Liang Shu-ming hsien-sheng ti ts'un-chih-p'ai" 梁漱溟先生的村治派 (Mr. Liang Shu-ming's village government group). [301], no. 17 (May 7, 1938).

528. Tso Shun-sheng 左舜生. *Chin san-shih-nien chien-wen tsa-chi* 近三十年見聞雜記 (Recollections of the past thirty years). Hong Kong, 1952.

529. ———"Chi Liang Chi ti tzu-sha" 記梁濟的自殺 (On Liang Chi's suicide). In *Wan-chu-lou sui-pi* 萬竹樓隨筆 (Random notes from the ten-thousand bamboo hall). Hong Kong, 1957, pp. 216–221.

530. Tsou Lu 鄒魯. *Chung-kuo Kuo-min-tang shih-kao* 中國國民黨史稿 (Draft

history of the Kuomintang). Taipei, 1965.

531. Tsou Lu-feng 鄒魯風, et al. "P'i-p'an Liang Shu-ming ti fan-tung chiao-yü szu-hsiang" 批判梁漱溟的反動教育思想 (Critique of Liang Shu-ming's reactionary thought on education). In [409], I, 166–173. Also [289], no. 10 (1955).

532. Ts'ui Te-li 崔德禮 and Liao Tou-hsing 廖斗星. *Chung-kuo wen-hua kai-lun* 中國文化概論 (Introduction to Chinese culture). 2 vols. Taipei, 1968.

533. *Ts'un-chih* 村治 (Village government). Peiping, o.s. 1.1—2.2 (Mar. 15, 1929—Apr. 15, 1930). Monthly. n.s. 1.1—3.5 (June 1, 1930—Aug. 1, 1933). Fortnightly, irregular after 1931.
   a. "Fa k'an tz'u" 發刊辭 (Inaugural issue editorial), o.s. 1.1 (Mar. 15, 1929):5. Probably written by Wang Hung-i.
   b. "Liang Shu-ming ch'i-shih" 梁漱溟啓事 (Announcements from Liang Shu-ming), n.s. 1.1 (June 1, 1930).
   c. "Ho-nan ts'un-chih hsueh-yuan t'ing-pan hsiao-hsi" 河南村治學院停辦消息 (News of the suspension of the Honan village government academy), n.s. 1.9 (Oct. 16, 1930).
   d. "Shan-tung-hsiang-ts'un chien-she yen-chiu yuan chü-pan hsiao-hsi" 山東鄉村建設研究院舉辦消息 (News of the establishment of the Shantung rural reconstruction research institute), n.s. 1.9 (Oct. 16, 1930).
   e. "Shan-tung hsiang-ts'un chien-she yen-chiu yuan chieh-yeh hsueh-sheng fu-wu pan-fa chi kung-tso chuang-k'uang" 山東鄉村建設研究院結業學生服務辦法及工作狀況 (The mode of service and work situations of the Shantung rural reconstruction research institute graduates), n.s. 3.2/3 (Jan. 20, 1933).
   f. "Lu sheng-fu hua Tsou-p'ing Ho-tse wei hsien-cheng chien-she shih-yen ch'ü" 魯省府劃鄒平菏澤爲縣政建設實驗區 (Shantung provincial government designates Tsou-p'ing and Ho-tse as hsien government experimental districts), n.s. 3.4 (Mar. 25, 1933).

534. *Ts'un-chih chih li-lun yü shih-shih* 村治之理論與實施 (Theory and implementation of village government). Peiping, 1930.

535. *Tu-li p'ing-lun* 獨立評論 (Independent critic). Peiping, nos. 1–225 (May 21, 1933—Nov. 1, 1936). Weekly.

536. *Tu-shu tsa-chih* 讀書雜誌 (Reader's miscellany). Peking, nos. 1–16 (1922–1923). Monthly.

537. T'u Hao-ju 涂浩如. "Wen-hua chih hsueh-shu ti yen-chiu shu-lueh" 文化之學術的研究述略 (Brief description of academic investigations of cultures). [436] 11.15 (Aug. 1, 1960).

538. T'u Hsiao-shih 屠孝實. "K'o-hsueh yü tsung-chiao kuo-jan shih pu-liang li-ma?" 科學與宗教果然是不兩立麼? (Is it true that science and religion cannot coexist?). [133] 6.1 (June 1922):1–13.

539. *Tuan-chü shih-san-ching ching-wen* 斷句十三經經文 (The punctuated thirteen classics). Taipei, 1955.
   a. Hsiao ching 孝經.

540. *Tung-fang tsa-chih* 東方雜誌 (Eastern Miscellany). Shanghai, 1904–1960.

541. *Tung-nan p'ing-lun* 東南評論 (Southeastern critic). Nanking, 1923-1924. Fortnightly.

542. Tung Shih-chin 董時進. "Chih Liang Shu-ming shu" 致梁漱溟書 (Letter to Liang Shu-ming) [271], April 4, 1952.

543. T'ung-meng-hui documents. Kuomintang party archives. Ts'ao-t'un, Taiwan.
   a. "Chung-kuo t'ung-meng-hui ching-chin fen-hui wen-tu-pu chien-chang" 中國同盟會京津分會文牘部簡章 (Regulations of the secretariat of the Peking-Tientsin branch of the Chinese revolutionary alliance).
   b. "Chung-kuo t'ung-meng-hui ching-chin fen-hui chang-ch'eng" 中國同盟會京津分會章程 (Constitution of the Peking-Tientsin branch of the Chinese revolutionary alliance).
   c. "Chung-kuo t'ung-meng-hui Ching-Chin fen-hui chün-cheng-pu jen-yuan hsing-ming chi-kuan lü-li-piao" 中國同盟會京津分會軍政部人員姓名籍貫履歷表 (Curriculum vitae of the members of the military department of the Peking-Tientsin branch of the Chinese revolutionary alliance).
   d. "Chung-kuo t'ung-meng-hui Ching-Chin fen-hui chün-shih-pu chan-hsing chien-chang" 中國同盟會京津分會軍事部暫行簡章 (Peking-Tientsin branch of the Chinese revolutionary alliance's military department's temporary regulations).

544. *Tzu-yu chung* 自由鐘 (Liberty bell). Hong Kong, 1970. Monthly.

545. *Tzu-yu-jen pao* 自由人報 (The freeman). Hong Kong, 1954-1957. Daily.

546. *Tzu-yu pao* 自由報 (Freedom journal). Kweilin, 1942-1944. Daily.

547. Ulam, Adam. *The Unfinished Revolution*. New York: Vintage Books, 1960.

548. Van Slyke, Lyman P. "Liang Sou-ming." M.A. thesis, Stanford University, 1958.

549. ———*Enemies and Friends: The United Front in Chinese Communist History.* Stanford: Stanford University Press, 1967.

550. Wang Ching-ju 王靜如. "Wo-men ti hsiang-ts'un yun-tung yü hsien cheng-ch'üan" 我們的鄉村運動與現政權 (Our rural movement and the present regime). [272] 2.11 (Nov. 30, 1932).

551. Wang Hsin-ming 王新命 et al. "Chung-kuo pen-wei ti wen-hua chien-she hsuan-yen" 中國本位的文化建設宣言 (Manifesto on cultural reconstruction on a Chinese base). In *Hu Shih yü Chung Hsi wen-hua* 胡適與中西文化 (Hu Shih and Chinese and Western cultures). Taipei, 1967, pp. 127-131.

552. Wang Hung-i 王鴻一. "Chien-she ts'un-pen cheng-chih" 建設村本政治 (Establishment of village-based government). [533], o.s. 1.1. (Mar. 15, 1929):1-6.

553. ———"Min-chu cheng-chih hsia k'ao-shih hsuan-chü liang-ch'üan ping-yung chih ching-shen" 民主政治下考試選舉兩權並用之精神 (Spirit of simultaneously implementing powers of election and examination under a democratic government). [533], o.s. 1.2 (Apr. 15, 1929):1-3.

554. ———"Chung-kuo wen-hua chih chung-hsin wen-t'i" 中國文化之重心

問題 (Essential problems of Chinese culture). [533], o.s. 1.3 (May 15, 1929):1-5.

555. ———"San-shih-nien lai chung-huai so-chih chih tzu-p'o" 三十年來衷懷所志之自剖 (Self-analysis of the purpose I have harbored these thirty years). [533], o.s. 1.11 (Jan. 15, 1930).

556. ———"Ch'ing-nien chih ch'u-lu" 青年之出路 (Prospects for youth). [533], o.s. 1.11 (Jan. 15, 1930).

557. ———"Chung-kuo min-tsu chih ching-shen chi chin-hou chih ch'u-lu" 中國民族之精神及今後之出路 (The spirit of the Chinese people and its outlet in the future). [533], n.s. 1.5 (Aug. 1, 1930).

558. ———"Wang Hung-i hsien-sheng i-yen" 王鴻一先生遺言 (Mr. Wang Hung-i's dying words). [533], n.s. 1.5 (Aug. 1, 1930).

559. Wang Jo-shui 王若水. "Liang Shu-ming so-wei li-hsing shih shen-ma?" 梁漱溟所謂理性是甚麼？(What is Liang Shu-ming's so-called li-hsing?). In [409], II, 123–137. Also [333], Oct. 23, 1955; [289], no. 11 (1955).

560. Wang Po-p'ing 王伯平. "Wo-men nu-li ti liang-tien" 我們努力的兩點 (Two items we are working on). [272] 2.9 (Oct. 21, 1932).

561. ———"Pen-yuan shih-yen-ch'ü chih she-li yü chin-hsing" 本院實驗區之設立與進行 (Establishment and progress of this institute's experimental district). [272] 2.21 (Feb. 21, 1933).

562. ———"Hsiang-ts'un yun-tung chih niao-k'an" 鄉村運動之鳥瞰 (Overview of the rural movement). [375] 10.31 (Aug. 7, 1933).

563. Wang Shao-sheng 王韶生. "Hsu Ming-hung chuan" 徐名鴻傳 (Biography of Hsu Ming-hung). In "Feng-shun hsien-chih kao" 豐順縣志稿 (Draft gazetteer of Feng-shun hsien). Unpublished manuscript shown to me by the author in Hong Kong.

564. Wang Shih-yuan 王士元. "Chi wu shih Liang Shu-ming hsien-sheng" 記吾師梁漱溟先生 (My teacher Mr. Liang Shu-ming). Chuan-chi wen-hsueh 傳記文學 (Biographical literature) 24.4 (April 1974):39–48.

565. Wang Te-chou 王德周. "Liang Shu-ming hsien-sheng wang na-li ch'ü-le?" 梁漱溟先生往那裏去了？(Where has Mr. Liang Shu-ming gone?). [206], Aug. 18, 1924.

566. Wang Tzu-sung 汪子嵩 and Chu Po-k'un. "P'ing i-chiu-san-ling-nien Liang Shu-ming ho Hu Shih ti cheng-lun" 評一九三〇年梁漱溟和胡適的爭論 (Comment on the 1930 debate between Liang Shu-ming and Hu Shih). In [409], II, 148–155. Also [359], Sept. 21, 1955.

567. Wang Yang-ming 王陽明. "Nan Kan hsiang-yueh" 南贛鄉約 (Village covenant for southern Kiangsi). In Wang Yang-ming ch'üan-chi 王陽明全集 (Collected works of Wang Yang-ming). Taipei, 1971.

568. Wei Cheng-t'ung 韋政通. Chung-kuo wen-hua kai-lun 中國文化概論 (Outline of Chinese culture). Taipei, 1968.

569. ———Ch'uan-t'ung yü hsien-tai-hua 傳統與現代化 (Tradition and modernization). Taipei, 1968.

570. ———Ch'uan-t'ung ti t'ou-shih 傳統的透視 (Penetrating look at tradition). Taipei, 1969.

571. Welch, Holmes. *The Practice of Chinese Buddhism*. Cambridge, Mass: Harvard University Press, 1966.

572. ———*The Buddhist Revival in China*. Cambridge, Mass.: Harvard University Press, 1968.

573. *Wen-hua hsien-feng* 文化先鋒 (Cultural vanguard). Chungking, 1.19—5.20 (Jan 14, 1943—Jan. 15, 1946). Tri-monthly.

574. *Wen-hua tsa-chih* 文化雜誌 (Culture magazine). Kweilin, 1.1—3.4 (1942–1943). Monthly.

575. *Wen-i-pao* 文藝報 (Literature and art news). Shanghai, 1950–1977.

576. *Wen shih che* 文史哲 (Literature, history, philosophy). Tsinan, 1954–1957. Monthly.

577. Williams, Raymond. *Culture and Society, 1780–1950*. New York: Harper and Row, 1958.

578. Wood, Allen. *Bertrand Russell: The Passionate Sceptic*. London: Unwin Books, 1963.

579. [Wu] Ch'ao-jan [吳] 超然 and [?] T'ien-p'ei 天培. "Tui Tsou-p'ing chiao-yü hsien-chuang ti hsun-shih" 對鄒平教育現狀的巡視 (Inspection of the present condition of Tsou-p'ing's education). [272] 6.11 (Mar. 1, 1937).

580. Wu Chih-hui 吳稚暉. "I-ko hsin hsin-yang ti yü-chou-kuan chi jen-sheng-kuan" 一個新信仰的宇宙觀及人生觀 (Cosmology and philosophy of life based on a new faith). In [352], II, 120–130. Also *T'ai-p'ing yang* 太平洋 (Pacific Ocean) 4.1, 4.3, 4.5 (August, October 1923, March 1924).

581. Wu Ching-ch'ao 吳景超. "Fa-chan tu-shih i chiu-chi nung-ts'un" 發展都市以救濟農村 (Develop the cities to relieve the villages). [535], no. 118 (1935).

582. ———"P'i-p'an Liang Shu-ming ti hsiang-ts'un chien-she li-lun" 批判梁漱溟的鄉村建設理論 (Critique of Liang Shu-ming's rural reconstruction theory). In [409], I, 11–19. Also [333], July 11, 1955; [289], no. 9 (1955).

583. ———"P'i-p'an Liang Shu-ming ti Chung-kuo wen-hua lun" 批判梁漱溟的中國文化論 (Critique of Liang Shu-ming's theory of Chinese culture). In [409], II, 86–105. Also [166], no 10 (1955).

584. Wu Ching-fu 吳敬敷. "Tsou-p'ing chien-wen lu" 鄒平見聞錄 (Record of my visit to Tsou-p'ing). [449] 2.4 (Sept. 26, 1934).

585. Wu Ching-hsiung 吳經熊 et al. *Chung-kuo wen-hua lun-chi* 中國文化論集 (Collection of essays on Chinese culture). Taipei, 1967.

586. *Wu-chou jih-pao* 梧州日報 (Wuchow daily). Wuchow, Kwangsi, 1942.

587. Wu I 吳怡. "Liang Shu-ming yü Feng Yu-lan" 梁漱溟與馮友蘭 (Liang Shu-ming and Fung Yu-lan). [546], no. 1636 (July 20, 1976).

588. *Wu-nien-lai Ho-nan cheng-chih tsung-pao-kao* 五年來河南政治總報告 (General report on the past five years of political work in Honan). Kaifeng, 1935.

589. Wu Shih-ch'ang 吳世昌. *Chung-kuo wen-hua yü hsien-tai wen-hua wen-t'i* 中國文化與現代文化問題 (Chinese culture and contemporary culture).

Shanghai, 1948.

590. Wu T'ing-ch'iu 吳廷璆. "P'i-p'an Liang Shu-ming ti fan-tung ti li-shih kuan-tien" 批判梁漱溟的反動的歷史觀點 (Critique of Liang Shu-ming's reactionary view of history). In [409], II, 30–49. Also [392], October 1955; [289], no. 11 (1955).

591. Yang Chia-lo 楊家駱. Min-kuo ming-jen t'u-chien 民國名人圖鑑 (Pictorial biographical dictionary of eminent Chinese of the Republican period). n.p., 1937.

592. Yang Hsiao-ch'un 楊效春. "Ts'ung hsiang-ts'un chiao-yü ti kuan-tien k'an-k'an Shan-tung hsiang-ts'un" 從鄉村教育的觀點看看山東鄉村 (A look at rural Shantung from the perspective of rural education). [208] 20.5–6 (November–December 1932).

593. ———"Hsieh kei tsai hsiang-hsia kung-tso ti t'ung-hsueh" 寫給在鄉下工作的同學 (Letter to students working in the countryside). [502], nos. 25–26 (Jan. 6, 13, 1935).

594. ———"Lai-hsin" 來信 (Letter). [371], July 2, 1938.

595. Yang Jen-shan 楊仁山. Yang Jen-shan chü-shih i-shu 楊仁山居士遺書 (Works of Yang Jen-shan). Peking, 1923.

596. Yang K'ai-tao 楊開道. "Chung-kuo hsiang-yüeh chih-tu" 中國鄉約制度 (China's village covenant system). [533], n.s. 3.2/3, 3.4 (Jan. 20, Mar. 25, 1933).

597. Yang Ming-chai 楊明齋. P'ing Chung Hsi wen-hua kuan 評中西文化觀 (Critique of views on Chinese and Western cultures). Peking, 1924.

598. Yang Tuan-liu 楊端六. "Lo-su hsien-sheng ch'ü Hua kan-yen" 羅素先生去華感言 (Heartfelt words on Mr. Russell's leaving China). [540] 18.13 (July 10, 1921):7–11.

599. Yang Tzu-hu 楊子湖. "Tsou-p'ing hsien hsiang-ts'un chiao-yü shih-yen-ch'ü kung-tso" 鄒平縣鄉村教育實驗區工作 (Work of the Tsou-p'ing hsien rural education research district). [502], no. 69 (Feb. 12, 1936).

600. Yang Yu-chiung 楊幼炯. Chung-kuo cheng-tang shih 中國政黨史 (History of political parties in China). Shanghai, 1937.

601. Yen Chi-ch'eng 嚴旣澄. "Shao-nien Chung-kuo tsung-chiao wen-t'i hao p'i-p'ing" 少年中國宗教問題批評號 (Criticism of the religious issue in Young China). [440] 3.2 (February 1922): 1–12.

602. ———"P'ing Tung Hsi wen-hua chi ch'i che-hsueh" 評「東西文化」及其哲學 (Critique of Eastern and Western cultures and their philosophies). [440] 3.3 (March 1922): 1–10.

603. Yen Fu 嚴復, trans. "Chung-kuo chiao-yü i" 中國教育議 (Views on Chinese education), by Alfred Westharp. [610] 2.3/4.

604. Yen Huan-wen 閻煥文. "Lun wen-hua-hsueh hsiao-shih" 論文化學小史 (On a short history of the study of cultures). [216] 1.3 (May 25, 1944).

605. Yen, James Y.S. [Yen Yang-ch'u 晏陽初]. "New Citizens for China." Yale Review 18.2 (February 1929).

606. ———The Ting Hsien Experiment, 1930–1931. Ting hsien, 1931.

607. Yin Shun 印順. T'ai-hsu ta-shih nien-p'u 太虛大師年譜 (Chronological

biography of the venerable T'ai-hsu). Hong Kong, 1950.

608. Yü Lu-hsi 于魯溪. "Shan-tung hsiang-ts'un chien-she yen-chiu-yuan nung-ch'ang chi-hua" 山東鄉村建設研究院農場計劃 (Plan for the Shantung rural reconstruction institute farm). [272] 2.3 (Aug. 21, 1932):11-23.

609. Yuan Fang 袁方. "P'i-p'an Liang Shu-ming ti hsiang-ts'un chien-she yun-tung" 批判梁漱溟的鄉村建設运動 (Critique of Liang Shu-ming's rural reconstruction movement). In [409], I, 57-71. Also [285], September 1955.

610. *Yung-yen* 庸言 (Justice). Tientsin, 1912-1914.

611. Zung, G.S. "Marshal Feng and Rural Reconstruction." *The Chinese Recorder* 19.8:523-525.

Interviews (Chinese characters are not given for persons whose names have already appeared in the previous section of the bibliography)

612. Chang Chih-wen 章之汶. Taipei. Sept. 12, 1969.

613. Chang Hung-chün 張鴻鈞. Tunghai University, Taiwan. June 9. 1970, Apr. 19, 1971.

614. Ch'en Ch'i-t'ien. Taipei. Aug. 13, 1971.

615. Ch'en K'ai-szu 陳開泗. Taipei. Mar. 2, 1971.

616. Ch'en Li-fu 陳立夫. Taipei. May 19, 1971.

617. Ch'en Wen-chung 陳文仲. Chia-i, Taiwan. Nov. 6, 11, 1971.

618. Ch'i Chung-ch'üan 漆中權. Peitou, Taiwan. July 28, 1971.

619. Chia Ch'ung-yen 賈崇言. Taipei. Oct. 9, 15, Nov. 11, 16, Dec. 20, 1971.

620. Ch'ien Mu. Taipei. Sept. 7, 1971.

621. Chou Shao-hsien. Taipei. Mar. 20, May 27, 31, June 20, July 20, 21, 27, 28, Aug. 1, 1970; Mar. 1, May 26, 27, 31, July 1, 19, 20, 21, 23, Aug. 1, 8, 16, Sept. 3, 10, 18, Nov. 10, 18, 1971; Feb. 3, 14, 1972.

622. Hu Ch'iu-yuan. Taipei. May 18, 1971.

623. Hu Ying-han. Hong Kong. Aug. 18, 20, 24, 28, 30, Sept. 3, 7, 26, 30, 1970.

624. Ku I-ch'un 顧翊羣. Taipei. Mar. 21, 1970; May 19, 1971.

625. Leng P'eng 冷彭. Taipei. Oct. 15, 1971.

626. Li Han-san 李漢三. Taipei. July 17, 1971.

627. Liu Hsin-huang. Taipei. Apr. 27, 1971.

628. Li P'u-sheng 李樸生. Taipei. May 8, 12, 1971.

629. Li Tsung-huang. Taipei. Apr. 30, Sept. 2, 1971.

630. Liu Tse-min 劉澤民. Taipei. July 31, 1971.

631. Liu Li-kuang 劉禮光. Hsinchu, Taiwan. Apr. 14, 1971.

632. Lo Shu-ming 羅漱溟. Taichung, Taiwan. Nov. 12, 1975.

633. Mou Tsung-san. Hong Kong. Sept. 21, 1970.

634. T'ang Chun-i. Hong Kong. Sept. 25, 1970.

635. Tseng Chao-sen 曾昭森. Hong Kong. Sept. 8, 1970.

636. Wang Shao-sheng. Hong Kong. Aug. 18, 19, 24, 26, Sept. 1, 3, 4, 5, 10, 19, 1970.

637. Wang Yun-wu 王雲五. Taipei. Oct. 25, 1971.

638.   Wei Cheng-t'ung. Taipei. July 26, 1971.

639.   Wei Li-chiu 衛禮九. Taipei. Oct. 9, 1971.

640.   Yang, Martin (Mou-ch'un) 楊懋春. Taipei. July 9, Aug. 6, 1971.

Index

√ J. of Phg Soc's V.1 I face. 2 (1985)
Max Weber in Asian Studies